D1554617

AMORAL POLITICS

AMORAL POLITICS

The Persistent Truth of Machiavellism

Ben-Ami Scharfstein

STATE UNIVERSITY OF NEW YORK PRESS

Production by Ruth Fisher
Marketing by Fran Keneston

Published by
State University of New York Press, Albany

© 1995 State University of New York

For information, address State University of New York Press,
State University Plaza, Albany, NY 12246

Library Of Congress Cataloging-in-Publication Data

Scharfstein, Ben-Ami, 1919–
     Amoral politics : the persistent truth of Machiavellism / Ben-Ami
Scharfstein.
          p.   cm.
     Includes bibliographical references and index.
     ISBN 0–7914–2279–8 (alk. paper).—ISBN 0–7914–2280–1 (pbk. :
alk. paper)
     1. Political ethics—History. 2. Political leadership—Moral and
ethical aspects—History. 3. Machiavellianism (Psychology)—
History. I. Title.
JA79.S3166 1995
172—dc20   94-8609
                                                                    CIP

10 9 8 7 6 5 4 3 2 1

For my mother's hundredth birthday

God help you if the scepter slips from your grasp . . . no one but the king may touch it. And it would hardly be a pretty sight to see a king stretched out on the floor to reach the scepter fetched up under some piece of furniture—or, when it comes to that, the crown, which could easily fall off your head if you bend over.

Italo Calvino, A King Listens

❮CONTENTS❯

ix

INTRODUCTION

This book tries to explain how and why politics is so often and so naturally amoral. It also undertakes to explain the relation between the morality or amorality of the political leader and that of the ordinary individual. In doing so, it treats the political theory and practice of the non-Western civilizations, principally those of China and India, with the same detail, seriousness, and measure of respect as those of modern Europe. It should by now be clear that we can only profit intellectually by drawing the experience of these other civilizations into our own. The act of drawing it in is far more important than any particular conclusion we can at first reach with its help.

The theory and practice dealt with here are all related to what I call *Machiavellism*, by which I mean the disregard of moral scruples in politics, that is, the political use, limited only by expediency, of every kind of deception and force. As I use it, *Machiavellism* is obviously a theoretical construct that fits no one person exactly, not even, as the text makes clear, Machiavelli himself—individuals are much too diverse to fit any such abstraction exactly. I want to be more careful, finally, than I may sound at first: while the abstraction helps to identify any political justification of amorality, it does not imply an original sin, a fixed, unchanging characteristic. Instead, like the concepts of love and hate, it represents something that is fundamental to human life and takes inexhaustibly different forms, each with its own consequences.

As it happens, in each of the three civilizations there were periods in which theory and practice related to one another in a particularly memorable way, one that has helped to define the nature of politics. Therefore the first part of the book is devoted to the description of the theorists and practitioners of politics in each of the civilizations during such a memorable period. To make the context of political theory and practice clear, I have in each case set the historical background, explained how the respective thinkers saw, judged, and sometimes affected their own history, and described the persistence of their thought in their traditions. In all this description, I have tried to reflect the best contemporary scholarship, but in scholarship as in political theory, much remains controversial.

In spite of the attention that is devoted to the varying political contexts of the three civilizations, it becomes obvious that it is reasonable to use the same term, *Machiavellism*, to characterize the amorality preached and practiced in all of them. The likeness is particularly impressive because these civilizations were so nearly independent of one another. Their likeness furnishes the evidence for a main thesis, which is modified and supplemented by a number of subtheses, to be taken up later. The main thesis is, simply, that Machiavellism is integral to political life of every kind. This thesis appears evident, I am sure, to anyone who has engaged much in politics, and it can be taken with a dismissive shrug of familiarity. But personal experience alone is a poor substitute for wideranging investigation and the variety of thought and practice that history reveals. Furthermore, the historical evidence leads to the conclusion, which I think is inescapable, that political or ethical theories that do not take Machiavellism into serious account are inadequate to human affairs in general and are of doubtful relevance to actual politics. In other words, I argue that the thinkers who make neatly schematic pictures of humanity should struggle more with the rationally intractable facts.

To test this view, I go on to examine it in the light of the evidence given by the so-called preliterate peoples, whether organized in kingdoms, chiefdoms, or stateless societies. I then go briefly into the ethologists' discovery in recent years that social life among the nonhuman primates is often ruled with the help of Machiavellian tactics, that is, by means of force and at least somewhat conscious deception.

Having come to the conclusion that political and ethical theories are too often distant from life as it is actually lived, in the second half of this book I discuss and, in a sense, judge Machiavellism with the help of actual examples and in the light of both philosophy and the social sciences. Since I do not want to arouse undue expectations, I must immediately make it clear that this part of the book is not a systematic treatise or a critical survey of current thought but a set of brief essays— answers to questions I asked myself—linked by the attempt to stay close to human reality and to use ideas without concern over the academic discipline from which they come. I wrote this second half because I was unable to survey the evidence I gathered without reacting to it and because I hoped that my reaction might lead readers to think beyond my brief analyses and preliminary conclusions.

I

MACHIAVELLISM DESCRIBED

~1~

The Machiavellis Introduced

Having introduced my thesis, I am obliged to document it, as I do in the following chapters, which explore a number of quite different human landscapes. Here, before the exploring begins, I want to defend wide-ranging comparisons of the kind I am making and then to characterize Machiavellism and introduce the Machiavellians—the Machiavellis, as I call them—with whom the following chapters deal. For the moment, these thinkers can be little more than names, but by taking them out of context it is easy to show what is common to them, what makes them all Machiavellis in spite of their differences in time, culture, and personality. In the course of this introductory discussion, I propose that the Machiavellis, with their overwhelming urge to understand political power, were able to assess politics more accurately than could thinkers whose sight was averted from political reality by their moral ideals, metaphysical principles, or need to build a system.

First, a word on the legitimacy of taking political theory and practice out of context. It is likely that my attempt to describe a transcultural Machiavellism will be criticized as implausible because, by ignoring the unique context of each civilization, I compare what is essentially incomparable. Such an objection rests on a misunderstanding of the limits of the idea of uniqueness. It is true, or at least irrefutable, that each civilization is unique; but there is no good reason to stop with civilizations. To be exact, everything human, for that matter, everything biological, is unique. To restrict ourselves to the human, a moment's thought should make it clear that even identical twins can never be exactly identical. Like other human beings, they are both the same and different, though more subtly different.

3

It should be altogether clear that all human beings, simply in being human, are always unique and, at least in nuances, very different from one another, but, in being human, are always very much alike. If not for their uniqueness, we could neither recognize them as human nor relate to them as individuals; but if not for their likeness to one another and to ourselves, it would be impossible to relate to them as, like ourselves, human beings. Physiologists or doctors will discover significant differences between the people they are most familiar with and those who live in a very different environment; but, even so, the resemblances will be great enough to make it possible to use the analogies to distinguish and understand the differences. Psychologists, too, discover pronounced differences but are likely to find (in fact have found) that the basic signs of emotion (smiling, laughter, a pained look, weeping) are largely (not completely) the same (in fact, people born blind smile for the same reasons as others—they have not learned to smile by watching others smile).[1]

On the basis of such analogies and whatever historical and anthropological reading I have done, I make the unremarkable assumption that human traits like kindness and cruelty, love and hate, altruism and egoism, cheerfulness and bad humor, and ambition and lack of ambition are universal. Even though such traits come to expression in different kinds of acts or avoidances and are accentuated or minimized by different social circumstances, they are always present (I assume) and are recognized, on the background of the prevailing culture, for what they are. The differences between kindness and cruelty and truth-telling and lying, the traits we will refer to most, are universal.

Now what are we to take as more real, true, or important, the uniqueness of the individual or the individual's likeness to others? Because groups of individuals, too, are uniquely individual, we can add the question: Is the uniqueness of every family, clan, town, city, country, and civilization more real, true, or important than the likeness between the individuals who constitute them all, including civilizations and mankind as a whole? A similar question can be asked about the uniqueness and likeness of the members of analogous groups—about their family-membership, clan-membership, and so on, up to their membership in civilizations as different as those to be discussed here. I mean—to speak of families only—how important is the likeness conferred on people by the fact that they belong to families and are fathers, mothers, children, and so on, as compared with their unlikeness as members of different kinds of families?

Surely the only reasonable answer to the question, What are we to take as more real, true, or important? is that, as asked, the question is absurd because, to make sense, it would have to be modified to something like, Are we to take uniqueness or likeness in such-and-such a particular respect as more or less important for such-and-such a particular purpose? This purpose might be the diagnosis of a disease or, in an instance more relevant to the present theme, the loyalty, that is, the depth of identification, of people with a state whose survival, in a moment of crisis, depended on their readiness to come to its defense.

With respect to what I am calling *Machiavellism*, my first response to the question of likeness and difference is this: In each of the three civilizations, as in the "tribal" cultures I deal with later, the difference between kindness and cruelty, altruism and egoism, truthfulness and lying, ambition and lack of ambition, and, of course, ruling and being ruled were very clear; and in China, India, and Europe, the difference was reflected in a bitter debate between the Machiavellians and the anti-Machiavellians, between, generally, the defenders of a morality with a single standard and the defenders of a *raison d'état* with its implication of a moral standard for the ordinary person different from that of the state and state's leader. It is this common likeness and common debate that justifies the use here of the term *Machiavellism*.

But this is only half of what should be said, because, once the likeness has been identified and exploited for whatever points one wants to make, it is quite legitimate to pay attention to the differences, declare the term *Machiavellism*, with its presumption of uniformity, misleading, and then begin—on the background of the likeness now perceived as oversimple—to make out the unique qualities of each civilization (or period, thinker, politician, or event). Nothing in the emphasis on either likeness or uniqueness prevents the recognition of the other of the pair; in both thought and practice, the existence of the one requires that of the other. This mutuality of likeness and uniqueness is what makes it possible for us to learn general truths and practical habits, and, at the same time, how and when to modify or abandon them. Here, my interest is clearly to establish and make intellectual use of the likeness between the Machiavellism of the three civilizations, and yet I describe the contexts and individuals in enough detail to make possible the verdict, opposite to mine, that the Machiavellism each civilization displays is unique to itself.[2] A more useful response to the opposite possible verdicts might be to distinguish different conditions, types, and consequences of Machiavellism; but such a response does not, in itself, escape the danger of identifying theoretical distinctions with actual occurrences.

Much of what I have to say could have been based on western sources alone. But if you ask why these strangers—ancient Chinese, Indians, and others—are needed in our company, the answer is that their strangeness, in many ways real, is superficial when it comes to their advocacy of deception and force. It is just because they are really variants of ourselves that they make it easy for us to see ourselves more clearly and, in Machiavellism, more cruelly than we prefer. They serve as what may be called *un*distorting mirrors. Unless we see ourselves in them, we are likely to excuse our less attractive traits as accidents of time and place that will change when we learn to become our true selves. But though we may think that we are really more beautiful than we have seemed till now—the beauty lies, after all, in the beholder's hopes—we learn that as true humans we are also true animals with the animal goal of power for ourselves and our kin, whom we defend— hate them or love them—against those of other kin groups.

Is this rhetorical, reductive exaggeration? Hardly so, though in time I will qualify because there are many facts to absorb and arguments to be considered before a balanced judgment can be attempted. Machiavellism is too deeply involved in human life to be unravelled quickly. Amoral though it is, it absorbs morality by accepting the moral rules that do not endanger the group or, above all, the state, which is based on the more artificial, nongenetic kinship of many kin groups. Typically enough, what does or does not endanger the group or state is determined by the leader, who voices what is, or what he proclaims to be, the collective will. Although this will is limited by habitual morality, the limits are violated with the help of excuses of many convenient sorts.

The rare candid Machiavelli goes so far as to proclaim that where the state is concerned, no excuses are needed; being essential to human life, it should be defended irrespective of moral rules. In other words, because the state makes moral rules possible, it is superior to them, or, to put it differently, the state, the source of morality, is the supreme moral value. Therefore, argues the candid Machiavelli, the state is empowered to use every means, including every form of deception and force, in order to protect its life. In practice, it is argued, a government can remain viable only if it acts in accord with the Machiavellian principles that allow it to subordinate everything else to the state's health or power. This is because, as I have been saying in the Machiavelli's name, the welfare of the many who make up the state transcends the welfare of all individuals except the ruler, without whom the state cannot exist. An equivalent justification is that the most tyrannical social order is better than social chaos. Therefore, by a simple reappraisal of terms, it becomes possible to argue that what is immoral for the individual is moral for the state, and even that the basic importance of individual morality is that it helps to maintain the state. By this argument, individual morality is approved because the more honest, industrious, and brave the citizens, the stronger the state and the better the chance that the ruler, whose ruling principle is effective political action, will remain in power and aggrandize whatever is possible for his own and his state's glory.

Machiavellism tends to be shy of public exposure. Leaders do not commonly avow it in public, either because they have not made their peace with it—they act by its rules, but it makes them uneasy—or because the avowal would subvert their ability to make use of its tactics. For the same reason that the liar, to lie effectively, wears an honest face, the Machiavellian leader prefers to wear an unchangingly moral face. Or, often, he restricts his more open Machiavellism to international relations, in which his tactics are approved by his subjects or citizens because they promise them a common gain. However, even when active in politics, the candid Machiavellians who are the main subject of this book are not themselves full rulers but subordinates or theoreticians who offer leaders their advice. Their preference to remain subordinate and act as the ruler's faithful advisers rather than his competitors hints at a possible quandary in Machiavellian thought.

Granted the ruler's desire for an industrious, brave, and loyal population, it stands to reason that the political doctrines taught in his name should be anti-Machiavellian, not only for the sake of the state's internal life but, as far as possible, to justify its external politics as well. God or gods are invoked to enhance an earthly army with superhuman weaponry, but they are equally useful in their role as the judges who are most likely to rule in the state's favor. Their presumed ability to declare what actions are just is important because justice, by which the accepted principles of fairness are said to be enforced, is always proclaimed to be the ruler's aim.

The kind of justice most useful to state and ruler is driven home by means of a suitable legendary history. Children accept this history because they know no better; and they are taught, more or less successfully, to grow up into consenting adults. Everyone is exhorted to be compliant, faithful, honest, and otherwise decent, and, to make compliance attractive, is promised a social, psychological, or religious reward—social approval, self-approval, or the favor of heaven. But while Machiavellism in its main, political sense prefers conventional morality for ordinary citizens, it does not assume that this morality is easy to inculcate. On the contrary, because its appraisal of human nature is negative, it anticipates that people will very often be selfish, cowardly, aggressive, aggrandizing, lying, and venal. So it is taken for granted that ordinary individuals will use the Machiavellian kind of tactics against one another and, if possible, against the state. When it seems expedient, the Machiavellian leader therefore tries to exploit the individual's Machiavellian tendencies or, when expedient, to suppress them by brutal punishment.

Apart from ambitious, faithless citizens, the state has as its other internal Machiavellian rivals any leaders or groups that assume that its right to existence defines or transcends the claims of morality. The state's most natural, most serious rival is religion, which sees itself as the ultimate moral authority. Later, in the last chapter, I will give an extended example of how a religion, like a state, develops Machiavellian characteristics.

So far, I have been calling Machiavellism by the name that European political history has made appropriate, but, as this book shows in detail, it has a Chinese and an Indian analogue—in China called *Legalism* and, in India, *Political Science*, as *arthashastra* may be translated. The differences between the European, Chinese, and Indian forms will become clear, but what is above all important (here, at least) is their underlying likeness.

Let me take a first step and introduce the protagonists of Machiavellism in the three civilizations. For China, these protagonists are three in number: Shang Yang, Han Fei, and Li Ssu, all of the fourth and third centuries B.C. and all grouped together retrospectively under the name of *Legalists*. For India, the leading protagonist is the Brahman Kautilya, whose systematic book, called the *Arthashastra*, is dated somewhere between the fourth and first centuries B.C. For Europe, represented by Italy of the Renaissance, there are Machiavelli himself and his friend and doctrinal critic, Guicciardini.

Can the appearance of Machiavellism in the three civilizations be explained by the influence of any one on the others? There were contacts, we know, between China and India even before the fourth century B.C., and there were contacts, especially after the conquest of Alexander the Great, between India and Greece, from which Renaissance Italy got so much of its culture. But the texts themselves on which we will draw show, by their rhetoric, their organization, the particulars on which they dwell, and the traditions they reflect, that they are quite independent of one another. They therefore furnish us with an extraordinary historical experiment in what I take to be universal traits of human politics.

To show in a concentrated way that this conclusion fits the evidence, I will now compare the doctrines of the Machiavellis I have introduced. To avoid misrepresenting them, I put their ideas mostly in their own words, as far as translation conveys them. The comparison takes into account (1) likeness in social and political backgrounds, (2) likeness in conceptions of human nature, (3) likeness in conceptions of the ruler's function, and (4) a number of the common stratagems they recommend.

(1) *The likeness of the Machiavellis' social and political backgrounds:* As one would expect, the more closely one looks at these thinkers in their backgrounds, the more different they are, the more they become three individual Chinese, a single, vaguely individual Indian, and two Renaissance Florentines, quite different from one another in status and personality. But if one is willing to back away and view them from the neutralizing distance that makes their comparison rewarding, the similarities are striking.[3]

These Machiavellis, who all regarded their thought as immediately useful, were all experienced in politics. Shang Yang, Li Ssu—as powerful an instigator of change as ever lived—and the Kautilya to whom the *Arthashastra* is plausibly attributed were strong-minded ministers. One of the Machiavellis, Han Fei, was briefly an adviser to the same emperor as Li Ssu but soon, so to speak, failed to death. Of the two Italians, Machiavelli was an experienced diplomat who was ousted for his republican sympathies, while Guicciardini was for a time a ruler in almost his own right.

Apart from their direct political experience, what stimulated these men to think as they did was a political situation similar in its broad outlines: many neighboring states, large and small, in alliance and conflict with one another, so that at each of their courts there was a ferment of fears, hopes, and intrigues. In each of the three civilizations, there was also a tradition of political analysis varied enough for the exponents of different views to draw on; and there was an active intellectual culture that bred thinkers of different kinds who were eager to put their theories to the test. Naturally, the more Machiavellian among them were sooner or later denounced by the others. Kautilya, whose book is a comprehensive manual of government, was denounced mainly by Buddhists and Jains, who refused to distinguish between morality and political practice. But the ancient Hindus, unlike many of their descendants today, seem to have accepted the manual as the summation of the science of government; and although the text itself was lost for a long time, other, widely known books continued to teach its doctrines.[4]

(2) *The Machiavellis' conceptions of human nature:* Looked at closely, their conceptions of human nature may not always have been self-consistent, may have changed in time, and are certainly different from one another. But for this general account it is enough that all six Machiavel-

lis make an estimate of human nature that is negative. Because they assume that human nature is bad or weak—meaning open to temptation, self-centered, lazy, cowardly, vindictive, or the like—they demand rigorous laws and exemplary punishments. This demand is expressed in the following four passages, the first two from Han Fei, the third from Kautilya, and the fourth from Machiavelli. The Rod of which Kautilya speaks is a symbol of authority and a synonym for rule by means of punishment or threat of punishment:

> It is the people's nature to delight in disorder and detach themselves from legal restraints. However, if they pursue ease, the land will waste; if the land wastes, the state will not be in order. If the state is not in order, it will become chaotic.[5]
>
> Severe penalty is what the people fear, heavy punishment is what the people hate. Accordingly, the wise man promulgates what they fear in order to forbid the practice of wickedness and establishes what they hate in order to prevent villainous acts. For this reason the state is safe and no outrage happens.[6]
>
> The Rod, used after full consideration, endows the subjects with spiritual good, material well-being and pleasures of the senses . . . If not used at all, it gives rise to the law of the fishes. For, the stronger swallows the weak in the absence of the wielder of the Rod.[7]
>
> A wise prince . . . is more merciful than those who, through too much mercy, let evils continue.[8]

Having a negative estimate of human nature, a Machiavelli is sure that love is a less effective instrument of government than fear. Sometimes the Machiavelli adds that the use of fear really expresses the ruler's love and, by imposing peace and justice, eventually causes his subjects to love him. The following passages, which express these ideas, are taken, respectively, from Shang Yang, Han Fei, Kautilya, and Machiavelli. In the quoted passages, Kautilya is milder than the others; elsewhere, all six object to ruthlessness so unconsidered that it defeats its own purpose:

> If penalties are made heavy and rewards light, the ruler loves his people and they will die for him; but if rewards are made heavy and penalties light, the ruler does not love his people, nor will they die for him.[9]

I can see that the sage in governing the state pursues the policy of making the people inevitably do him good but never relies on their doing him good with love. For to rely on the people's doing him good with love is dangerous. . . . [10]

The (king), severe with the Rod, becomes a source of terror to beings, the (king), mild with the Rod is despised. The (king), just with the Rod, is honored.[11]

The wise prince makes himself feared in such a way that, if he does not gain love, he escapes being hated. . . .[12]

(3) *The Machiavellis' conceptions of the function of the ruler*: The Chinese emperor was supposed to rule by the grace of Heaven, that is, by the life that Heaven had infused into his dynasty. In India, apart from the Buddhists and Jains, kingship was regarded as having been founded by the supreme being; and sometimes the king was identified with the god supposed to have founded his dynasty. The more modest Indian belief, according to which the king was not himself a god, resembled the European belief that kingship had been established by God and that the king's rule was the natural imitation of rule by God. Both in India and (usually) in Europe, kingship was therefore assumed to be the only natural form of government. However, the king was believed to be obliged to share the regulation of society with the religious authorities. In China, the Confucians came to assert that their morality should take precedence even over the will of an emperor. Kautilya and the other Indian writers on *arthashastra* did not reject the idea that religion had an independent right to existence, but to them, as to Machiavelli and Guicciardini, institutional religion was important only because it could help or hinder the welfare of the state. The Chinese Machiavellis, who had to make their peace with the traditional forms of Chinese ceremony and religiosity, probably felt the same.

It was only in Europe, beginning in the independent cities of Greece and republican Rome and continuing in the Middle Ages, that the idea developed that a community had the right to govern itself; and only in Europe did there develop a clear, consistent belief in the right to revoke the social contract—the best-known expressions of this right came after Machiavelli's time.[13] Therefore, among the Machiavellis we are discussing, only Machiavelli and Guicciardini applied their political theory to republican states, which they favored, as well as to kingdoms and tyrannies.

Machiavellis, of course, agreed in stressing that the ruler, by the virtue itself of his position, must be acknowledged as preeminent in the state; sometimes they dreamed of men who were fit for such preeminence. The following excerpts from Han Fei and Kautilya are evidence of the stress:

> Nothing is more valuable than the royal person, more honorable than the throne, more powerful than the authority of the sovereign, and more august than the position of the ruler.[14]

> For the king trained in the sciences, intent on the discipline of the subjects, enjoys the earth alone without sharing it with any other ruler, being devoted to the welfare of all beings.[15]

I do not believe that Machiavelli, who went back to republican Rome for his ideal, ever wrote an equivalent to this passage. It is true that he composed a panegyric on the notorious Cesare Borgia, but this praise is the opposite of Han Fei's and Kautilya's in the sense that it is a glorification not of the ruler's position as such but of Cesare's personal qualities. Machiavelli praises Cesare as a prince who is as severe or magnanimous as the occasion demands, who can replace old customs with newer ones, who knows how to compel princes to help him graciously or harm him reluctantly, who is, above all, able

> to win friends, to conquer by force or by fraud, to make himself loved and feared by the people, followed and respected by the soldiers. . . . [16]

The closest equivalent in Kautilya is the praise of the ideal king, who is not identified with any historical personage. Pious qualities aside, the king is

> born in a high family, endowed with good fortune, intelligence and spirit, given to seeing elders . . . not breaking his promises, grateful, liberal, of great energy, not dilatory, with weak neighboring princes, resolute . . . [and having the energetic qualities of] bravery, resentment, quickness and dexterity.[17]

Kautilya's ruler is basically dedicated to war. As will be explained later, this ruler is conceptualized as a natural aggressor encircled by natural enemies. Machiavelli's prince, as the second quotation shows, is equally concerned with the making of war:

The king . . . is the would-be conqueror. Encircling him on all sides, with territory immediately next to his is the constituent called the enemy.[18]

A wise prince . . . has no other object and no other interest and takes as his profession nothing else than war and its laws and discipline; that is the only profession fitting one who commands.[19]

According to Han Fei, the ruler who fails is the one who neglects laws and prohibitions, disregards defence works and other essentials, and has a strong interest in ideas and plans. But this last trait, which, for reasons that will be explained, spells failure to Han Fei, is necessary for a successful ruler as Kautilya and Machiavelli see him. The kingly ideal of Han Fei shows a peculiarly alert Taoistic nonactivity:

By virtue of resting empty and in repose, he waits for the course of nature to enforce itself so that all names will be defined of themselves and all affairs will be settled of themselves. Empty, he knows the essence of fullness: reposed, he becomes the corrector of motion.[20]

(4) *Some stratagems recommended by the Machiavellis:* The Machiavellis are at their natural best in suggesting political stratagems. One feels that it is the invention of ways to get around political obstacles and of dirty tricks and counter-tricks that particularly (though by no means exclusively) fired their imaginations. In one Machiavellian matter, that of spying, Han Fei and Kautilya go far beyond Machiavelli himself. Unlike them, he does not hold that every person should be encouraged to spy on every other and does not emphasize the need for a great network of secret agents. Also unlike Han Fei and Kautilya, he does not dwell much on the means for thwarting the treachery of the ruler's intimates. Maybe the reason is that, in spite of all Machiavelli's difficult experiences and his negative estimate of the people of his times, he tends to trust them more and finds it easier than Han Fei and Kautilya to advise his prince to put trust in his ministers.

Observe how suspicion rules the immediately following quotations from Han Fei, who advises the ruler to discover his ministers' views by keeping his own completely secret, and advises, with drastic finality, that the ministers be forbidden to exchange views with one another. He also gives the ruler the advice, usual among Machiavellis, to attribute all successes to himself and all failures to someone else. Like the other Machiavellis, he has an acute sense of the possible sources of danger—it takes one Machiavelli to assume the presence of others of his kind—and he knows that the closer the relationship, the greater the danger:

> The ruler must not reveal his views. For, if he reveals his views, the ministers will display their hues differently . . . Place every official with a censor. Do not let them speak to each other.[21]

> How to get rid of delicate villainy? By making the people watch over one another in their hidden affairs.[22]

> In the case of merits the ruler gains the renown and in case of demerit the ministers face the blame so that the ruler is never at the end of his reputation.[23]

> Favorite vassals, if too intimate with the ruler, would cause him personal danger. Ministers, if too powerful, would overturn the august position of the sovereign. Wives and concubines, if without distinction of rank, would cause legitimate sons danger. Brothers, if not subservient to the ruler, would endanger the Altar of the Spirits of Land and Grain.[24]

In one matter Kautilya recommends greater precautions against treachery than even Han Fei. He advises the king not only to spy on his ministers, as on everyone else, but to test them by putting them to the strongest possible temptations. He also favors carefully considered "silent punishment," by which he means assassination by unknown agents. Of course, the king's wives and sons are assumed to be a main source of danger:

> After appointing ministers to ordinary offices . . . [the king] should test their integrity by means of secret tests . . . When he has set spies on the high officials, he should set spies on the citizens and country people.[25]

> He should employ "silent punishment" towards his own party or that of the enemy, without hesitation[26]

> A king protects the kingdom (only) when (he is himself) protected from persons near him and from enemies, first from his wives and sons.[27]

Machiavelli's advice on uncovering the true nature of minsters, while reasonable, is far less Machiavellian than Han Fei's. For example, he advises a prince that a minister who thinks mainly of himself can never be good at his work.[28] Quite like Han Fei, he advises the ruler to avoid blame and take only credit:

> Wise princes have affairs that bring hatred attended to by others, but those that bring thanks they attend to themselves.[29]

With this small sample of stratagems, I conclude my introduction to the shared ideas of the Machiavellis. To complete the comparison and, I think, to make the Machiavellis' agreement the more impressive, I add a description of their individuality as thinkers.

All the Machiavellis make the impression of forceful men with experience in the tactics they recommend. Kautilya stands out for his encyclopedic motives and detailed, usually dry text, written in the style of the Brahman pandit he is. Unlike the others, he means to put on record the whole of the tradition of political science, responding with his own interpretations to those of his predecessors. Also unlike the others, he makes next to no use of history, and writes, so it seems, not to answer any pressing contemporary need but to give advice for any and all times. Surprisingly, there are no direct references in his *Arthashastra* to the king he is supposed to have served or the political events he himself experienced.

The other Machiavellis write what are, at least in part, tracts for their times, occasionally about very specific matters. The advice Han Fei gives is for a particular emperor at a particular time, and his generalizations are meant to support the tactics he recommends. When Machiavelli writes, he is often thinking of what is happening in Florence or somewhere else nearby, and he gathers just those historic instances that will verify his argument of the day—an argument Guicciardini may oppose with examples chosen for an opposite purpose. It would be most unfair to accuse these thinkers of not reflecting seriously on their own and others' experience, but their thinking was often short-range, and they wanted their ideas to be put into immediate practical use.

Not only did the Machiavellis have a relatively uniform message, but they were almost alike in avoiding any attempt to create a metaphysically based philosophy. Kautilya was engaged in completing a science, Indian style, that is, amassing legal and sociological details, and not in what we would consider a philosophy; and Machiavelli and Guicciardini had little interest in any but practically useful political rules, or, in Guicciardini's case, in a well-schooled alertness rather than uniform rules, which could only be misapplied, he thought, to an always changing history. The two Italians were not interested in creating a system of thought or even in remaining closely consistent in the arguments they made at different times. They knew that the abstractions of political thought, although inescapable, were too rigid to encompass the inexhaustible variety of the here and now; as distinguished from political thought, political wisdom may flaunt its little apothegms, but it deserves its name only if it can adapt to individual, that is, unique cases. So the question to themselves of Machiavelli, Guicciardini, and their likes had to be, Is this advice useful here and now? and not, Is the advice I am giving now consistent with what I advised in an earlier, apparently similar case?"

The Machiavellis must have showed some consistency of character, because they must have been (and must partly remain) intelligible as persons. This consistency was reflected in their general attitude toward politics, but not in any special concern with the consistency of the larger abstractions in which they expressed themselves from time to time. In this lack of concern they resembled many of the other well-known thinkers of their times. The lack shows that the Machiavellis I am discussing do not belong among the philosophers, or shows them to be only primitive philosophically. Knowingly self-refuting philosophers such as Montaigne, Kierkegaard, and Nietzsche care enough about consistency to be brazen in their defiance of it, but our Machiavellis do not find it necessary to defy what they are not much interested in.

The only one among the Machiavellis who is likely at times to makes the impression of a philosophical mind—in a perhaps relaxed philosophers' sense of the word—is Han Fei, because of the way he combines Legalism with Taoism. I will later explain the not unreasonable meaning of this combination. In Han Fei's case, however, it makes for what an unkind critic might call practical foolishness tinged with paranoiac suspicion. Yet it is just this combination that creates the possibility of depth, the result of the conjuncture in him of different lines of thought—of the quietistically mystical and the politically practical, or the disabused and the idealistic. Some of Han Fei is high-flown rhetoric directed at an emperor for a personal purpose not unlike Machiavelli's in his dedication of *The Prince*. Some is only a listing of aphoristic political warnings saying, watch out for this problem and for that, all not, I suppose, very helpful in practice though interesting enough to read and calculated to inspire a general suspiciousness. The book of Han Fei Tzu also contains commentaries on and illustrations to the philosophy of

Lao Tzu; some sound as if they may have been written by a different person.

The only protagonists of Machiavellianism to whom the reader can feel close are the two Florentines, Machiavelli and Guicciardini, of whom Machiavelli is the warmer. Both are skilled writers, both are close to our times, and both are revealed in reports, memoirs, and letters to which we have access. Machiavelli appreciated the freedom to express dissenting opinions. To him, the clash of opinions that represent different social interests was a creative political force, provided it was contained within the framework of the law. The Chinese and Indian Machiavellians were ready enough to tolerate differences in local culture, but the political order they envisaged was one determined by the will of the ruler.

In the preceding comparisons, I have left out much that might have been added, but there is enough for the general conclusion: Each of the three distinct civilizations gave rise to a relatively sophisticated body of thought that advocated the use of deception and force to maintain the state, in disregard of ordinary moral standards. I should stress that those who held this view did not mean to argue against the morality observed in everyday life. All these Machiavellians held ordinary religious views, and although they had no compunctions about using religion for state purposes, there is no sign that their acceptance of religion as such was cynical. To them, politics was a field that had to take other matters into consideration, politics and religion being different pursuits with necessarily different principles.

However this may be, the likeness in Machiavellism between the three civilizations raises the possibility that such thought is natural to civilized life as such. Politics as in fact practiced seems to give rise to such a point of view. In other words, what gives the Machiavellian position its (hypothesized) universal relevance is the degree of its truth to universal political experience.

This conclusion leads to a contrast between the Machiavellis and most philosophers as political thinkers. The Machiavellis claim that they are only pointing out the rules by which states in fact live or die. Having made and illustrated this claim, they ordinarily feel no need to justify their principles any further but go on to practical strategy, which interests them more. This makes for a philosophical primitivity—a few general, quickly expressed ideas supported by a choice of probably biased examples. Yet there is a cardinal trait in which the Machiavellians have the advantage over even the philosophers who were influenced by them—in Europe, notably Hobbes, Spinoza, and Hegel. This advantage is the obverse of what I have considered to be the Machiavellians' philosophical primitivity.

The explanation is simple. As I have pictured it, Machiavellism is a utilitarian doctrine based on a notion of the good of the community, whose members are regarded as so weak and untrustworthy that they need leaders who are firm, flexible, and prepared to be ruthless. The contest for leadership within and between countries is by nature unrelenting, with the victory often going to the most clever, insightful, flexible, brave, ruthless, attractive leader—but often also to the luckiest among the contestants, because, as experience teaches, the future can never be predicted in detail.

As it appears in the works of the Machiavellis, the temper of this doctrine seems to reflect the disillusionment taught by personal experience supported by a disillusioned reading of history. By the usual philosophical standards—Han Fei perhaps excepted—the doctrine is, I repeat, primitive or shallow. I mean that it is concerned with ambitions, suspicions, tactics, and practical experience but makes no sustained attempt to understand the universe or to penetrate into the nature of even the ordinary human beings about whom it makes such unflattering assumptions. But this shallowness by ordinary philosophical standards is Machiavellism's strength. When Hobbes makes the same unflattering assumptions about human beings, he does so in the framework of a mathematized quasi-materialism that tries to be perfectly logical, and with the help of a radical and (in intention) consistent theory of human speech. Spinoza's elaborate metaphysics does not leak much into his unsentimental political theory, but those who know his *Ethics* are aware of his belief that the true philosophy can be proved exactly and beyond doubt. This philosophy leads to the eternal intellectual love of God arising from the highest, third kind of knowledge.[30] In too summary words, Spinoza may be said to believe in absolute, unchanging, metaphysically provable truth and in some kind of union with God who is Nature. And Hegel, who considers Machiavelli's conception great and true, holds that everything is contained within the intricate synthesis of construction and destruction that comes to full conscious light only in his own philosophy.[31]

Each of these great philosophers makes an intellectually exciting, even genial construction of ideas; but in the end, each construction is a picture of the world that the philosopher has made to express his own, idiosyncratic view. In constructing, he is necessarily subjective in much the way in which a great painter is subjective. To the extent that the philosopher is ruled by his individual picture of the world, his image of human beings is made to fit his picture, which is very different from the world that ordinary experience or empirical science recognizes. That is why it is so easy to feel that these philosophic systems are artificial constructs. By their nature as powerful artificial constructs, they can stimulate and give refuge, but little is left in them of what we ought to recognize (along with Aristotle) as the incompleteness of even true principles and of the intrusion of chance into every life.[32]

Typically, the Machiavellians are truer to political experience, less drawn away from it by system, more alert to fate as the unexpected, more aware that history turns and twists often beyond our ability to master it. Machiavellism is less a system of thought than a collection of disabused opinions, examples, and parables meant to extend our experience of human life and make us alert to its dependence not on abstractions but on the variable nature of human beings living in an unpredictable world. Of course, the Machiavellism considered here is primarily the advice given by ambitious teachers to ambitious rulers—rulers at present most often identifiable as politicians—who in the West read Machiavelli with interest, I imagine, but soon dispense with him because they realize that their lives have taught them most of what he says, and that even he does not fit their particular problems closely enough to be helpful.

∼:2:∼

The Machiavellian Legalism of Ancient China

Historical Background

I n ancient China, it was myth, tradition, and history that the work of civilizing human beings was begun by the Three August Ones and completed by the Five Emperors. After them came the dynasties of more ordinary rulers, good and bad. The first dynasty was the Hsia, the historical existence of which is nebulous, after which came the Shang, which surely existed. The Shang was followed by a trio of dynasties, the Chou, Ch'in, and Han. It was during the course of these three that Legalism, the Chinese form of Machiavellism, took form as a doctrine and was put into actual practice.

If we begin to consider Chinese history, still uncertainly but historically, toward the end of the Chou dynasty, we find a world composed of perhaps 170 feudal principalities, often at war with one another and, not infrequently, with themselves—more than 540 interstate and 130 civil wars in a period of 159 years.[1] The ruling warrior-aristocrats were organized in lineages or clans, each with its capital, its temple, its cult sacrifices, and its veneration of ancestors. During the Chou's last period, that of the Warring States (403–221 B.C.), China's cities grew, its commerce developed, and its chariot-riding aristocrats were replaced by armies of foot soldiers and mounted archers. These armies came to be led by professional generals, men with no prior loyalty, who sold their services. There were also professional swordsman, retainers of the noblemen whose wars they fought and whose pride they maintained by their willingness to kill and be killed—both outcomes conferred on the retainers the honor of having avenged their lords.[2]*

As the more successful states grew, they mustered larger and more elaborate armies—the battle in the third century B.C. between Ch'in and Ch'u appears to have involved more than a million combatants—and the art of command grew increasingly complicated.[3] The at first oral teachings of the dangerous art of war were secret and remained so when put into writing.[4] These teachings were pervaded by a philosophy the aim of which was to teach the commanding generals a sagelike wisdom, an intuitive sensitivity to the interplay of forces by which they could turn the apparent chaos of battle to their own advantage. Wars between such sagelike commanders were understood to be intellectual combats that called for many virtues—intelligence, trustworthiness, humaneness, courage, and sternness—all made effective by the unequivocal clarity of the orders the commanders issued and the exactness with which they calculated rewards and punishments.

Their virtues, exercised only, it must be assumed, for the sake of the commanders' own armies, were supplemented by deception. Without deception, the theorists taught, no strategy could be carried out. It was essential, they said, for the enemy to be fooled into arrogance, and confused, surprised, corrupted, and divided. The greatest victory was to deceive or frighten the enemy into submission before battle had even been joined. Among methods of deceiving the enemy, Tai Kung's *Six Secret Teachings* advocated giving generous gifts to the enemy ruler, making secret alliances with his favorite ministers, and supporting his dissolute officials.[5]

In the long run, the most influential of the theorists was Sun Tzu, of the fifth century B.C. The book attributed to him, of which he may have written only the core, defines warfare as the art of deceit. To exercise it, one must pretend, seem unready when ready, far away when near, and near when far away.

---

*Because the historical documents for the period were wilfully destroyed, as will later be explained, Ssu-ma Ch'ien, the historian of the period, made use of a collection of historical anecdotes—rhetorical exercises in argument meant for the edification of rulers—entitled *Intrigues of the Warring States*. This collection "remains one of the limited group of books (Machiavelli's *Prince* is a Western example) the mere mention of which stimulates the flow of choleric humours in proper guardians of public morality—most particularly, one imagines, among those who have never read them." (See Crump, trans., *Chan-Kuo T'se*; p. 2 quoted)

If the enemy seeks some advantage, entice him with it. If he is in disorder, attack him and take him. If he is formidable, prepare against him. If he is strong, evade him. If he is incensed, provoke him. If he is humble, encourage his arrogance. If he is rested, wear him down. If he is internally harmonious, sow divisiveness in his ranks. Attack where he is not prepared; go by way of places where it would never occur to him you would go. These are the military strategist's calculations for victory—they cannot be settled in advance.[6]

Sun Tzu advocated knowing the enemy's situation by means of five kinds of spies, "local spies, inside agents, double agents, expendable spies, and unexpendable spies." He added, "When the five kinds of spies are all active, and no one knows their methods of operation *(tao)*, this is called the imperceptible web, and is the ruler's treasure."[7]

During the period I am describing, of the later Chou, the old allegiance of the vassal states to their Chou kings grew increasingly nominal and the area came to be dominated by a few independent nation-states, each equipped with a bureaucracy and a formal code of law. The great though temporary victor among them was the state of Ch'in. Its victorious progress was furthered by the duke of Chin's adviser, Shang Yang (d. 338 B.C.), one of the Machiavellis I named at the start. He led the armies of Ch'in to victories great enough to earn him a fiefdom and the title of lord of Shang. I leave the description of his reforms and his political thought for later, but it should be said, to begin with, that everything he did was for the sake of a strong state. Its strength, he was sure, had to be based on the peasants. Their two functions of fighting and tilling the soil had a natural relation to one another because the states were mostly agricultural, so that it made sense to keep the spring and summer, the time of growth, for agriculture, and the fall and winter, the time of decay and death, for war.[8]

Partly as the result of Shang Yang's reforms, the power of Ch'in continued to grow. It reached its climax under the First Emperor, whose adviser, Li Ssu, is another of the Machiavellis I have named. By 221 B.C., all the warring states had been incorporated into a single great empire. This spectacular accomplishment by a regime the Chinese later viewed as pure tyranny, created a stock topic for Chinese historians: Why did the Ch'in triumph so completely? One answer was the particular geography of Ch'in, which, cut off by mountains, was able to increase its strength without being disturbed. Other answers included Ch'in's success in developing agriculture, largely by means of its system of irrigation; its military technology; its administrative reforms; its severe and orderly government; and its readiness to disregard tradition, which allowed it to use the services of talented foreigners. But by all reckonings, the conquests of Ch'in also rested on a succession of ambitious, single-minded leaders.[9]

The political development I have described came to expression in views that were to become typical of Chinese thought. According to one such view, the rise and fall of dynasties is the result of shifts in the favor of *Heaven,* as the Chinese *T'ien* is translated. T'ien was the supreme god of Chou and, as such, the personal god of the Chou king. Later, the term often took on the impersonal character that fits the translation *Heaven.* Its impersonality, however, was not consistent, because people (including philosophers) might prefer to appeal to a personal god, so that T'ien could be either personal, impersonal, or both at once.[10] In any case, it turned into something like moral fate. The relation of T'ien to political success meant that moral actions had become more important (at least for certain thinkers) than sacrifices, for Heaven, interpreted as impersonal, rewards and punishes justly and reliably. Therefore a king who abandons moral norms no longer deserves to rule, and Heaven causes him to fall. Conversely, a king's ability to maintain his position is a sign of his basic rectitude. Such responsiveness of Heaven to morality was the explanation given for the fall of Shang and the rise of Chou.

The moral principles of the Chou were those necessary to a feudal society. Perhaps the most important of these was faithfulness to the ties of kinship, a faithfulness expressed in the Confucians' ritualized reverence for the ancestors of their lineages. Their feudally based morality also comes to expression in the honor paid to social superiors and in the modelling of all social obligations on the roles played by the different members of the family and clan. As in a family or clan, the inferior person has to serve and reverence the superior, while the superior has to justify his position by his concern for the welfare of all those socially below him.

Variant Readings of the Traditional Past

The Chinese soon learned to think about politics in relation to their past. Therefore the intellectual differences of the Chou and Ch'in thinkers, including the Legalists, are expressed in their differing interpretations of the mythical past. This past begins, it will be remembered, with Three August Ones.[11] The first of these is the Ox-Tamer, the August Fu Hsi, who first regulated marriage, taught hunting and fishing, built a thirty-five stringed lute, and invented the divinatory diagrams on which the *I Ching* (the *Book of Changes*) is based.[12]

The Divine Plowman, the August Shen Nung, continued to create civilization by clearing the fields with his red whip of fire, testing the various species of plants to discover which of them healed, and inventing the practice of trading. In his time, as primitivist philosophers liked to remind the others, human beings lived without rulers, armies, punishments, or inequality.

The third August One, Huang Ti, is also considered the first of the Five Emperors. In Ssu-ma Ch'ien, he appears as a true historical figure. The sole historian of early China, Ssu-ma begins his account with the Five Emperors. Out of respect for historical truth, he prefers to see them as merely human rulers who lived in a past so remote that it cannot be dated. He says that he assembled their records and chose from among them those that seemed most reasonable and reliable, which is to say, that fit a human measure.*

The August Huang Ti is the Yellow Emperor, whose color corresponds to that of the earth. The embodiment of sovereignty, he was celebrated as the inventor and patron of the crafts and the author of books on medicine, alchemy, astrology, and the martial arts. Then, after two further, shadowy emperors, there appeared Yao, the Confucian model of virtue, effortlessly "reverent, intelligent, accomplished, and thoughtful." Yao established the calendar and "regulated and polished the people of his domain" until they "all became brightly intelligent" and united in concord. His harmony was so profound that in his time people no longer died untimely deaths.[13]

Yao's most fateful decision was to share his power with the successor he designated, the remarkable Shun, a man of the people known for "mysterious virtue" and filial piety so unusual that he could live in harmony with an unprincipled father, an insincere stepmother, and an arrogant half-brother. Shun, says tradition, made wide-ranging admin-

---

*Behind Ssu-ma's list of rulers there lies the theory of the five phases or powers (or, put with a misleading fixity, elements), which are earth, wood, metal, fire, and water. Each of these is the power of a certain dynasty and is vanquished by the power of the dynasty that follows, until the cycle of five has been completed and begins again. By a later theory, subsequent, it appears, to the Ch'in dynasty, wood is the first and leading phase or power producing, in order, fire, metal, water, and wood again. Given this order, the Yellow Emperor could no longer be first in the list, which was headed with Fu-Hsi (wood) and Shen-Nung (fire), leaving Huang Ti, the Yellow Emperor, third in a list now comprising eight early rulers. Traditional lists of the first emperors varied. (See E. Chavannes, trans., *Les Mémoires Historiques de Se-ma Ts'ien*, vol. 1, p. cxci.)

istrative reforms, regulated the calendar, weights and measures, and the five classes of ceremonies, and also instituted examinations for officials. In addition, he put into force the statutory punishments, including banishment, the whip, the stick, and fines "for redeemable offenses." Inadvertent offenses and those ascribable to misfortune were to be pardoned, while presumptuous repeated offenders were to be sentenced to death. "'Let me be reverent! Let me be reverent!' he said to himself. 'Let compassion rule in punishment.'"[14]

The career of Shun, like that of Yü, whom Shun chose to follow him as ruler, was the historical evidence that the most humble of persons could rise to the highest level of worth and rank. Yü's greatest accomplishment was the overcoming of a catastrophic flood. For political debate, the central point of the succession was that Yao's choice of Shun and Shun's of Yü gave historical evidence that a ruler could and should hand his rule over to his worthiest minister, the rightness of the transfer in both cases being confirmed by the new ruler's success, that is, by the Mandate of Heaven. But this evidence was complicated by the fact that on Yü's death the people rejected the successor he had chosen, the best, he thought, to rule, and preferred Yü's son. This was evidence that, at a given moment in history, the people had decided to prefer hereditary succession and to found the first, Hsia dynasty. Given all the evidence, an argument on the best form of government could be based on any of the three historic precedents, that of a succession of sages, of a king who turns his rule over to a sage, and of hereditary succession.[15]

For political argument, it was essential to recall that Yao, Shun, and Yü had ruled not by force but by understanding and moral authority. Thinkers who honored tradition repeated that the authority that had emanated from Shun had been so great that he was able to rule merely by facing south, by assuming a reverent expression, or by singing the 'Song of the South Wind' to the playing of his lute.[16]

Although the virtuous Yü founded the Hsia dynasty, tradition said, dynasties must come to an end, and the Hsia's fund of virtue diminished until it was exhausted by Chieh, an emperor with the appropriate talent for doing evil. His talent was accentuated by his near-inhuman strength, his knowledge and verbal skill, and the extraordinary beauty of his wife, whose lust for luxury he was happy to gratify. His most infamous luxury was a lake of wine large enough for him and his courtiers to go boating on. Ministers who warned him of his extravagance were banished, imprisoned, or killed. Sure of himself, he boasted that he and everyone else would die only when the sun died; but then he dreamed of two suns fighting in the sky, no doubt a sign that the old dynasty's sun was contending with the rising sun of the dynasty that would replace it. Many grave portents showed that the Mandate of Heaven was now to be turned over to the Shang. But after a long rule ending in a king no less corrupt than Chieh, Shang was in turn replaced by Chou.[17]

The mythology of sage ancestors gave each philosophical school the chance to attach itself to the ancestors who best fitted its social ideal. Some Taoists chose Huang Ti, the Yellow Emperor, patron sage of alchemy, the very emperor who, in the eyes of Shang Yang and the Huang-Lao school (near-Legalists, to be described later) was the civilizing hero who organized the government and compelled compliance with its laws. The "Agronomists" and the "Primitivists," who preferred the simplest possible life, chose Shen Nung, as I have said. Confucians such as Mencius chose the parental, well-ordered, ceremonious Yao and Shun. The Mohists, who preached universal love and opposed ceremonialism, chose the same ideal rulers as the Confucians but praised them for their simplicity, Yü, for example, for toiling until he was shrivelled and shuffling with illness at his work of damming up the flood waters and regulating the river-flow—he was so preoccupied with this essential task, a story says, that he passed his own house three times yet failed to hear the crying of the son he had not yet seen.[18]

A time of disorder and contention, the later Chou was also the age in which Chinese philosophy came to birth. Not a few of the sages, military or philosophical, who participated in this birth wandered about with trains of students, looking for a ruler to advise. To show how Chou thinkers used the past to validate their social attitudes, I will cite five among them: Mo Tzu, Mencius, and Chuang Tzu, and the two Legalists, Shang Yang and Han Fei Tzu.

Mo Tzu (479–381 B.C.), whose utilitarianism justifies his dislike of ceremony, explains that, in the beginning, people lived in caves and suffered because of damp and cold. The sages therefore built them houses, not for beauty, but for shelter, and made clothing, not to please the senses or to impress, but to protect the body. Food was used only for nourishment. Before they knew how to cook

> primitive people ate only vegetables and lived in separation. Thereupon the sage [doubtless Shen Nung] taught the men to attend to farming and to plant trees to supply the people with food. And the sole purpose of securing food is to increase energy, satisfy hunger, strengthen the body and appease the stomach. (Mo Tzu, chap. 6)[19]

Mencius (Meng Tzu) (c. 372–c. 289 B.C.), the model Confucian for most of Chinese history, joins respect for tradition with compassion for the common man, of whose suffering he is intensely aware.[20]* He is bitter about those who, to win territory, slaughter men until the fields and cities are filled with corpses. Death, he says, is too light a punishment for such persons, regardless of whether they are (worst of all) specialists in war or specialists in contracting alliances or developing land. A tyrant always ends by being killed, Mencius is convinced, and his kingdom and reputation die with him (*Mencius* 4A.2.4, 14.2).

To Mencius, Heaven's Mandate, which he wants to actualize, depends on certain human potentials: compassion (suffering with and for others), humanity (benevolence to others), and deference (yielding to others).[21] He seems exceptional in believing that history operates, as Heaven wishes, in roughly five-hundred-year cycles of order and disorder. He believes that more than enough time has passed—over seven hundred years from the Chou dynasty—for a good king to appear, but that Heaven has evidently not yet wished for peace, and there is only himself, Mencius, to further it (7B.38.1–4, 2B.13.4–5).

In the longest passage in which he expounds his view of history, he begins with his idea of a sequence of periods of good and bad order, tells how, in Yao's time, the waters inundated the whole Middle Kingdom, so that snakes and dragons occupied it and the people, having nowhere to settle, lived in nests in the low ground, caves in the high ground, and platforms on trees. He tells how Shun employed Yu to tame the floods and drive away the snakes and dragons. But after the death of Yao and Shun, there arose a succession of oppressive sovereigns,

> who pulled down houses to make ponds and lakes, so that the
> people *knew* not where they could rest in quiet; they threw fields

---

*The antagonism of Confucius to a policy emphasizing punishment is evident in a well-known passage in the *Analects* (2.3) that reads (in Dawson's translation): "If you lead them by means of government and keep order among them by means of punishments, the people are without conscience in evading them. If you lead them by means of virtue and keep order among them by means of ritual, they have a conscience and moreover will submit." But as will be explained, Confucianism came to have a variety of overtones. Although the editing of the *Shu Ching (Book of History)* was ascribed to Confucius himself, its "Great Plan" chapter seems to represent an attempt, made in the late Warring States period, to use a Legalist vocabulary to express a predominantly Confucian position. Such a compromise fitted the temper of the Han Government, which gave the Confucian principles it accepted a pronounced Legalistic resonance. (See Nylan, *The Shifting Center*) out of cultivation to form gardens and parks, so that the people could not get clothes and food. *Afterwards*, corrupt speaking and oppressive deeds became more rife. (3B.9.3–5)

Mencius recalls that King Wu, helped by the duke of Chou, punished the evil ruler of his time and instituted his own, worthy rule. But the world fell into decay again, oppressive deeds became usual, and ministers sometimes murdered their kings and sons their fathers. Now, once again,

> sage sovereigns cease to arise, and the princes of the States give the reins to their lusts. Unemployed scholars indulge in unreasonable discussions . . . I am alarmed by these things, and address myself to the defence of the doctrines of the former sages. (3B.9.7–10)[22]

But Mencius remains steadfast in his belief that history teaches that "no one ever erred through following the example of the Former Kings" (4A.1.4).[23]

Chuang Tzu, whose book is a composite, expresses a variety of positions. By and large, however, he rejects what the so-called sages claim to learn from history. His contempt for sages and moral lessons is conveyed in the well-known fictional conversation between Confucius and Robber Chih. This conversation sounds as if it reflects the period (209–202 B.C.) when Ch'in had lost power and Han had not yet gained it.[24] I cite the conversation because of its claim that morality is honored in the breach even by its self-appointed guardians.

The story is this: Robber Chih, with his nine thousand followers, is the terror of feudal lords. Confucius is eager to reform this bandit king, who, unlike him, admires the peaceful anarchy in which he thinks humans first lived and hates what he thinks is the thievish civilization of his own time. When Confucius rebukes him, he recalls that people once nested in trees, gathered acorns, and warmed themselves by burning firewood. Knowing their mothers, he says, but not their fathers, they "lived side by side with the elk and deer." Plowing for food and weaving for clothing, they lived in perfect harmony and virtue. But then, continues Robber Chih, there came the Yellow Emperor, who, avid for civilization, fought a bloody battle with the dragonlike Ch'ih Y. Then came Yao and Shun with their hosts of officials, and then other, evil rulers. From that time on, the strong have oppressed the weak, the many have abused the few, and "all have been no more than a pack of rebels and wrongdoers." Turning to Confucius, Robber Chih says angrily:

And now you come cultivating the ways of Kings Wen and Wu,
utilizing all the eloquence in the world in order to teach these
things to later generations! In your flowing robes and loose-tied
sash, you speak your deceits and act out your hypocrisies, confusing and leading astray the rulers of the world, hoping thereby to
lay your hands on wealth and eminence. There is no worse robber
than you![25]

The book of Chuang Tzu is ambivalent about the Yellow Emperor,
whom later Taoists as well as the supporters of Huang-Lao (followers
of Huang Ti and Lao Tzu) saw as their patron. At one point, Chuang
Tzu criticizes the Yellow Emperor as the creator of culture, who "first
used benevolence and righteousness to meddle with the minds of
men." Yao and Shun, who followed him, "grieved their vital organs in
the practice of benevolence and righteousness, taxed their blood and
breath in the establishment of laws and standards," but failed to govern
as they had hoped. The situation continued to deteriorate, breeding
tyrants, robbers, and philosophical preachers, with the result that

> stupidity and wisdom duped each other, good and bad called one
> another names, falsehood and truth slandered one another, and
> the world sank into a decline ... The crime lay in this meddling
> with men's minds. So it was that worthy men crouched in hiding
> below the great mountains and yawning cliffs, and the lords of ten
> thousand chariots fretted and trembled above in their ancestral
> halls.[26]

The two Legalists, Shang Yang and Han Fei, learn a very different
lesson from the past. Shang Yang (d. 338 B.C.) says that at first people
discriminated against one another because they were partial to their relatives and became insecure because they wanted to protect their possessions. Preoccupied with discrimination and insecurity, they fell into
disorder, grew competitive, and relied on force. This shows that "the
guiding principles of the people are base, and they are not consistent in
what they value."[27] Shen Nung had been able to rule without the use of
punishment, but after he died, "the weak were conquered by force and
the few oppressed by many," so that, because the times had changed,
he was obliged to use force both at home and abroad.[28] Having no social
hierarchy at first, the people were so disorderly, says Shang Yang, that
the sages had to distinguish between nobles and others and to regulate
ranks and distinguish the idea of superior from inferior.

As the territory was extensive, the people numerous and all things many, they made a division of five kinds of officials, and maintained it; as the people were numerous, wickedness and depravity originated, so they established laws and regulations and created weights and measures . . . and the interdicts of the laws and regulations. [29]

The Legalist Han Fei Tzu (d. 233 B.C.), who has Taoist sympathies, thinks well of the early life of human beings but believes that their early amity has become impossible. Like Mencius and Chuang Tzu, he pictures people in the beginning as troubled by all the animals until a sage teaches them how to build shelters of wood. Grateful, they make him their ruler. Another sage teaches them how to make fire, and Yü saves them from a great deluge. Life then becomes idyllic because men do not have to till the soil—the seeds of grasses and fruits of trees give food enough—and because women do not have to weave—the skins of birds and animals are enough for clothing. There are so few people that they have more than enough, never quarrel, hardly need rewards or punishments, and govern themselves. But there comes a time when even the benevolent, righteous ruler loses his sovereignty.

Evidently benevolence and righteousness once serviceable in olden times are not so at present. Hence the saying: "There are as many situations as there are generations." . . . Men of remote antiquity strove to be known as moral and virtuous; those of the middle age struggled to be known as wise and resourceful; and now men fight for the reputation of being vigorous and powerful.[30]

What Han Fei learns from history is the lesson that effective government needs neither moral qualities nor sageness but authority, not trust but distrust, and reliable rewards and invariable punishments. "His theoretical formulations . . . might almost be taken as a prophecy outlining all the failures of government that were to be committed by all the muddle-headed rulers of the two-thousand-year imperial era commencing with the Ch'in and Han dynasties."[31]

The First Legalist, Shang Yang

The School of Law, Fa-chia in Chinese, is the retrospective creation of later observers.[32] We meet it first in Ssu-ma Ch'ien, where it is numbered among the six schools of Chinese thought and described as strict and merciless but right in setting the ruler high and the subject low, and right in making clear who carries just what legal authority. The text (written by Ssu-ma Ch'ien's historian-father) adds that the Legalists "judge all men alike by their laws," without favoritism based on familial closeness or social level. The historian's comment is that laws that judge men so "can serve as an expedient for a particular time, but they cannot be used for long."[33]

The term *fa* at first meant primarily *model* or *standard*, in the sense in which the carpenter's square and compass and the builder's plumb line are standards. *Fa* also meant *method* or *political method*. However, for the use made of it by the Legalists, the translation *law* or, more narrowly, *penal law* serves well enough. According to the Legalists, the idea of law is to be impartial and exclude any appeal to historic precedent, religious sanction, or morality, all of which it is meant to replace as the standard for judgment.[34]

The fact that it is the Legalists who most stress law and reward and punishment does not mean that such ideas were new or were not acted on by the later generations that execrated Legalism. The difference is that when non-Legalists recommended punishment, they did so in the name of morality. As has been pointed out, Confucius himself assumed that if the people's moral sense were not cultivated, they would lack a sense of shame and would prove cunning enough to defeat any law.[35]

The Chinese remembered Shang Yang quite well. We learn this from Ssu-ma Ch'ien, who says that in his time, the second century B.C., every family had a copy of the Lord Shang's laws.[36] The book ascribed to Shang Yang varies greatly in its style and refers to events that happened after his death, but it is generally agreed that it expresses his ideas and is basically authentic.[37] His biography by Ssu-ma Ch'ien is a consciously dramatic rendering of the facts he was able to verify, enlivened by the same devices, such as invented conversations, that were used by the Greek and Roman historians.

I skip the earlier part of Shang Yang's biography, which tells that as a young man he was interested in understanding social control by means of penalties and that he served the prime minister as an attendant. The stubbornness of his ambition is shown by the three successive attempts he made to gain the interest of the ruler, Duke Hsiao, who was so bored at their first interview that he fell asleep.[38] When the ruler was ready to listen to him, Shang Yang used historical examples to convince him that success was not guaranteed by following antiquity. "A wise man creates laws," he said, "but a foolish man is controlled by them . . . There is more than one way to govern the world, and there is no necessity to imitate antiquity, in order to take appropriate measures for the state."[39]

The ruler agreed, and Shang Yang prepared to put his radical reforms into effect. First, however, he had to convince the people that the new laws would be enforced. To convince them, he used a clever stratagem. Having put a thirty-foot pole near the capital's south gate, he had the people assembled and told them that he would give ten ounces of gold to anyone who could move the pole to the north gate.

> The people thought it strange, but there was no one who dared to move it. Thereupon, he said that he would give fifty ounces of gold to anyone who would remove it. There was one man, who removed it, and forthwith he gave him the fifty ounces of gold, to make it clear that he deceived no one.[40]

Having made himself believable, Shang Yang set about centralizing and rationalizing the state. He did this by dividing it into counties with their own appointed magistrates, by weakening the hereditary system enough to allow the people to buy and sell farmland, and by replacing taxation in labor by taxation in produce. To ensure public discipline, he used a tactic that became characteristic of China throughout its history: He divided the population into small units of five or ten families legally responsible for crimes committed by any person among them. He also standardized weights and measures and instituted honorary ranks for military achievements and for contributions of grain to the government. To enforce his new regulations, he proposed that the denunciation of a culprit should be rewarded as highly as decapitation of an enemy, concealment of a culprit as severely as surrender to the enemy, and failure to denounce a culprit by cutting the offender into two. According to his laws, people who tilled, wove, or produced grain or silk did not have to serve at forced labor; but those who engaged in an enterprise considered unproductive or who proved themselves lazy were to be enslaved.[41]

To Shang Yang, it was extremely important that the law be impartial, so that when the crown prince infringed it, he complained that the law was failing because it was not being observed by those in high places. Since it was impossible to punish the crown prince directly, he proposed that the crown prince's tutor should be punished instead and that his teacher, a different person, be branded. "The following day the people of Ch'in all hastened into the path of the law." And when the law "had been in force for ten years, the people of Ch'in greatly rejoiced" because robbery had ended, order prevailed, and the people were prosperous and "brave in war and timid in private quarrels." As a result, some of those who had once thought the laws inappropriate came forward to say that they had changed their minds. Shang Yang made a fully Machiavellian response. He condemned these people for daring to reveal that they had once opposed his laws and had them banished to the border areas. From then on, the people were afraid even to comment on the laws.[42]

Of Shang Yang's biography it remains only to tell that he had great administrative and military successes and a single but decisive misfortune. One of his successes was the capture of the rival prince he fooled into exposing himself by pretending that he wanted to conduct peace negotiations with him. The reason for his misfortune is as follows: The crown prince having infringed the law again, Shang Yang had his tutor's nose cut off. When the ruler, Duke Hsiao, died and the crown prince succeeded him, Shang Yang was accused of plotting a rebellion. He then actually rebelled, was defeated, and was "torn to pieces by chariots as an expiatory punishment." Following Chinese precedent, his family was exterminated.[43]

Shang Yang's views have already been expressed or hinted at. According to one of his statements, the state has three permanent functions, farming, trading, and the exercise of authority. These permanent functions give rise to other, parasitic, politically destructive functions, which lead people to live at others' expense, or to serve beauty, love, ambition, or virtue and, by doing so, to become soft.[44] A soft life is politically destructive, says Shang Yang, for which reason it is dangerous for a strong country not to wage war. Unless it does, the parasitic functions develop and enemies dismember it, as they do if there are too few farmers and too many merchants. Attacking traditionalism of the Confucian kind, Shang Yang insists that a country administered, as Confucians prefer, with the aid of "odes, history, rites, music, filial piety, brotherly love, virtue and moral culture" will either sink into poverty or fall prey to the enemy.

> A country that has no strength and that practices knowledge and cleverness, will certainly perish, but a fearful people, stimulated by penalties, will become brave, and a brave people, encouraged by rewards, will fight to the death . . . ; having no match, it will be strong, and being strong it will attain supremacy.[45]

Shang Yang often repeats that sound government can be maintained only with the help of consistent rewards and punishments. To be useful, the punishments have to be severe enough to cause disgrace or hardship.[46] To imitate ancient times, promote virtue, and give the people what they like, he says, is to lead the people into idleness, disorder, and suffering. But if you govern by punishment, the resulting fear will keep the people from committing crimes, and what they are allowed to enjoy will make them happy. "One always attains what the people like by means of what they dislike, and one brings about what they dislike by means of what they like." Therefore, "in an orderly country, punishments are numerous and rewards rare."[47]

In a passage that the translator of Shang Yang takes to have been written during the late third century B.C., the following summary of his doctrine is made:

> Law is the authoritative principle for the people and is the basis of government; it is what shapes the people. Trying to govern while eliminating the law is like a desire not to be hungry while eliminating food, or a desire not to be cold while eliminating clothes, or a desire to go east while one moves west.[48,]

The Confucian Teacher of the Legalists: Hsün Tzu

Apart from the teacher, Confucius himself, there were two great early Confucians, the one Meng Tzu (Mencius) and the other Hsün Tzu (c. 340–245 B.C.). Hsün Tzu's great early influence was in time supplanted by that of Mencius, but he was the most wide-ranging, rigorous, well-integrated, and rationalistic of the early Confucians, in fact, of all the early Chinese philosophers. He earns his place in this account because of his conception of human nature, which made him the appropriate teacher for his students Han Fei and Li Ssu. What could these two Legalists have learned from Hsün Tzu, who shares the Confucian's usual respect for decency? A partial answer is that Hsün Tzu comes to use the concept of *fa*, in the Legalists' way, to mean *law* and *political or administrative method*. Like the Legalists, Hsün Tzu also holds that punishment should have fixed standards, and, like them, believes that a country's power depends on its wealth and therefore on its inhabitants' frugality and their employment in the primary, wealth-producing occupations.[49] But Hsün Tzu's closeness to the Legalists rests most obviously on his conception of human nature, which he contrasts with that of Mencius, with his belief in instinctive goodness. Mencius, says Hsün Tzu,

> has not really understood man's nature nor distinguished properly between the basic nature and conscious activity. The nature is

that which is given by Heaven; you cannot learn it, you cannot acquire it by effort. Ritual principles, on the other hand, are created by sages; you can learn to apply them, you can work to bring them to completion. That part of man which cannot be learned or acquired by effort is called the nature; that part of his which can be acquired by learning and brought by effort is called conscious activity.[50]

Hsün Tzu's blunt conclusion is that man is by nature evil. In a well-known analogy he compares man's nature to a warped piece of wood that can be straightened only by setting it on a straightening board, steaming it, and forcing it into shape.[51] "Man's nature is evil," he says, "goodness is the result of conscious activity." Man is born with the desire for profit, which, if indulged, leads him into strife, discourtesy, and vanity.

He is born with feelings of envy and hate, and if he indulges these, they will lead him into violence and crime, and all sense of loyalty and good faith will disappear. Man is born with the desires of the eyes and ears, with a fondness for beautiful sights and sounds. If he indulges these, they will lead him into license and wantonness, and all ritual principles and correct forms will be lost. Hence, any man who follows his nature and indulges his emotions will inevitably become involved in wrangling and strife, and will end as a criminal.[52]

The Legalist Philosopher Han Fei Tzu

Han Fei Tzu (c. 280–233 B.C.) was a prince of the state of Han, Ssu-ma Ch'ien reports. "He was fond of studies in penology, epistemology, law, and statecraft, tracing his principles to the Yellow Emperor and Lao Tzu. Fei, being a habitual stutterer, was unable to deliver fluent speeches, but was proficient in writing books."[53] He and Li Ssu both studied with Hsün Tzu. Of the two, said Li Ssu, Fei was the more successful.

Concerned at the political deterioration of his state, Han Fei made repeated suggestions for reform, which the king ignored. Angry at the king of Han's indifference and poor administration, he composed his many political essays. When the king of Ch'in happened to read Han Fei's *Solitary Indignation* (on incompetent and untrustworthy officials) and *The Five Vermin* (on the types of men who destroy the state), he exclaimed that if only he could meet and become friendly with this man, when the time came, he would die without regrets. Li Ssu then said, "These are works of Han Fei." Later, Ch'in made an attack on Han, and the king of Han, afraid he would be conquered, sent Han Fei to Ch'in as a goodwill envoy. The king of Ch'in liked Han Fei, but his advisers Li Ssu and Yao Chia were very suspicious of him.[54]

Preserved in Han Fei's works is the first memorial he wrote for the king of Ch'in. In this memorial he says that his own state, Han, has served Ch'in and been its ally for more than thirty years; but if, nevertheless, Ch'in attacks Han, it will put up a strong defense and join other states in a formidable coalition. Why not be clever, he asks, and make the coalition impossible by bribing officials of one of its potential members, pacifying a second with a hostage, and attacking a third, whose alliance with a possible fourth would not be much of a danger? Once the coalition has been made impossible, any difficulty between Ch'in and Han can be settled by a mere official dispatch.[55]

Li Ssu, who advocated the conquest of Han, wrote a countermemorial. It begins by stating that it is true that Ch'in already has Han, but only in the sense that someone has a disease of the stomach or heart, because, although a vassal, Han has always been a menace to Ch'in and cannot be trusted if Ch'in is attacked. Li Ssu goes on to argue that Fei's plan would be catastrophic and proposes that he, Li Ssu, be sent to the king of Han to persuade him to come to Ch'in, where the king would be taken prisoner.

In the course of his argument, Li Ssu attacks his former fellow-student, who must have come to Ch'in, he says, to improve his position in the Han government by demonstrating that he could save it. Han Fei, he argues, uses his eloquence to embellish lies, invent plots, and try to win esteem by stimulating Ch'in and Han to become intimate.[56] Some time later, perhaps after Li Ssu had made an unsuccessful attempt to meet the king of Han, Li Ssu and Yao Chia wrote to their king:

> Han Fei is one of the princes of the Han State. As Your Majesty is now thinking of conquering the feudal lords, Fei will in the long run work for Han and not for Ch'in. Such is the natural inclination of human nature. Now, if Your Majesty does take him into service, and, after detaining him for a long time, sends him home, this will be a source of future trouble. It is best to punish him for an offense against the law.[57]

Are the documents I have been quoting from accurate? Considering the Chinese practice of incorporating official documents into their histories, perhaps so. There is no reason to doubt that the king of Ch'in agreed with Li Ssu, as Ssu-ma Ch'ien reports. Then, acting on his own, Li Ssu sent someone with poison to Han Fei, who was induced or ordered to commit suicide. Han Fei, we are told, had wanted to plead his case before the king but was denied an audience. When the king repented and sent him a pardon, he was already dead.[58]

Having followed Han Fei to his dismal end, we can turn to his political thought. Like Hsün Tzu, he argues that it is out of love that the ruler must work against the people's natural disorderliness and self-indulgence. "The triumph of penalty is the beginning of order; the over-flow of reward, the origin of chaos . . . Law is the origin of supremacy and penalty is the beginning of love.[59]

Because the people abhor toil and enjoy leisure, says Han Fei, it is all too easy for the land to lie waste and the state to grow chaotic; and therefore the prevailing tradition, which encourages disorder, must be discouraged. Afterwards, because the people are at times naive and at times intelligent, the law should be changed to fit each new situation.[60]

Han Fei rejects reasoning that, though eloquent, is unworldly, or absurdly dialectical, or beyond rational understanding. The most magnificent of theories can be impractical, he says. To drive this idea home, he repeats the parable of Yü Ch'ing, who once so impressed a carpenter with his reasoning that the house the carpenter then built fell down. "To seek for truth one must trust to practical means."[61] That is why it is wrong to advise rulers to show mercy and practice righteousness and love. When rulers accept such advice, they bring misfortune on themselves and their lands. Why so? Because even though the world thinks it good to give alms to the poor, when a ruler gives alms freely, some of those that get them are without merit, and the people lose the courage to face the enemy and refuse to work at home or on the land. Instead, they pursue private virtues, fame, high posts, and financial rewards. As a result, self-seeking ministers and bold rogues gain the upper hand—all the more, if the ruler hesitates to blame and punish.[62] Even a mother, so loving and compassionate to her little child, sends him, when mischievous, to the teacher, and when ill, to the doctor. In spite of all her compassion, she knows that she alone cannot save her child from penalties for misconduct or from illness or death. "If so, what preserves the child is not love." In any case, the relation between mother and child is love, while that between ruler and minister is only expediency. As for benevolence, it can drive the state to ruin no less easily than evil. Therefore the wise ruler knows that to rely on the people's love is dangerous. He governs in a way that makes it certain not that they love him, but that they do him good.[63] To put the matter analogically:

Without the severity of the whip and the facility of the bridle, even Tsao-fu [the renowned horseman] could not drive the horse; without the rule of the compasses and square and the tip of the inked string, even Wang Erh [the famous carpenter] could not draw squares and circles; and without the position of authority and power and the law of reward and punishment, even Yao and Shun could not keep the state in order. Now that the rulers of the present age thoughtlessly discard heavy punishment and severe censure and practice love and favor, to realize the achievement of the Hegemonic Ruler is also hopeless.[64]

According to Han Fei, although everyone approves of Yao and Shun, they weakened the principle of authority by reversing the relationship between ruler and minister. Yao did so by making his minister, Shun, his ruler, and Shun by making his ruler, Yao, his minister.[65] Nothing is possible, says Han Fei in his essay "Loyalty and Filial Piety," unless the ruler has statutory authority, *shih*, the authority of position inherent in the very structure of a state, which, to function properly, must have ingrained lines of command and obedience.*

In another essay, one of Han Fei's most interesting, there is a debate between a Legalist philosopher and a critic. The philosopher argues that the authority of position is enough to rule a state, so that the personality of the ruler is only incidental. Good as Yao was, says the philosopher, as long as he remained a commoner, he could do nothing. Chieh, however, though wicked, ruled the world because he possessed authority of position.[66]

The critic answers that authority is not everything, because to place unworthy men in high position can lead to outrageous, violent events and chaos. To make his point, he quotes the *History of Chou*, which says, "Do not add wings to tigers. Otherwise, they will fly into the village, catch people, and devour them."[67] Authority is essential, but it makes a great difference who exercises it.

---

*In the military writing of the period, *shih* means *conditions* (that prevail in two opposing armies), *prevailing circumstances*, *deployment* (of troops), or *advantageous (strategic) position*. The *Book of Lord Shang* adds the meaning *advantageous political position* or *authority of position*. In Hsün Tzu, unlike the Legalists, this authority is presumed to be the result of the people's will, that is, of self-evidently moral government. Among the Legalists, the term usually refers to the authority or power that accompanies and defines political status. For these distinctions, see Ames, *The Art of Rulership*, chap. 4.

Then Han Fei, who calls himself "some other critic," answers both philosopher and critic by making a distinction. He argues that if the term *authority, shih,* is restricted to nature, it is obvious that natural circumstances can create political order or chaos beyond the power of anyone, however talented, to change. But his concern is with the authority created by human beings, to which the qualities of the individual ruler are irrelevant. A simple calculation, he says, will show this: outstanding persons, good or evil, appear once in a thousand generations. "As a matter of fact, most rulers in the world form a continuous line of average men," who "neither come up to the worthiness of Yao and Shun nor reach down to wickedness of Chieh and Chou." When such ordinary rulers uphold the law and fulfill their high position, order prevails; but when they neglect the law and desert their high position, chaos prevails. If it were possible to neglect the position and wait for an outstanding ruler to appear, there would be one generation of order for every thousand of chaos. Conversely, if it were possible to fulfill the requirements of the position and wait for a Chieh or Chou to appear, there would be one generation of chaos for a thousand of order. Therefore it is true that *shih* is worth exercising and untrue that one must depend on the ruler's worthiness. To wait for Yao and Shun is as absurd as waiting for the best quality of rice and meat to save a starving person's life, or as waiting for an expert swimmer to come from far away to save a person drowning nearby. Han Fei concludes that, between them, the philosopher and his critic create a dilemma out of the alternatives they teach, but these alternatives are not exhaustive, while his own position is consistent and more reasonable than either.[68]

Much of Han Fei's thought is devoted to the factors that make or break a state. In an essay on portents of danger, he makes a comprehensive though disorderly enumeration that should be useful for a study of the rise and fall of monarchs. A state's ruin is likely, he says, under the following conditions: when families own more land than the ruler and when the power of his ministers is nearly as great as his own; when the ruler concerns himself with plans, ideas, and foreign friendships rather than with laws and defence works; when officials prefer study, sons prefer debate, and shopkeepers prefer foreign money, which they hide; when the ruler is fond of luxurious architecture, chariots, clothing, and curios; when the ruler believes in astrology, divination, and the like; when the ruler refuses to take advice except from ministers of high rank; when bribery and favoritism prevail; or when the ruler is tender hearted and indecisive, or greedy, or swayed by impractical debate and thoughtless wordiness, or unable to keep secrets, or proud, contentious, and unable to compromise. Han Fei continues, portent of ruin after portent, to the total of forty-seven, ending with, "If the ruler's sons-in-law and grandsons live behind the same hamlet gate with the commoners and behave unruly and arrogantly towards their neighbors, then ruin is possible."[69]

Han Fei's caution against the ruler's belief in astrology and divination seems to show that he shares the rationalism, very unusual for his time, of his teacher Hsün Tzu. The list makes clear that Han Fei prefers the ruler to be always alert to, not to say suspicious of, the people who surround him. His ministers, though necessary, are a constant menace, as are his consort, his concubines, and the son he has chosen to succeed him. Any of these may prefer that his life be short. It is dangerous for a ruler to trust anyone, says Han Fei, because trust breeds dependence. As for ministers, they are tied to him by nothing more than the force of circumstance, for which reason

> those who act as ministers never for a moment cease trying to spy into their sovereign's mind, and yet the ruler of men sits above them in indolence and pride. That is why there are rulers in the world who face intimidation and sovereigns who are murdered. If the ruler puts too much trust in his son, the evil ministers will find ways to utilize the son for the accomplishment of their private schemes.[70]

To detect the more subtle kinds of subversion, the ruler must get the people to watch one another. This can be done by implicating them in one another's crimes, so that the evil-minded will not forget how many people are watching them. The lesson is that "the most enlightened method of governing a state is to trust measures and not men."[71] However, adds Han Fei, it is important for the ruler to understand that even if he is as wise as Yao, without the support of the people, he will not accomplish anything great. Whatever his strength, the help of others is necessary—the keenest-sighted man cannot see his own eyelashes. Therefore the intelligent ruler accepts his own and others' incapacities.[72]

As a Taoist, Han Fei accepts that the Tao is the beginning of everything and that the ruler who holds fast to this beginning understands what everything comes from. The ruler therefore waits quietly for nature to define every function and settle every affair. Waiting quietly, he must not reveal his preferences because, if he does, his ministers will pretend to share his opinions and hide their own. Even if wise, he should let each minister act by himself and discover his own intelligence, and even if courageous, he should let each minister discover his own courage. Everyone will then occupy himself according to his particular ability.

> It is the Tao of the intelligent ruler that . . . he makes the worthy exert their talent and appoints them to office accordingly without being himself at the end of his ability; and that in case of merits the ruler gains the renown and in cases of demerit the ministers face the blame so that the ruler is never at the end of his reputation . . . It is the ministers who do the toil; it is the ruler who gets the spoil. This is the everlasting principle of the worthy sovereign.[73]

It is because the Tao, the principle of nature, exists in invisibility and functions in unintelligibility, says Han Fei, that the ruler should do nothing (*wu-wei*) and show nothing (*wu-hsien*).[74] Doing nothing and resting in darkness, he should observe the faults that others reveal by exposing themselves to the light. He should see, hear, and know, but never be seen, heard, or known. He should correct no word uttered by others, but compare their words with their deeds to see if the two coincide. And to ensure that ministers carry out policies without knowing the reasons for them, the ruler must appoint a censor for each official and forbid the officials to talk to one another. The ruler must keep the real reasons secret in order to prevent the tiger of subversion from coming into existence. If the ruler succeeds in being "too great to be measured," if functions and norms are set, laws and manners scrutinized, and punishments maintained, "there will be no traitor in the country."[75]

Han Fei's Taoist wisdom or cunning is of a kind the Chinese have often found suggestive, in and out of politics. Is it compatible with the other advice he gives, advice that implies a very active ruler? Han Fei's use of the idea of nonaction in politics appears to assume that, ideally, human affairs are self-regulating, or, to speak of the government, that the hierarchy is self-regulating when each official acts in exact accord with his function as defined by law. Everyone is held to account, and would-be transgressors are held in check by the threat of severe punishments for even minor infractions. The role of the officials is to be active; that of the ruler, to hold them together by his embodiment of authority and his ability to compare their performance with the definition of their offices. For him to say something is disruptive because he then deflects officials from their own natural understanding of their tasks. For him to exert himself, that is, to move in his own, particular direction, is to disrupt the natural movement of the system that revolves around him as its axis. And for him to take advantage of the system is to weaken the objective force of the authority that rules everything in an even, equal way. The ruler's silence is his wisdom, his lack of intention is his union with the *tao*, his distance from his ministers and people is his strength, his hiddenness is his safety. As the wholeness of the whole, the emperor must not attempt to be anything else.

But wholeness is not enough. In Han Fei's version, it needs to be guarded by a very inclusive suspicion. His advice to the ruler to remain inscrutable should be classed with the "roundabout, profound, magnificent, and exaggerating" language he rejects in other political advisers.[76] I say this because he seems ready to spin Taoist fantasies that give ordinary palace intrigues an aura of cosmogonic depth.

The Paradigmatic Legalist, Li Ssu

Li Ssu (c. 290–208 B.C.) is the paradigmatic Legalist because, with the collaboration of his emperor, he used power intelligently to create the political structure of the Chinese empire. To traditional Chinese, he is also the paradigmatic villain who tried to destroy the moral basis and cultural continuity of their lives. If, with the Chinese, we consider him and the First Emperor a symbiotic pair, we can describe him as the union of Yao's abilities and Chieh's evil disposition, as a Machiavellian genius on whom Heaven smiled brightly and briefly before it left him to be torn apart in the marketplace.

Ssu-ma Ch'ien begins Li Ssu's biography with the following story, which sounds too good to be true. Li Ssu, then a petty clerk, saw that the rats in the toilet ate filth and fled from people and dogs, while the rats in the granary were fat and fearless. His conclusion was that a person, like a rat, fails or prospers depending on where he places himself. With this thought in mind, he became a follower of Hsün Tzu and studied the methods used by emperors and kings.[77] Then he looked for the most promising ruler to serve and chose the king of Ch'in, whom he encouraged to pursue his goal "to swallow up the world and to rule with the title of Emperor."[78] He persuaded the king that the feudal lords who paid him allegiance might one day ally themselves against him, so it was best to break their power soon. Therefore, on Li Ssu's advice, the king sent secret agents equipped with gold and jewels to reward the feudal lords and officers who allied themselves with Ch'in. The agents were instructed that, if the lords proved unwilling, they were to initiate rifts between them and their subjects and, when possible, stab the recalcitrants to death. To take advantage of the opportunities created by these agents, the king sent generals to follow in their path.[79]

Afraid that the aliens in Ch'in would sow dissension, one of the king's ministers advised that all of them, including Li Ssu, be expelled. Unwilling to leave, Li Ssu submitted a memorial in which he gave instances from history of men who became outstanding ministers in the states to which they had emigrated. The foreigners in Ch'in were one of its important resources, he argued, adding that many of them preferred to be loyal to Ch'in, but that if they were expelled, not only would Ch'in be depopulated, but they would sow enmity against the king in the other feudal courts.[80]

The king rescinded the order of expulsion and, returning Li Ssu to office, kept him to the end as his counselor. Ch'in policies were so effective that the feudal states yielded one by one until "the world was finally united." The restless, superstitious, power-hungry King, well aware of the magnitude of his enterprise, took the title of First August (*Shih Huang Ti*) while the able, harsh, calculating Li Ssu received the rank of grand councillor (*ch'eng hsiang*).[81]

To make the universal state possible, Li Ssu abolished feudal estates and ranks and organized the empire into thirty-six provinces or commanderies (*chün*), each with its own governor, military commandant, and superintendent, while each province was divided into prefectures (*hsien*). To keep the former feudal lords docile, they were resettled at the capital in replicas of their old palaces; and to make it easier to keep the peace, all nonauthorized weapons were surrendered to the emperor:

> At a great banquet, he received all the weapons in the empire, and had them brought together at Hsien-yang. There they were melted into bells and bell supports, and made into twelve metal human figures. . . . The laws and rules and weights and measures were unified . . . and the characters used in writing were made uniform.[82]

The new empire's laws were unified by the application everywhere of the Ch'in code, which called for severe punishments (not unusual in other Chinese codes), collective responsibility (also not unusual), and a hierarchical administration (which must now have become much more complex). As we know from recently discovered texts, the local rules of the Ch'in code took up such details as the nature and use of official documents, the rules for appointing and dismissing subordinate officials, the weights and measures to be used in warehouses, and the amount of seed grain per area to be loaned to farmers.[83]

Now, after the unification, tax and convict labor could be used to build roads that spanned all China—the Ch'in imperial highways were longer by far than the Roman road system (of about A.D. 150). To make the roads more usable, cart wheels, which cut deep ruts into unpaved roads, were kept to a uniform gauge. The long linked roads, needed no less by merchants than by soldiers, were supplemented by an unbroken canal system, still in use, stretching from the north to the south of China. There was also the Great Wall—not the present one, mostly of the sixteenth century—a fortification, on which some three hundred thousand men worked for more than ten years, that dwarfed all previous human constructions. A telltale sign of Legalist principles was the appearance among the wall's builders of officials convicted of handling court cases unjustly.[84]

The unified empire was expanded by military conquests followed by colonization with convicts and others. In the long run, however, the extension of the empire may have been less important than the reform of writing, which countered China's great linguistic diversity by simplifying and standardizing the Chinese characters so that they carried the same meaning everywhere.[85]

Yet, despite all this, Li Ssu is remembered most vividly for the episode of the burning of the books, which occurred in 213 B.C. This act of censorship, unprecedented in its extent in China, was a catastrophe for Chinese culture, though not as great as appears at first sight. It was limited because the regime had too few years to carry it into effect, and because copies of the banned books were kept in the imperial archives (later burned by rebels). However, even if less catastrophic than usually supposed, the burning created a great cultural divide in China. It strengthened the antiquarian and historical passions of the Chinese and it stimulated the hunt for old texts and the close study of language and style needed to verify or restore what might otherwise have been lost. The search for lost classical books led to the suspicious discovery of so-called ancient texts, written in old, pre-Han script, which competed with so-called modern texts—those transcribed in modern script from scholars' memories. This contest between "ancient" and "modern" texts was to prove extremely important for later Chinese orthodoxy.[86]

I return to the fateful episode of the burning of the books. Li Ssu wanted them burned because they reminded their readers of dynasties, like Chou, that lasted because their kings gave fiefs to sons, younger brothers, and worthy ministers. Such reminders supported the criticism that the tried old ways were now being abandoned and the empire endangered, the danger being heightened by the flatteries lavished on the emperor by his ministers.[87] Seeing in this criticism an invitation to revive feudalism and make ill use of the sacred past, Li Ssu outlawed criticism altogether. The empire has been unified, he said, the distinctions of right and wrong have been laid down and a supreme sovereign has been put into office, yet there are those who rely on their private teachings and try to discredit the new laws. Inside the court, these critics make mental reservations, and outside, they criticize the laws in the streets. For the sake of the imperial power, all this should be prohibited. Li Ssu therefore wrote to the emperor requesting

> that all persons possessing works of literature, the *Shih* [collections such as the later *Book of Odes*], the *Shu* [collections of documents such as the *Book of History*], and the discussions of the various philosophers, should destroy them with remission of all penalty. Those who have not destroyed them within thirty days after issuing the order, are to be branded and sent to do forced labor. Books not to be destroyed will be those on medicine and pharmacy, divination by the tortoise and milfoil, and agriculture and arboriculture. As for persons who wish to study, let them take the officials as their teachers.[88]

Ssu-ma Ch'ien, sensitive to the loss of precious historical data, writes that these recommendations were accepted and carried out "for the purpose of keeping the people ignorant, and of bringing it about that none within the empire should use the past to discredit the present."[89]

In 212, a year after the burning of the books, there occurred the episode of the "execution of the literati," which involved Li Ssu but was not of his doing. It resulted in the putting to death of 460 scholars. This execution has been a byword of horror in China ever since (except quite recently).* In its traditional interpretation, the word for *put to death* is understood as *buried alive*; but the whole story may be one of the episodes later inserted into Ssu-ma Ch'ien's text in order to blacken the already black reputation of the First Emperor.[90]

For traditional Chinese, what remains of Li Ssu's biography is the cautionary ending of a classic tale of hubris. I abbreviate severely, leaving only enough to recall the drama of its betrayals and counterbetrayals. It begins with the sudden death of the emperor, after a reign of

---

*An approving history, published in China in 1973, says, "In burying the Confucian scholars alive, Ch'i Shih-huang only buried 460 reactionary Confucianists in Hsien-yang who 'used the past to attack the present.' Such a suppression was entirely necessary in order to 'emphasize the present while slighting the past' and to consolidate the unification" See Bodde, "The State and Empire of Ch'in," p. 72, footnote.

twelve years, at the age of only forty-five. To anticipate his death, the emperor had prepared a letter to his eldest son appointing him successor. But the eunuch-official in charge of the emperor's seal kept the letter and, arguing from historical precedent, persuaded another of the emperor's sons, Hu-hai, to assume the office of Emperor.

Asked to join the plot, Li Ssu is reported to have answered "How can you speak words that would destroy the state? This is not a fit affair for subjects to discuss."[91] Li Ssu eventually gave in, though less, it appears, to the eunuch's reasonings and precedents than to his threats. In league with Hu-hai, the two forged a letter in which the late Emperor accused his eldest son of disloyalty, passed the crown on to Hu-hai, and suggested that his eldest son commit suicide. The eldest, impeccably filial son obeyed the suggestion, or rather, command, made in his father's forged name. Then, following the eunuch's advice, the new Emperor tried to prevent rebellion by making the laws and punishments even more severe. The eunuch's further advice was to exterminate the ministers and exile the family of the former Emperor. He said, "Your Majesty will then recline on a lofty pillow, giving free vent to his desires, and favoring what he takes pleasure in."[92]

The quoted letters and conversations in this part of Ssu-ma Ch'ien's biography contain words suggestive of a later period. Because it is most unlikely that the conversations were recorded verbatim, it is natural to suppose they are literary inventions, maybe of Ssu-ma Ch'ien himself; but the Chinese have been unable to forget or minimize them. Whatever the whole truth, it appears likely that the eunuch, Chao Kao by name, and Li Ssu clashed, as is inevitable in such relationships. Li Ssu's attempts to see the emperor in private were unsuccessful, and then, alarmed (by events I omit), he pretended to agree with a speech the emperor gave and sent a memorial in which he says that a sage-king can remain in power for a long time only if he passes judgment personally, supervises and advances those who are virtuous, and keeps his authority out of the hands of his ministers. To persuade the emperor, Li Ssu quotes what Han Fei says about the bad results of misdirected affection—it is the affectionate mother who has a prodigal son—and gives Han Fei's advice on making punishments definite and severe.[93]

The emperor is said to have been delighted with Li Ssu's advice. The result was that officials who taxed heavily were regarded as intelligent and those who executed people freely regarded as loyal and responsible.[94] But though the emperor had accepted Li Ssu's advice, Chao Kao tricked Li Ssu into annoying the emperor, after which he remarked to the emperor that his grand councillor was dangerous, particularly because he lived outside the palace, where his authority was greater than the emperor's. Li Ssu defended himself and made counter-accusations, but the emperor had put his trust in the eunuch and was afraid that Li Ssu would kill him. "Chao Kao then had Li Ssu brought to trial, and Li Ssu was seized and thrown into prison." Ssu-ma Ch'ien has Li Ssu raising his eyes to Heaven, groaning, recalling the ministers who, though loyal, were executed, and enumerating the infamies of the present Emperor.[95]

Accused of plotting to revolt, Li Ssu was arrested and flogged so hard that, unable to bear the pain, he made a false confession of guilt. To avoid execution, he wrote a defense in which he reviewed all he had done, but Chao Kao, on the pretext that a prisoner cannot be allowed to submit a memorial, kept the defense from reaching the emperor. Chao Kao then delegated men of his own to pretend to be messengers sent by visiting imperial secretaries to get at the truth. When Li Ssu protested his innocence to them, Chao Kao had him flogged again. The result was that when the emperor did in fact send his agents to examine Ssu, Ssu, afraid of being flogged a third time, again falsely admitted his guilt. This made the emperor happy because, thanks to Lord Chao, he said, he now was sure of the truth.[96] From July 30 to August 27 of 208 B.C., Li Ssu was tortured, after which he was cut in half in the marketplace. His relatives to the third degree—defined, with some ambiguity, as his parents, brothers, wife, and children—were then exterminated.[97]

In the sequel, the emperor was tricked by Chao Kao into staying at a distant palace, which was attacked by soldiers masquerading, by Chao Kao's orders, as bandits. Their sight terrified the emperor and "Kao seized the opportunity to force him to commit suicide. He then took the imperial seal and hung it from his own girdle." Realizing that the officials would not accept him as Emperor, he conferred the seal on a younger brother of the late Emperor. Allowed only the diminished title of king, the new ruler was afraid of Chao Kao and had him stabbed to death and his relatives exterminated. After a few months, when rebel forces arrived, the ministers and officials threw off their allegiance to the king, who then wound a silk cord around his neck to show his readiness for suicide. The rebel commander spared him, but the commander's superior arrived, sacked the city, burned the palaces along with their libraries, and decapitated the king. "And thus it was that Ch'in lost the empire." The year was 206 B.C., fifteen years after the Ch'in empire had first been proclaimed.[98]

Ssu-ma Ch'ien ends his dramatic account by blaming Li Ssu for his disloyalty, apart from which, he says, he would have been classed with the virtuous princes who established the Chou dynasty.

Judgments and Reflections

Was Ch'in rule as harsh as Ssu-ma Ch'ien says, or has a later age inter-polated stories to justify its hatred of the dynasty? Scholars have their reasons for believing in such interpolations, but in the twentieth cen-tury it has become easy to take as sober possibilities stories that once sounded like vindictive fables. The Chinese have always thought them to be true, and passing judgment on the Ch'in has been a stock preoc-cupation of Chinese moralists. A famous old judgment, made soon after Ch'in's fall by the Confucian Chia I, says that the great empire became a joke when it was brought down in a revolution begun by a single com-moner. This happened, says Chia I, because Ch'in "failed to display humanity *(jen)* and righteousness *(i)* or realize that there is a difference between the power to attack and the power to consolidate."[99]

Morality apart, why did Ch'in fall? Would it have fallen so soon if the First Emperor's eldest son had inherited him? Was the fall the result of the administration's inability to cope with the sudden enlargement of China? A contemporary scholar thinks that pure Legalism would have been too inflexible to last, but that the later symbiosis of Legalism and Confucianism "gave the Chinese State the necessary combination of firmness and flexibility that enabled it to survive."[100]

Opposites though they were, Legalism and Confucianism—not to speak of Taoism and other modes of thought—did, in fact, join in com-plex composites of various degrees of internal coherence. This is evident in the so-called Huang-Lao school of thought (the name, as I have said, combines Huang Ti and Lao Tzu), which came to dominate the Chinese court during the early Han dynasty. The Taoism of the school is more purposeful or instrumental than Lao Tzu could approve. That is, the school emphasizes a Taoist-like "nonaction" in the sense of consider-ation for the interests of the people by lowering taxes, for example, and passing more humane laws. By the tenets of this school, the emperor binds himself to take action only if and when his subordinates suggest it.

The influence at court of Huang-Lao school ended abruptly about 140 B.C., on the accession of Emperor Wu. As the historian Ssu-ma Ch'ien tells it, the emperor's chancellor rejected "the doctrines of the Taoists, the Legalists, and the other philosophical schools and invited several hundred Confucian scholars and literary men to take service in the government."[101]*Perhaps a restored and confident central govern-

---

*Ssu-ma Ch'ien's historian-father writes that the teaching of the Taoists, by which he obviously means Huang-Lao thought, "is all-sufficient and embraces all things. Its method consists in following the seasonal order of the *Yin-yang* school, selecting what is good from the Confucian and Mohist teachings, and

ment now found Confucianism better for practical, political reasons. This is because the activist doctrine of Confucianism justified loosening the constraints the government had accepted in the interests of the people and, as then interpreted, justified the government's reclaiming of powers it had earlier ceded to local authorities.[102]

The most complete surviving documents of the Huang-Lao school, four silk scrolls unearthed from a tomb in 1973, make a more or less coherent synthesis of late Warring State and early Han thought. Central to this synthesis is the conception of nature as an impersonal order, an objective Tao, that encompasses human beings in its scope. To grasp nature in this sense, one must be tranquil, empty, nonactive (wu-wei), which means, approximately, without any personal bias. In this frame of mind, one fits oneself in with the natural order of things, one sees the constant norms of nature, and one acts in accord with the times. One also understands how language (rightly applied) and how the principles of morality and human laws all express the Tao, the natural order. As required by the Legalists, the law must be objective and impersonal; but as Legalists may be reluctant to admit, even the ruler, if he is to succeed, must abide by the same law.[103]

Other, sometimes amusing literary evidence of Han syncretism is given by a composite Han text, the *Huai Nan Tzu*, which joins Legalism, Confucianism, and Taoism as if they were the same.[104] It obviously prefers the Legalist lion to lie down with the Confucian lamb and the Taoist buffalo (Lao Tzu's mount). Like Legalism, it repeats that Yao as a commoner could do nothing while Chieh's commands were obeyed, and that law is the "level and marking line of the ruler."[105] Like Confucianism, it praises the civilizing work of Yao and Shun and repeats that benevolence and intelligence agree by nature.[106] And like Taoism, it claims that culture has "polluted" man's original nature.[107]

The differences between a Legalistic and Confucian outlook are extremely obvious; but if the measure of Legalism is administration by means of reward and punishment, regulation of the economy, military efficiency, territorial expansion, and a hierarchy of officials with the emperor at its head, then China of the Han dynasty remained rather Legalistic both during and after the predominance of Huang-Lao thought. We see the government's ideology in a basically Legalistic light in the greatest political debate of the times, which used arguments that recall the old confrontation between Legalists and Confucians. On

---

adopting the important points of the Logical and Legalist schools. It modifies its position with the times and responds to the changes which come about in the world" (Watson, *Ssu-ma Ch'ien*, pp. 44–45).

the one side were the "modernists," those who favored government control of natural resources, large-scale agriculture, and commerce. On the other side were the tradition-minded "reformers," who thought that state control was oppressive, that trade, especially in luxuries, was at the expense of the poor, that taxes should be collected in kind, and that small-scale agriculture should be the state's mainstay.

The government, which needed money to finance its frontier armies, had favored the modernists and taken over the production of iron and salt, regulated their prices, and made a handsome profit for itself. But iron grew too expensive and the iron implements supplied to farmers by the government were inferior, so there was a public outcry.[108] To settle the issue, the government summoned sixty representatives of the "reformers" to debate the government representative. Held in 81 B.C., the debate was recorded, with evident fairness, by a contemporary scholar.[109] Argued on both sides, Chinese fashion, by means of examples and counterexamples, the debate changed little in practice, but it is interesting for us because the government side echoes Legalist arguments and the reformist, Confucian ones.

In the debate, the lord grand secretary, the defender of government policy, argues against dispersing authority and leaving things to the anarchic actions of the people. He recalls that, long ago, when Shang Yang was chancellor of Ch'in, he was firm in establishing laws and harsh punishments and in creating orderly government and education. The result was that

> in his external policy he managed to obtain profits of a hundred fold and collected taxes on mountains and marshes. The state became rich, the people, strong; weapons and implements were kept ready, complete in every detail, and grain stores had a surplus . . . He was victorious in every battle and always captured his object of attack, absorbing his nearest opponents and crushing the distant.[110]

The literati "reformers" counter with the example of the prosperous reign under an emperor (Wen Ti, 179–156 B.C.) they regard as a model, while under their own regime, with its salt and iron profits, the people are in terrible straits. The opportunistic Shang Yang, insist the "reformers," was only temporarily successful, and for the sake of this fugitive success he had to rely on might and tyranny.

> He cheated his friends to accomplish his ambition, punished members of his ducal house to make his authority felt. He had no

compassion for the people, nor did he show any faith in his relations with the feudal princes.[111]

When the grand secretary answers, "White cannot hold its own in the presence of black; a Worthy or Sage cannot order things as he wishes in an age of anarchy," the Literati remind him that

the people of Ch'in hated the laws of Shang Yang more than they did their personal enemies. So on the death of Duke Hsia [his protector] they rose as one man and attacked him; east, west, north or south he found no place to flee. Looking up to heaven he said with a sigh, "Alas! Has the evil of my policy reached such an extreme?" . . . An object of mockery to the whole Empire, this man was killed by himself, not by others.[112]

While the terms of the debate certainly resemble those between the Legalists and Confucians of the Chou period, this time both sides agree on the need for a centralized empire with its ceremonial based on tradition; and this time neither side is ready to preach the irrelevance of character. Although the modernists resemble the Legalists, it is the reformers who repeat Shang Yang's and Han Fei's criticism of the luxurious life. In estimating these changes of position, one ought to remember that Legalism, unlike Confucianism, was only a retrospective creation, not a doctrine with a tradition to which its supporters needed to feel loyal. As history shows, there is nothing anomalous in a Confucian Legalist, Confucian Taoist, or even Confucian Taoistic Legalist; but this history belongs mainly to periods too late to discuss here.[113]

The formal death of Legalism was not the death of harsh government. When Ssu-ma Ch'ien comes to write his chapter The Biographies of the Harsh Officials," he recalls that

in the time of Ch'in, the net of the law was drawn tightly about the empire and yet evil and deceit sprang up on all sides; in the end men thought of nothing but evading their superiors and no one could do anything to save the situation.

When the Han dynasty arose, Ssu-ma Ch'ien goes on, "the law officials were honest and simple-hearted and did not indulge in evil . . . so we see that good government depended upon virtue, not harshness."[114] Yet Ssu-ma Ch'ien describes extraordinarily harsh Han officials. One of these is Wang Wen-shu, in his youth a grave robber, who managed to become an official and "had occasion to execute an extraordinary number of men." His courageous prosecutions of powerful and lawless families and his execution of the major criminals and their families were so shocking that "people no longer ventured out at night and there was not a single bandit left to set the dogs in the fields to barking."[115] Transferred to the post of military commander of the capital, he learned to twist the law cleverly to ruin "petty rogues" and intimidate powerful families.

> Knaves and evildoers were subjected to the most thorough investigation; most of them were beaten to a pulp in prison, and none was ever known to have refuted the charges brought against them and gotten out of prison alive.

The upshot was that the officials who "wanted to rule effectively began to imitate his ways," while the lower officials and the people began to think of lawbreaking as a trifling matter, so that the number of thieves and bandits kept growing, some joined in large armed bands.[116] To judge by this report, harshness fails as easily as it succeeds.

In his not dissimilar final comments on the harsh officials, Ssu-ma Ch'ien says that

> harsh penalties became increasingly frequent, so that the work of the government officials was gradually hampered and brought to a standstill. The high ministers . . . were so busy staying out of trouble that they had no time to think of anything but laws and regulations.[117]

Some of the harsh officials, Ssu-ma Ch'ien reports, were honest, some corrupt, but all were men of strong character whose reputation for cruelty fitted their calling. Too many of them were simply violent oppressors of the people. One of them "tore people limb from limb," another "sawed people's heads off," another "bludgeoned people into making confessions," another "executed people indiscriminately," two others "ruled like vipers or hawks," and another "beat people to death unless they bribed him for their release."[118] "Why bother to describe all of them?" asks Ssu-ma Ch'ien at the end of the chapter. It is more than clear that he does not think that either honest or corrupt harshness had been confined to the only openly Legalist government, that of Ch'in.

~:3:~

The Machiavellian Political Science
of Ancient India

Historical Background

As in the case of China, the period that concerns us is roughly a thousand years. It begins with Buddhism, which appears in the late sixth century B.C. and ends about the fifth century A.D. The chronology of the period is extremely vague, and there is no equivalent of Ssu-ma Ch'ien's history of China.[1] The result is that while everything of traditional India seems to be contained in its epics, mythology, and codes of law, to try to use them to create an image of social life or thought at any particular time and place is like trying to reconstitute the time, place, structure, and use of a building from stones that were taken from its ruins in order to construct other buildings at other unknown times and places. The effort can stimulate the greatest ingenuity, arrive at sometimes plausible results, but yields no real historical precision.

It is only with early Buddhism, Jainism, and the conquests of Alexander the Great that the chronological problem grows rather easier and history more nearly possible. The history we need to know begins about 321 B.C.—if the date is right, just one hundred years before the rule of the First Emperor of China was proclaimed. This is that year that the young Chandragupta, aided by his canny, unscrupulous adviser, Kautilya, defeated the Nandas, founded the Maurya dynasty, and created the first great Indian empire. The impression this king made is recorded in literature, but little that is surely authentic is known of him. Greek writers tell of an early meeting with Alexander the Great, who,

they say, wanted him killed because he offended him. Later, Chandragupta checked or drove back the troops of Alexander's prefects and of
his local successor, with whom he established friendly relations.

To match the Chinese story of the rats that teach Li Ssu, we have the
Indian story according to which Chandragupta learns his tactics from a
woman he overhears talking to her child. Seeing that the child eats the
middle of a cake of bread, throws away the rest, and asks for more, the
mother says, "You throw away the outside and eat the middle, the way
Chandragupta neglects the frontier and tries to conquer by invading a
country's heart, where his army is surrounded and destroyed." From
this lesson, Chandragupta learns to devour enemy territory by first
chewing up its outer areas.[2] Other fables illustrate Chandragupta's natural authority by telling, for example, that when he was in exhausted
flight from an enemy and fell asleep, an enormous lion came to lick and
revive him.[3]

What was India then like? The most extensive description is given
by the Greek Megasthenes, an envoy sent by Seleucus I (between 302
and 291 B.C.) to Chandragupta's court. What Megasthenes reports gives
an independent background to Kautilya's political doctrine. A witness
so valuable can be forgiven for sometimes believing in fables or sometimes making factual mistakes.*

Megasthenes says that the smallest but most honored class of people is that of the "philosophers." Some of the Brahmans among them
study nature and practice religion—their views are said to be somewhat like those of Greeks—and others act as the king's counsellors. The
majority of the population belongs to the class of cultivators. Mild and
gentle, they take no part in wars and do nothing but cultivate the soil
and pay taxes. The only occupation of the fighters, of whom there are
many, is war. There is also a class, Machiavellian in intent, of secret government inspectors, who report to the authorities whatever goes on
among the people. The final class described is that of magistrates and
administrators, who are chosen for their wisdom and uprightness.[4] The
army is led by the king, who in peacetime acts as a judge, performs sacrifices, and goes on hunting expeditions. It is noted that he sometimes
changes beds at night in order to frustrate attempts against his life. His
government is organized into boards of district, town, and war officials;

---

*For example, he tells the fable of the gentle-mannered men with no mouths
who live on the odors of roast meat, fruit, and flowers, and he makes the mistake of saying that there are no slaves in India and the mistake of describing
Indian occupations as if they were castes.

for example, the War Office has separate boards to administer the navy, transport and supplies, cavalry, chariots, and elephants.[5]

Megasthenes calls the capital city, Pataliputra, where he lived, "the greatest city in India." He says that it forms an oblong about 9 by 1³/₄ miles and is surrounded by a fortified wooden wall with 570 towers and 64 gates, outside of which there is a ditch some 60 feet deep. The magnificent palace, all of wood, is set in a park filled with clumps of native and exotic trees, ponds with enormous tame fish, and tame peacocks and pheasants. The people of the capital, who love bright colors, are very honest and trusting.[6] This praise is hard to reconcile with Kautilya's elaborate enumeration of punishments. If Megasthenes is right about the rarity of thefts, lies, and lawsuits, the reason may be not the native character of the inhabitants but laws as severe as those the Chinese Legalists recommend.

Chandragupta, whose India Megathenes describes, will return, along with Kautilya, as a protagonist in a Machiavellian play written long after his death. His glory as an empire builder contrasts with the tradition according to which he was converted to Jainism and abdicated during a famine and ended his life by starvation, a method approved for Jain saints.[7] His son, Bindusara by name, extended his conquests, leaving only the hostile area of Kalinga (today Orissa), which was conquered in a bloody war by his son, Chandragupta's grandson, Ashoka (c. 274–232 B.C.). The empire of Ashoka extended over all the sub-continent except its southern tip.

Ashoka stands out among the world's rulers for the greatness of his conquests but, even more, for his conversion to humaneness. An Indian historian says that his reign "forms the brightest page in the history of India."[8] Luckily, the evidence for Ashoka's views is literally inscribed on stone. It consists of some thirty-five so-called Rock Edicts placed along the borders of Ashoka's empire; of Pillar Edicts, on sandstone pillars, some forty to fifty feet high, set up in important cities and along roads; and of Cave Edicts, some of which dedicate caves as living places for Ajivika (atheistic, anti-Brahmanical) monks.[9]

In Ashoka's edicts, everything centers on the concept of *dharma*. I defer an exact explanation and suggest that it be understood for the present as *universal (moral) norm* or *moral law*. This is the criterion that Ashoka embraced after his conversion from war to peace. Ashoka, whose name means *sorrow-free*, explains his conversion in Rock Edict 13. The edict begins with a description of all the suffering he caused: In the eighth year of his reign, in the course of his conquest of the Kalinga country, 150,000 people were taken captive, 100,000 killed, and many times that number died as a result of the warfare. Immediately afterwards, he says, he became devoted to the *dharma*. Now he is now pro-foundly regretful at this slaughter, death, and deportation, and at the suffering caused the victims' friends, acquaintances, companions, and relatives. He now thinks, he says, "that even a person who wrongs him must be forgiven for wrongs that can be forgiven." The words *for wrongs that can be forgiven* mark the boundary of Ashoka's rather com-monsense magnanimity. So does his reminder to the "forest peoples" under his dominion that, despite his repentance, he still exercises the power to punish them for their crimes. Likewise, to the unconquered peoples bordering his empire he offers the assurance of his good will and his hope that they will trust, not fear, him. He is ready, he says, to forgive them "for offenses which can be forgiven."

Ashoka proclaims, with undoubted sincerity, "All men are my children." These words occur in the preface of an edict he posted in the territory of his former enemies. He goes on, "Just as I seek the welfare and happiness of my children in this world and the next, I seek the same things for all men." What follows is an exhortation to officials to judge without anger, cruelty, impatience, or inattentiveness, not to be "harsh or cruel but gentle" because, he says,

> sometimes in the administration of justice a person will suffer imprisonment or torture. When this happens, he sometimes dies accidentally, and many other people suffer because of this. (Kal-inga Edict 1)

One pauses at these prosaic but poignantly merciful words. How effectively Ashoka's exhortations were translated into the daily life of his citizens we do not know, but his faith in exhortation as such is very clear when he recalls (in Pillar Edict 7) that earlier kings tried but failed to induce people to follow *dharma* strictly. In contrast, he says, he has issued proclamations on *dharma* and ordered instruction in *dharma*, as a result of which the people will conform to it and make moral progress. His highest officials, including the provincial governors, are to expound and spread the precepts of *dharma*. They are to occupy them-selves with services for the good of ascetics and householders. Some of them have been ordered to look after the affairs of the Buddhist reli-gious orders, some to take care of the Brahman and Ajivika ascetics, some to work among the Jain monks, and some among other religious sects. These and other officials are to distribute or supervise gifts from himself and other members of his family.

Ashoka is not a humble teacher. He has become, he proclaims, a model for the people, who imitate his good deeds and have progressed in obedience to parents and teachers and in courtesy to ascetics, to the poor and distressed, and even to slaves and servants. Believing as he does in good words, he orders (in Rock Edict 3) that local, provincial, and state officials should tour their districts every five years to proclaim the precepts of *dharma*—an educational tactic reminiscent in particular of nineteenth-century China.

Although Ashoka proclaims his desire to help monks and ascetics of every sect, his interest is basically in what he calls "the ceremonies of dharma," by which he means kindness, reverence, peaceableness, and liberality. He accepts but shows impatience with the "diverse, trivial, and meaningless ceremonies" that mark sickness, marriage, birth, departure, and the like, to which women in particular have recourse (Rock Edict 9). There seems to be a hint of impatience with ritual that is not morally oriented. However, Ashoka's basic tolerance is beyond doubt. Verbally, at least, it goes beyond that of any ancient ruler with whom I am familiar. As he proclaims, he wants men of all faiths to know each other's doctrines, and he wants "growth in the qualities essential to religion in men of all faiths," for he believes that the "faiths of others all deserve to be honored for one reason or another. By honoring them," he says in Rock Edict 12, "one exalts one's own faith and at the same time performs a service to the faith of others."

Although Ashoka was a convert to Buddhism, his faith was of the relaxed kind good for a king who must have felt tolerance not only morally justified but also politically expedient for an empire that sectarianism could easily endanger.[10] He in fact often proclaims that he wants to do good not merely to relatives or residents of his capital, but to people everywhere of every class (Pillar Edict 6). Now, he says, his tours are moral tours on which he visits priests and ascetics, the aged, and the people of rural areas (Rock Edict 8). To know how his people are faring, he proclaims that officials can have access to him at all times—when he is eating or in his harem or inner apartments, attending to his cattle, or engaged in religious exercises. For the sake of emphasis, he proclaims that he is never quite satisfied with his work or his vigilance in public affairs. To this, he adds:

> I consider the promotion of the people's welfare my highest duty, and its exercise is grounded in work and constant application . . . Such work as I accomplish contributes to the debt I owe to all living creatures to make them happy in this world and to help them attain heaven in the next. (Rock Edict 6)

To extend mercy to all living creatures, Ashoka prohibits the slaughtering of any living creature at the capital city; earlier, he limited those killed every day for his own kitchens to two peacocks and a single deer (Rock Edict 1). He also decrees that the many animals he names in a long list should not be killed; that living animals should not be fed to other animals; that only on certain days should fish be killed or sold, cattle castrated, or horses and bullocks branded; and that forestland should "not be burned without reason or in order to kill living creatures." (Rock Edict 1)

The historic Ashoka inspires respect for his resolute principles, as distant as possible from Machiavellian amorality; but the Ashoka of Buddhist legend gives an inherently more ambiguous lesson on the relation between Buddhist humanitarianism and Machiavellian impulses or necessities. The Ashoka of the legend—which may reflect realities that the inscriptions omit—is said to have inspired the emulation of Buddhist kings in many countries.[11] The legend begins by making the young Ashoka so ugly that his father cannot bear to look at him and so evil that, when his father dies, he usurps the throne and tricks his elder brother, the rightful heir, to his death. Then, when his ministers, many of whom are contemptuous of him, fail his extreme test of their obedience—which is to cut down all trees that bear fruit or flowers and cultivate only thorn trees—he decapitates all five hundred of them. And when his many concubines, who do not enjoy caressing his rough skin, mock him by cutting down the ashoka tree he loves, he burns all the concubines alive. His search for an executioner to match his own evil temperament ends with a naturally, or unnaturally, cruel young man, who reviles his own parents, beats up children, and catches and kills ants, flies, mice, and fish. This executioner persuades Ashoka to build a prison in which the tortures imitate those suffered by persons reborn in (Buddhist) hell. All this insistence on Ashoka's ugliness and initial cruelty dramatizes his later turn to the good, but it also carries the implicit message that power is independent of appearance and morality and can be used to equal effect for good and evil.

In the legend, Ashoka's conversion is brought about by a young monk. Imprisoned, about to be tortured, the monk struggles with his fear of death and his revulsion against an execution he witnesses. He struggles with such power that he breaks "the bonds of existence" and attains the supreme understanding that will be followed, when he leaves this life, by nirvanic extinction.[12] Unaware of what has happened, the jailer throws the monk into an iron cauldron and, after repeatedly trying and failing to light the fire under it, looks inside and discovers the monk sitting cross-legged on a lotus. Ashoka is called by the executioner to witness the miracle, which the monk makes the more impressive by magical feats and the statement that Ashoka is destined to be a great Buddhist king. This is enough to convert Ashoka to Buddhism and Buddhist kindness. In response, the executioner wants to kill Ashoka—on the grounds that the king has promised that no one who has entered the prison will leave it alive—so Ashoka has his guards take the executioner to the torture chamber, where he is burned to death, after which the jail is torn down.

In the legend, Ashoka now gives massive proof of his piety by building eighty-four thousand Buddhist shrines, by making munificent donations to strengthen Buddhism, and by entertaining great numbers of Buddhist monks. However, he not infrequently uses less than saintly means. "A master of clever means," as the legend calls him, he threatens to execute many of the people of a city who insist on keeping too many boxes of Buddhist relics. When he is told of a Jain who has drawn a picture showing Buddha bowing to the Jain's teacher, he has the Jain burned along with his whole family, and he sets a price on the head of any other Jain who can be found. He also has his own wife burned and the inhabitants of a city killed for a cause more than adequate for an ordinary king but not for a saintly Buddhist.[13]

Why are such acts retained in the legend that recounts the life the greatest of Buddhist kings? A scholar answers that the inclusion of the acts reflects the feeling that to be a king is to be inevitably prone to such acts. While Buddhist thinkers reject the amoral doctrines taught in Indian political science, the legendary king is made to act like a real king, that is, he becomes enraged and bloodily vengeful, he kills heretics, and he uses the deceptive "clever means" of which he is considered a master.[14] To judge by his edicts, the real Ashoka would have been quite incapable of the acts attributed to his legendary counterpart.

The Buddhists had accepted the Indian vision of great, beneficent rulers of the world, "wheel rulers" whose *dharma*-wheeled chariots roll everywhere without obstruction. The Ashoka of the legend represents the particular variety of such a ruler who is unable to avoid the use of threats and force. Clearly, even the greatest of historic Buddhist kings is unlikely to rise to the level of a Buddhist saint; and in the legend Ashoka recognizes himself to be inherently less worthy than the Buddhist elder to whom he makes his obeisance.[15]

At the end of the legend, when Ashoka is on the verge of death, he wants to give a huge sum of money to a Buddhist monastery; but his son and heir apparent prohibits this use of state funds because, he says, "The power of kings lies in their state treasury; he should be restrained."[16] Ashoka then gives away the gold dishes on which his food is served, and when he is stopped from giving more of them away, gives away the substituted silver dishes and, after again being stopped, gives the substituted copper ones. Finally, left with half a fruit, he gives that away, too, while making mournfully resentful comments on the lord of men who has become no more than the lord of half a fruit, and on the servants who have stolen his sovereignty. At the very end, he renounces the glory of kingship, which is "as unsteady as a choppy sea," and claims the only kind of sovereignty that is safe from agitation, which is sovereignty over the mind.[17] Having understood how little kingship means in the end, he dies in peace.

To return from the legend to history, we can note that Ashoka ruled India for thirty-seven or thirty-eight years. Historians have attributed his success to the Mauryan practice of deposing or reducing the power of the rulers included in the empire, so that Ashoka could become the equally benevolent father of all his subjects. His tolerance and the development of cities and commerce may be supposed to have furthered his policy.[18] But however successful Ashoka himself may have been, after his death his empire quickly declined. Because of the script in which they were written, his edicts became unreadable and remained so until deciphered in 1837. Even then, they were not identified as Ashoka's—the inscriptions refer to him by honorific titles such as The Benevolent One or Beloved of the Gods; the one inscription that refers to him by the name Ashoka was discovered only in 1915. Buddhists continued to know him through his legend, but after Buddhism disappeared from India, he was forgotten there.[19]

The decline of Ashoka's dynasty has been blamed on a Brahmanical reaction against his pro-Buddhist policies (but he was careful to be fair); to the sapping of his military power by his bias against violence (but he was careful to remain realistic about the possibility of resistance to his rule); to economic pressures; to a bureaucracy so large and perhaps so new that the king had trouble with it, as he explicitly says (but his statements are on injustices that other kings might let pass without comment); to the lack of an administrative system relatively immune to a ruler's death; and to the lack of national feeling among the peoples that composed the empire. Perhaps "a state like that of the Mauryas was simply ahead of its time." But whatever the causes for the decline of his empire, Ashoka's idealism, translated into a tolerant but despotic paternalism, died with him, and it was his un-Ashokan successors who lost the empire.[20]

I will not dwell on the ironic contrast between the presumably Machiavellian Chandragupta and his *dharma*-loving grandson, Ashoka. I suppose that very nearly everyone would prefer Ashoka; but the whole Machiavellian problem can be encapsulated in this familial contrast between grandfather and grandson and in the question, Who, objectively, was the more successful?

Indian Views of the Origins of Government

In ancient India, theories of government were confirmed by cosmological myths. The framework of the theories is usually the Indian belief in a world that begins in near-perfection and grows progressively worse until, having arrived at its lowest, most degenerate stage, it is destroyed, only to be created and go through the cycle again.[21] In contradiction to the other, "orthodox" (Veda-accepting) Indians, Buddhists did not believe in a creator god, in the cosmic origin of the caste system (the four hierarchically arranged social orders), in the authority of the Brahmans, or in the divinity of kings, so none of these is confirmed by their cosmogony or their myths of the origin of human government.

We can follow the cyclical course of human degeneration, as Buddhists saw it, in a famous text ascribed to the Buddha himself. When the usual, manifest world passes away, he says, most beings are usually reborn in the World of Radiance, where they live "made of mind, feeding on rapture, self-luminous, traversing the air, continuing in glory" here for a long time.[22] There is nothing then but water and deep darkness. Then, as occurs in cosmic cycles, an earth-essence spread out on the water just as a skin forms on cooling milk-rice, and it had color like sweet ghee or cream and taste like clear honey.

Then someone with a greedy nature, inherited from a previous birth, tasted the sweet earth-essence, liked it, and began to crave it and eat it, and others imitated him. As craving overcame these beings, their luminosity faded and the moon and sun and then the stars and constellations appeared. The beings kept feeding on the sweet earth, and their bodies grew solid in proportion to the quantity they ate, until it became evident that some were good looking and others ugly; and when the better looking ones grew vain of their appearance, the sweet earth-essence disappeared, a fragrant earth appeared suddenly, and the beings' solidity, good looks and ugliness and the vanity of the good-looking were accentuated. The fragrant earth disappeared and a honey-sweet creeper appeared. The more they ate of this creeper and of the huskless, self-regenerating rice that replaced it, the more solid the beings became, and the more solid, the more good or bad looking. Then the women—those who had been women in an earlier life—became distinctively female and the men distinctively male. The women looked at the men too intensely, and the men at the women, and passion arose, burning fire entered into their bodies, and they had sex. Because what is now considered moral was then considered immoral, some beings threw ashes or cow-dung at them and shouted "away!" at them. The beings who had sex were kept out of villages and towns and hid their immorality in huts they built.

Someone with a lazy nature decided not to gather rice every morning and evening but to gather enough in a single journey for two meals. The others imitated him and extended the habit and came to store rice for as long as eight days. Because the beings ate stored rice, rice grew covered with powder and with a husk and no longer regenerated after it was reaped. Remembering that once they had been made of mind, had fed on rapture, had been luminous, and that the earth-essence and earth had been sweet and edible, the people lamented that evil customs had caused the rice to have husks, stop regenerating, and grow in clumps. They therefore decided to divide and demarcate the fields of rice.

Then a being with a greedy nature kept his own rice and took another portion and ate it. In spite of his promise, he repeated his offense a second time and a third. Some people hit him with their hands, some with clods of earth, and some with sticks. This is the way in which stealing, accusation, lying, and punishment became known. Grieving at what had happened, the people gathered and proposed that they choose someone, to be paid with a portion of their rice, to accuse whoever deserved accusation and banish whoever deserved banishment. They chose the handsomest, most attractive man among them to rule, and they gave him a share of their rice. The name they gave the ruler was Mahasummata, meaning *appointed by the people*.[23]

The myth continues: In this way, the class of rulers originated, naturally and rightly, from the same people as the others. The Brahmans were those who decided to reject evil ways and built leaf-huts in the forest in which to meditate. Those who were unable to meditate settled on the outskirts of villages and towns and compiled texts, so people called them *Reciters* (of the Veda) and considered them the lowest of the Brahman class—now they are considered the highest. Of those who remained, some, who had sex, had reputable occupations and originated the third class or caste, and some, who had cruel, mean occupations, originated the fourth, lowest class. Ascetics, too, had a quite natural origin. They were members of the four classes who, disapproving their own tasks, took up the homeless life instead.

The myth draws its moral: Any member of any of the four classes has a future in keeping with the morality of the life he leads. Anyone evil in deed, word, and thought will be reborn in a bad destiny, hell; anyone good in deed, word, and thought will be born in a good destiny, heaven; anyone both good and evil is reborn to experience both happiness and suffering; and anyone of any of the four classes who practices the seven things that lead to Enlightenment attains nirvana in this present life.[24]

Taken literally, this myth teaches how desire reduces the radiant, almost immaterial beings of the earliest world—"mind" is taken to be of very fine material—who commit no sins and need no ruler, to heavily material, sinning, quarrelling, unfortunate human beings of the kind we are familiar with. At this point, the myth shows its particularly Buddhist face: That a ruler is needed to make social life possible is decided by discussion like that in an assembly of Buddhist monks or a "republic" of the sort the early Buddhists knew. As Buddhists prefer, the first ruler is chosen not because of a god's will but because of qualities that fit him to rule. With the help of some perhaps humorously intended etymologies I have omitted, the myth shows that the system of social orders or castes is not sacred but the natural result of the development of social life. The original division into castes has nothing to do with cosmogony or heredity, as the Hindus claim; every social development is the result of purely natural law. Finally, everyone of every caste has the same natural reward or punishment for the morality or immorality of action, speech, or thought, and the same opportunity to arrive at nirvana.[25]

On the opposed, Brahmanical view, the system of the four social orders is integral to cosmic law, which is equated with the undisturbed functioning of the hierarchy of the social orders. Reality is identified with and supported by the power of sacrifice and the sacred authority of the king, who is related to the gods, even, sometimes, identified with the gods' king, the great Indra—even the gods need a king to lead them in their struggle against the disruptive powers of the universe. The human king is also said to have been descended from the divine-human father of the human race, Manu.[26]

In the great epics, the *Mahabharata* and the *Ramayana*, where violence, treachery, and political opportunism play their entertainingly destructive roles, the power of a king, abetted by the obedience of the people, is able to ensure peace and righteousness, for which reason kingly power and submission to it are "the eternal way of righteousness." This implies that "the actions of a king must always be truthful and benevolent. The kingdom will thereby be true, the world firmly established in truth."[27] Put with epic pathos (by a bard reciting to a king?), the primacy of the king must prevail because if kings did not exist, no creatures anywhere could exist, and because kings exist, other creatures do. Who dares refuse them homage? . . . Never should the king be scorned as being a mere mortal: He is a great divinity existing in the form of a man . . . A man who acts in opposition to the king never gains happiness, neither he himself nor anyone close to him—son, brother, friend.[28]

There is a perhaps unique passage in the *Mahabharata* according to which society began with a social contract that failed. In the beginning, we read, anarchy made people suffer so greatly that they agreed among themselves that they needed a king. But after they failed to elect one and to keep their agreement to expel wrongdoers, they appealed to Brahma to appoint a king, as he did. This story, which may be meant to refute the Buddhist story of the first king's election, implies that authority cannot succeed unless it is imposed from above.[29]

The characteristic structure of both Brahmanical and, later, Hindu thought appears in a well systematized form at the beginning of *The Laws of Manu*, the purported author of which is the Manu (*Thinking Being, Man*) from whom all human beings are traditionally said to be descended. The book begins with the full integration of cosmogony with the origin of human government: First there was the indistinguishable darkness, out of which the unmanifested, self-existent Lord caused the present universe to become manifest. He emitted semen, which became a golden egg as bright as the sun, from which was born Brahma, the grandfather of all people, and all the host of gods, whose essence is the ritual. The unmanifested Lord also made the names and conditions of everything in exact accord with the verbal and metaphysical truth, the Veda; and he emitted time and its divisions, the constellations and planets, and everything else, including inner heat, speech, sexual pleasure, and anger. In order to distinguish right from wrong, he yoked the creatures he had made to pain and pleasure. Then, for the sake of the prosperity of worlds and people, he created the priest from his mouth, the ruler from his arms, the ordinary person (the "commoner") from his thighs, and the servant from his feet. Then, splitting into a man and a woman, the Lord generated ascetic heat and emitted the Creator, who emitted the ten great sages, who emitted seven brilliantly energetic Manus—one for each Manu epoch—and after them, the gods, the great sages, and all other beings, each living being with its innate activity, internal consciousness, and experience of happiness and unhappiness, each living being caught in the terrible cycle of transmigration. Then the Creator, pressing time against time, vanished again into himself. In this way, by means of waking and sleeping, he brings to life and destroys this whole universe time after time.[30]

Manu having finished the account of the stages of creation, one of the great sages takes over and explains the nature of the world cycle, which is the measure of the night and day of Brahma.[31] A day of Brahma has four periods. The first is one in which religion is perfect, people are free from sickness, achieve all they want, and live four hundred years; but then, period by successive period, religion weakens and is destroyed by theft, lying, and deceit, and people live successively shorter lives. Everywhere and at all times, according to the law, the priest rules, because "he was born of the highest part of the body, because he is the highest, and because he maintains the Veda."[32] Created to make offerings to the gods and the ancestors, he guards the whole creation. "Priests are traditionally regarded as the best of men."[33]

Since *The Laws of Manu* is so important in the formation of Hinduism, its conception of the beginnings of human society has remained influential. In *The Laws of Manu*, just as in the Vedas, the caste system is built into the process of creation itself. Any weakening of religion or of its guardians, the priests, is considered to be a weakening of the force that sustains the visible universe. In this spirit, the sage who speaks for Manu describes the sacred origin of the human ruler. At first, he says, when this world was without a king and people scattered in fear in all directions, the Lord emitted a king in order to protect this whole creation. In order to make the king as he should be, he took the eternal particles of Indra, the Wind, Yama (Death), the Sun, Fire, Varuna, and Kubera (Wealth). Because a king has been made from particles of all these gods, each one with his particular powers, the king

> surpasses all living beings in brilliant energy, and, like the Sun, he burns eyes and hearts, and no one on earth is able even to look at him . . . Even a boy king should not be treated with disrespect, with the thought, "He is just a human being"; for this is a great deity standing there in the form of a man.[34]

From a great enough cultural distance, Manu's description of the king and his duties now takes on a note at once comical, didactic, and poetic: The various acts of the king encompass all the four periods of a world cycle. His behavior expresses the powers of all the gods, whose substance, the brilliant energy of all eight of them, he shares: The king showers benefits with the power that Indra showers monsoon rains, absorbs taxes with the power that the sun absorbs water, penetrates everywhere with his spies with the power that the wind moves about everywhere, restrains his subjects with the power that Death restrains friend and foe at the right time, seizes evil men with the power that Varuna binds sinners, delights his subjects with the power that the full moon gives delight, turns his majesty's heat against evildoers with the power that fire burns all, and supports all living beings with the power that the earth supports them all.[35]

Yet this hyperbolical empowerment of the king, conclusive though it sounds, is not enough in Manu's eyes to challenge the supremacy of the priest, the first- and best-born of all human beings. Therefore Manu warns the king that "even during the utmost extremity, he should not make priests angry," or else the priest "could instantly destroy him, with all his army and vehicles.[36] Despite the godly particles he incorporates, the king cannot compare with the Brahmans, whose property is the Veda and whose formulaic power sustains world and gods alike.

The Law of the Fishes and the Cynicism of Kings

There is one great fear, shared with Chinese thinkers and with Europeans such as Hobbes and Kant, that qualifies all Indian political thought. It is social chaos, which in India is called *the law of the fishes*, that is, the law by which the stronger fish eat the weaker. It was the law of the fishes that was supposed to have caused the people still without government to turn to the gods to give them moral instruction and appoint them a king.[37] The institution of kingship stood between them and anarchy, but they never forgot the threat. Think of a state without a king, says a wise man in the *Mahabharata*, of the robbers that overwhelm it, of the abduction of women, of the strong who would roast the weak like fishes on a spit. Without the protection of a king, people would be like fishes in shallow water and birds in a void who, after they rove as they like for a while, attack and destroy one another.[38]

Think, too, of the fear of anarchy as expressed in descriptions of the last, declining age of a world cycle. Even under a king, people might feel they were living on the edge of chaos, and many of the fears expressed in accounts of the end of days are evidently heightened versions of actual experiences or actual fears. To give a sense of the more human evils attributed to the last, evil age, I recall something of a text in which a sage describes what will happen (and has already happened in previous cycles) "when little time remains of the last thousand years" and "all men in general becomes speakers of untruth."[39] As always in traditional India, anarchy first of all means caste confusion: The Brahmans stop sacrificing and studying, stop making the offerings to the fathers, stop praying, and eat anything at all; and the serfs (the *shudra*) pray, gather wealth, or practice the laws of the ruling class.

In this version of end of days, the world will turn upside down, politics will go awry, and "many barbarian kings will rule the earth with false policies, being given to evil and lies."[40] As the age draws to its end, women will bear too many children, be too short, throw off all morals, and have intercourse by mouth. Brahmans will take money from kings who have committed the crime of Brahman-murder and made false accusations; and greedy Brahmans will flaunt the law falsely and plunder the land for alms. Householders, afraid of taxes, will become thieves, and false hermits will live off trade, while merchants will use false measures, and the evil will prosper. Furnished even with small capital, the arrogant will grow rich. Students of the Veda, greedy for possessions, will misbehave in their hermitages, drink liquor, and have intercourse with the teachers' wives. Overrun by impostors, no hermitages will be left. Man-eating tigers will lurk in city parks. Girls will get pregnant at the age of seven and eight and boys of ten and twelve will become fathers.[41]

It was the threat of such everyday disasters that led to conclusions of the kind we have already heard. One conclusion, we know, was that a king should be worshipped like a god and obeyed whatever happened because to have no king was worse than having the worst king.[42] Another was that a king's refusal or inability to play his protective role would lead to his downfall. A third conclusion, the most drastic of all, was that there was a right to kill a disastrous or outrageous king. *The Laws of Manu* voices the threat we have heard against the king who, for whatever reason, angers the priests. Other passages in this book say that if the king is lustful, partial, and mean, he will be destroyed by the very kind of punishment he metes out; that many kings, together with their entourages, have been destroyed through lack of humility (probably to Brahmans), and that a king who tolerates someone bent on violence incurs hatred and is himself destroyed. This last sentence is followed by the hint that the members of the higher castes may take up arms when calamity has been brought down on them.[43]

In one place in the *Mahabharata*, the conclusion is more explicit: In a crisis in which the king loses his ability to protect, the king, if wise, should recover his power by means of his spiritual strength, his *brahma*, alone, for he has lost all other power, and the Brahmans, the knowers of Veda, should collaborate in increasing his spiritual strength—old Vedic texts know of magic rituals to return a king to power.[44] However, if disorder and caste confusion have taken over, then all castes should take up arms. Even more categorical is the statement that a king who has promised but failed to protect the people should be killed by them like a rabid dog.[45]

There is a further surprising and, it seems, antimythical conclusion in a passage of the *Mahabharata*. This passage says that it is the king who by his actions creates the age as either the best age, the intermediate age, or the worst age. This conclusion sounds as if it comes not from believers in the traditional *dharma* but in the newer, more practical study of politics. Even if the conclusion is meant figuratively, whoever wrote it was liberated from the notion that the succession of ages, each with its characteristic level of morality, was caused by fate alone. The king's responsibility for his subjects is such that he is rewarded in heaven or punished in hell for the merits or sins by which he affects the welfare of his people—rewarded or punished far more heavily than an ordinary person.[46]

In a degenerate age, it is said, there are "times of distress" during which righteous and unrighteous are reversed. For example, by reversal of right and wrong, a king is allowed to kill the inhabitants and destroy the mines of an enemy's state.[47] Whatever the examples, the Indian belief that we live in the most degenerate of ages fits the Machiavellian attitudes we find in the epics. Take an example of a Machiavellian attitude from the *Mahabharata*: A Brahman, a great expert in Veda who has become a great archer as well, offers his services to his good friend, as he thinks, now a king. The Brahman greets the king with, "Recognize me, your friend!" but the king answers contemptuously that the Brahman's mind is not very sound—no king anywhere strikes up a friendship with someone so poor and so little fortunate. "As time ages men, so it wears out their friendships," the king says.

> Sure, we were friends before, but our friendship was based on what power we had ... I was friends with you, good brahman, because it served my purpose. No pauper is friend to the rich, no fool to the wise, no coward to the brave. An old friend—who needs him? It is two men of equal wealth and equal birth who contract friendship and marriage, not a rich man and a pauper ... An old friend—who needs him?[48]

When this passage was written, the doctrines of Indian Machiavellism must already have been well known; but the king's remarks, however crude, are so close to what a cynic may naturally think that they do not need the support of any presumed science. However, the *Mahabharata* also contains more subtle Machiavellian advice: The king is told that his highest secret is to lack trust in others, and that he should hide his desire or anger in order to have the chance to attack and destroy an unsuspecting enemy. His instruments should be smooth, reverential talk, oaths, and tears. There is no way in which, as a king, he can avoid cruelty; he should strike his enemies down while talking amiably and, after he decapitates them, mourn them. He must have as many faces and appearances as the peacock's tail has colors.[49]

This rather more subtle advice is likely to have been derived from the science of politics, to which we now turn, at first by way of a contrast between the sociopolitical views associated respectively with *dharma* and *artha*.

Righteous Kingship or Practical Kingship—Dharma or Artha

The root sense of the word *dharma* is *what is firm, what supports or sustains*. Understood broadly, as I have said earlier, *dharma* is the law of cosmic and social existence that sustains the world. In the earliest religion, it is mostly the rules and practice of ritual, but, as time goes on, it becomes identified with the righteous activity that keeps society stable and just. As the rule of righteous activity, *dharma* makes explicit the duties owed by the members of the different social orders, each order having the righteousness that expresses its relation to the others. Because it requires discipline, this righteousness needs to be reinforced, as the literature makes clear, by the considered punishments the king imposes on those who violate their order's duties. To create discipline, the king needs God's gift to rulers, the rod or *danda*, the symbol of the ruler's ability to protect, punish, and coerce. The king who fails to punish the violators of *dharma* is himself guilty. However, as king, he is exempted from the guilt of killing enemies in battle and sometimes, to keep him from interrupting his work, from ceremonial impurity. *Dharma* implies the superiority of the Brahmans, who are therefore not taxed (their tax is their pious behavior), have the right of way, and enjoy various immunities. The one restriction that appears in almost all texts is that they are not allowed to take another person's life, land, or woman.[50]

Artha is quite different from *dharma*, although, as social life makes necessary, the two overlap. *Artha* means *profit* or *wealth*, or, more narrowly and exactly, *means of subsistence* in the basic sense of *inhabited (and therefore productive) land*. The science that deals with *artha* is *Arthashastra*, defined as "the science of the means of acquisition and protection of inhabited land."[51] Given such a definition, it is natural that it should include a good deal of economics and be translated *political economy*; but as a rule, the translations *the science of politics* or *the art of government* fit its subject matter more aptly. There are two narrower but often almost synonymous terms, which I repeat because they say something about the Indian conception of politics. They are *the principles of coercive authority (dandaniti)* and *the conduct of kings (rajaniti)*.

I have taken the above definition of *arthashastra* or science of politics from the *Kautilya Arthashastra*, the oldest and fullest book devoted to it. The author's name poses something of a riddle. It may well be that of his clan, but because *Kautilya* means *craftiness*, it may be the name of a type—what English drama calls a Machiavel—rather than of an individual. But just as Kautilya quotes his predecessors, his successors quote him, and the book attributed to him has a structure, flavor, and position of its own, so it makes sense to regard its author as an individual and suppose him to be connected, at least by knowledge and sympathy, with the individual named Chanakya or Vishnugupta, the crafty adviser of King Chandragupta. The connection is made in the *Arthashastra* itself, which ends with the statement that it was "composed by him who, in resentment, quickly regenerated the science and the weapon and the earth that was under the control of the Nanda kings." Although this identification may be a later addition, it is accepted without question in a later text on the same subject, whose author (Kamandaka, of the fourth to eighth century A.D.) makes obvious use of the *Kautilya Arthashastra* and says that the master of his thought is Vishnugupta, he who, after the Nanda king's destruction, raised Chandragupta to the throne and recovered the essence of statecraft from the ocean of political science.[52]

Historians have drawn details of Chanakya's life from a drama in which he is a central character, but the drama, to which I will return, was written some six hundred years after the events that it portrays—a longer time than elapsed between the historical life of Joan of Arc and Shaw's *Saint Joan*. The uncertainty about the author of the *Arthashastra* makes it the harder to establish its date.[53]* However, none of the arguments over its date or the identity of its author have weakened its stand-

---

*The book mentions China, so it seems very unlikely to have preceded the establishment of the Ch'in empire. When it discusses the counterfeiting of coins, it knows nothing of the easy method of counterfeiting by casting, so it seems unlikely to be later than the first century B.C., a date that is also roughly plausible because of the denominations of the coins it names. However, if one assumes that the book has interpolations, such evidence may establish only the date of the fragment in which it is found.

ing as a basically accurate picture, unique in extent and detail, of life in ancient India, especially of the Maurya period. Therefore, although Machiavellism has had a long, varied career in ancient India, it is reasonable and economical to choose the *Arthashastra* to represent it.

The *Arthashastra* does not confine itself to Machiavellian doctrine but covers almost all life as an high administrator might see it; it more nearly resembles the Ch'in or Han code of law than a Legalist's essay or memorial to the throne. The first of its fourteen books deals with the rather miscellaneous topic of training. Most of it relates to the king and his ministers, his spies, his envoys, and his sons, who are assumed to be threats to his life. The following books deal with the heads of the government departments, civil and criminal law, secret government activities, foreign policy (in war and peace), and the strategy and tactics of war. The book ends by characterizing the logic of scientific explanation, which is understood in the terms of Indian rhetoric and debate.

To Kautilya, the science of politics is meant wholly for practice. There is little if anything explicitly philosophical about it except the framework in which it sets itself at its beginning and end. There is also little if anything exactly historical. A few memorable incidents are recalled: To warn the king—any king—against uncontrolled sensuality, Kautilya recalls a particular ruler who violated the daughter of his chaplain and was destroyed by the chaplain's curse, another who whipped Brahmans by mistake and was destroyed, and kings who were destroyed because they were extortionate or overbearing. However, all these incidents are drawn from the two Indian epics and echo more of the storyteller's dramatized morality than the historian's care for fact. It says something of the nature of Kautilya's project that he finds no clearly historic examples at hand but only incidents whose storybook nature maintain his characteristic distance from history.[54]

In some respects broad minded, Kautilya wants to take account of both local tradition and traditional law (*dharma*), and he often insists that the king should cultivate public opinion. This should be easy for the ideal king he describes. This king is taught by the science of politics to remain in full control of his sensuality, which he is advised to indulge but "without contravening his spiritual good and material well-being." The assumed balance between the spiritual and material seems violated by one statement, which is: "'Material well-being alone is supreme,' says Kautilya. For, spiritual good and sensual pleasures depend on material well-being." Is the statement a sign that Kautilya has let his guard down or allowed an aphorism repeated incautiously from somewhere to creep into the text?[55]

The education Kautilya prescribes for the ideal prince shows the thoroughness a careful adviser prefers. The roles given the prince are primarily sacramental, moral, and military. As shown by the suggested course of his day, his duties are not untaxing. In the order of day's eight parts, they are: the early-morning discussion of defense measures and of finances; the examination of the affairs of citizens and country people; the bath, meal, and study; the acceptance of cash revenues and the assignment of duties to department heads; the dispatch of letters to the council of ministers and the reception of information brought in by spies; the review of elephants, horses, chariots, and troops; the deliberation of military plans with the commander-in chief; afterwards, his day ended, the king "should worship the evening twilight."

Then begins the prince's almost equally strenuous night, also divided into eight parts: the interview with secret agents; the bath, meal, and study; the ceremony of going to sleep, to the accompaniment of music (sleep takes two parts of the night); the awakening to music and the pondering over the science of politics and the work to be done; the consultation with councilors and dispatch of secret agents; the reception of blessings from priests, preceptors, and chaplain, and consultations with his physician, chief cook, and astrologer. Then, "after going round a cow with her calf and a bull," the prince should go on to the assembly hall.[56]

Kautilya wants rural areas (composing most of inhabited India) to be administered with care. The economic welfare, industriousness, and loyalty of the farmers must be cultivated, he says, and their chiefs should be intelligent. He recognizes the importance of religion by specifying the duties of the royal chaplain, sacrificial priest, and preceptor, and advises that astrology, omens, and propitiatory and magical rites should be used to foresee, avert, or remedy calamities. No doubt recognizing what custom tended to grant, he advises that Brahmans be settled on tax-free lands, forest retreats set aside for Vedic study, and temples constructed. But though religion is to be respected, it is also to be used for political purposes.

Kautilya advises the king that secret agents masquerading as holy men should spread propaganda to favor the king and (as will be seen) mislead his enemies. He also advises that, when opportune, the king's agents should confiscate a temple's treasury. A different example of exploitation of religious faith is Kautilya's advice that an enemy king is most easily assassinated when visiting a holy person or shrine, to which he can be enticed for the purpose of assassinating him.[57]

Kautilya's Science of Punishment and Suspicion

With these recommendations by Kautilya, we move from his non-Machiavellian to his Machiavellian advice. I summarize the Machiavellian kind under the following headings: the science of politics as the proper use of coercive authority; the use of secret agents to test the ministers' loyalty and punish them discreetly; the use of spies at home and abroad; the protection of the king against the crown prince and other dangerous persons; and the geopolitical nature and strategies of war.

The science of politics as the proper use of coercive authority: Kautilya first creates a general framework for his recommendations. He opens with a brief discussion of the relationship between the traditional "sciences." Traditionalists, he recalls, propose the Vedas as the basic science because, they hold, philosophy is only a special branch of Vedic study; but others say that only economics and politics are basic sciences; and one of his predecessors claims that politics is the basic science because everything undertaken by the other sciences depends on it. Kautilya's own opinion is that the Vedas, philosophy, economics, and politics are all interdependent and essential (this contradicts his earlier cited statement that economics is basic).

The first of the enumerated sciences, philosophy, is the rational investigation of what is better and worse in the other sciences; it illuminates them, steadies the mind, and fosters proficiency in speech and action. It is noteworthy that Kautilya's conception of philosophy is liberal enough to include the *Lokayata*, which is often opposed for its sophistry and is identified in later sources with radical materialism.[58]*

As described by Kautilya, the science of politics, which alone concerns us closely, teaches the king the use of the Rod, ensures the pursuit of philosophy, religion, and economics, and makes possible the orderly

---

*Because Kautilya supports traditional religion and because philosophy as he sees it is "investigating by means of reasoning," it seems best to assume that the *Lokayata* he refers to was a school of logic (whose logic was put to use that outsiders considered sophistical). That the logic might cast a confusing light on religious dogma should not have disturbed him any more than did the political exploitation of religion he advocated. Whoever composed the *Arthashastra* makes the impression of a shrewdly practical observer rather than an observant Hindu.

In Kautilya's account, the "science" of religion is constituted by the sacred canon (the three Vedas), which establishes the four castes and four stages of life that, properly observed, lead to individual bliss and social prosperity. The science of economics, he says, deals with agriculture, cattle raising, and trade, the income from which maintains the king's rule and army.

maintenance of worldly life. Succinctly, politics teaches that a king too severe with the Rod is terrifying, a king too mild in its use is despised, and only a king who uses it justly is honored. "If not used at all, it gives rise to the law of the fishes. For, the stronger swallows the weak in the absence of the wielder of the Rod."[59] The pursuit of the just mean is not in itself Machiavellian, but what follows from it, in Kautilya's exposition, often merits the name very well.

The coercive power or Rod the *Arthashastra* prescribes is actually a code of law. Kautilya means to comprehend in it the whole of life and not only the legal provisions that furnish my examples. The *Arthashastra* contains rules for marriage, inheritance, property, debts, and deposits. It is sensitive enough to human relations to include regulations against verbal injuries, whether defamation of body, character, learning, profession, or country. If the insult is, in fact, true, if, for example, the person defamed as one-eyed or lame is really so, the fine is lower. Defamation of superiors is fined more four times more than defamation of social inferiors.[60]

The punishments prescribed in the *Arthashastra* are often brutal by modern standards. Though their frequent brutality is in keeping with the Machiavellian conception that excessive mercy creates social chaos, it would be unfair to criticize them without comparing them with what prevailed in other premodern legal systems. The need for due process and for exceptions is clearly recognized.[61] Intentional crime is distinguished from the unintentional, and accused persons whose innocence is corroborated by witnesses are cleared of guilt. If not cleared, they are tortured, but the use of torture has many exceptions. That is, it is forbidden to torture persons suspected of small crimes, or to torture Brahmans or ascetics, or those who are minors, aged, sick, intoxicated, insane, overcome by hunger, thirst, the fatigue of travel, or the like, and, under no circumstances, pregnant women—the long list must be the result of much accumulated experience. A Brahman can be punished by being branded, so as to indicate the nature of his crime, and exiled.[62]

For very grave offenders there is a choice of punishments that range from various kinds of beating to a "needle in the hand," the burning of one joint of a finger, "heating in the sun for one day," and "a bed of *balbaja*-points on a winter-night."[63] Some kinds of sheerly accidental killing are excused and others are punished by death (though recognized in India, justifiable homicide is not dealt with by Kautilya). For murder, the punishment is death with torture; but the longer the victim survives, the lighter the punishment, which is changed to a fine after the victim survives seven days. For the worst of murders, of mother, father, son, brother, or teacher, the head is first doused with boiling water, to remove the skin, and then set on fire. For rebellious acts, the punishment is the setting on fire of the rebel's hands and head, or if the perpetrator is a Brahman, blinding.[64]

The use of secret agents to test the ministers' loyalty and punish them discreetly: Kautilya recommends an extraordinarily thoroughgoing use of secret agents. As usual, he speaks concisely and drily, but his enumeration of practices—attested to, though in less detail, by other Indian sources—has the eloquence of its own pitiless ingenuity. Kautilya begins by prescribing tests by temptation of the king's new ministers. The first test, of piety, uses secret agents to tempt the minister to revolt after the king has seemingly dismissed his chaplain because of the chaplain's religious scruples. To pass the test, the minister must prove more loyal to the king than to religion and refuse the invitation to revolt and install a more pious king. By the second test, of material gain, the commander of the army is seemingly dismissed for supporting evil men, after which it is suggested that the minister take a large material reward and join a common rebellion. By the third test, of love, a wandering nun, really a secret agent, who has won the ministers' confidence and is respected in the palace, suggests privately to each minister that the (chief) queen has fallen in love with him and requests an assignation, her promise of love being reinforced by the promise of wealth. By the fourth test, of fear, a seeming conspiracy leads to the ministers' imprisonment, after which one of the king's agents secretly suggests to each minister that the king is behaving wickedly and, as everyone agrees, should be killed and replaced.[65] (Though I am expounding rather than criticizing Kautilya, at this point I cannot refrain from a parenthesis of objections: Obviously, ministers who could pass these tests would be paragons of loyalty; but one supposes that if the tests were in fact carried out, discreet whispers would reveal them for what they were and might turn the mock conspiracy into a real one. More clever than realistic, the tests seem to me to be the amusement of someone playing at Machiavellism. If more than amusement, they suggest an intolerably heightened suspiciousness—what would be the reaction of ministers who knew of the possibility of such tests, and what thoughts would pass through the mind of the king who knew that they might know about them? This situation recalls Stalin's paranoiac mock-trials, to be taken up later.)

Kautilya continues: After the body of ministers has been proved loyal, the king should set up a secret service. While the use of secret agents is ascribed to a Buddhist king and mentioned in the epics, Kautilya's is the only thorough Indian account. He recommends that some spies or secret agents—often a more appropriate term—should be assigned to stations, and others, the "mobile agents," should work alone.

The agents assigned to stations, which are supervised by the king's ministers, are recruited from a wide range of the Indian careers or professions of Kautilya's time. Some are clever students and some are intelligent and "honest" apostate monks, provided with money and assistants, who can pass themselves off as ordinary wandering monks. Others are intelligent and trustworthy but impoverished farmers, who can play the part either of householders or of the farmers they were in the past; or are intelligent and trustworthy but impoverished traders, who can continue to act the part of traders. Lastly there are hermits with shaven heads or matted hair who want steady employment and who can act the part of ascetics (though allowed secret meals as big as they like) and direct other agents, these other agents pretending to be traders' assistants who have become the pretended ascetic's adoring disciples. These "disciples" of this unholy "holy man" should announce that he can make anyone prosperous. To inspire faith in him, the "holy man" should astonish potential believers with his knowledge of what is going on in their families, the knowledge to be passed on to him by his pretended disciples' signals. This "holy man" should also predict events that are made to happen by other secret agents. Further, he should arrange for the livelihood of the more able of his (true) believers, pacify with money and honor those who have good cause to be resentful, and arrange for the death of those who are either resentful without good cause or who act in a way injurious to the king.[66]

When Kautilya describes who should be chosen as mobile agents, he brings up a whole motley of human types. He explains very little, but the kinds he chooses demonstrate the psychological acuteness that underlies Indian political thought. The mobile agents, he declares, are to be recruited from among people who have no close relatives and who need support for their study, study of the meaning of bodily marks, magical lore, the creation of illusions, the interpretation of omens, and so on—including, significantly, the art of human relations. Mobile agents, says Kautilya, are to be of three character types, each with an appropriate function: bravos, audacious men who, for the sake of money, are willing to fight even an elephant or other wild animal; poison givers, who are cruel, idle persons without affection for their kinsmen; and wandering nuns, whether Brahman or heretical, that is, female ascetics or mendicants, who are poor, widowed, and bold, who are looking for steady employment, and who are treated with honor in the palace.

Given a credible disguise and cover story, these mobile agents should spy on all the high officials. The audacious men, in the guise of umbrella bearers, water carriers, drivers, and the like, can easily spy on officials out of doors. The poison givers, in the guise of cooks, waiters, barbers, valets, and the like, or of deaf or dumb or blind persons, freaks, idiots, actors, dancers, musicians, or professional storytellers can spy indoors. If a female nun is denied entry into the homes of those she is assigned to spy on, some other agent can gain entry by pretending to be the mother of a servant, or a female artist, singer, or slave, and can then smuggle out the information in songs, recitations, and notes hidden in musical instruments, or by means of signs; or the agent can get out by pretending to be ill or mad, by setting fire to something, or by administering poison to someone.

Naturally, agents are sometimes fallible and sometimes corrupt. It is only when the reports of three agents are in agreement that they should be given credence. Agents who always make mistakes should be done away with quietly. Tight security must be observed within the spy system itself: The agents' reports are brought to spy stations and there put into alphabetic code by assistants who neither know nor are known to the agents (or, by an alternative explanation, brought where coding assistants and other station employees do not know one another).[67]

The danger of treason being constant, Kautilya proposes an assortment of remedies, many of them fatal. Should it be discovered that some great official, one too powerful to suppress openly, is treasonous, it is possible for a secret agent, for example, to incite the treasonous official's brother against him while the king himself encourages the brother by offering him the official's property, Once the brother has killed the treasonous official, he should be executed for the crime of fratricide. Or a secret agent can lead the treasonous official's son to believe that he is in fact the king's son kept (as a hostage?) in the official's home for fear of that same official. The king himself should then honor the son in private and tell him that if not for fear of the official, the king would install him immediately as crown prince. When this encouragement leads the son to murder his treasonous father, the king should have him executed as a parricide. Or a woman agent can win the confidence of the treasonous official's wife by giving her love potions intended to heighten the husband's love and then substitute poison for the love potions. Or an agent disguised as a holy man can kill the traitor in the course of a rite conducted to help the traitor attain his desires. Or a physician can diagnose a malignant illness and cheat the traitor with poison in medicine or food. And so on, as the relentlessly scheming imagination suggests.[68]

The use of spies at home and abroad: After the king has set spies on his high officials, he should set them on the ordinary inhabitants of his country. One of the functions of these spies or agents is to create favorable public opinion. For instance, they should stage a debate wherever large numbers of people meet. To begin the debate, one of them should complain loudly that the king oppresses everyone with fines and taxes. To answer the complainer and those who agree with him, the other agent should remind the audience that, long ago, when the people were oppressed by the law of the fishes, they made Manu their king and promised him one-sixth of their grain and one-tenth of their goods and money. Maintained by this agreement, the agent should say, kings guard their subjects' well-being and security. The agent should point out that those who refuse to pay fines take on themselves the kings' sins, just as incompetent kings take on themselves the sins of their subjects. Even forest-dwelling ascetics agree to this and pay their share of grain to the king who protects them. To drive home the importance of kings, the agent should add that those who slight them will undergo divine punishment.

It is also the business of the secret agents to investigate and improve local administration: Disguised as ascetics, they should discover to what extent those who live on the king's bounty, the grain, cattle, or money they receive from him, actually help him in local affairs and restrain rebels and repel enemies. To strengthen his position, the king should reward local rulers or dignitaries if they are contented, calm those who are discontented, and divide those who might turn against him. For those who, despite his efforts, remain discontented, there is an effective cure: The king should appoint them collectors of fines and taxes, so that after they have incurred the inhabitant's dislike, he can have them secretly done away with, or, alternatively, arrange an insurrection against them or post them to mines and factories. To guard against locally important persons who are so greedy, angry, frightened, or proud that enemies can seduce them easily, secret agents disguised as fortune-tellers or astrologers should uncover their mutual relations and their contacts with enemies, so that the king can reward the contented and manage the others "by means of conciliation, gifts, dissension, or force."[69]

Since people are often unwilling to give the information needed for administering them, the information should be collected by secret agents. Disguised as householders, these agents should count the fields, houses, families, and individuals in the villages in which they are stationed and accumulate helpful information relevant to taxes, occupations, departures and arrivals, antisocial activities, and possible enemy spies. Likewise, agents disguised as traders should investigate the quantity and price of whatever is produced in mines, waterworks, forests, factories, and fields, and everything pertaining to imports and exports. To guard against fraud, agents disguised as ascetics should investigate the honesty of farmers, cowherds, traders, and department heads. And to guard against subversion, agents disguised as veteran thieves should investigate why thieves and enemy agents enter, stay, and leave any place whatsoever. Given the help of such methodical spying, an administrator will be able to look after the countryside in his charge.[70]

There are also the enemy territories to investigate and influence. For this purpose, double agents—their sons and wives kept as hostages to ensure their loyalty—should be sent to find employment with the enemy king and uncover the enemy's double agents. The need for care is so great that spies should be sown not only in enemy but also in allied and neutral countries, each kind of spy to be given the most plausible disguise; and counterspies should be stationed wherever they will be most helpful.[71]

These spies have much to do because it is to the king's advantage to discover all the persons of consequence within the enemy country who are disaffected for any reason. As usual in Kautilya's systematic text, the types of persons involved are enumerated. There are persons who have become disaffected for all kinds of reasons: some have been cheated, humiliated, removed from favor, defeated in a contest, distressed by banishment, or hindered from carrying out their duties; some have been deprived of inheritance, honor, or office; and some have suffered because their women have been molested or because they have been been imprisoned and fined; and so on. There is also the person who had been frightened because, for example, he has committed an offense of a kind for which someone else has been punished, because he has made a sudden fortune, or because he is disliked by the king or hostile to him. And there is the greedy person, greedy because he is poor, because someone has taken his property, or because he had made rash investments. In terms of personality, the disaffected include the conceited person, the person who craves honor or resents the honor done his enemy, the fiery-tempered person, the violent person, and all the others who have not received what they think they deserve.

At this point we again meet the agent in holy man's guise. This, says Kautilya, is because each of the disaffected persons should be egged on by the "holy man," the king's agent, to whom he is devoted. This agent should say that the king of the disaffected person's country, being ignorant of political science, charges about like a drunken elephant with a drunken driver and threatens to destroy his subjects. But this elephant, says the agent, can be hurt by inciting a rival elephant against him. Kautilya advises that the enraged person should be incited by such means, and the frightened, greedy, and proud by arguments that fit their particular temperaments. In this way, the agent can win over all these kinds of disaffected people, whom he should use to further his subversive purpose, all the while setting spies to watch over them.

To Kautilya, the most desirable object of all this subversion is conquest. For that reason, after having won the allegiance both of his own subjects and those of his enemy, the king should deliberate on the feasibility of taking his enemy's territory by conquest.[72]

The protection of the king against the crown prince and other dangerous persons: In considering the king's protection, Kautilya recalls the view that the king must guard against his sons from their very birth because princes, like crabs, devour their begetters. One of Kautilya's predecessors suggests that princes should be killed silently before their father grows to love them. Others argue, as Kautilya recalls, that precautionary killing is too cruel, so a prince should be confined in a place where he is no threat. Kautilya then recalls the suggestion that the prince be kept so engrossed in pleasures that he is too preoccupied to become hostile to his father. But this is a living death, says Kautilya, because, if the royal family's princes are undisciplined, the family will disintegrate as soon as it is attacked.

Other suggestions are considered: Some contend that when the prince is ready for it, secret agents should tempt him with hunting, gambling, wine, and women, and should suggest to him that he attack his father and take over the kingdom, while another agent should undertake to dissuade him. Kautilya answers that "this awakening of one not awake is highly dangerous," besides which an immature person, such as the prince must be, accepts what he is told. Therefore he should be instructed only in what is best for his spiritual and material good and guarded by secret agents faithful to him. Instruction by means of experience is the most effective. So if the prince is eager for women, the agents should bring him women of a kind that make him abhor illicit sex. If he longs for wine, they should frighten him with drugged wine, and if he longs to gamble, they should pit him against expert cheats whose superiority will teach him to dislike gambling. By a similar method of countering desire, if the prince entertains the idea of attacking his father, the agents should pretend to agree but then dissuade him on the grounds of danger, punishment in hell, or the anger of the subjects. Kautilya brings up other educational expedients in case of need, none of them drastic, and says that if an only son is evil by nature, the king should try to get him to bear a son, that is, a grandson who may prove better, or try to get sons from some selected daughter. Kautilya ends this discussion by making the point that a sound family oligarchy "is difficult to conquer and remains on the earth for ever."[73]

Considering all the dangers he may face in his own palace, the king "should take precautions against fire, poison, and serpents" and against the treachery of the queen and of persons admitted into the palace. Every object entering or leaving the palace should be examined, recorded, and transported under seal. The rest of the precautions the king should take, against poisoned food, garments, or flowers, against plunging into crowds or insufficient guards, I leave to the reader's imagination.[74]

To appreciate the difference between the incomplete Machiavellism of *The Laws of Manu*, which was influenced by *arthashastra*, and the usually thoroughgoing Machiavellism of Kautilya, it is instructive to compare their respective advice to kings on precautions against poison. *Manu* has a brief five sentences beginning with the advice to have poison-dispelling Vedic verses chanted over the king's food. He says nothing about the methods of administering poison or recognizing its appearance and effects, and nothing, except by brief indirection, on having the food tasted in advance. Kautilya, in contrast, is silent about Vedic chanting but requires frequent tasting, speaks of the possibility of poisoning drinks and water, describes the appearances of many poisoned foods and other substances, tells what the symptoms of poisoning are, requires the attendance not only of physicians but of experts in poison cures, and also assumes that antidotes are kept among the king's medicines. *Manu's* few sentences on precautions are there only to complete his description of the king's behavior, whereas Kautilya takes the matter with the full seriousness of someone who expects the ruler he advises to use poison and to be its intended victim.[75]

The geopolitical nature and strategies of war: Kautilya thinks that, for a successful king, war is the most natural of activities, and he defines such a king—one with superior qualities, material resources, and a successful policy—as the would-be conqueror. By definition, therefore, all the immediately adjacent territories are those of the enemy and all territories on the further side of the enemy are those of the ally. Therefore, also by definition, a powerful neighboring ruler is an enemy ruler and a weak one is a vulnerable enemy ruler. Beyond these natural enemies there are natural allies.

This conceptualization belongs to the formal scheme, invented by Kautilya's predecessors, of the conqueror or aggressor in the middle,

encircled by the enemy (the enemy group of kings), who is encircled by
the ally (group of kings), who is encircled by the second enemy (group
of kings), who is encircled by the second ally (group of kings), and so
on. Outside of the whole circle of circles is the neutral king, who is capable of either helping any of the kings or suppressing any one who has
no ally. As constructed in *Arthashastra* style, the standard type of circle
of states comprises twelve kings: In the middle is the conqueror or
aggressor, then, facing him, there are groups of five kings who are,
alternately, his foes and his friends, the strength of their enmity or
friendship proportionate to their distance from him; and then, in the
aggressor's rear, there are groups of four kings, alternating between
foes and friends of different degrees; and beyond all these there are two
neutral kings.[76]

Proceeding scholastically, we discover that there are six types of
foreign policy by which the state can govern its relations with its neighbors. These types are peace, which requires a treaty; war, which
requires doing injury to the enemy; neutrality, which means remaining
quiet; marching against the enemy, which is the result of growing
strength; seeking protection from a powerful king, which requires surrender to him; and "dual policy," which is simultaneous peace with one
state and war with another.

When the king considers the three possible conditions of his state,
decline, progress, and equilibrium, he decides what policy is expedient:
When in a condition of decline relative to the enemy, he should make
peace; when prosperous, he should make war; and when neither he nor
the enemy can harm the other, he should stay quiet. In every case, expediency is the guide. He does not remain at peace because of a benevolent attitude but, on the contrary, may prefer to remain at peace in order
to ruin the enemy's enterprises by the success of his own. Or he can
exploit the mutual confidence created by peace to use secret or occult
means against the enemy; or by paying higher salaries or granting
favors or exemptions, he can entice away the enemy's most able person-
nel.

Another of the many possibilities is that peace will detach the
enemy from his allies, who may then become the king's allies instead.
Or the king may lend his troops to an enemy to attack the other states
in the enemy's circle, and when the others become hostile to the enemy,
the king can join them and destroy the enemy whose ally he had seemingly become. Such possibilities imply that it is often best to be at peace
on one border and at war on another. Regardless of the course he takes,
the king should try to carry out the policy toward the circle of sur-

rounding states that helps him most to change decline into stability and stability into progress.[77]

There are many considerations to take into account in determining foreign policy. For example, if a weaker neighbor meets all the king's demands, the king should make peace with him because "heroism born of grief and resentment make one fight bravely like a forest fire." Besides, such peace puts the king in a favorable light in the eyes of the other members of the weaker king's circle.[78] The king should also keep the peace with an enemy whose dissident subjects refuse to take his side because they either are afraid of being retaken by the enemy or are afraid of war as such. Analogous considerations should direct the king if he is either weaker than or equal in strength to his neighbor.

How should the king come to terms with his neighbors? As always, concise in form and fertile in expedients, Kautilya suggests that one can come to terms with stronger states by means of marriage alliances, by the payment of tribute, and by the surrender of a large part of his army, of forest products or other goods, or of territory. It may well be expedient, he says, to cheat the enemy to whom one surrenders by overestimating the value of what he will actually get, by sending secret agents or robbers to operate in the surrendered territories, or by removing everything of value from these territories.[79]

Considerations of justice sometimes become those of expediency as well. For example, when there is a choice between attacking a strong but unjust king and a weak but just one, the aggressor king should attack the strong, unjust one. The reason Kautilya gives is the obvious one that injustice creates disloyalty; and justice, loyalty. The subjects of the strong, unjust king "drive him out or resort to his enemy," while the subjects of the weak but just king give him every support when he is attacked and follow him if he is forced to flee.[80] This conclusion is accompanied by criticism of all the varied forms of injustice of a wicked king, who in being wicked shows himself to be foolish and impoverishes his subjects and causes them to kill him or to go over to the enemy.

Victory, says Kautilya, brings with it rewards some of which are dangerous. Such danger makes it better to hold relatively poor territory with inhabitants who can be won over rather than rich territory with stubborn, permanent enemies. Likewise, territory whose people are disunited is preferable to territory whose people join together in potentially dangerous bands. The policy to adopt for conquered territory should be a varied one. The conqueror should be intelligently conciliatory and protect the ordinary inhabitants everywhere, though he should demand that deserters and other harmful persons be handed over to him. To conciliate whoever can be conciliated, he should give gifts of land, money, girls, and promises of safety. He should also give good positions to those who have the energy, forcefulness, or intellect to be helpful in the administration of the conquered territory.[81]

The actual tactics of war recommended by Kautilya are hard to summarize because, though detailed and practical, they lack any guiding principle. They include directions for setting up and guarding a military camp, for marching from the camp, for guarding the troops while on the march, for various forms of covert warfare, and for encouraging one's troops. There is something that appears especially contemporary in Kautilya's recognition of the importance of means by which an army's morale is kept high. To encourage his troops, the kings is advised, he should collect them and personally request them to attack the enemy, saying among the rest, "I receive a wage like you; this kingdom is to be enjoyed together with you." The minister and chaplain should encourage the troops by pointing out how well prepared they are. And

> bards and panegyrists should describe the attainment of heaven by the brave and the absence of heaven for the cowards, and sing praises of the caste, corporation, family, deeds, and conduct of the warriors. Assistants of the chaplain should speak of the use of sorcery and black magic, mechanics, carpenters and astrologers should speak of success and failure in their own works and failure in those of the enemy.[82]

Then, after the ranks have been softened by honors and money, the commander-in-chief should address them and offer them generous rewards for killing enemies, from one hundred thousand (of I do not know what monetary denomination) for killing the enemy king to twenty for an ordinary infantryman. In the rear, physicians should be stationed with surgical instruments, apparatus, medicines, and bandages, as well as "women in charge of food and drink and capable of filling men with enthusiasm."[83]

There follow directions for the grounds suitable for fighting; for the varied functions of the infantry, cavalry, chariots, and elephants; and for the arrangement of the battle array in wings, flanks, and front; and so on.

I end my account of Kautilya with a few war stratagems taken from his cornucopia of suggestions and with two of his aphorisms, chosen not quite at random. The stratagems occur in a section entitled "Concerning the Weaker King," to which sort of king Kautilya gives the advice neither to bend like a reed nor to mobilize all his troops. Instead, says Kautilya, the weaker king should find shelter with a stronger one or take refuge in an unassailable fortress. He can, of course, fight with the weapons of diplomacy. Or he can assassinate the enemy's generals by egging them on to quarrel over young, extremely beautiful prostitutes. He can also use secret agents to give poisoned wine to an already intoxicated officer, or to mix poison with the fodder and grass for elephants and horses. Or the enemy should be panicked during a night battle by the striking of as many drums as possible and the loud announcement of victory. Or the king's camp should be entered and the enemy king killed during the ensuing panic.

A few more expedients for the weaker king: If his fort is under siege and he fails to break out at night, he can escape in the guise of a heretical monk; or he can be carried out disguised as a corpse; or, dressed as a woman, he can follow a funeral procession. If the fort is captured, he can remain concealed in a hollow inside the image of a god or in a hollow wall or underground room. Then, when they are no longer looking for him, he can enter the king's room at night by an underground passage and kill him while he is asleep. Or, when the enemy king is asleep, secret woman agents should drop snakes or poisonous fire and smoke on him. The details are varied and sometimes surprising, but the general nature of the reasoning is familiar.[84]

The first of the two aphorisms I have mentioned is a reminder of the most Machiavellian side of Kautilya: "An arrow discharged by an archer may kill or not kill; but intellect operated by a wise man would kill even children in the womb." The second aphorism is one that is interesting because of its sweeping nature and its likeness to the advice given by Han Fei, which it resembles in its rather paranoiac air and impracticality:

> The wise (king) should guard others from others, his own people from his own people, his own people from others, and others from his own people, and always guard himself from his own people and from others.[85]

Machiavellian Drama and Fable

Indian literature reflects the attitudes both of those who endorsed "the science of politics" and of those who morally opposed it. Citations from the two great epics have already shown this dual reflection. The literature of the fourth to eighth centuries A.D., when Sanskrit literature flourished, often mentions and sometimes concentrates on political

ideas in relation to morality. Although this literature, too rich to be followed here, adds nothing to the basic views already discussed, it does
contain strong attacks on Kautilya's advice.[86] For example, in the seventh century A.D., Bana, a great writer familiar with Buddhism, asked if
there is anything righteous in those who accept the authority of the
cruel science of Kautilya, taught by hard-hearted priests

> whose desire is always for the goddess of wealth that has been
> cast away by thousands of kings; who are devoted to the applica-
> tion of destructive sciences; and to whom brothers, affectionate
> with natural cordial love, are fit victims to be murdered.[87]

Kautilya's message was also conveyed in works with literary pretensions. One of these, a metrical book written by the Jain saint
Somadeva in the tenth century A.D., shows how far Machiavellism can
lead even a Jain, whose religion, like Buddhism, reaches complete
mercy to all living things. Somadeva writes, among the rest, "A person
devoted to compassion or who is always in grief is unable to protect
even an object placed on the palm of his hand." Whoever "does not hit
adversaries hard" is "dead even though alive."[88]

For practical reasons, I confine the rest of my account of the relevant literature to two works, the play *The Minister's Seal*, most likely
written in the late fourth century A.D., and the famous collection of
fables called the *Panchatantra (The Five Books)*, probably compiled by
about A.D. 500 from stories many of which were probably much earlier.

The Minister's Seal, written by Vishakhadatta, is dedicated at its
end to "my Chandragupta, our most gracious king."[89] The reference is
to Chandra Gupta II—historians often divide the name to distinguish
him and his father, Chandra Gupta I, from Chandragupta Maurya. The
play was much commented on in later India as a study of character and
an instructive example of political science. It takes place after the defeat
of the last ruler of the Nanda dynasty. We find that the crown prince of
this dynasty has survived and some of the former Nanda subjects are
still loyal to the dynasty, but that the most dangerous Nanda survivor
is their prime minister, Rakshasa, an especially able and loyal person.

The most impressive character in the play is none other than Kautilya—here known as Chanakya—who is eager not to kill but to win
over Rakshasa to the Maurya side. For this purpose he makes the most
devious use of his secret agents. Rakshasa, on his part, plays a counter-
game, the object of which is to use secret agents to persuade King Chandragupta that his prime minister, Kautilya, is too eager to rule.

However, Chanakya, who learns of the plot against him, stages a mock quarrel with Chandragupta, the Maurya king, whose order he countermands for theatrical purposes. Chandragupta pretends to be angry, Chanakya speaks to him with a staged insolence, leaves in a show of fury at the king's ingratitude, and pretends to resign. In the meanwhile, an agent of Kautilya creates genuine distrust between Rakshasa and his prince. This distrust grows when a letter is discovered, one that has been forged in Rakshasa's name and sealed with his briefly stolen seal. The distrust is heightened when Rakshasa is discovered wearing a jewel sold him by Kautilya's bidding, a jewel once owned by the last Nanda king and now taken to be the price that was paid Rakshasa for treachery. Rakshasa is sent away in disgrace. Even then, however, he remains loyal. What finally gets him to change sides is the chance offered him to save a loyal friend from death on condition that he serve the Maurya side as minister in place of Kautilya. As minister, he will be able to restore his now captive prince to his ancestral land. Pressed so hard, Rakshasa accepts the offer.

This plot, much of which I have omitted, is the framework on which a drama of great deception and great loyalty is played out. Oddly, deception supports loyalty and loyalty deception, and both win out. The loyalty exists on both sides, because Kautilya, the great deceiver, remains wholeheartedly devoted to his king. His loyalty is proved by the lengths he is willing to go to gain the services of the rival who will displace him. And this rival, Kautilya knows, is necessary to the Maurya side because of his passionate, inspiring loyalty.

Here are a few illustrations from play's text: In the prologue, we hear a fearful actress call Kautilya "Kautilya of the crooked mind." Soon afterwards, Chalakya (Kautilya), who is just setting his stratagems in motion, muses that only a person such as Rakshasa "who joins wisdom and courage to loyalty can increase a king's fortune." Later he compares Rakshasa to a rogue elephant in rut "roaming the woods in a frenzy of exuberant power" and adds, "I shall capture you with my wits, and rope you in for you to serve at last as the Maurya's beast of burden!"

I end with the grateful words of King Chandragupta, who says to himself after Kautilya has won the game:

Indeed, I am ashamed that the well-nigh invincible army of the enemy has been vanquished by my minister without bloodshed . . . Even without cording a bow a king may be able to vanquish all that is vincible on earth while sleeping, as I did, if his guide, wakeful in all matters, watches over his affairs.

Then the king approaches Chanakya and says, "My lord, Chandragupta bows to you!"[90]

The *Panchatantra* begins with a dedication to six previous authors of books on the science of conduct *(nitishastra)*, beginning with Manu and ending with Chanakya the wise.[91] It explains its own existence with the story that a king named Immortal Power had three stupid sons, all of them unwilling to learn. His advisers were at their wits' ends, but a Brahman promised to teach them the art of intelligent living within six months. He took them home, made them learn the five books he had composed, and proved as successful as he had promised. "Since that day," the book says, "this work on the art of intelligent living, called *Panchatantra*, or the *Five Books*, has travelled the world, aiming at the awakening of intelligence in the young."

This has turned out to be no idle boast. It has been said that, with the exception of the Bible, the *Panchatantra* is the most widely disseminated book in the world. There are some two hundred versions in some sixty languages—including old ones in Arabic, Greek, Hebrew, Latin, Slavic, Turkish, German, Italian, French, Spanish, Swedish, English, Georgian, and Dutch. Since the *Panchatantra* represents itself as teaching the Indian science of politics, since it quotes from the *Arthashastra*, and since it gives a faithful representation of the spirit of this science, it is no exaggeration to say that Kautilya, made humorous and universally palatable, has reached the world as a whole and has given even children an education in Machiavellian attitudes.

I will summarize only one story, from the first book of the *Panchatantra*, which I choose because it offers such a good representation of the clash between morality and the arthashsatran principle of the priority of the ruler. In the story, a lion gives asylum, kingly asylum, to a camel. When the lion is wounded and becomes unable to hunt, his adviser, a crow, urges him to eat the camel, but the lion, quoting *Dharmashastra*, says that the gift of safety is the noblest gift of all. To this the crow answers that the lion is mistaken because the great sages allow sins for one's own good. Explaining himself, the crow says that for the sake of the family, one of its members may be sacrificed. Likewise, for the sake of a village, a family may be sacrificed, and for the sake of a state or a territory, a village may be sacrificed. Furthermore, as the sages teach, the whole world may be sacrificed for one's own sake. Convinced, the lion kills and eats the camel. Then, however, struck with remorse, he complains that the loss of a wise servant is the death of kings.

To this the crow answers that if the king is to prosper, anyone who threatens his life, even a brother or friend, must be killed. If the king is merciful, he is ineffective and must be abandoned. A kingdom, explains the crow, cannot be governed by the usual standards because the vices of ordinary men are the virtues of a king (in verse, "To ruling monarchs let no trace / Of common nature cling; / for what is vice in other men, / Is virtue in a king"). Royal policy, the crow continues, is difficult because "a king's policy, like a harlot, takes many guises: it is at once true and false, harsh and gentle in speech, cruel and compassionate, avaricious and generous, lavish in spending and yet taking in great amounts of wealth from many sources."[92]

In saying that anything may rightly be sacrificed to save one's own self, the crow dissents from the *Arthashastra*, to which the king, not the private individual, is central. I will later contend that the message of the crow poses a natural dilemma to anyone who tries to judge the justice or wisdom of Machiavellian reasoning.

◢:4:◣

The Machiavellism of Renaissance Italy

Historical Background

The political fragmentation of Renaissance Italy corresponded to the breaks in its geography, the variations in its culture, and the differing histories of its cities.[1] To some of these cities, independence was a traditional right; some even believed that their municipal institutions had been granted to them by God, who had made them by nature free. In their contests with the emperors, the cities defended themselves physically with the usual swords and spears and intellectually with arguments drawn from Roman civil law. By this law, they contended, they were entitled to the same independent juridical standing as a guild, monastery, or university. The argument of Azo of Bologna (d. 1230) was that the Roman people had transferred its power to the emperor only conditionally, so his power was by right no greater than that of the people as a whole. The arguments of Aristotle's *Politics*, translated into Latin a generation after Azo's death, gave the cities the means with which to question the superiority of monarchy as a form of government.[2] Because arguments alone were ineffective, many of the cities fell into the hands of hereditary rulers, who saw themselves as bulwarks against chaos and tyranny. Florence and Venice, however, succeeded in remaining independent and guarding their old liberties, an accomplishment that was explained by their loyalty to traditional forms of government.[3]

The constant, somewhat desultory warring of the Italian city-states, fought by bands of professional soldiers, must have stimulated the local pride evident in Renaissance culture, which demonstrated present glory along with a bid for future immortality. The humanists or literati were themselves mostly members of the glory-hungry ruling class, and the more individual artists depended on patrons from this class.[4] Many of the humanists and artists came to believe, proudly and polemically, that their culture, though interrupted by the Middle Ages, was continuous with that of ancient Rome. As proof of the continuity, old books that had been isolated in monasteries became the sources of a still plausible wisdom, and Hellenistic statues, whole or in fragments, stimulated the unashamed celebration of the human body. But neither the hunger for glory nor the recovery of classical culture could prevent Italy from being unstable and inhumane—writers mourned that the evil of *Fortuna* was magnified by the evil consciously inflicted by human beings on one another.

To return to civic politics, especially Florentine, by the beginning of the fifteenth century, the citizens of Florence had come to see themselves as members of a free city whose traditions went back to republican Rome and its "mixed" form of government.[5] In the optimistic atmosphere of this period, men such as Bruno Bruni (c. 1370–1444) preached civic humanism, which implied that it was a need and duty for self-respecting citizens to hold office. Given such an ideal, it was natural for a talented young aristocrat to aim to become an orator or a lawyer, that is, someone trained for political debate. The preferred political ideal was the Roman republic and the preferred moral guide Aristotle's *Ethics*, which Bruni translated again into Latin in 1417.

To Aristotle, as to the young aristocrats who believed in civic virtue, happiness was an activity in accord with the highest excellence. Aristotle's descriptions of liberality and magnanimity fitted the aristocratic temper of the times, and it was easy to agree with him that in order to demonstrate one's virtue one must have external goods, the means by which the virtue could be exercised. "What kind of happiness would it be," it was asked, "for a man to see his father dying of hunger and not have the means to help him?"[6] The Florentine aristocrats were ready to agree with Aristotle that "the magnificent man is like an artist; for he can see what is fitting and spend it tastefully" on public, lastingly beautiful works, which are like votive offerings.[7]

Under the rule of the Medici, which began in 1469, Florence changed again. Difficult economic conditions and the weakening of the civic ideal led to a revival of interest in the goddess Fortuna and in the contemplative life, to be lived in or even above the pure realm of philosophy. In contrast with civic humanism, it became natural to think of politics as a pursuit to be avoided. Writing in 1470, Alberti makes the point by contrasting the family with the state. The family, he says, is based on love, faith, and kindness, while the state is often based on treachery and hate. It has become evident that power rules, not right, he says, and that the precepts of civic humanism are impotent. The higher magistracies are filled not by lot, as they should be, but by selection of the retainers of the powerful. The wise man therefore retires from civic life to the villa in which he studies peacefully—a parallel to the Confucian literatus who, for moral reasons, retires from public service. The political ideal, if any, is that of the philosopher-king.[8]

This new implausibility of republican ideals was the result of their manipulation in favor of the Medici, the ruling family of Florence. Civic precautions against tyranny had been made quite carefully. In order to prevent favoritism, the names of all eligible citizens were written on slips of paper and put into the red leather bag from which the names of those to hold government offices were drawn. To ensure quick rotation of office, tenure was limited to a period of from two months to a year. Other precautions included a rule that no holder of an office was eligible for another for some time, and a rule that no more than a single member of the same family could hold office at the same time. But all such precautions were circumvented. The officials who judged eligibility for office would put into the red bag only the names of adherents of the Medici, and district assemblies were likely to be attended and run by patricians.[9] The Medici had evidently learned a policy of divide and rule that kept the city in their hands.

Such was the Florence into which Niccol Machiavelli (1469–1527) was born. Of his early life we know next to nothing, but it is significant that his father worked as a lawyer, was a student of the classics, and was friendly with distinguished scholars. One senses the father's influence in Machiavelli's interest in law, in his conviction that the greatest benefactors of humanity are the great lawgivers, and in his advocacy of republican rule in spite of the possible advantages of royal or aristocratic government.[10]

During Machiavelli's adolescence and early manhood, the ruler of Florence was the cultured, poetic, lavish, shrewd, tyrannical Lorenzo de Medici. When Lorenzo died in 1492, the city was left in the hands of his son, Piero; but Piero's rule was soon ended because the Florentines were angered by his easy submission to the invader of Italy, Charles VIII of France, and Piero fled to Venice. The influence of the Medici was then replaced by that of the Dominican friar Girolamo Savonarola. His fame, established by his denunciations of priestly and princely corruption, was heightened by the French invasion, because the Florentines identified it with the catastrophe he had prophesied. With Savonarola's encouragement, a Florentine republic was instituted. The troubles that

Florence then underwent were followed by a loss of faith in Savonarola, who accepted and then shrank from an ordeal by fire to prove that his attacks on the church were justified.[11] Savonarola's end, abetted by his political enemies, was death in 1498 by hanging and burning.

Happy at the flight of Piero de Medici, who had shown himself arrogant and rash, the aristocrats were willing to avoid civil war by sharing power with the others. They did this by means of a so-called Grand Council, which was set up in order to become the soul of the body politic, as Florentine rhetoric described it. Larger than any earlier representative body, it was copied from the Grand Council of Venice, a city internally harmonious and externally powerful because, it was believed, its constitution embodied the political wisdom of the Greek and Roman past. Of the some seventy-thousand inhabitants of Florence, some three thousand (one out of every four or five males twenty-nine or more years of age) were to serve in the Grand Council. The members of the Grand Council elected the captains of fortresses and castles, while the most important officials were chosen by a method that combined election by this council with choice by lot. A great deal of thought was invested in the attempt to keep the city from falling into the hands of a tyrant or an oligarchy.[12]

As things turned out, however, elections were often won by aristocrats, sometimes because their names were well known, and members of the middle class came to doubt the usefulness of the electoral method they had favored. After Savonarola's execution, the constitutional problem became particularly troublesome. Moreover, the need to raise money to pay the condotierri, buy off enemies, and keep up the current war against Pisa, caused conflict between the two dominating sides in the Grand Council. Then poor harvests, repeated wars, rising prices, and unemployment made the population restless, and there were fears of secret conspiracies; the political atmosphere was filled with complaints and suspicions. Not all members of the Grand Council proved able to get the "benefit of office" they had expected. Within the Grand Council, the soul of the city, the old ruling class, composed of cosmopolitan bankers, merchants, and cloth manufacturers—known collectively in Florence as *the rich, the great, the nobles,* or *the first citizens*—confronted the far more numerous, more provincial shopkeepers, small businessmen, and artisans, all members of what the Florentines called *the middle classes (mezzani), the common men (populari), the people,* or, simply, *the mass (moltitudine)* (of the Grand Council). There were also those ineligible for the Grand Council, called, variously, *the poor, the plebs,* or *the mob (vulgo).* The confrontation of the two main sides in the Grand Council made the hoped-for integration too difficult to accomplish.[13]

The concerns of Florence were not only external. The protocols of its executive boards show how troubled they were by external politics, which was Machiavelli's main professional concern. The protocols deal with such problems as whether to ally Florence with France or with Milan and the Church States, which resisted France; or whether to request the intervention against France of some other power, such as Spain or the Holy Roman Empire, both at the time headed by the same emperor. And then in 1494, when Pisa, the seaport of Florence, revolted, outside powers tried to force Florence into alliance by giving Pisa support but promising to withdraw it if Florence agreed to end its neutrality and side with the power in question.

We see by the protocols that the Florentines, although confident of their cultural superiority, were cautious in foreign affairs, preferring to defer decisions on which power to ally themselves until they were sure which would win. To enjoy, as was said, "the benefit of time," they usually tried to stay neutral.[14] In awe of the outside powers and thwarted by their incalculable motives, the Florentines tried to guess the future by deciphering the nature of the powers' rulers. They supposed that by means of rational decisions—reasons (*ragione*)—they would be able to understand the rules of human behavior, which could be learned from their own, Florentine history, and even better from that of ancient Rome. Because of their devotion to classical literature, even the most common sense rule became impressive to them if supported by a quotation from a classical or old Christian source. But "their cry for *ragione* was the corollary of a feeling of constant intervention of the incalculable," *Necessita*, from which there is no escape, and *Fortuna*, which is whimsical, frowns on some, smiles on others, but leaves room for human initiative. "When there are favorable opportunities and man then does not try his luck, *Fortuna* will leave him."[15] With the usual human inconsistency, the Florentines tried to enlist fortune on their side by turning sometimes to human intelligence and sometimes, especially when intelligence seemed insufficient, to religious processions, distributions of alms to the poor, a miracle-working statue, or a day of prayer.[16]

During this period of crisis, the aristocrat Bernard Rucellai tried to revive the tradition of the philosophical academy and opened his gardens to discussions held by aristocrats, scholars, and humanists. The two subjects most discussed in the gardens were history and politics. Many looked back with nostalgia to what they recalled as the peace, prosperity, and flourishing art of the time of Lorenzo the Magnificent.

Convinced of Lorenzo's greatness, Bernard wrote that Lorenzo had owed his success not to fortune but to his extraordinary intelligence. As the aristocrat and political writer Francisco Guicciardini said later, "The Rucellai gardens sparked the flame which burnt the city."[17]

In answer to the prolonged crisis, Guicciardini wrote a proposal to revise the laws of Florence. Drawing on the Greek and Roman history, he suggests that after various forms of government have been studied, one ought to put everything together in a single heap and give form to the mass, reshape it, and dissect it "the way a baker treats flour."[18] Guicciardini remains aware of the faults of the past, and he wants to imitate it only in what withstands critical examination. He wants to reestablish the dominance of the aristocrats, not because of their inherited status but because of their superior ability to govern. Yet Florence, he says, should remain a republic because its citizens have become so accustomed to this form of government.[19]

Guicciardini's position changed along with events, as we find in his changing assessments of Lorenzo the Magnificent. At first, in his early work, *Florentine History*, he sees Lorenzo neither as an evil tyrant nor as a paragon of leadership but as someone whose prudence and liberality are balanced by his arrogance, cruelty, and, above all, his suspiciousness. In a later work, Guicciardini argues that a state can exist only if it uses force, so it is irrelevant whether or not it is tyrannical; the only criterion to apply is that of the well-being of its members. Granted that the efficiency of a government depends on the exact circumstances in which it functions, he says, the Medicean system must be judged to have been better than the more democratic government that followed. Lorenzo's intelligence, foresight, and care in the administration of justice, as well as his attempts to keep every social group satisfied, now appear to overshadow his vices, because, says Guicciardini, his rationality and desire for the good of the city were enough to allow him "to eliminate, to a certain degree, the power of chance and fortune."[20]

In the last writing in which he takes up Lorenzo, *The History of Italy*, Guicciardini speaks of him with almost unremitting praise. It may be supposed that this praise reflects the current desire of the aristocrats, who had come to power on the death of the republic in 1512. Now Guicciardini echoes the victorious aristocrats' criticism of the earlier popular government but also expresses his desire to restrain the new regime's absolutism. The drift of his thought is clearly in favor of the powers that once were, not those that are.

By this time, it is usual for the younger aristocrats to believe that politics is ruled only by force of arms. Since Italy is helpless against foreign invasion, the use of mercenaries is increasingly criticized and that of a citizen army advocated, by Machiavelli among others. The importance of a state is measured, it is now argued, by the amount of money at its command, but far more so by the power of its army. Determination by means of force is taken to be as necessary in the internal life of a state as in its external affairs. While older aristocrats still hope to regain their control of the city, the younger ones are mostly content with the new Medici government and the way it controls Florence behind a republican facade even more transparent than that of the earlier Medici. Young aristocrats close to the Medici ruler think that discussions about different forms of constitution are a waste of time. "Wise men," one of them says, "make no revolutions." Even Guicciardini, who is opposed to absolutism, writes, "Every government is nothing but violence over subjects, sometimes moderated by a form of honesty." On this premise, it might be best, someone suggests, that the Medici kill all those able and willing to oppose them. Why not tear away the veil of republicanism and freedom, the duke of Florence (1492–1519), another Lorenzo, is asked, and rule quite openly? Guicciardini, who reports the question, responds, "Such a procedure would, in the course of time, emerge as being full of difficulties, of suspicion, and finally of cruelty."

Despite the prevalent belief in force, there are no extreme acts. Instead, Lorenzo and his friends write verse and compose plays; the Rucellai gardens, with a younger Rucellai as host, flourish; and great civic displays are joined in by Florentine painters and sculptors in demonstration of a golden age of peace and beauty—guarded by force sufficient for its purpose. As the song of a Medici procession says, "From iron was born a gold age." The song goes on, "One age follows another in this world / And changes good into bad and bad into good."[21]

Views on the Origin of Human Society

Machiavelli's interest in classical literature began early. In his youth, we know, his father would buy or borrow classical books, among them Aristotle's *Ethics* and Cicero's *De officiis*, to which I will later refer. The father notes in a diary entry that he has sent his adolescent son with a barrel of wine to help pay for the binding of Livy's history of Rome, to which Machiavelli's *Discourses* was to be a commentary.[22] Considering his home atmosphere, his Latin school education, his later studies, and his literary style and interests, Machiavelli was a humanist and, as such, saw the Greco-Roman past as immediately relevant to his own time.

Machiavelli's idea of mankind's origin was based on Greek and Roman literature, into which the biblical account had to be fitted, how-

ever awkwardly.[23] In "Tercets on Ambition" Machiavelli tells how after
Adam and Eve had been driven from paradise, a hidden power
unfriendly to human beings sent down two furies, Ambition and Avarice, along with various pestilent companions (much like those
assigned to the furies in Hesiod's *Theogony*). The furies, writes Machiavelli, made Cain malignantly ambitious, so "the first violent death was
seen in the world, and the first grass red with blood!" Since then, the
evil seed has matured and evil's cause has been multiplied, so that
"there is no reason for men to repent of doing evil."[24]

It is hard to tell how literally Machiavelli took these words.
Although he detested the church, there is no sign that he disbelieved in
Christianity. But the cause he gives, the power that sustains itself
among the stars, is more astrological and pagan than Christian. It therefore seems that Machiavelli's biblical tradition is not so much assimilated into his idea of human development as it is used to express his
feeling that human beings are evil and difficult to reform.

Greco-Roman tradition gives Machiavelli basic options not unlike
those given by Chinese and Indian mythology. The options include: ini-
tially perfect human beings who degenerate; primitive, animalistic
human beings who progress by their own successive efforts; cyclical
degeneration and regeneration; theories of irregular catastrophes followed by new beginnings; and, from the Stoics, a theory of the periodic
conflagration and renewal of the world. As in China and India, the theory of degeneration serves those who think badly of human nature; the
theory of progress serves those who think well of it; and cycles allow a
measure of belief in both bad and good. Incidentally, the earliest Greek
beliefs are as difficult to date as the corresponding Chinese and Indian
ones, and they raise the same problem of distinguishing between individual fantasy and a widely held conviction.[25]

Hesiod's *Works and Days* (c. 800 B.C.), the first of our sources, gives
two accounts of the development of humankind, both of which insist on
degeneration. In the first, Hesiod explains that the tribes of men on
earth lived without harsh toil or deadly illness until Zeus repaid
Prometheus' theft of fire for them by sending down the lying, treacher-
ous, painfully attractive Allgift (Pandora). She freed countless troubles
and sicknesses from the jar in which they had been enclosed, leaving
only Hope inside, secure under the jar's lip. By one interpretation,
Hope is still available there to humans, or, by an opposite interpretation, is now unavailable to them.[26]

At this point there begins "another tale" to show "how gods and
mortal men have come from the same starting-point." We learn that
there have been four races, each created on a successive occasion by

Zeus, the first of gold, whose members "lived like gods, with carefree heart, remote from toil and misery." For them, as for the Buddhists of the good age, "the grain-giving soil bore its fruits of its own accord in unstinted plenty." Since the time when the earth covered this race up, its members have remained in the vicinity of mortal men as good spirits who watch over them. There follows an episodic process of degeneration that goes from the crime-rife, irreverent silver race to the fierce bronze-clad race, whose members destroy themselves, to the heroic demigods, also victims of their own wars, and to the fifth, human race, which is the unfortunate or iron race. The members of this iron race "will never cease from toil or misery by day or night." They will turn gray at birth and will be careless of their social relationships, of that of child to father, of guest to host, and of comrade to comrade. They will sack one another's towns and forget to thank the oath-abiding or righteous but honor the miscreant and criminal.

> Men in their misery will everywhere be dogged by the evil commotions of that Envy who exults in misfortune with a face full of hate. Then Decency and Moral Disapproval will join the immortals and abandon mankind, "and there will be no help against evil."[27]

This account, which at its start resembles the Indian myths of degeneration from a perfect state, has an odd discontinuity. When Hesiod reaches the human race, which is worse than any other, he breaks out emotionally with the wish that he had died before it started or would be born after it were over. Nothing is said about what might come later.

As compared with the tales of degeneration, there are Greek tales of progress from a brute animal state, in which human beings have no clothing, no houses, no language, and no social skills and are the victims of wild animals and disease. We find echoes of such a tale in many Greeks: Xenophanes, Aeschylus, Sophocles, Euripides, Critias, Protagoras, Democritus, Isocrates, and others. The tale establishes that the technical skills of human beings developed and they learned to speak and live together, often with the help of Prometheus, who comes to be a symbol of human inventiveness.[28] In a variant of the tale, Protagoras (Plato's Protagoras, that is) tells a story according to which Prometheus found human beings "naked, unshod, unbedded, and unarmed" and for their sake stole fire and skill in the arts. Human beings then discovered articulate speech and names, got food from the earth, and invented houses, clothes, shoes, and bedding. However, they lacked the ability to live together in peace until Zeus, afraid that the whole human race would be destroyed, sent them Hermes to teach them respect for others and justice, so that they could live together in an orderly way and create bonds of friendship.[29]

The most famous example of a cyclical theory is that in Plato's *Republic*, where a parallelism is established between typical individuals and the successive types of the city. Social life begins in the relatively simple, idyllic city, based on economic interdependence. Because of avarice, this first type of city degenerates into the larger, more luxurious, more complex aristocracy—although second in the descending line, this state is described as the balanced, ideal city. Aristocracy degenerates into timocracy, timocracy into oligarchy, oligarchy into democracy—which is much like the Athens of Plato's time—and democracy into tyranny. It seems reasonable that Plato saw the cycle not as literal but as a typological scale of values for the city-states of his time. Plato adds a long, very obscure (almost surely farcical) calculation for times of ideal procreation. The calculation serves to explain that even the best of states degenerates because "for everything that has come into being destruction is appointed."[30] There may be a hint here of a repetitive cycle or progress that is stopped and started again from time to time. Aristotle remarks in passing that "probably each art and science has often been developed as far as possible and has again perished." Aristotle also considers and rejects as impossible the cosmology according to which the world undergoes an unending sequence of creations and dissolutions.[31]

The idea, broadly like the Indian, that there are periodic world conflagrations and renewals is primarily Stoic—not that every Stoic accepts it or that there is a fixed version.[32] As put in one report, the Stoics believe that

> at certain fated times the entire world is subject to conflagration, and the world is reconstituted afresh. But the primary fire is as it were a sperm which possesses the principles of all things and the causes of past, present, and future events.[33]

The Stoic fire is intelligence itself, God itself, a self-directing vitality. The sequence of world conflagration, world creation, and world conflagration is a cycle of God's life in which he purifies the world, enters into his fiery, spiritual self, emerges to reconstitute the orderly development of all things—whose life he is—in the best possible whole, and then retreats to his pure self again.[34] The Stoics draw the conclusion that it is possible that after the lapse of enough time we will return to ourselves again, or even that everything *must* return exactly an infinite number of times—"for again there will be Socrates and Plato and each one of mankind with the same friends and fellow citizens."[35]

Making a distinction worthy of Buddhists, Stoics who believe in this exact return sometimes claim that each recurrent being is not identical with its previous equivalent but indiscernible from it—the person that (re)appears is not Socrates himself but someone indiscernible from Socrates. If so, the distinction between one world and another can be preserved by assuming changes to be small or "accidental" and therefore indifferent to the necessary excellence of the whole—for example, Dion with a mole and without it, so that nothing essential would differ but one world could be distinguished from another.[36]

Machiavelli's conception of history is adopted, though without acknowledgement, from Polybius (c. 200–118 B.C.), who wants to explain how one form of government is transformed into another. Polybius recalls Plato and other, unnamed philosophers, then launches into his own, purposely simple version. This begins with the catastrophic destruction that at times wipes out all human culture. "Such disasters, tradition tells us, have often befallen mankind, and must reasonably be expected to recur."[37] In the course of time, the population renews itself from its survivors as if from seeds, increases in numbers and, for the sake of protection, forms herds. "In this situation it is inevitable that the man who excels in physical strength and courage should lead and rule over the rest." Such rule may be called *monarchy*, which develops into kingship when families and social relations are developed and "for the first time mankind conceives the nature of goodness, of justice, and of their opposites."

Polybius goes on to state that human beings are able to create moral conceptions because, as "the only creatures to possess the faculty of reasoning," they begin by reflecting on one another's conduct, imagining themselves in one another's positions, and grasping something of the meaning of justice. "When reason becomes more powerful than ferocity or force," their monarch develops into a king. The people assume that the king's descendants will continue to cherish his principles, but they may become dissatisfied with his descendants and choose kings not for physical strength but for judgment and powers of reasoning.

It is possible, Polybius thinks, that the ancient rulers by inheritance might have been tempted by the superabundance at their disposal to indulge their appetites for luxury, honor, and even lawless love. Such vices provoked hatred on the one side and anger on the other, the result being tyranny, which provoked conspiracies against the tyrant and the institution of aristocracy. But the descendants of the aristocrats, who inherited their fathers' authority, had no experience of misfortune and no tradition of civic equality or freedom of speech and therefore became avaricious or lawless and transformed the aristocracy into an oligarchy. The oligarchy created hatred, resentment, and the institution of democracy as a reaction. However, in a new, forgetful generation, democracy, too, degenerated, turned bestial, and ended in despotism. "Such is the cycle of political revolution, the law of nature according to which constitutions change, are transformed, and finally revert to their original form."[37]

This is the determinedly secular account that Machiavelli adapts in two variations, the one in the first chapter of his *Discourses*, where he explains the origin of cities, and the other in the second chapter, where he explains the cycle of governments. Machiavelli is more rapid and less thorough than Polybius, and he makes use of the parallel examples of Athens and Venice and Alexandria and Florence. Then, in his second chapter, he compares Sparta and Florence as cities that from the beginning "governed themselves by their own judgment, either as republics or princedoms."[38] Having enumerated the six kinds of government in the cycle derived via Polybius from Plato, Machiavelli denounces them as "pestiferous by reason of the short life of the three good and the viciousness of the three bad" and turns to such lawgivers as Lycurgus and Solon. These were prudent enough to establish a mixed form of government designed to make the state more solid and stable by mixing princedom, aristocracy, and popular government in the same city. In Rome, says Machiavelli, there was no such lawgiver, but "so many unexpected events happened, on account of the disunion between the plebeians and the Senate, that what an organizer had not done was done by Chance."[39]

Fortuna and Umori

Machiavelli's adoption, like Polybius, of an informal cyclical theory is especially clear in the passage of *The History of Florence* in which he says that when countries

> come to their utmost perfection and have no further possibility for rising, they must go down. Likewise, when they have gone down and through their defects have reached the lowest depths, they necessarily rise, since they cannot go lower. So always from good they go down to bad, and from bad rise up to good. Because abil-

ity brings forth quiet; quiet, laziness; laziness, disorder; disorder, ruin; and likewise from ruin comes order; from order, ability; from the last, glory and good fortune.[40]

This passage raises the question why countries that have risen as far as possible *must* go down, or why those in the worst possible state must *necessarily* rise. Is there something in this flux and reflux that Machiavelli assigns to necessity or fate? The same question is relevant to Plato and Polybius. Polybius, who is generally rationalistic, deals with the problem explicitly, but not, it must be said, very successfully. The great theme of his *Histories* is the Roman unification of the world he knew. It is a theme adequately dealt with, he says, only by means of a universal history that presents in a single synoptic view the convergence caused by Fortune in world affairs. He adds:

> Although fortune is forever producing something new and forever enacting a drama in the lives of men, yet she has never before in a single instance created such a composition or put on such a show-piece as that we have now witnessed in our times.[41]

This passage tells us that Polybius wants to match the universality of his history to the uniqueness of the great conquest he has chosen to relate. What, however, does he imply when he speaks of Fortune as a woman putting on a show? A translator's note to this passage says "Polybius' conception of Fortune here is of a force in the universe which takes pleasure in change for its own sake, and also acts as a dramatic producer, fashioning a design out of men's destinies." But is Fortune a goddess playing freely because, having no constraints, she does as she pleases—as the child-god Krishna plays, or as Shiva plays, or as Nicholas of Cusa's God plays, so to speak, in manifesting the perfect freedom of perfect volition?[42]

Later in the *Histories*, Polybius speaks of phenomena so unusual that "it is impossible or difficult for a mortal man to understand," in which case it is reasonable enough "to escape from the dilemma by attributing them to the work of a god or of chance." Accepting public opinion is then natural, as are attempts to appease the divine powers by prayer, sacrifice, or queries to the gods asking, "what should we say or do to produce a change for the better?"[43] Polybius objects strenuously to regarding as acts of God any events whose causes we are able to discover. He gives a significant example, the shortage of children in contemporary Greece. This shortage leads to a decrease in the population, the desertion of some cities, and the decline in agricultural production.

The answer to this problem does not lie, Polybius insists, in turning to the gods for salvation but in changing the people's own will or in passing appropriate laws. Only such events as the great failure of the Macedonians against the Romans or as the Macedonians' great courage and success in fighting on behalf of a hateful man baffles our intelligence and inclines us to speak of an infatuation sent from heaven along with the wrath of the gods.[44]

Polybius uses *Fortune (Tyche)*, *god*, and *gods* synonymously and confines their field of influence as much as rationally possible. Sometimes he speaks of what we should call *chance*, sometimes he speaks of acts of God but without any religious implications, and sometimes he appears to believe in god or gods or Fortune and the just punishments they impose.[45] It all seems the kind of muddle that uneasy theologians and philosophers try to cure, with incomplete success.

Machiavelli puts us in a similar difficulty, which he compounds by using sometimes developed stretches of the astrological language that was widely used in the Renaissance.[46] In *The Prince* he has a theologically unresolved relation, characteristic enough of his time, between Fortune and God. He says he is well aware how many have believed and continue to believe that "human affairs are so controlled by Fortune and by God that men with their prudence cannot manage them—yes, more, that men have no recourse against the world's variations."[47]

Machiavelli adds that he himself now and then inclines in some respects to these beliefs, but in order not to annul human free will, he judges that fortune leaves a half of our actions, more or less, under our control.[48] For although Fortune can act like an angry, flooding river, when the weather is quiet, people can take precautions and build embankments and dikes. Machiavelli concludes that people are only successful when in close harmony with Fortune; and he adds, in an unfortunate sexual metaphor, that Fortune being a woman, to keep her under, she must be cuffed and mauled—boldness is more likely to master her than caution.[49]

There are suggestions in Machiavelli, theologically even more problematic than the pairing of Fortune and God, of astrological influences not only on individual events or fates but on a general decline from the high point of perfection and a general rise from the low point of decline.[50] In his "Tercets on Fortune," Machiavelli may be more than rhetorical—who can judge this exactly?—when he speaks of Fortune suddenly reversing the wheel to the rim of which you are bound, or of the inability to change wheels "because to attain this is denied by the occult force that rules us."[51] Elsewhere (in "The Golden Ass"), Machiavelli is more explicit and sounds more astrological. The planets wander without any rest, he says, and nothing on earth always remains in the same condition.

> From this results peace and war; on this depend the hatreds among those whom one wall and one moat shut up together; from this comes your suffering ... And those humors which you have found so hostile and adverse are not yet purged; but when their roots are dry, and the heaven shows itself gracious, times happier than ever before will return.[52]

In this passage, Machiavelli augments his astrological vocabulary with the theory of humors, widely accepted in his time, by which he often explains the differences between individuals, social groups, and even countries. By this theory, one's personality is determined by the predominance of a certain humor—of blood, which makes for a sanguine or buoyant personality; of phlegm, which makes for a sluggish, phlegmatic one; of yellow bile, which makes for a quick-tempered or choleric one; and of black bile, which makes for a melancholic one. Characters in literature and life are often interpreted as representatives of a single humoral type or nature. A serious imbalance explains an individual's pathology, and, for Machiavelli and those who share his belief, explains the pathology of a group, city, or nation. To rule effectively, one must satisfy the humor of one's subjects, or the humoral structure of a particular city or country. But political success, Machiavelli is convinced, needs more than an understanding of the humors. It needs action that is in conformity both with one's own and others' humors and with the wishes of Fortune. And because the humors determine what we and everyone else desires, politics is conducted for the satisfaction of desires.

In *The Prince*, when Machiavelli wants to explain the fundamental division of an urban population, he says that in every city one finds two diverse humors. One is the result of the rejection by the people of rule and oppression by the nobles. The other is the desire of the nobles to command and oppress them. *The Discourses* and *The History of Florence* have equivalent passages.[53] Machiavelli is even ready to speak of the social groups of a country as its humors, or to speak of the conflicts between states as between contrary humors. Politics is therefore a study in humoral metaphysics and psychology, and the unity of a city or state demands one like that of the different humors in a healthy body.[54]

To return to Machiavelli's notion of Fortune or Fate, two conclusions suggest themselves. The first is that his attitude toward history and politics is far more secular than religious. This is evident from his characteristic modes of reasoning but makes for a difficulty because Machiavelli is clearly religious. He believes in God, the creator and judge, to whom his probably late oration "Exhortation to Penitence" gives eloquent, sincere-sounding praise; he invokes God's name in customary ways in his papers; he mentions God often, in customary ways, in his letters; and he believes that religion helps to discipline armies— "in whom," he asks "ought there to be more fear of God than in a man who every day, being exposed to countless perils, has great need for his aid?"[55]

The second conclusion is that Machiavelli's secularism is deeply tinged with the pagan attitudes of Greece and Rome, including astrological and humoral notions and the notion of the power of (an unchristian) Fortune. I deliberately use the word *attitudes* because Machiavelli enjoys ridiculing the fears caused by astrologers just as much as he enjoys ridiculing demonic possession and other superstitions. However, like Polybius and like the skeptical-believing Kant, he remains interested and marginally believing. He shows this when he says that hardly anything important ever happens in a city or region that has not been "foretold either by diviners or by revelation or by prodigies or by other celestial signs."[56] He does not understand how this happens but inclines to accept that it is due to the compassion and ability to foresee of spirits—the intelligences that fill the air above us—who warn men with such signs so that they can prepare themselves.

The line in Machiavelli between skepticism and belief is therefore often thin, and his pagan attitudes and astrological and humoral notions surely affect him, though in an indeterminate way. They mark his distance from a contemporary social scientist; but instead of undermining his native shrewdness or his belief in well-conceived, purposeful activity, they are the medium by which he expresses his view that too many factors are involved in politics for anyone to understand them completely or master them for long, except, that is, if luck is on one's side—a lesson that every contemporary social scientist and politician has to relearn.

Machiavelli and His Two Masterworks

When Lorenzo the Magnificent, the Medici ruler of Florence, died in 1492, Machiavelli was twenty-three years old. From exactly June 19, 1498 until November 7, 1512, he served the republic of Florence as an official of the chancery, which administered the government's internal and external affairs. As an administrator, Machiavelli prepared voting lists, lists of nominees for civic positions, wrote the minutes for meetings of the deliberative assembly, and so on. As a correspondent of the chancery, he kept in touch with foreign states, with Florentines, diplomats, and citizens abroad, and with officials and citizens in subject territories. Furthermore, he was sent on diplomatic missions, notably to France and Germany; and in 1507, he was made general administrator of the militia.[57]

Machiavelli's experience of political life was therefore rich. For a man so filled with curiosity about people, it was enthralling, but for a man with such energy and hope for change, it was profoundly frustrating. He kept learning how little Florence and he, its diplomat, were able to do: He learned that the political efforts of states as weak as Florence were often futile, that the usually smooth language of diplomacy was deceptive, that political promises were worth little if anything, and that the mercenary soldiers that Florence employed were unreliable—at Pisa they simply deserted. To survive, he learned, a state has to be strong on its own and depend on its own soldiers and not, like Florence, skimp during peacetime and in emergencies turn to condottiere.[58]

Machiavelli's missions to the French court, beginning in 1500, taught him particular unpleasant lessons about the French. They are, he writes, better disposed to receive money than shed blood. "In adversity they are abject, and in prosperity they are insolent. They are fickle and light-minded, and have faith only in success."[59] He reports to his government, in a similar vein, that the French, blinded by power and the desire for immediate advantage, "have consideration only for those who are either well armed, or who are prepared to pay," so Florence, unprepared to pay and ordinarily without troops, is to them nothing but a *"Ser Nihilo* (Signor Nothing)."[60] But despite the mediocrity and errors of its king, says Machiavelli, France has an extraordinarily good constitution and is strong because unified and centralized. Its parliament mediates the conflict between the people and the *grandi*, so that the king is able to remain nonpartisan. But the French infantry, except for the Gascons, is cowardly, and the Gascons have for some years "shown themselves better thieves than soldiers."[61]

Machiavelli does find admirable foreigners, the inhabitants of the independent German cities and the Swiss communities. They are free and unafraid; their freedom rests on the equality of their citizens and their fearlessness on their fortifications and arms. True, says Machiavelli, Germany is disunited and its emperor has poor political judgment, but the people of its free cities want only what is absolutely necessary, and they are, as he repeats in his later writings, brave, unassuming, devout, and honest because—unlike the corrupt Italian republics struggling for survival among the great powers—they have the ancient civic virtues.[62]

From the weaknesses of Florence, the two-facedness of the French, and the civic virtues of the Germans, Machiavelli learns to become more Machiavellian. He advises his Signory to give Cesare Borgia some of the troops he demands but to inform him that the number is twice what has really been sent. It is safe to cheat Cesare, because he will be unable to get accurate information on the troops' numbers. In other small instances of Machiavellism, he sends the Signory a letter, carried by Cesare's own envoy, with a coded passage advising the signory to ignore Cesare's demands; and he tells both the enemies and supporters of the Peruginian tyrant, Giovampagola Baglioni, that they are right.[63] Tricks like these, if successful, overweigh such small failures of diplomatic secrecy as the message hidden in a courier's boot so long that it is illegible by the time it gets to him.[64]

As his mission requires, Machiavelli's dispatches to Florence are filled with analyses, but also with possibly unwanted advice and apologies for his frankness. The advice and frankness are motivated, he once says, by the fear that saying nothing will harm Florence, while making a mistake will harm only himself.[65] His colleagues' letters very often praise his dispatches but sometimes complain that he does not report news regularly or soon enough, or that not everyone appreciates his views on Cesare Borgia.[66] His colleagues caution him not to grumble too loudly about his own superiors. Once, while waiting in Verona for the imperial court, he writes to a friend that he is marooned because no one there knows anything about anything, and so, "in order to seem alive, I go one fantasizing tirades that I write to the Dieci."[67] These words show that to feel alive, he has to be engaged in diplomatic activity and analysis, and that, as an analyst, he is a faultfinder (whose dissatisfaction with his leaders can be sensed even when not openly voiced). A historian who loves Machiavelli speaks of him as someone who condemns his associates in his heart but nevertheless wants to go on associating with them.[68] For the good of his career, Machiavelli was too impatient, critical, and independent. His attitude toward his republic can be summed up as one of simultaneous devotion and rejection.[69]

Machiavelli kept this attitude for the rest of his life, and it appears detailed and accentuated in his last important work, *The History of Florence*, which ends with the death of Lorenzo the Magnificent in 1492. In its preface, Machiavelli writes that in order to delight or teach, history must be presented in full detail. He continues:

If the experiences of any republic are moving, those of a man's own city, when he reads about them, are more moving and more useful; and if in any republic internal dissensions were ever worth noting, in that of Florence they are especially noteworthy.[70]

Machiavelli goes on to say that in Florence, unlike Rome and Athens, there were many sorts of factional strife: First there were factions among the nobles, then between the nobles and the middle class, and then between the middle class and the masses; and often a victorious faction would itself split into factions. Later in the *History*, Machiavelli stresses "the serious and natural enmities between the people and the nobles, caused by the latter's wish to rule and the former's not to be enthralled." Such enmities kept Rome disunited and, *mutatis mutandis*, have kept Florence divided. But the people of Rome, unlike those of Florence, were willing to share power with the nobles. The debates in Rome were terminated by law,

> those in Florence by exile and death of many citizens; those in Rome always increased military power, those in Florence wholly destroyed it; those in Rome brought that city from an equality of citizens to a very great inequality; those in Florence brought her from inequality to a striking equality.[71]

The result, says Machiavelli, was that in Rome the excellence of the citizens was turned into a pride so great "that she could not keep going without a prince," while in Florence, the military ability and boldness of the nobility were destroyed and did not, in compensation, arouse the ability or boldness of the people. The result was "that Florence grew always weaker and more despicable" and arrived at such a condition that a wise lawgiver could easily "reorganize her with almost any form of government."[72]

So far, we have taken up Machiavelli's devotion to and rejection of the Florentine republic. When the republic was destroyed and the rule of the Medici restored, in 1512, the republic's gonfalonier, Piero de Soderini, was ousted. Some nine weeks later, Machiavelli was dismissed, even though most of the other chancery officials were left at their posts and even though he had always acted for the government and not for any faction or individual. However, he had been in the confidence of the gonfalonier, Soderini and had no doubt made influential enemies, and he hated the aristocrats who had destroyed the republican government.

Banished from Florence but compelled by a surety of a thousand
florins to remain on Florentine territory, Machiavelli underwent further
humiliation in 1513, when his name was found listed as a likely supporter of two conspirators against Medici rule. He was arrested, questioned, and given the *strappado* torture—his arms tied behind him and
a rope fastened to his wrists, he was hoisted up and suddenly released,
so that he stopped, just short of the ground, with a very painful jerk.
The torture was not extreme and, having nothing to confess, he con-
fessed nothing, was released, and spent the rest of his life in exile on his
small estate not far from Florence. Longing, as his letters show, to
return to political life, he was reduced to writing instead, mostly about
politics.

For all his critical views and the pessimism about human beings
that will be described, Machiavelli makes the impression of a warm person, one who enjoys imagining serious Machiavellian acts more than
committing them (unless they are regarded as including marital infidelity). His most prominent probably Machiavellian act was the writing of
The Prince, which contradicts, or appears to contradict, his long-stand-
ing preference for republics over principates. Quite possibly, although
this too is debated, he worked on his republic-loving *Discourses* and his
"tyrant"-loving *Prince* at the same time. That is, in early 1513, after the
episode of his imprisonment and torture, communing equally with his
anger and his old teachers, his books, he wrote most of the first part of
The Discourses on the First Decade of Titus Livius, in which he justifies his
preference for republics, especially the republic of Rome he idealizes.
Then, some time between July 1513 and early 1514, he wrote almost the
whole of *The Prince*, in which the deliberate pace of the earlier book,
worked out section by section, becomes the rapid, improvisatory one in
favor of the man of the hour, the perfect prince, who is exhorted to use
everything—the evident favor of God and Church, providentially
headed by a Medici, Italian valor, and new military tactics—in order to
redeem Italy from its stinking barbarian tyranny and unite it as Moses
freed the enslaved Hebrews, as Cyrus rescued the Persians from the
Medes and founded a Persian Empire, and as Theseus united the scattered communities of Attica into the Athenian state.[73]

In *The Prince*, Machiavelli takes the transparently self-serving
view that princes, especially if new, may find greater loyalty and help
in men who were at first feared as dangerous to their rule than in men
who were at first trusted.[74] The reason for turning from the *Discourses*
and its republicanism to *The Prince* is quite open. As its dedication to the
Magnificent Lorenzo de' Medici shows, the reason is "the wish to gain
a prince's favor" and prove his loyalty to him by means of the gift that

he, Machiavelli, most treasures, which is "an understanding of great men's actions, gained in my lengthy experience with recent matters and my continual reading on ancient ones." And if, Machiavelli continues, the prince ever turns his eyes to low places, he will perceive how long Machiavelli has undeservedly borne "the burden of Fortune's great and steady malice."[75] Machiavelli's hope is plain enough, but there is no evidence that the prince ever read Machiavelli's book; if he did, he saw no reason to satisfy its author's hope.[76]

The Discourses, written, probably, between 1513 and 1517, is dedicated to Zanobi Buondelmonti and Cosimo Rucellai, the first a friend who took part in the discussions in the Rucellai gardens and the second a person who presided over many of them. Machiavelli says he gives this book as the greatest gift possible to him, the gift of everything he knows and has learned in the course of his "long experience and steady reading in the affairs of the world." He is avoiding the usual custom, he says, of those who, blinded by ambition and avarice, address a work to a prince whom they praise extravagantly instead of blaming. So he chooses not princes but those whose innumerable good qualities entitle them to be princes. At the beginning of the book proper, Machiavelli excuses his poor talents, slight experience of present affairs, and feeble knowledge of ancient ones, and then boasts that, driven by his natural eagerness to benefit everybody, he disregards the trouble to which he may be subjected and determinedly enters "upon a path not yet trodden by anyone."[77]

Both The Prince and The Discourses share the same conviction that no government can be effective unless it makes use of force. For the prince, Machiavelli recommends war and its disciplines and discounts personal qualities such as honesty and clemency in favor of qualities that ensure political effectiveness. But whereas The Prince stresses the need for a ruler, The Discourses is based on the premise that a republican government is superior by nature, though not under all circumstances.

In favor of republicanism, Machiavelli says in The Discourses that what makes cities great—great like Athens after it freed itself from Pisistratus' tyranny, and, above all, like Rome after it freed itself from its kings—is the ability to seek the common good, which is considered important only in republics. What benefits a prince usually injures his city, and what benefits the city injures him. Therefore, when a tyranny is established over a free community, it grows poorer and weaker. And if it happens that a courageous, conquering tyrant arises, he is unable to honor the best of his citizens unless he is willing to fear them, and so his conquests benefit not the city of which he is the tyrant but only himself. That is why ancient peoples strove with such great hatred to overthrow tyrants and so loved free government and liberty. Free countries prosper and have larger populations because marriages in such countries are freer and more attractive to men, who are sure that they can become prominent by means of their abilities, and who father children willingly because they do not fear that their patrimony will be taken from them. Riches multiply in a free country because men gladly increase what they believe they will be allowed to enjoy (2.2).

One of the important theses of *The Discourses* is that, for republics, conflict is constructive. Machiavelli says that three hundred years of dissension in Rome between the nobility and the people did not often lead to exile or bloodshed. This dissension educated citizens to act honorably and led to laws and institutions helpful to public liberty. Even though the people are ignorant, they are able, as Cicero says, to grasp the truth and yield when someone worthy of trust tells them the truth (1.4). It is true that the enmities between the Roman people and the Senate caused the ruin of free government, but these enmities were an "evil necessary to the attainment of Roman greatness" (1.6). When partisan hatreds can be discharged in a lawful way, a republic is made firm and solid (1.7).[78]

As he shows in *The History of Florence*, Machiavelli regards the public dissension in Florence as having been very destructive, but he continues to believe that dissension creates the possibilities of a more flourishing life (and eventual death).[79] At least for Rome, his impulse is to defend the multitude, as he does against Livy's charge that the multitude either serves humbly or domineers arrogantly. A more proper comparison, he says, would be between law-breaking princes and people and between law-abiding princes and people. In the still-uncorrupted Roman republic, the multitude was neither humble nor arrogant but "kept its place honorably." A well organized people is likely to be more stable, prudent, and grateful than even a prince who is thought wise; and a lawless prince will be less grateful, variable, and prudent than a people. What is decisive is respect for the laws. Think of the differences between prince and people: The prince may be better in establishing laws and forming communities, but the people are much better in maintaining what has already been organized. An uncontrolled people can be easily led back into a good way, but a wicked prince can be remedied only by the use of steel. An unrestrained people can behave foolishly and produce a tyrant, but a bad prince is himself the tyrant (1.58). *The Discourses* ends in the caution that, to be kept free, a republic requires new acts of foresight every day, acts of a wise physician who knows how to deal with an unexpected emergency (3.49).

The Discourses is more carefully thought out than *The Prince*, represents Machiavelli more faithfully, and, to most readers, has a bias more attractive than the princely or tyrannical bias of *The Prince*, which implies, as Kant would say, the perpetual childhood of its citizens.[80] Yet it is *The Prince* that has been much the more influential of the two, which is to say, the more successful, and success is the measure that Machiavellism might be supposed to propose for itself no less than for the governments of which it speaks.

Man Is Evil

Machiavelli is so convinced that humans are evil that he sometimes adopts a secular version of the black, Augustinian belief that Adam's sin has corrupted and convicted all his offspring and produced, Augustine says,

> gnawing cares, disquiet, griefs, fears, wild joys, quarrels, law-suits, treasons, angers, hatreds, deceit, adultery, fraud, theft, robbery, perfidy, pride, ambition, envy, murders, parricides, cruelty, ferocity, wickedness, luxury, insolence, impudence, shamelessness, fornications, adulteries, incests, and the numberless uncleannesses and unnatural acts of both sexes, which it is shameful to so much as mention.[81]

Machiavelli can be just as vehement as Augustine, even though his inventories of sins are put in a more discriminating style and suggest autobiography as much as tradition. His extreme stress on human evil seems out of place in so usually warm (if complaining) a person. The early poem "Tercets on Ambition" is all dyed in Augustinian blackness. Human beings sinned, says Machiavelli, from the beginning; even when they were all still naked and destitute, with no distinction between rich and poor, their ambition led to the first death, that of Abel. In rhetorical, bitter words, he accuses the human spirit of being "insatiable, arrogant, crafty, and shifting, and above all malignant, iniquitous, violent, and savage." Experience and study alike have convinced him that "every man hopes to climb higher by crushing now one, now another, rather than through his own wisdom and goodness." If unrestrained by law or force, we are jealous of others' success and instinctively do them harm. Thinking of war, he says "Wherever you turn your eyes, you see the earth wet with tears and blood, and the air full of screams, of sobs, and sighs."[82]

These last words are more than rhetoric, as is made clear by a letter Machiavelli sent from Verona on November 26, 1509, the year he wrote his tercets. Speaking of invading soldiers, Machiavelli says that he hears and sees things more terrible than he has known of before.[83] Strengthened by such experience, his belief in human cruelty could only have been confirmed by his later imprisonment and torture, to which he reacted in two sonnets he addressed, though perhaps did not send, to Giuliano de Medici (the ruler to whom Machiavelli would dedicate *The Prince*). Giuliano was a likely target of the would-be assassins with whom Machiavelli was imprisoned. The sonnets describe the shackles on his legs, the hoist of rope on his shoulder, the walls exuding lice, and, most disturbingly, the prayer chanted for the two condemned conspirators, whose fate, decapitation, he is afraid he will share. The possible irony of some of the sonnets' lines may distance but does little to erase the underlying horror.[84]

The Prince again describes humans negatively, as "ungrateful, changeable, simulators and dissimulators, runaways in danger, eager to gain."[85] *The Discourses* takes this estimate of human nature to underlie the making of laws:

> It is necessary for him who lays out a state and arranges laws for it to presuppose that all men are evil and that they are always going to act according to the wickedness of their spirits whenever they have free scope. . . . [86]

The conclusion is that familiar to us from Shang Yang, Han Fei, and Kautilya: The only reliable way to influence human beings to be good is to make laws that force goodness on them, that is, make it difficult to be anything but good. "So we may say that, just as hunger and poverty make men industrious, it is the laws that make them good."[87]

Force and Deception, Lion and Fox

Machiavelli's defense of the intelligent use of force and deception is quite explicit. Of the classical sources for the defense, Machiavelli certainly knew Plato, Thucydides, and Cicero. What Plato says about it in *Republic* is too familiar to repeat, but it should not be forgotten that Socrates, as Plato represents him, recommends the "opportune falsehood" or "noble lie" for educating even the rulers of the ideal republic. Socrates also remarks that the republic's rulers will probably "have to make considerable use of falsehood and deception for the benefit of their subjects." Amusingly, while he advocates lying "for the benefit of the state," he strictly forbids anyone but rulers from having anything to do with the "sin" of lying.[88]

Thucydides' demonstrates the amorality (or Machiavellian "morality") of the *raison d'état* both in his narratives and in the words that he, like Ssu-ma Ch'ien, puts in the mouths of the persons on whose actions he reports. In the famous dialogue between the inhabitants of Melos and the Athenian envoys who urge them join their confederacy, the Athenians contend that when such "matters are discussed by practical people, the standard of justice depends on the equality of power to compel." Later in the dialogue, the Athenians say:

> Our opinion of the gods and our knowledge of men lead us to con-clude that it is a general and necessary law of nature to rule wher-ever one can . . . We are merely acting in accordance with it, and we know that you or anybody else with the same power would be acting in precisely the same way.[89]

The story ends when the defiant Melians, weakened by treachery from within, surrender unconditionally and their men of military age are killed and their women and children sold as slaves.

Reconstructed from scattered remarks in his history, the position of Thucydides himself is more complex. He is proud of the power of Athens but wants it to be used with care. Because he is alert to the dif-ference between each situation, he praises some cities for moderation and others, which acted under other circumstances, for boldness. The Melian dialogue appears to express not his condemnation of the Athe-nians but his pessimism about human nature. The Athenians, too, he seems to think, were participating in the natural process by which their imperialism forced them to go from one conquest to another and to eventual defeat. Athens might not have been tempted into disaster if it had retained Pericles' integrity and his flexible, unoppressive, way of control. But ambition, spurred on by success and greed, public and pri-vate, led the Athenians to forget until too late that they, too, could fail. Wisdom is something the individual can attain, Thucydides teaches, while the "human nature" displayed by groups of people does not lead then to act rationally. It is evident that Machiavelli profited from both Thucydides' narrative and his incompletely articulated but always real-istic attitude.[90]

Cicero is equally useful to Machiavelli. Like him, he loves repub-lican Rome. like him, he, too, prefers a mixed constitution, one designed to win the cooperation of the masses; like him, he takes the lawgiver's role to be fateful; like him, he recognizes the need for military power to defend the state; and, like him, he advocates the use of religion for state purposes. Further, Cicero, like Machiavelli, emphasizes the importance of the state's cohesion, stability, and elemental will to survive; believes in the cyclical rise, corruption, and decadence of civilization; and—to add the decisive Machiavellian trait—recognizes that the state must be defended by expedient, otherwise immoral means.[91]

Cicero's more Machiavellian problems are explained in his book *On Duties (De Officiis)*. His doctrine there resembles Machiavelli's in three explicit emphases. The first is on the limits to be observed in keeping good faith; the second, on the ways in which a leader can avoid being hated and despised; and the third, on the importance in politics of fear as compared with love. More cautious than Machiavelli, Cicero accompanies each discussion of the need to breach ordinary ethical principles with the reminder that no liberty should be taken that is not absolutely necessary, and he continues to recommend trust and honor. Using a comparison that was to become famous in Machiavelli's version, he says, "There are two ways in which injustice may be done, either through force or through deceit; and deceit seems to belong to a little fox, force to a lion. Both of them seem alien to a human being; but deceit deserves a greater hatred" (*On Duties* 1.41).

Rather than agree to the commission of an expedient but apparently dishonorable act, Cicero prefers to consider its exact conditions and see if it can be redefined as honorable. Ordinarily, he says, killing a man is dishonorable, but the recent killing of a tyrant who was a close friend—he means Caesar—is not an instance in which the benefit of the act overcame honor but one in which there was an honorable result from the benefit—translated exactly, Cicero says, rather vaguely, that the honorable "followed upon what benefitted" (3.19). Cicero then gives examples from ordinary life of honorable acts, such as keeping promises, standing by agreements, and returning deposits, that lose their honorable quality under certain circumstances. The honorable quality is lost, for example, when the promise is to commit an evil deed, or when the agreement reached is to return a sword to someone who has meanwhile become insane, or when a deposit was put in the hands of a person who later became the enemy of one's country (3.96). But Cicero admits the moral problem involved in making a slight violation of fairness for the sake of an extremely important result (3.81).

Cicero seems to have taken his stand when he states resolutely that "nothing is either beneficial or expedient that is unjust," even if the rewards are great (3.76, 79). With equal resolution, he sets the limits of what a wise or decent man should be prepared to do. *Raison d'état* is no absolute excuse, for "some things are so disgraceful or outrageous, that a wise man would not do them even to protect his country" (1.159); and "there is a limit to revenge and to punishment" (1.33). Often—not always—promises given to an enemy must be kept even in time of war, because war, too, has its laws (3.107).

Yet Cicero is open to arguments from expediency, and this openness erodes the clear limits he tries to draw. Promises should not be kept, he says, if disadvantageous to those to whom they were made, or if they are the result of deception, or "if they harm you more than they benefit the person to whom you have promised." In a lawyerly summary of the problem, Cicero writes that there are doubtful cases in which it can be argued that it is honorable to do only what seems beneficial—even dishonorable not to do what seems beneficial—and that cases of at least apparent incompatibility between the beneficial and the honorable need to be adjudicated (3.56).

On the issue of fear against love, Cicero recalls, without explicitly naming, Caesar's assassination, which shows, he says, that no degree of influence can stand before the hatred of a large number of men. Hardly any tyrant has escaped death at their hands, he recalls. In a free city, there always comes a time when the people rise up in silent judgment or in secret elections; and when freedom is suspended, she bites back the more fiercely. "Fear is a poor guardian over any length of time; but goodwill keeps faithful guard for ever" (2.23) In both private and public affairs we should make a choice that best preserves safety, influence, and power, "so that fear may be absent but love preserved" (2.24).

Such is Cicero's position, to which (I think) Machiavelli, though an objector by nature, would not have objected much because Cicero was thinking of the Roman republic that both men cherished, not of Renaissance Italy. There is not, therefore, a great contradiction when Machiavelli insists that experience in his time shows that princes who have not valued their promises much and have used cunning trickery have conquered those who insisted on honesty. Nor is there an insurmountable contradiction when, reversing Cicero's judgment, Machiavelli says that, if the choice must be made, "it is much safer for a prince to be feared than loved" because of the ungrateful, inconstant, selfish nature of men. Even so, Machiavelli agrees with Cicero that, to be safe, the prince must curb himself and at least escape hatred.[92]

Machiavelli is doubtful about rules of war and claims that because the human kind of fighting, which is according to laws, is often not enough for a prince, the prince, like a lion among wolves, must adopt animalistic force. Men are bad and do not keep their promises, he says, so that promises to them need not be kept; and therefore the prince must also play the fox, though his foxiness must be well disguised to allow him to deceive those who let themselves be deceived.[93] Acting in this way, he need not ask himself Cicero's question, "What difference does it make whether someone changes from a man into a beast or remains in human form while possessing the savagery of a beast?" Nor need he ask himself Cicero's second question, "Can worry, anxiety, fears by day and night, and a life full of treachery and dangers, be beneficial to anyone?" (*On Duties* 3.82, 83)

If we change Machiavelli's exemplary fox into a jackal or crow, his lion and fox become the lion ruler and jackal or crow adviser of the *Panchatantra*. But while the *Panchatantra* gives only fabulous examples, Machiavelli claims to have met a true lion-fox in the person of Cesare Borgia. By his well-known cruelty, says Machiavelli, Cesare succeeded in uniting the Romagna and making it peaceful and loyal. Machiavelli devotes much of the long seventh chapter of *The Prince* to Cesare, describes his career, ending in failure, and says that he not only cannot censure Cesare but proposes him as a model for all rulers to imitate. This is because he was courageous, had a great aim, and knew all he had to know: how to conquer by fraud or force, how to make himself loved and feared by the people and followed and respected by the solders, how to destroy those who endangered him, and how to replace ancient with new ways. All told, he was a princely paragon whose one, unfortunately fatal error was to allow a person he had injured to be chosen as pope. This error was compounded by his illness, the blow given by Fortune.

Machiavelli's choice of Cesare Borgia as his hero sets a problem because, as the emissary of Florence, Machiavelli had stayed in Cesare's court during negotiations that had been quite hard on Cesare. At that time, Machiavelli had reported that Cesare not only relied too much on Fortune but was unable to make up his mind, a trait incompatible with the decisive planning attributed to him as hero of *The Prince*. The obvious difference in emphasis leaves his readers with two possibilities, both of which may hold true, the one that Machiavelli purposely created an artificial, near-infallible hero out of the resourceful, brave, cruel, devious, but quite fallible adventurer he happened to know, and the other that because he needed a good contemporary exemplar—especially one who had learned to rely on his own troops—he saw Cesare in retrospect as more heroic, in the Machiavellian vein, than he had thought him when he had been in his company.[94] In his image of Cesare, Machiavelli is deducing lessons from his own recreation of history.

Granted such a hero for his own times, and granted the evil nature of man, Machiavelli concludes that a wise prince is not troubled by being accused of the cruelty "by which he keeps his subjects united and loyal," because this cruelty is really kindness. By giving a very few examples of cruelty, the prince "is more merciful than those who, through too much mercy, let evils continue." From mercy there arise serious, murderous disorders that harm the whole public, while the wise prince's executions affect only individuals. Moderated by prudence and kindness, the wise prince is able to keep the balance between recklessness and the sharp distrust that would result from unmeasured cruelty.[95]

It is claimed (by de Grazia) that Machiavelli is unique in portraying human beings as rational brutes, creatures whose rationality does not imply any inborn impulse to do good.[96] If we accept this simplification of Machiavelli's not very simple impulses, his problem is how to persuade, force, or trick such brutes into the approximate amity and solidarity that human beings need even though they so often wreck them. Using old and new examples, Machiavelli tries to give enough insight into the relation between statecraft, history, and human nature for his goal to be more nearly attainable. His prefers a necessarily tumultuous republic, in which the leaders and the people limit one another's power and together demonstrate the prudence, courage, and enterprise needed for civic unity and glory. In such a republic, he believes, people acting for their individual good are likely to be acting for the common good as well. He sees it as his duty to recall what was once rightly done in Roman times because he hopes that someone more loved by heaven than himself may be able to do it rightly again.[97] The example of the ancient Romans shows that it is exaggerated to assume that men are evil and malicious under all circumstances. But despite the hope this concession reflects, Machiavelli has suffered the fate appropriate to the heroizer of Cesare Borgia: He has become the paradigm of the villainous hero who encourages the ruler to sacrifice truth and justice on the altar of expediency.

Machiavelli's Machiavellian Friend

Machiavelli and Guicciardini had known and, no doubt, distrusted one another in the days of the republic, when Guicciardini was part of the aristocratic opposition to the republic's leader, Soderini.[98] But the dislike of both for the Medici's subsequent rule over Florence helped to make them friendly later.[99] The years of Guicciardini's rise were those in which Machiavelli succeeded in reinstating himself in the graces of the Medici—it was the Medici pope Leo X who commissioned *The History of Florence* in 1520. Favored by the same pope, Guicciardini was made governor of Modena and Reggio, which were under papal control. Both cities were economically depressed, politically disturbed, and infested with armed gangs. Like the ideal Legalist ruler, Guicciardini proved both effectively ruthless and just, a terror to disturbers of the peace and an object of respect to the law-abiding. When a new pope, Clement VII, the Medici patron of Raphael and Michelangelo, was elected in 1523, Guicciardini was made president of Romagna, the Papal States north of the Apennines. Now, in Italian terms, an important ruler, he wrote to the pope of his success in Romagna:

> I came to this province, torn by strife, with the intention and hope of reorganizing it and I have made no small beginning, having immediately on my arrival reduced it to the greatest terror and obedience ever known . . . I will reduce it to a condition where severity and mercy may be used fairly and without disorder resulting.[100]

Later, during the great crisis of his life, Guicciardini composed two speeches on himself, one in indictment and the other in defense. In his defense he argues that he had given impartial justice and security, and that his luxurious house, servants, and German mercenary guards had been needed to give his rule the ambiance of authority. His personal lot as ruler had been all work and worry.[101]

The problem of the hour had come to be the hostilities between Francis I, king of France, and the Holy Roman Emperor Charles V, who was simultaneously, the king of Spain. Alarmed by the success of Charles in Italy, the new pope followed Guicciardini's advice and formed a coalition including France, Venice, Milan, and Florence. But Charles' army defeated the coalition. In 1527, when its commander was killed and its mercenary soldiers were unpaid, Charles's army sacked Rome, with much accompanying cruelty.[102] The pope then retreated to the Castel Sant'Angelo, where he was, in effect, a prisoner. Many saw this turn of events as a sign of God's wrath against a corrupt church.

One result of the downfall of the pope was the overthrow of the tyranny of the Medici in Florence and its replacement by a republic, which had religious and antioligarchic enthusiasms like those of Savonarola's time. Guicciardini's career was, of course, ruined. Now a private citizen, he returned to Florence, where, like other Medici supporters, he was made to pay special imposts. Charged, as well, with having taken for himself monies sent by the city to the coalition armies, he was cleared in an official inquiry. Now confined to political reflection, Guicciardini began to work on a history of Florence and to write or rewrite his Machiavellian observations, the *Ricordi*, which were intended to instruct his family.

Just then there was still another turn of the wheel of political fortune. The treaty finally signed between Charles and Clement specified that Charles was to restore Medici rule in Florence. Afraid of the reaction of the republicans, Guicciardini left the city. When the emperor's army besieged it, the Florentines defended themselves heroically for almost a year. Out of concern that this unrelenting defense would result in the city's destruction, Guicciardini got Clement to offer the Florentines favorable terms. Not only did the Florentine government reject the terms but it also made the charge that Guicciardini had conspired against the city, for which reason he was officially exiled and his property confiscated.

When Florence surrendered in September 1530, the pope charged Guicciardini with punishing its leaders and putting its affairs into order. The houses around Florence had been destroyed for miles, the common folk had almost vanished, and his own property had been destroyed or damaged—even his fine chairs had been sold. Consumed by anger, Guicciardini did all he could to ensure that the punishment of the leaders of Florence was merciless. Some members of the former government were tortured and beheaded; some were exiled or otherwise punished; and when the gonfalonier's death sentence was commuted to life imprisonment, Guicciardini complained.[103]

Guicciardini must have felt his harshness to be a satisfying conjunction of private revenge with public good. After a few years service as Lord Lieutenant of Bologna, he became the adviser of the dissolute Alesandro de' Medici. Alesandro was murdered by a kinsman and was followed as ruler by Cosimo de' Medici, who dismissed Guicciardini from his employ. Retired from public life, Guicciardini made his bid for literary immortality with the *History of Italy*. This well-documented work deals with the period Guicciardini knew from personal experience and could consider—therefore and nevertheless—with near dispassion.[104] One attentive reader says that this history has "the nobility and sadness of a classic epitaph." A rather less approving reader speaks of Guicciardini's "obstinate passion for clarity" and his concentration on the passions of rulers.[105]

The History of Italy gives almost no leader unqualified praise. Guicciardini holds that most of military leaders of the time were unimpressive because of their ignorance of military science, their cowardice, or their egotistical desire for fame. His judgment of political leaders is more often favorable but nevertheless critical: Lodovico Moro had megalomanic ambitions that ruined him and Italy; Soderini veered from overconfidence to panic; Pope Leo X was sexually shameless, frivolous, and scheming; Clement VII was fatally indecisive; Francis I of France was too enchanted with the trappings of power; and Charles V was the helpless tool of his advisers. When Guicciardini looks for human perfection, he turns, like Machiavelli, to the Romans. It was easier for them to be perfect, he says, because they lived at the beginning of their history, after which corruption sets in.[106] Sometimes he explains the travail of Italy as God's punishment for corruption, sometimes he speaks of overambitious, cruel rulers, and sometimes he blames lack of prudence. But even good and prudent people can fall into disaster, because fate, Fortuna, makes all human affairs unstable. Except for self-interest, which is constant, fate transforms human personalities as well as events. Events and motives influence one another because the occurrence of an event creates a new human intention that leads to an action that, in the absence of the event, would not have been considered.[107]

Having risen, fallen, risen, and fallen again (I have not retold all his political ups and downs), Guicciardini had learned from his own life "what children and unlettered men know: that prosperity does not last and fortune changes." Experience has taught him, he writes, that probably everyone who preaches liberty has his own interests in mind, and if a partisan of freedom thought he would be better off under an absolute government, he would rush into it.[108] Yet he remains optimistic enough to hope that the discovery of America will reveal a world free of the torment of avarice and ambition.[109]

Guicciardini thinks of himself as more realistic than Machiavelli. In his unfinished *Considerations on the "Discourses" of Machiavelli*, he agrees that government by the people keeps tyranny at bay, but he belittles the people's ability to make decisions of importance. Not only are they too ignorant, in his view, but they are restless and easily misled by ambitious men and traitors. Worse still, "they are fond of persecuting well qualified citizens for they need novelty and disturbances." For this reason, matters they must decide in order to keep their freedom, such as the election of magistrates and the creation of laws, should come to them only after they have been well digested and approved by the magistrates and the senate; but, to keep the balance even, the decisions of these authorities must be approved by the people before they come into force.[110]

Guicciardini also takes issue with Machiavelli's remarks on the greater wisdom and constancy of the multitude than of the prince by

Always deny what you do not wish to be known, and affirm what you wish to be believed, for even when there is much evidence and even certainty to the contrary, a bold statement or denial often sows doubt in the mind of those who hear it.[118]

Guicciardini also advises that when it is decent and possible, you should hide your displeasure with others because you may in the future have to use these very people, whose help it will be hard to get if they know you are dissatisfied with them.[119] More psychologically balanced than Han Fei, Guicciardini knows the psychological rule that telling persons secrets inspires their reciprocity. True, "it is often a mistake to talk too much even with friends" about what ought to be kept secret, but people are inspired to confide in you by the belief that you are confiding in them, and if you tell them nothing, you lose the possibility of learning anything from others. So, as always, you must distinguish between persons, circumstances, and times.[120]

About cruelty, Guicciardini comments that Alexander the Great, Caesar, and others who understood political life in this respect, "never showed mercy which they knew might spoil or endanger the fruits of their victory, because this would have been madness." Their mercy was kept for the instances in which granting it was safe and led others to admire them the more.[121] Elsewhere he explains that as a governor he avoided cruelty or excessive punishments "because apart from certain exemplary cases it is enough, in order to maintain terror, to punish crime lightly as long as you make it a rule to punish all crimes without exception."[122]

I have saved for the last Guicciardini's comment on human nature, which I find so striking because it would almost fit into the mouth of Hsün Tzu or Han Fei. Other things being equal, he begins, all men are more inclined to good than evil.

Yet man's nature is so weak, and so frequent are the occasions which invite one to evil doing, that men easily allow themselves to be driven from what is good. For this reason the legislators invented rewards and punishments simply to hold men firm in their natural inclinations, through hope and fear.[123]

Machiavellian Echoes, Literary and Philosophical

European Machiavellism was not created by Machiavelli, but he soon became a very noticeable thorn in the flesh of the orthodox moralists, and before long his name became a byword for insidious evil.[124] It was toward the end of the sixteenth century that *Machiavellist* and *Machiavellian* came into use as highly pejorative words. For dramatists, Machiavellism was the kind of perfidy that fitted the current fashion for a criminal hero. When Italian editions and manuscript translations of Machiavelli appeared in Elizabethan and Jacobean England, the government refused to allow the printing of either the original text or translations of *The Prince* or *The Discourses*.[125]

The perfidious Machiavelli appears in the prologue to Marlowe's *Jew of Malta*, produced about 1590, where he comes on stage and bares his doctrine in the words "Might first made kings, and laws were the most sure, / when like the Draco's they were written in blood." In such plays as *Henry VI*, *Richard III*, and *Othello*, Shakespeare portrays the evil hero with an eloquence, ferocity, and complexity that make the historic Machiavelli pale by comparison. In *Henry VI* (Part III 3.2), the deformed Duke of Gloucester, the future Richard III, says he will account this world a hell until he wears the glorious crown of England and boasts that he can smile and murder while he smiles, wet his cheeks with artificial tears, play the orator, deceive, conquer, add colors to the chameleon, change shapes with Proteus, "and set the murtherous Machiavel to school." In *Richard III*, this self-appointed teacher to Machiavelli demonstrates the strength and weakness of a great but evil will. For Richard III is no merely one-dimensional symbol, but a blackly witty, active, attractive, intelligent person who nevertheless suggests the devil, as he is called in the play, or an Antichrist. Driven on by the lust for power that destroys him, he begins the process of his destruction with his accession to the throne, the process turning the play into a non-Machiavellian morality play. Toward the end, like a Cesare Borgia, he loses control.[126]

If Richard represents evil exercised on a political stage, Iago, in *Othello*, represents evil delighting in itself, evil always concealed, depending on the trust of others, and working by means of insidious, persistent deception. He is not, he says, what he is (1.1.65). "What Iago does is to prove that, in the right context, anyone can be made to believe anything," suspect anything, and become a brute or hypocrite.[127]

From the first, political writers more usually attacked than defended Machiavelli. Both attacks and defenses might take on a predominantly religious color. In an early attack (written in 1539 but published only much later), Reginald Pole took the author of *The Prince* to be one of the privy councillors of Satan, that is, of Cromwell, the demon-inhabited transmitter of Machiavellian doctrines. The influence

and indeed the preservation of his people?" Surely such a ruler under such circumstances deserves and may hope to gain the favor of God.[138]

My own reaction to Montaigne's reaction to such quandaries is that of all the thinkers we have consulted, it is he who has the least qualified and most nuanced sympathy with the human condition, including that of the ruler with a strong conscience. Machiavelli is capable of sympathy, but Montaigne shows it more often, more subtly, and more deeply. This difference should not obscure the extent to which Montaigne agrees with Machiavelli.[139] In a larger sense, Montaigne loves nothing more than the truth, as he says and demonstrates; but the truth is also, he says, that he, like everyone else, dissembles, and that dissembling is sometimes prudent and even necessary—politics is impossible without it. It is hard to disentangle the humor, irony, and truth in Montaigne's statement that his memory is too weak for public life because he is unable to lie consistently and convincingly. He insists that lying is an "accursed vice" because "it is only our words which bind us together and make us human." But despite the examples he gives of lying that fails or treachery that arouses remorse, he concedes that "to deprive wiliness of its rank . . . would be to misunderstand the world." He is also willing to adopt the ordinary mode of thought that distinguishes between what is useful and what is decent.[140] And although he professes sympathy for the prince who is unable to lie, he elsewhere says that anyone whose morals are conspicuously higher than those of his time "must either distort and blunt his rules" or "have nothing to do with us." As he shows clearly enough when he wants to, he does not believe that the princes who deserve God's favor will in fact gain it.[141] Still further likenesses with Machiavelli include his satirical attitude toward fantasies of ideal states based on the assumption that people can become highly moral, and his preference for a "mixed" form of government that combines the virtues and lessens the weakness of democratic and oligarchical forms of government.[142]

Unsystematic though he is, Montaigne has considerable insight into political philosophy. As a Machiavellian, though of the gentler sort, he shares the perception of the inconsistency and ambivalence of life that philosophers of a more abstract cast of mind too often miss.

Francis Bacon (1561–1626), who experienced both high office and political disgrace, declares that he is indebted to Machiavelli as one of those "who openly and unfeignedly declare or describe what men do, and not what they ought to do."[143] In Bacon's eyes, the rules of government have a strong resemblance to those of nature. In contradiction to Guicciardini (whose thought he knows), Bacon states that it is the virtue of Machiavelli's kind of writing that it is likely to be controlled by the particulars from which it is derived rather than by prior abstractions. Such writing is apt for application to the "variable argument of negotiation and occasions." Drawn from particulars, it knows the best way to return to them.

> For when the example is the ground, being set down in an history at large, it is set down with all circumstances, which may sometimes control the discourse thereupon made and sometimes supply it, as a very pattern for action; whereas the examples alleged for the discourse's sake are cited succinctly and without particularity, and carry a servile aspect toward the discourse which they are brought in to make good.[144]

Bacon writes frequent Machiavellisms. In the first of his *Essays*, "On Truth," he praises the truth aphoristically with the eloquence one would expect of so diligent an investigator and says, "The knowledge of truth, which is the presence of it; and the belief of truth, which is the enjoying of it; is the sovereign good of human Nature." But he also says, "A mixture of a lie doth ever add pleasure," the absence of which would "leave the minds of a number of men poor shrunken things, full of melancholy and indisposition."[145] In the essay "Of Simulation and Dissimulation," Bacon enumerates the advantages and disadvantages of both and concludes that the best combination is "to have openness in fame and opinion; secrecy in habit, dissimulation in seasonable use, and a power to feign, if there be no remedy." Like Machiavelli, he holds lawgivers in especial honor for their ability to "sow greatness to their posterity and succession." Like all the Machiavellis, he holds "that no nation which doth not directly profess arms may look to have greatness fall into their mouths." The intimate of two monarchs, he notes like Han Fei and Kautilya that kings must exercise care and circumspection because they are endangered by the neighbors, their wives, their children, their clergy, their nobles, their merchants, their commoners, and their "men of war."[146]

Of the great philosophers close to Machiavelli in time, the most like him in political thought are Hobbes, whose resemblance to Machiavelli he himself never mentions, and Spinoza, who acknowledges the likeness. Hegel, too, acknowledges the importance of Machiavelli. Although he is the most strenuous of anti-Machiavellians, I add Kant to this group of philosophers because his morality is based on a similar assessment of human nature and makes a similar demand for the unqualified obedience of subjects to their ruler.

Machiavelli was interested not in advising a tyrant as such or a mere ambitious oppressor but in correcting an impossible political situation. Italy, says Hegel, needed a drastic cure, and

> gangrenous limbs cannot be cured with lavender water . . . You must come to the reading of *The Prince* immediately after being impressed by the history of the centuries before Machiavelli and the history of his own times. Then indeed it will appear as not merely justified but as an extremely great and true conception produced by a genuinely political head with an intellect of the highest and noblest sort.[156]

According to Hegel's reasoning, a nation, a *Volk*, can be created only when it is conceded that the moral idea of a community requires the understanding that, implicitly, a human plurality is a single will. Otherwise society becomes a collection of isolated, dehumanized individuals. Once that is admitted, "we can recognize the necessary function of tyrannical authority in the founding of a political community. No one can become a tyrant without a considerable mass of popular support," which is often

> a conscious recognition of a directly felt authority that overrides one's own conscious will and preference . . . This truly spiritual authority is what Machiavelli understood and analyzed in *The Prince*. The "Prince" must secure his own power by all the violent means that ordinarily count as crime; but what raises him from the status of despot to that of tyrant is his vision of the sovereignty and independence of the *Volk*, which cannot exist unless lesser local authorities are destroyed . . . When the tyrant's work is done, he appears automatically as a despot. Then, it is the tyrant-slayers who are heroes.[157]

Hegel is sure that "state-power must always contain a tyrannical element, and that those who exercise it must know when to display their tyrannical power fearlessly." Correspondingly, the subject must learn to be obedient and give the will of the prince the force of law, so that once "the habit of thinking legally is established, the personal will of the tyrant is superfluous." When this will is superfluous, "the tyrant is overthrown unless he has already become a constitutional monarch."[158]

Kant (1724–1804) is, in basic ways, the opposite of Machiavellian: He demands truthfulness without limit, regard for humanity as an end in itself, and a will so absolutely good that it is independent of reward and punishment. But Kant thinks about human society in a spirit surprisingly like that of the Machiavellians. By nature, he says, man is social but also unsocial, because he wants everything to go according to his individual will. Knowing himself, he expects opposition. It is this opposition that

awakens all his power, brings him to conquer his inclination to laziness and, propelled by vainglory, lust for power, and avarice, to achieve a rank among his fellows whom he cannot tolerate but from whom he cannot withdraw.[159]

Kant continues that if man is to live among others of his kind, he must have a master. With, I suppose, a suppressed smile, he says, "How it may be with the dwellers on other planets and their nature we do not know," but human nature here on earth is such that, unless for a master, man continues to be too tempted by all his animal impulses. The master required is one who will force him to obey a universally valid will, which alone makes each person free.

The highest master should be just in himself, and yet a man. The task is therefore the hardest of all; indeed, its complete solution is impossible, for from such crooked wood as man is made of, nothing perfectly straight can be built.[160]

I remind the reader that the crooked-wood analogy is common to Hsün Tzu as well as to Kant. But despite man's crookedness, Kant believes in the moral absolute and therefore in God (Hsün Tzu's Heaven). He is therefore tempted to believe in a secret plan by which nature makes use of each human being's instinctive reactions in order to create an eventually perfect state, one in which human capacities will be fully developed. Yet the old Kant, in whom the the younger Kant's more genial qualities tend to be obscured, is ready to say that "everyone almost hates the other . . . *Homo homini* not *deus* but *diabolus*."[161] Although conscious of the moral law, human beings consciously deviate from it, with the result that "the propensity of evil is . . . woven into human nature."[162] Therefore "man is evil by *nature*," meaning that "evil can be predicated of man as a species." We know this not from the concept as such of the species but from experience, which teaches us "that we may presuppose evil to be subjectively necessary to every man, even to the best." The moral disposition of humans is such that the moral law forces itself on them, but instead of obeying it unconditionally, as they

and to privilege memory for everything sacred even when writing has come into use (India is again an example, though far from the only one).

By whatever general names we call these non-Chinese, non-Indian, non-European societies, when we shift our attention to them, we are faced with the difficulty that the evidence at our disposal is inadequate. This is true because the number and variety of the societies is so great, because written records are for the most part lacking, and because really careful observation is mostly recent. Often we depend on isolated observers who may not have penetrated deeply into the culture they studied. Most elusive is the anthropologist's reaction to the absence of history for most of the societies. The assumption that used to be made that the "old days" reconstructed by an anthropologist represent an almost unchanging traditional life was always more convenient than plausible. The assumption is the more distorting because contact with trained anthropological observers came long after the transforming, often devastating influence of western civilization had been exerted. Furthermore, because it is easier to make external observations than to attain an intimate understanding of tribal life, the discussion of Machiavellism here will almost necessarily lay more stress on what is externally observable, such as public aggression and war, than on personal qualities. It will be as obvious in this as in previous chapters that my stress on Machiavellian and anti-Machiavellian traits does not allow a balanced picture of any of the societies.[3]

None of what I have just said should be construed as a general devaluation of anthropology. It does no more than reflect the critical tendencies of contemporary anthropologists toward their own past. Although, following them, we are much more aware of the fallibility of their predecessors (and of ourselves), anthropology displays an enormous gamut of human possibilities. It would therefore be a great pity, an intellectual lapse, I think, not to make use of anthropological evidence—it would like discarding all the evidence of history because it is elusive and problematic. I acknowledge that the difficulties I have mentioned are so great that I cannot pretend to sum up the relevant anthropology in accurate generalizations. All I can and should do is search out trustworthy examples—the trust is always subject to withdrawal—to show whether or not Machiavellism prevails beyond the great civilizations I have discussed, and whether or not there are any truly non-Machiavellian societies, that is, societies in which socially justified fraud and force are at a minimum.

To make this test of the extent of Machiavellism, I accept the anthropologists' crude but helpful distinction between kingdoms, chiefdoms, and stateless societies. I begin with the kingdoms, sometimes really empires, because these most resemble the states we have already dealt with; and among the kingdoms, I choose those the existing literature has most emphasized, the ancient ones of South and Central America—represented here most strikingly by the Aztecs—and those of Africa—represented here most strikingly by the Zulus.

The kingdom of the Incas comes first. Most of what I report about them is drawn from the comprehensive summary of a seventeenth-century Jesuit historian.* In the fifteenth century, two great Incas (*Inca* is the Quechua word for *ruler*) established an empire, extending from central Ecuador of today to central Chile, of perhaps ten million subjects ruled over by an elite composed of Incas by birth.[4] To justify their conquests, the Incas made use of the legend that all other peoples had originated from them, the Incas, and were therefore obliged to serve them. Another justification was that their father, the Sun, had sent them to the world to teach human beings how to serve and honor him and his representative on earth, the godlike Inca reigning at Cuzco, sacred center of the universe.

To minimize disobedience and revolt, the Incas settled thousands of families from conquered territories elsewhere and replaced them by an equal number of families from distant but geographically similar areas. Settled in subjugated capitals, where they had no familial ties, the transplanted families were meant to form a garrison that would be repressed by the natives if it turned disloyal. To make the conquered populations as uniform as possible, the Incas demanded that they learn the Inca language, laws, and rites. And to keep track of what was going on in their empire, the Incas had topographical maps drawn and recorded the age, social position, marital status, and tax status of everyone. Populated areas were divided into two parts and the residents of the part labelled superior were given ceremonial preference everywhere. The object of the division was to stimulate competition in rites, festivities,

---

*He is Bernabé Cobo (1580–1657), author of the *Historia del Nuevo Mundo*. Although he draws on living informants and direct observation, most of his book is paraphrased from sixteenth-century descriptions, many confined to manuscript. What he says of Inca institutions comes mostly from reports that are regarded as basically trustworthy (though many of them have been lost). Despite his missionary zeal, Cobo was a serious historian and did his honest best to uncover the truth. To do so was and remains difficult—the early accounts often contradict one another, and the testimony of the Inca on their history and customs is likely to have been idealized, either because of their pride or because they wanted to represent themselves favorably in the eyes of their conquerors. See Father Bernabe Cobo, *History of the Inca Empire*, pp. ix–xix, and *Inca Religion and Customs*, pp. xi–xx.

a dynasty was compiled by its successor). In the words of the Mexica rulers:

> It is not suitable that all the people know the paintings. Those who are subjects [the people] will be corrupted and the country will go astray, because many lies are preserved for, for many in the paintings have been hailed as gods.[13]

In the course of the establishment and downfall of the Tepanec state, authority grew more centralized and the pursuit of war more important. Power was consolidated in at least two of the Aztec cities, Tetzcoco and Tenochtitlan, by a severe, objective system like that recommended by the Chinese Legalists. That is, the old, more relaxed attitude toward conduct was sharply modified by a code in which responsibilities and punishments were clearly defined and uniformly executed, exceptions being for the most part ruled out; a codex shows erring judges being strangled.[14]

The three city-states that had won their independence together made up the confederation that ruled the joint Aztec empire, but the Mexica, the most warlike of the three, were the dominant partners.[15] While becoming independent and creating an empire maintained by the threat of retaliation, the Aztecs (as I will call them from here on) had learned to dedicate themselves to war.[16] From their point of view, war had become an endlessly repeated condition in the absence of which life would lose its savor and earnestness; and human sacrifice, which relied largely on war, became an increasingly important instrument of their unity and power. We cannot grasp the Aztecs' preoccupation with war unless we understand their need for very many sacrificial victims—at one long ceremony in 1487, twenty thousand victims, who were slaves, prisoners captured in war, and persons given in tribute, are said to have had their hearts torn out (moral repulsion joins historical second thoughts to make the number hard to accept).[17]

Why so many sacrifices? Strangely from our point of view, the Aztecs believed that the sun and the powers of the earth had to be fed with blood. According to an Aztec myth, when the gods were about to create the sun they understood that the creation would be useless unless the sun were provided with human blood and human hearts as food. Therefore, at the same time that the gods created the sun, they created war to provide him with sustenance and keep him from being extinguished. Other gods besides the sun, those of fertility, for instance, also needed sacrificial sustenance.[18]

The Aztecs called the wars between their own cities *flower wars.* They were fought between the harvest and planting festivals, when men could be spared from working the land. The object of these wars was the accumulation of captives to be sacrificed to the gods, who did not fail to inform the priests when they were hungry and thirsty again. Given the information, the ruler would call for volunteers, who were the warriors who felt the need to prove their manhood. Such warriors fought the battle with their neighbors, like a tournament, at stipulated times on a stipulated battlefield. In a fairly typical flower war, the imperial army took seven hundred prisoners and lost four hundred men of its own.[19] Other occasions that called for victims were the ceremonial installation of a new ruler and the dedication of a new temple, the victims being perhaps foreigners taken by the Aztecs themselves in war or delivered to them as tribute by a subject people. The victims might be treated with a mixture of cruelty and ceremonial courtesy; their sacrifice was usually preceded by torture.[20]

Should such wars be considered Machiavellian? In attempting to see things from an Aztec point of view, we might argue that the "flower wars" were a religious phenomenon, prompted by the belief that the gods, who assure the beneficence of nature, would die if not fed on human sacrifices. The Aztecs, we might argue, proved the genuineness of their by belief drawing sacrificial blood from their own bodies as well as those of captives. The argument would be more impressive if the Aztecs had not sacrificed so few, relatively, of their own people and had not foraged so widely for victims among other tribes, and if they had not at times wrecked the towns, burned the fields, raped the men, and murdered the women of the neutral and even vassal states through which they passed on the way to and from battle.[21] The killings are estimated to have been

> explicitly about the dominance of the Mexica and their tutelary deity: public displays to overawe the watcher, Mexica or stranger, in a state theater of power, at which the rulers of other and lesser cities, allies and enemies alike, were routinely present.[22]

A reflective historian doing his best to understand Aztec imperialism lists as factors: the lust for power; the craving for riches—of the elite for land and of others for tribute that benefitted artisans and added glory to military leaders; the sense of being destined to rule; a cosmology that encouraged bloodthirsty fanaticism and a religion that supported a compulsive will to power.[23]

As in ancient China and India, agriculture and war were the essential occupations of the larger African states. The Ashante, of southern Ghana, are an example. Their state was founded by revolt late in the seventeenth century. Their empire, built up by conquest and deportation, had a capital out of which some 250 administrative chiefs governed some 750,000 inhabitants. The Ashante took their tribute in slaves, whose sale served to buy smelted iron, copper, and guns; but they waged war mainly, we are told, for the sake of political domination. Not dissimilarly, the Yoruba kingdom, or, rather, empire, of Oyo (in present-day Nigeria) made use of its army, especially its cavalry arm, to conquer territory and capture slaves, some for export and others, only semi-slaves, for resettlement around the capital. The Yorubas' slaves served the king, manned the standing army, cleared land, and worked in mines.[32]

Kingship in Africa, too, had mythical and metaphysical explanations: The king contained within himself the metaphysical power to sustain the order necessary for human life; and his status expressed his ability to keep nature and society in balance.[33] The mythical version given by the Yorubas was that the first human beings were created at Ife, the Yorubas' country. According to the myth, in the beginning there was only the sky, in which the gods lived, and the primeval ocean below. Two gods who were brothers found a complicated way to make land, on which they settled; but they quarrelled violently, and the other gods joined the fight. The sky god, Olorun, heard out both sides and settled the fight by giving one of the gods, the first king of Ife, the earth as his dominion. The other god was given the power to mould human bodies and became the creator of mankind. The founders of the sixteen original Yoruba kingdoms were the sixteen sons of the king of the Earth. This descent makes a Yoruba king sacred, for which reason he used to be isolated in his palace. When he appeared once a year at the sacrifice to Ogun, the god of iron, he was concealed so that only his crown and its egret feather were visible. In another festival, he made three sacred visits to a shrine during which the city's inhabitants had to stay at home with their windows closed.[34]

For our purposes, the most instructive example of Machiavellism in an African ruler is provided by Shaka or Chaka (c. 1787–1828), who created the Zulu empire by his conquest of what is today the territory of Natal. To the Zulus he remains the greatest of heroes:

> His name is frequently invoked in Zulu councils, his example is cited as a supreme authority. Any criticism of Shaka can, and often does, earn a sharp rebuke from Zulu elders and statesmen.

He is the subject of eulogistic praise chants and poems; the hero of more than one African novel. The Zulu people have erected a monument in his honor at the site of his Dukuzi kraal.[35]

Much of the account I am about to give depends on the indispensable but imperfect testimony of two traders, Nathaniel Isaacs and Henry Fynn. The testimony is imperfect because Isaacs was interested in making as strong an impression as possible, while Fynn, who wrote more soberly, buried his original notes in his brother's grave and had to depend on a distant memory of events.[36] But even if much of their testimony is discounted, Shaka's rule remains an object lesson in the use of force for the creation of a state.

The name *Zulu* was originally that of a lineage with only a few thousand members. Some time around the beginning of the nineteenth century, when the local population was growing and land becoming relatively scarce, a chieftain named Dingiswayo (He Who Was Caused to Wander) succeeded in conquering a large number of neighboring chiefdoms. His justification was that the chiefdoms were constantly at war with one another. Such war, he said, could not be the desire of the First Being, so it would be better if one great king ruled over them all. When an enemy captured and killed Dingiswayo, his place was taken by Shaka, who with Dingiswayo's help had become the head of the small Zulu chiefdom.[37]

Shaka's childhood had been difficult. His mother's temper had led her and Shaka to be banished from the court of her husband. Not only did Shaka grow up a fatherless stranger, but he was mocked and attacked because of his appearance (little crinkled ears and a stumpy penis are mentioned). However, as a young man he proved himself a hero in battle, and he conceived of a new kind of warfare. To ensure victory, he formed a standing army in which all men under forty were enrolled, every one of them compelled, while a soldier, to remain celibate—bouts of sex in enemy territory excepted. Shaka replaced the usual long throwing-spears with short stabbing-spears, much more effective at close range, drilled his soldiers in formation fighting, and developed tactics to envelop and destroy the massed enemy. The result was that in the course of six years of fighting, from about 1818 to 1824, he defeated tribe after tribe and consolidated his rule over a large area. Around his kingdom he created a wasteland in which everything that might serve as food was destroyed, making both escape and invasion far more difficult. It has been estimated (unreliably) that a million or more people died as the result of his wars.[38]

me how to rule the Zulus; for your ideas on that subject are as foolish as a man who urinates against the wind.[51]

As even the exponents of Machiavellism would predict, Shaka
was assassinated. When two of his brothers were killing him with their
assegais, he turned to them, says a version—a legend?—with the question, "Children of my father—what is wrong?" Another version has
him die while he makes the prophecy that the white men will overrun
the country.[52] In Isaac's version, which is less heroic, when Shaka was
stabbed by his brothers, he ran away, was stabbed again by his servant,
a member of the conspiracy, fell at the conspirators' feet and

> in the most supplicating manner besought them to let him live
> that he might be their servant. To this however, no heed was
> given, they soon speared him to death, and then left him to exe-
> cute a similar deed on the chiefs who were with him.[53]

The fratricides explained to the people of the royal kraal that they
had killed Shaka because of his atrocities at his mother's funeral and
because they wanted to preserve the nation of the Zulus and allow them
to live in peace (the implication being that the men would no longer be
subject to full-time military service.) One of the two brother-fratricides,
Dingane, murdered the other and took Shaka's place as chief, promising to avoid Shaka's cruelty and initiate a milder regime.[54] Dingane was
welcomed as a liberator by troops returning, afraid to be punished,
from an unsuccessful campaign, and he was supported by traditionalists, who had been too cowed to express themselves openly. However,
he enjoyed none of the respect and even affection that Shaka had com-
manded. Shaka's passions had been war and dominion, says Isaacs,
while Dingane's were women, luxury, and ease.[55] One of the larger,
previously independent chiefdoms rebelled. Dingane demanded subordination, but the revolt spread, and Dingane decided he had to renew
the terror. Political opponents were killed, a chief who had been a favorite of Shaka was tricked into expressing his hatred of Dingane and was
killed, and most of Shaka's favorites were replaced by chiefs loyal to
Dingane. Executions now became common, including those of people
killed for coughing while he ate, having an erection in his presence, or
saying they were disappointed that Dingane had not kept his promises.
Dingane killed as freely as Shaka had done, but often "in a more treach-
erous and crafty manner."[56]

Although surrounded by flatterers and glorified everywhere by
praise chants, Dingane's despotism was not really unlimited. After he

tricked and killed a group of Boers, the Boers defeated him severely and his brother revolted against him, splitting the nation. In 1840, he was killed.[57] But even his brother, who proved to be distinctly milder, observed that "The Zulus are only ruled by being killed"—an exaggeration, perhaps, but by no means an idle one.[58]

Aggressive and Antiaggressive Chiefdoms

A chiefdom is defined as intermediate between a kingdom, which is highly organized, and a stateless society, which has a minimal organization. Though ambiguous, the term is hard to dispense with and may serve for such provisional ends as this discussion of Machiavellism. Looked at in the abstract, chiefdoms, like kingdoms, may seem to depend on war for their inception and continued existence. An anthropologist who embraces this conclusion supports it with a comparison of warfare in chiefdoms of America and Oceania—his particular examples are from the Cauca Valley in western Colombia and the archipelago of Fiji.[59] In both areas, warfare, often motivated by the desire to conquer territory, was frequent and acute. Fiji, a land of many despots, had frequent ruleless and ruthless wars.

In the chiefdoms of North America, warfare seems to have been inseparable from tribal culture, even though its usual form was small-scale raiding. Contact with the Europeans stimulated war between whole tribes made more mobile by horses and more deadly by firearms.[60] Among many Indian tribes, the individual acquired prestige by fighting. "No young man ever thought of getting married or of being accepted as an adult citizen until he had slain an enemy and brought back a scalp to prove it."[61] This ethos of pride through aggression was typical even of the confederacy of the Iroquois Five (later Six) Nations, founded to put an end to hostilities between the confederated tribes. These tribes were often successful in maintaining their own harmony and equality of rights; but although their unanimous agreement was needed to wage war, they were not shy of it, and their insistence on the individual's freedom did not keep their war parties from rigorous obedience to their captains.[62]

In the Southeast, warfare between unrelated groups was conducted in order to retaliate, terrorize the enemy, and give young warriors the chance to attain glory. This warfare could lead to prolonged hostility and frequent raiding, as it did between the Cherokees and the Iroquois. Much of the warfare was conducted to avenge a killing and fulfill the male relatives' obligation either to kill the killer himself or one

lent to the concept they use for a well-made, well-balanced object *(kete-pepi)*. They believe that "the peaceful man is treated peacefully by others" and that "after death, only the peaceful man lives in the [paradisal] Village in the Sky." But their peacefulness is not so much a matter of abstract justification as of the particular ways in which they express themselves and act.[70] Because their society is mostly unstratified, their chief is simply the father who takes care of and provides for "his children." This father not only works hard but, ideally, "never displays anger, never engages in gossip, never makes witchcraft accusations, and never participates in witch killings, no matter how severe the provocation."[71] However, this communal father is troubled by anxiety over the possible jealousy of other tribesmen and by his fear of witches whose jealousy might prove fatal to him.

To many of the Xinguanos, anger is frightening and suggests a force as much out of control as a raging fire, a thunderstorm, or the kind of pepper so agonizingly hot that whoever eats it writhes helplessly on the ground. They refrain from eating most game animals because "they have too much blood," which is defiling. Persons bleeding seriously are ritually impure, and killing is wrong not only in itself but also because it produces blood. The non-Xingu Indians are considered "wild," violent, which is to say, not really human, for they split skulls, kidnap children, burn villages, and make wars as if celebrating festivals; and they are ugly and malodorous, sleep like animals on the ground, defecate in the water, and, like animals, attack without provocation (as they, in fact, attacked the Xinguanos). The Xinguanos who, a generation ago, succeeded in killing the men of an outside tribe that had attacked them and might have attacked again, received no special honors, were required to take blood-decontaminating medicines, and were regarded as having participated in a morally exceptional though justifiable act against morally deficient Indians. Such wild Indians make "a dramatic moral counterpoint for the ideal of peaceful behavior" because, even when physically distant, they are kept constantly in mind, not least by the child who is warned not to behave like a wild Indian.[72]

Some of the villagers, those "who don't have feelings for others," are rumored to practice witchcraft. Village gossip makes a great deal of witchcraft rumors, and village courtesy is augmented by the fear of offending possible witches. After someone dies, well-paid witch hunters identify the witch who is responsible. If the alleged victim was a young man, his relatives may carry out a brutal execution of the "witch" accused of his death. This striking breach of the dominant peace is possible because the executioners, their courage raised by magical spells and objects, are quite sure of the righteousness of their act. It appears that the prevailing fear of violence only masks the prevailing suspicion of witches. Anyone may at some time fall under suspicion and, and if aware of it, lives in fear; so that the hard-won peace of the Xinguanos is always under threat. But they understand that revenge against witches violates their essential value, and some of the Xingua-nos say that the killings of witches were not only ugly but in most cases based on insufficient evidence.

Somehow, ethnocentrism, the fear of losing self-control, the fear of offending others (especially possible witches), the imagery of blood, and the stereotype of the wild Indian have joined to create a peace that is real but distinctly uneasy. But the Xinguanos are able to assimilate newcomers into their peaceful way of life, and there are signs that their demonization of the Indians outside of their area can be changed.

Violent Stateless Societies

The most dramatic contrasts between violent and peaceful behavior are exhibited by "stateless societies."[73] In stateless societies, which have no formal authorities or formal structure of government, murder is perpe-trated, vengeance is taken, and feuds are carried on. But these forms of aggression may be confined to individuals or kin groups and not involve the organized aggression, the war, of one whole social group against another.[74] Such abstinence from true war has been ascribed, for example, to the aboriginal Australians and the Eskimos (or Intuit, as many now prefer to be called). As usual, one must beware of exagger-ated polarization. Contrary to the claim that the Australians knew no true war, it appears that (occasionally prearranged) fighting between tribes or clans was usual among them in early times. It was more usual, however, to send out expeditions to avenge the killing, perhaps by sor-cery, of a fellow tribesman, to avenge a "wrong" marriage, or to kill a runaway wife and her lover. In the area of the Western Desert, such an expedition might enter the victim's camp stealthily, encircle him by sur-prise, chant the formula of vengeance and, at the formula's last word, spear him dead.[75]

For the Eskimos, too, a simple verdict is impossible. Archaeolo-gists have uncovered Eskimo armor and weapons and speak of the emergence, perhaps a thousand years ago, of an Eskimo warrior cult and of armed confrontations between the Eskimos and the Chukchi (a genetically identical people) in the twelfth to fourteenth centuries. Before the coming of the Europeans, there were feuds among the Eskimo-Aleuts, and Aleuts and Pacific Eskimos organized war parties

into a fight. Boys fight with spiked bracelets, grown men of the same village, with clubs alone (a death might start a feud that would split the village) and of different villages, with spears, which are easily fatal.

As one would expect, even among the Nuer there are methods of settling hostilities. The killing of anyone from the same village or a nearby one is relatively easy to settle because there are ties of kinship among neighbors and because an active feud would disrupt daily life too seriously. For this reason, compensation in cattle is likely to be accepted. In any case, the main intercessor is the "leopard-skin chief." He may utter exhortations and threats to make it easier for a dead man's kinsmen to yield without dishonor, but his authority depends on the willingness of both sides to settle the affair.[79]

The Yąnomamö are, if anything, even more aggressively militant than the Nuer.[80] Ferocity *(waiteri)* is the quality they value, and they exhibit it in their internal conflicts and chronic wars, village against village. Boys are encouraged to fight, dragged back to a fight they run away from, and cheered on when they roll in the dirt pounding one another and screaming. Young men show their competitiveness by temper tantrums, by beating their wives, and by trying to seduce the wives of others while showing extreme anger at the seduction of their own. Afraid that when injured they will say or do some unbefitting their honor, young men may practice groans to correspond with arrow-wounds in different parts of the body and may carefully memorize the defiant words they will utter if mortally wounded.[81] The lethal frequency of Yąnomamö violence is shown in the estimate that about 40 percent of adult men had participated in the killing of another person, and that the warriors among them had participated in the killing of up to 16 people.[82]

Much of the violence takes the form of graded contests, which begin with relatively innocuous chest-pounding duels, in which the contestants alternately hit one another as hard as they can with a closed fist (a rock sometimes hidden in it). The prelude to these, as to other contests, is a serious enough injury, or boasting and bluffing that continue until the individual or group must take action to remain credibly brave. Fights once started for any reason can take on lives (and deaths) of their own. If a chest-pounding duel has been prearranged to mark a feast, it may, however, end in mutual chanting, hugging, and vows of friendship.

Club fights are usually the outcome of the challenge issued by an enraged husband to a seducer. They are fought with eight- to ten-foot poles, again, as in the chest-pounding duels, by giving each opponent his turn to hit the other. When blood begins to flow, the spectators enter the fight, clubbing away wildly in support of the person they favor. If someone is killed by a village neighbor in such a fight, the killer flees to another village; if the death results in a fight between men from different villages, a war soon follows.

Spear fights, which are very rare, are more serious. They are pre-arranged between villages not angry enough for them to kill one another with bows and arrows. Raids of one village on another are still more serious. The raiders hope to discover someone to kill outside the raided village. If they succeed in killing anyone or are detected, they retreat, leaving alternating pairs of men to cover them. If a woman is captured, unless she is related to the captors, she is raped and then given to one of the men as a wife.[83]

The most Machiavellian form of Yąnomamö violence is the "dastardly trick" (nomohori). In one instance of such a trick, a raiding party pretended to teach the men of a village how to pray to a spirit believed to give machetes and cooking pots. When the village men knelt in prayer, the raiders killed them, captured their women, and fled. In another trick, the people of a certain village were invited to feast in a different, ostensibly friendly village that was really in league with an enemy village. The guests were treacherously murdered and their women abducted and given to the plotters' confederates. Those who escaped were shot from ambush.[84]

The anthropologist Chagnon, who became famous (some would say, infamous) for these descriptions of the Yąnomamö, has come to the conclusion that among human beings, as among other animals, there is a biological contest over reproductive success. "Among humans," he says, "prestige leads to power, and power appears to lead to high reproductive success." He claims that this correlation, which he takes to be typical of "despotic" societies, holds among the Yąnomamö, who are always intimidating one another and testing one another's status in a complicated dominance hierarchy of prestige and power. Among the Yąnomamö, he says, the most esteemed men are the headmen, who have (or have had) more wives and more offspring than others. He adds:

> A recent analysis of marital and reproductive correlates of Yąnomamö men who are unokais (those who have killed someone) indicates that they, compared to same-age non-unokai, have over twice as many wives and over three times as many children.[85]

Chagnon's views have been contested, sometimes fiercely. One response is to argue that although Chagnon may be right with respect to the Yąnomamö, human societies have evolved many other standards of success, and the Yąnomamö's very unusual adaptation must have been the result of circumstances of equally unusual difficulty. Anthropologists who have conducted field research among Yąnomamö in other areas have found them to be much more peaceful, and Chagnon himself has discovered that the Yąnomamö of the highlands, whom he has investigated only lately, are much more peaceful than those of the lowlands, who figure in the description I have given.[86]

Antiviolent Stateless Societies

Very peaceful stateless societies are less well known than very aggressive ones but are quite as interesting and far more hopeful (to the non-Nietzcheans among us).[87] There are only a few stateless societies that qualify, especially if one makes the condition that they not only teach the value of peace but also act, internally and externally, in an unmistakably peaceful way. Among the examples of such rare peaceableness—antitheses of the Nuer and Yąnomamö —there are the Buid, a highland group of Mindoro Island in the Philippines, and the Semai, who live in the steep river valleys of the central Malay Peninsula.

Like the Nuer, the Buid value the autonomy of every individual, whether a child or an adult, but they do not equate individualism with the courage to fight for one's honor. Instead, they regard the fear of danger as quite reasonable and think that an aggressive person has a mind too weak to control emotion or is afflicted by a spirit that stimulates aggressiveness. Instead of proving his virility by his readiness to fight, a young Buid acquires prestige and makes conquests by means of the love poetry he recites.

To retain their freedom as individuals, the Buid minimize their dependence on particular persons or groups, and so they move easily from one community group to another. In describing the Buid, the anthropologist Thomas Gibson explains that their very strong obligation to share is to the community as a whole, not to particular individuals. He says that their conversation, their work in the fields, and even their easy marriages and easy divorces are best described "as the sharing of speech, labor and sexual intercourse." This is because, preferring autonomy and equality, the Buid try to avoid the closeness to individuals that leads either to competition, dominance, or indebtedness. If they quarrel or become violent, they fall prey, they believe, to the evil spirits that feast on them just as they, the Buid, feast on pigs.[88] To them, violence is evil in every situation.

The Semai are equally averse to violence. Although they suffer no less than any other small society from jealousy, gossip, theft, property disputes, and marital infidelity, their disputes never lead to violence. Faced by difficult issues, they insist on talking in order to smooth things out and avoid trouble. An offender is forgiven out of "pity" and the fear of losing the results of the offender's work. Typically, the Semai react to the disputes they have over land and trees by saying, "These quarrels don't matter for us, because we all die soon; but they are important because they will result in dissension over our children and grandchildren."[89]

Such an approach is effective among the Semai because, like the Buid, they require every person to help everyone else in the community. As they see, the purpose of the community is to nurture all of its members, whose survival it alone makes possible. When someone is frustrated, the community, a band of some hundred persons, protects itself by alleviating the frustration. A formal meeting begins and ends with a declaration of interdependence such as, "We are all siblings here; we take care of one another. When I couldn't hunt, you took care of me; when you were sick, I fed you."[90]

This mutuality is the more important because the forest world outside is filled with threatening forces, which are guarded against by the taboos and rituals that accompany everyday activities such as gardening, hunting, eating, or children's play. Spirits that appear in dreams and ask to become kin are solicited by the dream songs they teach and are asked to help overcome illnesses and to protect against the malevolent spirits that prey on the Semai.

We see that instead of falling back on their individual resources, the Semai stress their mutual affiliations and their dependence on the community. To them, to be good is to help the others, and to be bad is to fight, get angry, and quarrel. By this standard of good and bad they judge one another and teach the next generation that violence neither settles disputes nor solves difficulties of any kind.[91]

The descriptions of small peaceful societies like the Xinguano, the Buid, and the Semai allow us at least one important preliminary conclusion. It depends on the evidence, which I have not presented, that neighbors of all the exceptionally peaceful societies—neighbors that live under at least fairly similar conditions—have different, more violent personal and social ways of life. This appears to rule out a purely environmental, that is, geographical theory of social development. Each society constitutes a world the violence or peace of which depends largely on the ethos it has evolved out of its own perceptions.

On Some Further Tribal Machiavellisms

The internal permutability of human societies leads to the common but not negligible observation that no matter what rules are set, individuals find all kinds of tactics for evading them. As a writer on the anthropology of law has said, "The making of rules and social and symbolic order is a human industry matched only by the manipulation, circumvention and unmaking of rules and symbols."[92]

A direct example of such unmaking is the following: When the Arusha of Northern Tanzania—a stateless agricultural society—take part in the settlement of a dispute, they admit frankly that it may be necessary to act

> in what otherwise would be regarded as disapproved, unethical ways. As a conscious obligation, men may give false evidence or suppress pertinent but damaging evidence. It is an obligation not only to show up a fallacious argument or false evidence by the other disputant, but also deliberately to upset or confuse the other and his supporters by interruption, cross-questioning, twisting his argument, raising false issues or appealing to irrelevant emotion, precedence or other considerations.[93]

An example of a different kind is given by the Lovedu, of the Transvaal, to whom absolute honesty and truthfulness are less important than smooth social relations. They think it is wrong to say no when a relative asks for help but right to evade the request by always agreeing to give the relative the goat he wants but always failing to find the goat. Such an estimate of wrong and right expresses the Lovedu conviction that

> truth is not always good in itself nor is a lie always evil. Lies are objected to when they are socially inconvenient, yet not only is it expected that a man will lie to get out of difficulties but there are cases in which lying is prescribed, as when children are told to lie to strangers if asked about village secrets. To keep tribal secrets and the secrets of initiation schools is of far greater importance than to tell the truth.[94]

For the same reason, smooth social relationships, the Mbuti pygmies of Zaire, who found it essential to cooperate with one another in hunting, settled their disputes not primarily for the sake of justice in the abstract but for the sake of peace. This seems to be the reason why they had relatively few explicit rules and punishments. Mostly, they managed to put infractions out of mind, divert attention from the actual cause of a dispute, recall other incidents to spread blame more widely, and claim that what had happened was an "accident." An infraction such as incest, too serious to be dissipated in this way, might be met with tears and threats, and might be punished, as it was in a reported case, by a brief ostracism. Ridicule was another form of social control, and exile might be imposed, for instance for a hunter's excessive claim of authority in the hunt.

When asked why they had no chiefs, lawgivers, or councils, the Mbuti answer was that they were the people of the forest. For them, the forest was the standard of judgment, "the chief, the lawgiver, the leader, and the final arbitrator."[95] Although the forest was the good provider, it might punish the Mbuti, they said,

> by causing storms, trees to fall, ill health, and poor hunting. What displeased the forest was "noise"—trouble, dispute, or discontent, the result of laziness, aggressiveness, disputatiousness . . . For the Mbuti, to dwell upon individual blame was secondary to the maintenance of harmony and could be counterproductive, deflecting people from their most vital task, living in harmony with their forest.[96]

The Mbuti strategy for survival was the subordination of rules to what has been called "situational adjustment." Societies—such as that of the egalitarian Cheyenne Indians—whose strategy for survival relies on categorical rules and serious punishments work out a series of exceptions that allow the rules to command without becoming too destructive. Candor compels the additional remark that, despite the rule that all rules have exceptions and are violated, there appear to be rare societies that have categorical, strictly observed rules, make next to no allowance for intent, and, in sacred matters, allow no excuse of accident—an example offered is that of the Walbiri (or Walpiri) of Australia, a people among whom there are no groups or individuals with clear, permanent judicial functions, although there are likely to be ritual leaders. Yet the Walbiri have a clear sense of the law, and they have established norms (instituted eternally in Dreamtime), distinct offenses of both commission and omission, and distinct punishments, up to death. Of course, none of this prevents the Walbiri from continuing to bicker, make accusations, and brawl. The strictness of their rules and the reported absence of exceptions to them make it hard for us, a great cultural distance away, to grasp just how the Walbiri retained their pleasure in living.[97]

Tricksters and Other Tribal Machiavellis

Our distance from "tribal" societies is too great for us to have an exact understanding of their attitudes toward truth (do we know even our own exactly?) and how and when they violate them (being human, they must break as well as make their moral rules). But we can get some insight into their modes of thought by paying attention to the stories they repeat for their own amusement and edification. With respect to Machiavellism, the most ubiquitous and interesting character in unwritten literature is the trickster, as he is called. The mythical embodiment of all Machiavellian traits, the trickster (only rarely female) is through and through deceitful, egotistical, greedy, and cruel, and he takes malicious pleasure in violating the rules of decency and any and all religious taboos. He is by nature lecherous—much more unscrupulously so than the merely human characters of Machiavelli's *Mandragola*—and able by his magic to undergo transformations to achieve his selfish ends or escape the punishment that others rightly try to inflict on him. Like any other Machiavellian, he can be stupid and fall into the very traps that he sets for others. His example therefore teaches those who hear about him that at all times and places there are Machiavellis to take advantage of other people, and that they sometimes succeed and sometimes fail. To go deeper, the trickster, who is most often divine or semidivine, embodies the implicit belief that deceit and cruelty are inseparable from the nature of things. In other words, nature itself has a strong, so-to-speak Machiavellian strain, an amorality in the absence of which the spontaneous impulses of humans would not have been preserved or human society created.[98]

These generalizations should be fortified by a few examples of trickster or equivalent tales. Among the Native Americans, the most widely known of the tricksters is Coyote, clever, bestial, insatiably and even incestuously erotic, and generally contemptible, but also, in satisfying his own wants, very helpful to others. According to a group of Coyote tales, at the time when human beings were created, they were offered a way of renewing their youth, but out of pure meanness, Coyote kept them from becoming immortal. Ironically, he was then unable to save his own son from dying. In a Winnebago cycle, Coyote sends some mothers, who are human raccoons, to find nonexistent plums while he minds their many children. As soon as the mothers are out of sight, he kills the children and boils and eats them. When the mothers return and find that their children are dead, he magically changes his appearance, pretends to search for the culprit, and claims to have killed him in a hole. When the mothers go down the hole to find the killer's body, he stuffs the hole's entrance with hay, sets the hay on fire, pulls out the burned raccoons and says, "Now is the time that I will eat some fat."[99]

The last trickster story I repeat is about the Polynesian Maui. As told on the atoll of Manihiki, Maui went to his ancestor, the god of fire Tangaroa, who showed him how to make fire by rubbing two sticks together. Out of jealousy, Maui played Tangaroa a fatal trick and then, to escape his own parents' anger, revived him; but Tangaroa was now scarred and weak, his pride, beauty, and magical power gone. Yet it was Maui who brought the gift of fire and of cooking to the human world.[100]

As I have intimated, the fact that the trickster is also often a culture hero is significant. It implies that the power to change things radically, for instance by creating human culture, is the same as the power to defy rules and habits and act out of spontaneous, natural egotism. Although it takes culture to be good, the underlying idea is not un-Taoistic. It is an idea that parallels the Machiavellian theme that to create anything politically memorable, such as a great Chinese empire or a Zulu nation, the leader must be bravely, unrestrainedly selfish, and use any means, however ruthless, to accomplish some great social aim. In other words, great egoism, like nature, which it echoes, has a power to construct no less than to destroy.

Of African tales, I might have chosen from among the many about the trickster Anansi, the Spider, who not only dupes everyone who can possibly be duped but is bold enough to steal the sun. But because of its explicit moral, I prefer to repeat the Congolese story of the origin of the difference between human beings and apes. The story goes back to the time when apes and humans were the same, except that some of them wore no clothes. The naked ones, ridiculed by the others, retreated to the forest and were the chimpanzees. In the story, a man gets lost in the forest. Frightened by leopards, he takes refuge in a tree and is too afraid to come down. He is saved from possible starvation by an ape who takes pity on him and shows him the way to the village. In apparent gratitude, the man invites the ape to visit him. The ape agrees, but when he arrives at the man's home, the man, who has no intention of sharing the meat simmering on the fire, sends the ape out with a basket to bring back water. When the ape comes back, after many failures to keep the water in the basket, the meat has already been eaten. The moral of the tale is "Never expect gratitude from people; they are greedier than apes."[101]

A Tale on Ingratitude and a Tale on Overambitiousness

The tale on ingratitude that follows is a dilemma tale. It is called so because it poses a moral dilemma that amuses and stimulates the Africans who hear it.[102] Its importance lies not in its solution, which is meant to be inherently contestable, but in the active discussion it arouses, discussion pursued in the light of communal tradition. In other words, the tale is a dramatic means for working out the moral implications of tradition. The dilemma tale I retell, called "The Snake, the Farmer, and the Heron," is a chill reminder that Africans were familiar with the self-serving behavior that is rightly associated with Machiavellism.

According to the tale, a snake that was being chased by some men asked a farmer to save its life. To hide him from his pursuers, the farmer bent down and allowed the snake to enter into his belly. But when the farmer asked the snake to come out, it refused because it had found itself a place to stay. The man was about to go home, the snake inside him, when he saw a heron. He whispered to the heron what had happened and the heron advised him to squat and keep straining. Then, when the snake stuck out its head, the heron caught it, pulled it out all the way, and killed it. But the farmer was still uneasy because he was afraid the snake might have left some of its poison inside him, so the heron advised him that the cure for the poison was to cook and eat six white fowls. When he heard this, the farmer said, "You're a white fowl, so you'll do for a start." He seized the heron, tied it up, and carried it to his hut, where he hung it while he told his wife what had happened. "I'm surprised at you," said his wife. "The bird does you a kindness, rids you of the evil in your belly, saves your life in fact, and yet you catch it and talk of killing it." With that she released the heron and it flew away. But as it left, it gouged out one of her eyes.

The story ends ends with the words, "That is all," followed by the moral, which the Africans who heard it must have thought plausible enough to merit discussion, "When you see water flowing uphill, it means that someone is repaying a kindness."[103]

Because this tale is impossible to forget, it is only just to append another from Africa, memorable for its very different, anti-Machiavellian moral. According to the tale, the king of Beggar Town died and the kingmakers chose Aiyeyemi to replace him because Aiyeyemi had everything that fits a man to be king—money, mouth, and personality. However, not satisfied with the prospect of owning the world, Aiyeyemi wanted to be the commander of heaven as well. How? The sacred Oro spirit, who was about to appear at the initiation ceremony, had forbidden women to be present. But because Aiyeyemi's senior wife insisted on knowing the secret, Aiyeyemi hid her in the basket on which his feet rested during the ceremony. When the ceremony began, the kola nut refused to answer the priests' attempt at divination. The god of divination was consulted and revealed Aiyeyemi's transgressions. Oro, his voice thunder, split the wife in two like a fork, and the priests drove out Aiyeyemi and chose someone else to be king. The story shows, say those who tell it, that when life is good to us, we act badly. A song at the end puts the modest moral that we should "Enjoy the world gently" because "If the world is spoilt, / No one can repair it."[104]

Ethological Machiavellism, Especially of Primates

Whatever a more comprehensive review might show, it is clear that the Machiavellism we recognize in the political life of the great civilizations is found in many "tribal" cultures as well, even those we describe as stateless. There is good reason to go further and extend the concept of Machiavellism from human beings to other primates, though probably not all of them. The subject might be pursued more deeply and connected with the "struggle for survival." But this "struggle," to give it too human a name, is based on genetics and is far too complex to be taken up here. Therefore, after a brief reminder of the basic background and two ethological parallels that are too intriguing to omit, I will go on to primates, mainly the chimpanzees.

Beginning on the genetic level itself, it seems, we find both symbiosis and competition. Most genes act together to further the life of the organism whose development they rule by the directions they encode. In this sense, genes are symbiotic. But so-called selfish genes increase their frequency at the expense of other genes and even of the organism as a whole—at the extreme, they cause the death of the individual and end their own chance for further transmission.[105] Everywhere in biology, we find such cooperation (in the form of symbiosis, mutual benefit, "altruism," and mutuality of host and parasite) and such competition.[106] The mutual help of social insects like bees, termites, and ants (and, as well, of naked mole-rats) is so highly developed that the individual insects (or mole-rats) have been considered parts of a superorganism, which is the whole community or colony.[107]

The various forms of animal mimicry make especially interesting parallels to human deception. It ought not to be necessary to stress the word *parallels* except that some people feel demeaned by having human traits compared with those of animals. They may not object to calling human cruelty *beastly*, though in this sense humans are more beastly than beasts, but deception may seem to them to require the cleverness and self-consciousness that they attribute to humans alone. But what I mean by a parallel is simply the kind of response that an organism, given its situation, would be likely to make *if* it were clever and self-conscious rather than merely instinctive.

Instinct is a global concept that is hardly illuminated by the notion that that the act it characterizes is automatic. However, speaking of biology in general, human deception is to animal mimicry as conscious awareness is to animal instinct. This is clear if we think of a few often-cited examples. A parent bird "deceives" a predator that comes close to its still undiscovered nest and is drawn away by the bird's helpless-seeming, tantalizing zigzag or its fluttering to the ground and dragging of its outstretched, apparently broken wing. The example of the cuckoo shows mimicry and parasitism that change to fit the improving defenses of the birds that are its victims. When one kind of bird tries to "deceive" or discover the "deception" of the other, the relationship is parallel to that between criminals and detectives, or that of potentially enemy countries whose means of attack and defense evolving together.

Consider for a moment longer the relation, as studied in England, between the cuckoo and the reed warblers that are its victims. The female cuckoo watches the reed warblers build their nest. Some days later, during the warbler's laying period, she waits quietly near the nest and, when both parents are away, glides down to the nest and, in no more than ten seconds, lays her own egg in it and flies off with a warbler egg in her beak. The cuckoo's timing is right because, as experiments show, warblers reject eggs put in their nest before they themselves have begun to lay. The cuckoo is also right to remove only one egg because if she removes more, the warblers may abandon their nest. And although the warbler-cuckoo is a much larger bird than the warbler, its egg is only slightly larger than the warbler's and like enough in shape and greenish color to deceive the warbler most of the time. Sometimes a second cuckoo lays an egg in the same nest and flies off with an egg—especially a mismatching egg, perhaps that of the first cuckoo. The cuckoo's egg hatches faster than the warbler's, and the cuckoo chick, balancing each warbler egg on its back, pushes it out of the nest. Now alone in the nest, the cuckoo's chick looks different from the warbler's and is much larger, but it is accepted and fed by the warblers.[108]

Though the cuckoo's tactics are instinctive, they are as cunningly adapted to their purpose as those of Ligurio, whose deceptions in Machiavelli's *Mandragola* capture Lucretia for Callimaco.

The "Machiavellism" of the cuckoo does not compare with the conscious human variety nearly as well as that of the primates.[109] In primate research, anthropomorphism is the great seducer, and researchers try to resist it, with a difficulty that seems to increase as they grow more experienced. To the question if primates are self-conscious or able to plan or deceive, the researchers now answer with a qualified, sometimes highly qualified yes and with professions of how much they still need to learn. So while it is admitted that monkeys can predict one another's actions and the effects they and other monkeys have on one another, it seems unlikely, researchers say, "that monkeys take into account each other's thoughts, motives, or beliefs when they assess what other individuals are likely to do next." However, chimpanzees seem better able "to recognize thoughts as agents of actions, and much of their behavior seems designed to alter or control other individual's states of mind."[110]

To give an instance of such recognition in chimpanzees, one of them who knows where food is hidden may lead others away from it and come back to eat it as soon as they are out of sight. Or one of them may make a conciliatory gesture to an opponent, only to turn suddenly aggressive as soon as the other comes within arm's reach. Or, to give an example from baboon life, a female baboon approaches and grooms a male who has caught an antelope he does not want to share, and as soon as he relaxes in enjoyment of her attentions, she snatches the carcass and runs.[111]

Field research has made it clear to what a degree chimpanzees resembles human beings. In a recent summary of her experience, Jane Goodall has written of the chimpanzee as

> a creature, *a being*, with a very high level of intellectual sophistication, much greater than was thought even ten years ago, a being whose emotional states are quite similar to our own and who is capable of feeling pain, sorrow, happiness, a being who can trust and whose trust is very easy to betray.[112]

However, these humanly familiar qualities are allied with the less sympathetic, humanly familiar qualities of deception, aggression, competition, and even war (war in the sense of the tribal raid in which isolated members of a rival group are attacked and, if possible, killed).[113] Prolonged and careful observation has shown that chimpanzees make friends and enemies, who may change, and take part in changing alliances. The basic rules of their friendship and enmity are "one good turn deserves another" and "an eye for an eye, a tooth for a tooth"; but the reasons for friendship and enmity can be as elusive as they are among ourselves.[114*]

What we may call, for caution's sake with quotation marks, the "political," "Machiavellian," nature of chimpanzees is most apparent in the nearly universal desire of the males to rise in the dominance hierarchy. Like Nuers or Yạnomamö , they go through a series of contests that begin early in life, require the help of allies, and end only for those who achieve old age. Just as it is possible to ascribe the aggressiveness of the Nuers or Yạnomamö to new, pathological stress-reactions, it is possible to ascribe the vigor of the chimpanzees' dominance struggles to new, to them abnormal stresses. One such stress might be the presence of the researchers who feed them, and another, the stress created by the inability of the chimpanzees, their living grounds hemmed in by human beings, to split into groups that do not interfere with one another.[115]

The evidence for this skepticism about dominance struggles appears to me indecisive. Chimpanzee societies do develop differently, and their social life and degree of aggressiveness do vary with time, place, and circumstance. However, the existing evidence shows that the organization of chimpanzee societies is largely by means of struggles for dominance. A high rank earned by a male in such struggles gains him deference, which he must maintain without relaxing, and gains him greater ability to monopolize a female, that is, prevent other males from mating with her. Yet there is no very clear relation between rank and success in mating, and females make their choices for reasons that are often mysterious to their human observers.[116]

---

*There must be a rule that all early plausible generalizations are misleading. While it is often assumed that chimpanzees are closer to human beings than are the other primates, in such a crucial "altruistic" trait as food-sharing, chimpanzees are less human than such New World monkeys as marmosets and tamarins. Unlike chimpanzees, the monkeys appear to mate for life and share responsibility for children. "The apes rarely give food without being prompted, and begging takes several forms, some of which are prolonged." But the monkeys "spontaneously offer food, accompanied by a specific invitational call. Possessors give up food quickly, with little or no resistance," their "food sharing being embedded in a rich, cooperative family life." See McGrew and Feistner, "Two Nonhuman Primate Models for the Evolution of Human Food Sharing" (p. 239 quoted).

The quest for dominance can lead to the deliberate use of clever-ness instead of strength. Goodall tells of two males, Mike and Figan, who were particularly successful in using intelligence to rise to the top of the hierarchy. Mike used all kinds of human artifacts to enhance the threat of his displays—chairs, boxes, tripods, and the empty kerosene cans that he rolled, sometimes two together, to make a frightening noise.[117]

To give a close example of the struggle for dominance among chimpanzees, I summarize what Goodall tells us of the alliance, fol-lowed by rivalry, between the dominant Figan and the younger Gob-lin.[118] When Goblin first became independent of his mother, Figan would attack him; but he followed Figan around, watching what he did and often grooming him, until Figan grew quite tolerant of his presence. Goblin challenged adult females without any help from Figan, but when he began to challenge males, Figan would charge over to help him, until Figan's presence alone seemed to inhibit the other males and give Gob-lin the advantage. With this help, Goblin became dominant over all the males except Figan himself. There came a time, however, when Goblin, instead of hurrying to greet Figan, began to ignore him; and when Figan became lame from sores on his fingers, Goblin began to threaten and hit him as he passed. Figan relied increasingly on allies, but after Goblin drove him up a tree and kicked him off it, Goblin controlled the situa-tion. The tables were turned in a great fight, when Figan, joined by three allies, attacked Goblin, who escaped badly wounded. Figan then regained his dominance, but not to its previous degree. Things changed again as Goblin slowly regained confidence and, in the absence of Figan, was able to terrorize the others. Ten months after the great fight, he once more began to challenge Figan. Figan, whose best friend had disap-peared, spent a good deal of time in the company of his two other allies but could not really trust them to support him, and he became more and more intimidated. Finally he disappeared, whether because of illness or the attack of a neighboring enemy group. Goblin went on pursuing dominance with more and more violence. He disrupted grooming ses-sions of the senior males and later attacked the groomers, charging even innocent bystanders, and pounding his human observers. Because of such persecution, the heaviest of the males became abjectly subject to Goblin. Goblin then began to groom the male, share food with him, and reassure him, until they became friends. Finally—this story took from 1976 to 1984—the other males gave up and Goblin became the undis-puted dominant male. Their hierarchy struggle temporarily settled, the other males grew calmer.

In telling this story, I have not explained how Goblin, who had observed Figan closely, learned to use his intelligently threatening tactics. Goblin obviously prevailed because of his boldness, intelligence, and, above all, his extraordinarily persistent will to dominate. As usual, when the relationships of dominance and submission became clear and every individual was clearly placed in the group, the general level of aggression grew lower, threats more often took the place of attacks, and the community was at relative peace with itself. But dominance is always subject to challenge, youngsters are always moving up, and the contest of wills continues and flares up at critical times in a way that again creates tension in the group as a whole.[119]

The tactics I have described were those of one group alone, the chimpanzees at Gombe. Their behavior was in some ways quite different from that of the group studied in the Tai Forest of the Ivory Coast. As I have said, no one group of chimpanzees acts very much like another.[120]

We have come to this point by way of Shang Yang, of Han Fei and Li Ssu, of Kautilya, of Machiavelli and Guicciardini, and of others, including named and nameless tyrants and tricksters. Would the shades of these Machiavellis, if they survive in their presumed hells, recognize their counterparts in such nonhuman beings as Figan and Goblin? Luckily, we can go on without waiting for the answers.

II

MACHIAVELLISM DISCUSSED

~:6:~

Moral Abstractions and Human Realities

I turn now to discussion and judgment. As I have contended, the discussion of Machiavellism is not furthered by confining it to philosophical abstractions. In the long run, it is neither realistic nor fruit-
ful to separate the basic issue, the relation of politics to morality, from
morality as a whole, nor from social life as a whole. To understand the
relation as best we can, we need to join the abstract clarity of philosophy
with the empirical competence of the social sciences. It is true by definition that thought in any discipline is denatured if it does not remain
within the discipline's boundaries, but the need to stay within these
boundaries creates the need to cross them; they are theoretical and
mark nothing fixed in the the empirical world that is their quite unthe-
oretical object. Medicine is a good example of the relation between the
divided disciplines it makes use of and the undivided individuals for
whose sake it is used. Although it depends on many sciences, medicine
can hardly be one of them because it must unite them unscientifically in
order to help the doctor to reach an informed subjective judgment. Like
medicine, the study of morality in politics can gain by crossing boundaries that do not correspond with the opinions and acts of the undivided persons who are the only ones we meet outside of books.

I mean to try something of what I claim is needed, but not by writing in the style of a treatise or survey. I will not summarize and react
critically to the views, one by one, of prominent philosophers and social
scientists. It is a sign neither of contempt nor ignorance that the text
does not mention Isaiah Berlin, Friedrich Hayek, Jürgen Habermas, or
Michel Foucault (the older, more sober one). I have chosen these names
because I thought of them first, but I stop with them and add no philos-

ophers, philosophers of law, anthropologists, sociologists, or psychologists because any brief choice I make will be unjust.[1] Like any true bookworm, I have burrowed into more than a few books. At this point, however, I find it more promising to allow a thought the freedom to follow its own sometimes associative path, without the obligation to refer to anything but examples to make it plausible and empirical evidence to give it support.

I have organized the two chapters that follow in accord with the questions that arose in my mind as I was describing Machiavellism in various societies, including one of anthropoids. The questions are direct, simple, and difficult. The answers I give constitute no more than a free sketch, the spirit of which I value more than the letter. The questions are as follows:

1. Why has the problem of Machiavellism been solved so rarely?

2. Why are people often ready to accept Machiavellian violations of basic virtues such as truthfulness and fairness?

3. Why are some Machiavellis willing to argue openly, against their own interests, for the use of deception in politics?

4. Why are people often ready to adopt or condone political practices they know to be amoral?

5. Should leaders, Machiavellian or not, be expected to sacrifice their welfare for that of the people they lead?

6. How can we understand the reckless boldness of great Machiavellian leaders?

7. Does an established moral tradition make it more difficult for a Machiavelli to succeed?

8. Does history teach whether or not Machiavellism has been successful?

9. How adequate is the Machiavellian description of political life?

10. Have philosophers raised any decisive arguments against Machiavellism?

After I have finished answering these merely difficult questions, I will put the final, impossible one:

11. Does the prevalence of Machiavellism rule out the likelihood of a better political future?

To begin, then:

Why has the problem of Machiavellism been solved so rarely?

The answer is that the question is misconceived: Machiavellian behavior is not a human problem but a human characteristic. Cheating in politics (or elsewhere) is not a problem that can be bared theoretically and then solved and legislated or educated out of existence. To approach Machiavellism as a problem is like asking, If people suffer from anxiety, why not learn to do away with it? Buddha asked much the same question, on suffering in general, and gave a solution, but one that normally requires a long succession of lives to reach its full effect. Buddhism apart, how can we respond as human beings, for good or ill, if we are never anxious or afraid? When the anxiety is excessive, we can hope to reduce it, but although the psychologist is ready to say how much is excessive, what he regards as such may be indispensable to the anxious person's accomplishments. I imagine that psychologists and psychiatrists would regard the attempt to abolish anxiety altogether as doomed to failure and, if not, as dooming the persons whose anxiety was abolished. So to think of Machiavellism as a particular problem with a particular solution is like trying to analyze a fundamental human trait in order to rid ourselves of it, as if the condition of being human were a medical syndrome with a drug to cure it or a puzzle whose formulaic solution we might discover if lucky or clever enough. What could such a formula be used for? Science-fiction psycho-surgery or atomic or genetic substitution to remove the old biological "instructions" by which our organism operates? Or could the formula be imprinted on infants who would grow up looking like people but acting like angels (of the nonrebellious kind)?

Machiavellism is no illness, genetic anomaly, or performance that contravenes fantasies of angelhood. Its tactics are an inescapable accompaniment of every real or possible social system, whatever its ideological pretensions. "All's fair," they say, "in love and war," and though there are rules for love that are observed by the timid or austerely moral, and rules for warfare that generous victors or frightened losers may honor, the statement is more often true than not. But Machiavellian tactics are not confined to literal loves and wars. The love and strife that enter into all ambitious efforts call up the same all's fair—the force of the ambition can be measured by the readiness with which it dismisses scruples, or, in more stubbornly moral persons, is tempted to dismiss them. Since conscience is usually reinforced by fear, Shakespeare's Richard III is not altogether wrong to profess that "conscience is but a word that cowards use."[2]

If not ourselves Machiavellis, big or little, we are recognizably their kin. The Machiavellian unscrupulousness from which we suffer is imposed on us by people who, but for the grace of parents or circumstances, are like ourselves, or more like us than we prefer to think. We know that parents and circumstances can change things radically, but not so much that we cannot imagine our kinship to the Machiavellis or feel jealous of their power or attracted to them because, like creative artists, they can disregard the fears that confine both our fantasies and our accomplishments to our imagination

There is no use in thinking that people would act ideally if only they listened more closely to this or that preacher of the good. What must concern us here is how people, not angels, act, and why, when they are candid, they are apt to to regard their ethically questionable actions as natural and necessary. When their sins seem likely to escape the surveillance of outside judges, their inward judge winks agreement to exceptions to most rules. So if we try to understand the social aspects of life as we in fact live them, we are faced not by a puzzle in intellectual consistency but by an empirical condition that affects all our relations with others.

This answer is brief and rhetorical because all the pages that follow explain it further.

Why are people often ready to accept Machiavellian violations of basic virtues such as truthfulness and fairness?

The answer is that people often prefer to lie or half-lie, that fairness is ambiguous, that conscience is selective, and that conspicuous virtuousness, when thought socially disruptive, can isolate those who display it. For although virtues such as truthfulness and fairness are so basic that human life would be impossible in their absence, people allow or prefer their leaders to use Machiavellian tactics because they, the people, find such tactics necessary at times for themselves, even if only on the minor scale that ordinary lives allow. It is for this reason, among the others that will be discussed, that people assume that such tactics are also necessary in politics.

I begin with the virtue of truth-telling and its violation, lying. In theory, Machiavellism has the same neutral attitude to truth as it does to force. That is, to the Machiavelli the truth has no value in itself but, like untruth, is there for use as a means to success in politics and elsewhere. To understand how this attitude fits in with that of most, not especially Machiavellian people, we should ask ourselves why we tell the truth, why we depart from it, and why a utilitarian view of truth-telling and lying is more illuminating than conventional praise and blame.

To deal with these questions, it is helpful to make a clear though oversimple distinction between two aspects or uses of truth. I call the one aspect *discovery and communication*, and the other *social attentiveness and reciprocity*. As I see it, the first of these aspects, the discovery of the truth, has a number of reasons. One is directly practical: a person tries to discover whether it is true that a certain material bears the weight that is meant to be put on it, or, to vary the instance, whether it is true that something can be bought for a certain price. Another, allied reason for the discovery of the truth is the strong, strongly socialized curiosity of the kind that drives a scholar or scientist to try to understand something as deeply and in as much detail as possible.

Once discovered, a truth of whatever aspect is ordinarily communicated to others. The most fundamental reason for us to communicate the truth is to create ties with others by sharing experience with them and interesting them in what we know, feel, or have. As social creatures, we may also have the desire to share experience, even distantly, by helping others who are searching for understanding, or, as is typical of scholars and scientists, by taking part in the joint process of discovery.

It is clear that the attempt to discover and communicate truth in any sense is made impossible by lying, made equivocal by suspicion, and made perplexing by exaggeration or the withholding of information. Anyone who acts on misinformation, who has been directed to take the literally or figuratively wrong road, is, of course, angry at the wasted effort and all the angrier to discover that the misinformation was intentional, in other words, a lie. This is the reason why scholars or scientists who lie, whether for the sake of fame, revenge, or material reward are regarded by their fellow scholars or scientists as especially blameworthy. For such persons to lie in scientific matters is blameworthy not because lying is wrong as such but because they lie in a way that, for the scientific or scholarly community, is knowingly antisocial. Scientists and scholars face more than enough obstacles apart from the difficulty of the intellectual problems they set themselves, and the lying of their fellows troubles them not only by suggesting that lies can be professionally rewarded but by putting the reliability of their whole enterprise into question. A lying scientist betrays the individuals with whom he has scientific dealings and, even worse, the joint effort to advance science by uncovering new truths to modify the old. There really is an unspoken pact by which all the scholars or scientists who deal with the same area agree to work with a well-defined care to the same cumulative end. There is even an unexamined expectation, I feel, that the work of all scholars and all scientists will in time converge in some utopian structure of verified knowledge.

There is still another reason for the anger of such persons. A scientist or scholar may have been driven on by fantasies of success like those of any other ambitious person, but whoever is a scientist or scholar by nature is subject to an extraordinarily powerful need to appease curiosity and, having appeased it, to provoke it again: he or she lives for the one emotion that distinguishes the investigator's life, the pang of insight, and, if it comes, for a repetition of it; and each repetition involves the hope for still another, for a stronger integration into the community of those who value the insight, and for the accompanying renewal of self-esteem and public esteem. In the absence of elemental curiosity, there would be no such emotions, nor any scholars or scientists. The liars among the scholars and scientists threaten the emotions themselves with futility.

In the sense I have described, discovering the truth and communicating it truly so that people know what road to take or how to continue their research is different from the social attentiveness and reciprocity that mark ordinary conversation. As I mean it, the function of such attentiveness and reciprocity is to give people the personal information they need in order live together with the others. They feel that it is essential for them to know what other people have been saying and doing, how they have been reacting to events and to one another, and how their relations are, as always, changing. To tell the personal truth is a great social virtue because it maintains our everyday reliability and therefore our usefulness to others as sources of intimate information. The virtuousness of this telling of the truth is drilled into us and becomes more or less embedded in all our consciences.

Just here, in this embedding, everyone without exception encounters a difficulty. This is because the social truth conflicts with the exaggeration, concealment of truth, and outright lying that are hardly less necessary to social life. It is not only the Chinese, the Arusha, the Lovedu, and the Mbuti pygmies who sacrifice the truth for the sake of smoother social relations. When someone breaks a social rule, the transgressor is likely to try to escape censure or punishment by denying the transgression, and the denial, even if unconvincing, is often easier for others to accept than the truth, recognition of which is apt to create more conflict than the community can easily bear. The community is held together by rules, but also by mutual tolerance of their transgression. Whoever insists on telling the unvarnished truth—whether it is what he or she knows or thinks is so or feels at the moment—may be compulsively truthful or may enjoy the others' dismay, but in either case disturbs the always fragile local peace.

What must also be considered is the web of mutual respect that is woven by the smiles and small fibs that express one's pseudo-interest, pseudo-esteem, pseudo-love, pseudo-obedience, pseudo-devotion, pseudo-adoration, and pseudo-piety. Because one is impressionable and one's feelings change, it may often be unclear even to oneself what subjective or objective truth underlies the misleading expressions that help unite us in a community of mutual concern. To this web of solidarity in social dissimulation, I should add the common interest in evading laws set by distant authorities, an interest that can transform an illegal act or religious sin into a local virtue that unites the transgressors in the intimacy of their joint defiance. A full study of such relationships could no doubt be subsumed under a theory of communicative dissimulation (an ironic complement to Habermas's theory of communicative action and openness).

Although easy to sense, the conflict between the need to tell and to avoid telling the truth is most often only implicit. Likewise, the need to lie (in which I include exaggeration and the withholding of the truth) is revealed much more often in act than by verbal acknowledgement. The revelation in act becomes apparent when one discovers, often slowly and painfully, that the very people who teach and enforce the virtue of speaking the truth—parents, teachers, officials, policemen, judges, rulers, and maybe gods—themselves resort to deception, sometimes for benignly social and sometimes for selfish ends. And so one learns by example, consciously and unconsciously, how to tell the truth and how to lie in acceptable proportions. For in ordinary life, telling the truth, withholding the truth, exaggerating, and lying are activities that limit and regulate each other and form a person's subtly unified idiom, which eludes easy moral characterization in itself and, to complicate matters, may have an unobvious relation to the way in which the person acts. That is why official morality, the kind advocated in catechisms and simplistic philosophies, though necessary as a public standard, is an extremely primitive instrument for characterizing human beings. The difference between the moral reality and its catechistic measurement is like that between a person's completely individual face and the distances that calipers measure between that individual's features. Of course, amoral intentions may turn out to be just as distant from reality as moral ones. That is, there are similar distances between the pretensions of a Machiavellian ruler and what in fact happens under his regime. The people under his rule know how to thwart, evade, and turn to their own advantage the regulations that he sets: Machiavellian catechisms are no more infallible than others.[3]

Summarily, the social relationship between those who mostly tell the truth and those who often lie might be put in this way: Unless we usually supposed that others were telling the truth, our ability to act, individually and collectively, would be paralyzed. Even the ability of the liars to lie effectively depends, of course, on the degree to which the others are prepared to believe them. But most people realize that it is impossible or damaging to tell the truth all the time, and some learn to lie for their own advantage rather often and, in extreme cases, as much as they can get away with—or more. So truth-telling and lying have to reach some viable, though necessarily changing, balance. For the survival of the group, it is no doubt useful that it contains talented truth-tellers, talented liars, and talented fantasists—persons whose imagination is so powerful that their ability to distinguish truth from lie or fantasy is minimal. Most socially able of all, I assume, are the persons, paragons of a kind, who can temper their truthfulness, lying, and fantasizing to the demands of each particular occasion.

Because the boundaries of the truth are often unclear, because social pressures are complex, and because consciences are of different kinds and degrees of severity, the desire to tell the truth and the desire to be socially comfortable conflict in quite variable ways. In people with strong consciences, the usual compromise is apt to be a limited but distinctly uneasy conformity with social expectations. The problem is complicated by our ingenuity in deceiving ourselves; the sincerity of a deception makes it all the more convincing.[4]

The conflict between truth and lying is perennial and has no clean intellectual or emotional resolution. However, there is an even more interesting conflict between the desire to discover and communicate the truth—to know and share what one knows—and the desire to forget, exaggerate, and lie so as to combine a decent measure of credibility with a socially sufficient friendliness and, along with it, an acceptable defense of one's own interests. This conflict shows itself, among the rest, in our mixed feelings toward the Machiavellian analyses of human conduct. These analyses are prima facie justified by their nature as discovery and communication of the truth about human conduct, but they put a strain on sociability because they put most human actions in a light that makes them either ineffectual, unreliable, egotistical, or suspicious, and because—in contradiction to conventional ethics—they equate success with the readiness to use guile and ruthlessness.

Now for the virtue of fairness: Although philosophers often think less of what we are than of what they would prefer us to be, their path of abstraction has the virtue of simplicity and clarity, so I propose to follow it for a while to see what emerges when we begin with simple abstractions but remain aware of the Machiavellian possibilities.[5] Suppose we try what I take to be the most plausible of the abstractions on which an ethical theory can be based, which is that people want to be treated in a way they perceive as fair.[6]* Given this assumption, the first question is how the fairness should be calculated. In actual life, it is only in some simple matters that fairness can be seen in terms of arithmetical equalities: For the same work at the same level of expertness, it is fair to give the same pay; and generally, every single person deserves the same measure of fairness, ounce or pound, as every other. Aristotle, who thinks rather in this way, transmitted the idea to both European and Muslim philosophers. After equating what is just with what is lawful and equal or fair, and what is unjust with what is illegal and unequal or unfair, he says:

> Now since an unjust man is one who is unfair, and the unjust is the unequal, it is clear that corresponding to the unequal there is a mean,

---

*This is the basis of John Rawls's thought in in his well-known book, *A Theory of Justice*. The book's object is to use the idea of justice as fairness in order to raise the level of abstraction of the idea of the social contract (p. 3). In *Political Liberalism*, Rawls admits that his earlier book took too little account of the plurality of views necessary in a modern democratic society. He therefore addresses the question, "How is it possible that there may exist over time a stable and just society of free and equal citizens profoundly divided by reasonable though incompatible religious, philosophical, and moral doctrines?" (p. xxviii). Like Kant, Rawls begins in abstractions, in the conditions that should, abstractly, prevail if "a well-ordered democratic society" is to exist. While Rawls's thought is serious and humane, I should prefer to begin with actual situations and tease out from them what happens and why what people actually do fits what they want or say they want, and how ideals also serve as utopian refuges or incitements to Machiavellian activity. Why set aside, as if unworthy of serious thought, the question what prevents any ideal society from existing? Is the question too obvious, too difficult, or too discouraging— discouraging to those who suffer rather than profit from the unideal reality? It is not the absence of suitable abstractions that prevents the existence of "a well-ordered democratic society."

namely that which is equal; for every action admitting of more or less admits of the equal also. If then the unjust is the unequal, the just is the equal—a view that commends itself to all without proof; and since the equal is a mean, the just will be a sort of mean too.[7]

When such an arithmetic of fairness is attempted, it quickly grows either arbitrary or incalculable. By what numbers are we to divide, multiply, or set up proportions? Not only is it unreasonable to calculate a child as equal in everything relevant to an adult, but fairness requires that one decide exactly how and exactly when a child becomes a legal or moral adult. Also, rules have to be made for fairness to the sick and old, for women (if only because they bear children), for men (if only because they do not), and maybe for the rich and the poor, the highlanders, midlanders, lowlanders, and outlanders, and all the other many categories that need special consideration. This is much too complicated to be done at once or done solely by the fiat of legislators. The remaining arbiter, tradition, has had the time and the adjudicators to decide the rules of reciprocity, one detail after another, in accord with its slowly reached perception of many different specific occasions and persons. Every tradition recognizes very many nuances of fairness and, within practical limits, puts them into effect.

Of course, the ruling tradition is interpreted in various ways and is not acceptable to everyone, and there are always complaints that tradition is out of accord with another, truer perception of fairness, which can itself become incorporated into a subtradition. The Hindu believers in the caste system have been in such a conflict with the populistic or mystical groups that have objected to it. In China, the Confucians, who believed in a hierarchical notion of reciprocity, were in such a conflict with the Buddhists, who in principle believed in everyone's equality. In Europe there have been repeated conflicts between different social views and strata, like those, for example, that preferred and that denounced slavery (whether slavery by outright possession, debt-slavery, or wage-slavery). It was a conflict between different interests and conceptions of fairness that was expressed in the demands of medieval communes to be allowed to govern themselves, in defiance of God's supposed preference for kings. Other conflicts between traditions were expressed in demands that led to the revolutions of the postmedieval Western world: the Glorious Revolution in England, the French Revolution, the American Revolution, the antimonarchical and Marxist revolutions in China, and the Russian Revolution.

The point is that when larger social matters are in question, traditions themselves turn out to be ambiguous. It then becomes difficult to avoid the social disorder that tradition is meant to suppress and to find a mutually accepted criterion of fairness by which to interpret the tradition itself, or the criterion by which to replace one tradition of fairness by another—as the Vedic tradition was replaced for many by the Buddhist or Jain tradition. The sense of abstract fairness always becomes enmeshed in the difficulty of estimating it under particular circumstances. Rules of fairness cannot be constructed *ab ovo* by any automatic, self-evident intellectual procedure.

The simplest, least culture-bound principle of fairness has always been some version of the golden rule: I agree to be treated so on condition that everyone else is also treated so, and I agree to treat each of the others as each of them treats me—the contrasting Biblical, Confucian, or Buddhist precept to love the other as oneself cannot be more than a strained metaphor. The golden rule, which is involved in the ideas of natural law, due process, and equal protection by law, must have had many versions. One of them is Confucian, another, Talmudic. When Confucius was asked by a disciple if there is a single word that can guide one's conduct, he answered, "It is perhaps the word "shu" [using oneself as a gauge]. Do not impose on others what you yourself do not desire."[8] When the Talmudic sage Hillel was asked by a proselyte to put the whole Torah, the Law, as briefly as possible, he answered, "What is hateful to you do not do to your fellow . . . The rest is commentary." Hillel said, likewise, "Do not . . . judge your fellow until you come into his place."[9] It was at about the same time that Jesus said, "Whatever you wish that men would do to you, do so to them; for this is the law and the prophets."[10]

But to state the abstract rule of fairness is one thing and to put it into effect, another. When do people actually perceive themselves to be treated fairly? For one thing, their perception depends not only on the implicit acceptance of reciprocity by everyone concerned, but also on the trust they are able to repose in those who appear to accept it. Even if they are by nature or experience prepared to grant their trust, it will not be extended to everybody and surely not equally, so the granting of trust always poses the question of who is trustworthy and to what extent. In other words, if I am to be fair, it will be only to someone I am able to trust to be fair to me; and this someone is likely to be a person I recognize as enough like myself to feel easy (or uneasy) in trusting, a person with whom, at least for trusting, I can identify myself or relate to with some confidence in my judgment.

Let me first raise the (still abstract) question of fairness as it applies to the individual. I put the individual first because the relation of persons to their leader, which is basic to Machiavellian conceptions, is to him not merely as a leader but as an identifiable individual; and the leader's relation to other leaders is one also between individuals. To go still further in equating individual and group, when we trust or distrust a collective entity such as a nation or tradition, we do so in virtue of our ability to relate to it as if it were a person, a unique individual in whom we invest our emotions. This is because the quality of our attachment to nations and other large, impersonally named groups takes its earliest cues from our attachments to particular persons and, by assimilation, to *their* attachments to persons, nations, and institutions.

As for trust, it has a general aspect that psychologists have called *basic trust*. This rests on the individual's feeling, which stems mostly from the earliest human relationships, that the attitude of others is good and that cruelty, lying, and exploitation are not the norm. Since the earliest relationships vary greatly, there are great differences among individuals in readiness and even ability to trust others. By nature or experience, some are trusting, others suspicious. All of them, trusting and suspicious, may agree on an abstract rule of fairness, but some will find only a few persons worthy of it, and others, in effect, no one at all: "Yes," these last say in effect, "we would grant our trust if there were anyone who deserved it, but we have found nobody."

Those whose sense of trust is low may well tend to be amoral—trusting so little, expecting to be cheated or exploited, it is easy for them to be generally hostile and to justify their own cheating or exploitation of others: "I am decent," they say, "but why should I allow everyone to take advantage of me without defending myself?" The trusting persons learn to be rather afraid of the untrusting; they may suspect them of projecting their own untrustworthiness on others. Besides, the trusting find that the untrusting rob them of something of their natural pleasure in human relationships. Among Machiavellians, even those with a normal conscience in private life regard people who naturally trust others and are naturally kind as naive and, unless they learn better, unfit to hold important public office. The Machiavellian type feels that non-Machiavellians do not fit well into the real world, while the anti-Machiavellian type, of the kind that finds emotional closeness essential, feels that the Machiavellians lack not only morality, but also faith and compassion. Considering the two types at their extremes, each is right about the other.[11]

We can test this remark briefly by recalling the attitudes of criminals. As expected, they have weak or unusually selective consciences and little sense of trust. For example, a criminal who has learned of his classification as a psychopath (having an "antisocial personality disorder") agrees, as the definition implies, that he feels no guilt or loyalty. He says,

The thing is that I'm going to be me until the day I die; and you simply can't tolerate me. By "you" I mean society in general, not just you the judge or you the person . . . I'm lacking in a feeling for other people just as a one-armed man is lacking a limb.[12]

Even if the criminal has a relatively strong, though necessarily very selective, conscience, he or she most likely feels (as many reformers have also felt) that society is corrupt, that the rich are often useless and exploitive, that the powerful aim only to help themselves, and that criminals act much like noncriminals but are morally superior in their candor. As a perceptive criminal said of the prison officials he knew,

I've met no one, anywhere, any time, with whom it wasn't perfectly obvious, usually sooner than later, that in the end the main person he was doing it for was himself . . . He was hoping for once in his life to have put a criminal straight.[13]

This particular criminal was able to find a rare straight person or two to admire; but it is not clear how, being intelligent, he might be convinced by an abstract argument of a kind that did not apply to the people he knew or the world he lived in. Nor is it clear to me how he could be proved wrong by means of any of the verbal procedures by which criminologists or philosophers "prove" anything. There was no one he could fully trust, not even himself. His example shows that the question, Who is enough like me to trust? is the twin of Who is enough like me to suspect? Both questions require the same feeling of likeness or identification.

A first obstacle to trust must therefore be unfamiliarity. A stranger is suspected before being trusted; and this order of suspicion before trust holds true not alone of strangers but of any strangeness, strangeness in psychological type, appearance, profession, language, or religion. Symmetrically, a stranger in any sense tends to believe that others do not trust or understand him—in the double sense of feeling with him and of grasping his point of view. It is therefore plausible for a criminal to argue that a straight person almost automatically thinks that he, the criminal, would like to join straight society, but that the straight person is mistaken because the criminal prefers to be just what he is.[14] A criminal is likely to be bored merely to vegetate, as he sees it, in a steady job and merely to exist among merely conventional people.

To an experienced criminal, prison is hardly more than an occupational risk he must be willing to take. As a particular criminal says, he is willing to gamble away a third of his life in prison to be able to live the other two thirds as he wants.[15] Criminality is his habit, his bent, his preference, and, when successful, his pride. His attitude toward moralists is like that of Robber Chih, who says to Confucius, "You speak out your deceit and act out your hypocrisies . . . to lay your hands on wealth and eminence." To Robber Chih, as to less picturesque criminals, most so-called good men and all politicians are only con men who take over and exploit the official mechanisms of society. In a milder but nevertheless strong protest, Diderot has his ebulliently amoral character, Rameau, say that virtue is cold and often cruel:

> People praise virtue, but they hate it, they run away from it. It freezes you to death, and in this world you've got to keep your feet warm. Apart from which, it would make me bad-tempered, inevitably. Why is it that the pious people we see are so often hard and irritable, so difficult to get on with? It's because they're forcing themselves to do something that isn't natural to them. They're unhappy, and when you're unhappy, you make others unhappy too.[16]

Montaigne, who would not have disagreed with Rameau if he had had the malicious pleasure of hearing him, would have answered him, along with Robber Chih, in a psychological and sociological vein, that

> our being is cemented together by qualities which are diseased. Ambition, jealousy, envy, vengeance, superstition and despair lodge in us with such a natural right of possession that we recognize the likeness of them in the animals too—not excluding so unnatural a vice as cruelty, for in the midst of compassion we feel deep down some bitter-sweet pricking of malicious pleasure at seeing others suffer it . . . If anyone were to remove the seeds of such qualities in Man he would destroy the basic properties of our lives. So, too, in all polities there are duties which are necessary, yet not merely abject but vicious as well: the vices hold their rank there and are used in order to stitch and bind us together, just as poisons are used to preserve our health.[17]

Why are some Machiavellis willing to argue openly, against their own interests, for the use of deception in politics?

To change the tense of the question to the past, the answer is that some of the Machiavellis were unaware that their theories would be published; but the answer is also that their theorizing shows what is, in them, the paradoxical desire to discover and communicate the truth. The Machiavellis did their best to show that consistent truth-telling, like ordinary kindness, works against political success and, if indulged in by a leader, thwarts his purposes and is likely to be socially destructive. Imagine, they might ask, what chaos would be created by a leader who let no emergency prevent him from saying, without evasion or exaggeration, just what he knew to be the truth. What the theorizing Machiavellis tell us is uncomfortable. Yet as social analysts, though not as actors in real life, the Machiavellis were anti-Machiavellian, because they were so open in disclosing the unpalatable social realities that are normally, by Machiavellian preference, hidden from public view. How could they have expected to remain effective Machavellis after they had bared their views and stratagems?

To make this point in a more discriminating way, let me return to the familiar theorists. Shang Yang was both ideologue and implementer. There is no explicit information on why he put his ideas into writing, but Ssu-ma Ch'ien has him approve the saying, "Pleasing words are adorned, direct words are real; bitter words are medicine, sweet words cause disease."[18] Han Fei is said to have written his works out of anger at the Han king's failure to accept his advice and out of frustration at the choice of incompetent, self-seeking ministers. Insofar as the advice he gave was on the institution of competent government, there was every reason for him to publicize his views; but when he showed himself to be fully Machiavellian, in his advice to the king of Ch'in and in many of his essays, he was furthering his career by disclosing what, as a potential implementer, it would have been wiser for him to conceal. Besides, when he gave rulers the advice to deceive, he could not help drawing suspicion on his own motives—someone who finds it easy to tell others to lie must be himself willing to lie easily. As for Kautilya, if he had had the desire to build his system of rules on a developed hierarchy of principles, or if he had been more interested in the principles than in the serried array of consequences, he might be considered a sociologist. His writing makes one feel that he was concerned to demonstrate his acuteness and sense for useful detail more than his ruthlessness. Whereas Han Fei may have dreamed of being the inscrutable ruler placed at the still center of the web of politics, sensitive to the least tremor of its threads and able from there to rule everything and everyone with no effort, Kautilya was more the planner and systematizer of details. And Machiavelli, both the discoverer of the unpalatable truth and the enthusiast for Italy, would have liked to have been the adviser, on Machiavellian principles, of an intelligently ruthless and grandly beneficent prince; but he seems to have been too warm a man to reach more than an imaginative identification with a radically Machiavellian ruler. Unlike him, Guicciardini showed the ability to be ruthlessly Machiavellian in practice; but he, too, felt the discoverer's need to put down and communicate what he had discovered, some of his reflections limited, however, to his own family.

No one of these Machiavellis felt any anomaly in telling the truth as he saw it or in proposing his faithfulness to a ruler he advised to be suspicious of everyone, advisers included, who was close to him. Shang Yang taught and acted according to the rules of merciless but, as he believed, objective truth. When Han Fei wrote advice for a ruler, he did not have to worry that he was informing the ruler's enemies of anything of which they were unaware—it is more the ruler's than the plotter's danger to fall into complacency. While Han Fei himself was an object of suspicion to Li Ssu and the emperor, it is reasonable to conjecture that neither Han Fei nor Li Ssu thought that their Machiavellian memorials would become known outside the court. The memorials' inclusion in Ssu-ma Ch'ien's history comes in a later era, and their notoriety is the work of their Confucian enemies. Kautilya was merely acting the methodical, practical thinker. And although Machiavelli took pride in *The Prince*, he himself did not have it published.

I imagine (but do not know) that, in the last analysis, each of these Machiavellis would have wanted his work published even if he had thought that he was advising potential enemies; or he would have at least wanted it published after he could no longer be an actor or adviser in politics. I say this because each of them was proud of his insights into the political process and because such pride asks to be confirmed by general recognition among those the writer imagines as a knowing audience. The Machiavellian theorist is caught in an existential dilemma: he wants to be praised for what he should leave hidden unless he wants to be blamed.

Despite the complications I have outlined, the interest of the Machiavelli in communicating the political truth is such that, as the name of a kind of theory, the word *Machiavellian* should stand for an attempt to arrive at truth, not falsehood. Evidently, the word—implying the revelation of the political need to deceive—arouses quite as much dislike for its truth as for the falsity it describes and, within reason, recommends. The result is that such words as *Machiavellian* and *anti-Machiavellian* are confined to a definition that is too categorical. Just as there is nothing to prevent a person from being Machiavellian in one sense and the opposite in another, there is nothing to prevent anyone from being Machiavellian and anti-Machiavellian at the same time. This happened in ancient China and happens now.

Why are people often ready to adopt or condone political practices they know to be immoral?

The answer is that the impulse to follow a leader and the need to belong to a group can fix or overrule much of what we feel to be moral, that is, of what our conscience approves. To explain, I go back to the human tie of trust, this time to the analogy between the trust among individuals and the trust they have for their group, nation, or leader. How does the group or leader gain the trust of the individual? In the long run, not by abstractions, theories, declarations, or even by deeds as such. Instead, the trust is a psychosocial perception whose exact quality could be described only by something like a combination of history, economics, sociology, and individual and social psychology. In a practical sense, this trust, so immediate in response and so complicated to analyze, can be the accomplishment only of a society, not of any individual within it.

The possibilities are many: The group or nation may or may not trust its leaders and may or may not believe that rules and customs are being observed as they should be. If the group does accord its trust to a leader, the trust implies that the leader has a Machiavellian attitude toward all other groups. That is, a group's members assume that it will be defended when necessary at the expense of other groups. Loyalty to the group means that the group comes first, largely because its members insist that they do. A father is a father because he defends *his* children, not those of others. Therefore, even a leader who is not himself particularly ambitious or ready to be cruel or deceptive knows that he had best be Machiavellian toward outside groups because that is what is expected of him and makes him, if not a good person, a good leader. He is *required* to act in a way that in a private person is considered unethical; but (as I have said) because a private person's ethical life appears to depend on the stability of the group, the leader's act that is unethical in the private sense is granted the status of an act that is ethical in the higher sense, that of the act that makes ethics at all possible.[19]

Consider: One's ethical sense or conscience determines how and to what extent one approves of oneself; one's kind of conscience and self-approval are fixed by one's early personal relationships and the group to which one is most deeply related; and so one's ethical evaluation of oneself must also depend on the perspective from which the group views everything that affects it. It is reasonable to go further: For the many people who are highly dependent on the good opinion of others, what conscience says about an act depends on who suggests or performs it. Therefore conscience tends to be equivalent to social conformity with the opinions and acts of the majority of whatever group is closest and most important to us. Even in extreme cases of the violation of ordinary morality, this tendency to conform is more likely to exact its price in inward suffering than to inspire actual disobedience. Mostly we conform, and when we refuse to, we mostly do so in company with the particular nonconformists with whose refusal we find ourselves moved to conform.[20]

Let me give two convincingly researched examples of the conjunction of conscience with conformity, both examples taken from the history of Nazi Germany. The first is Robert Lifton's *The Nazi Doctors: Medical Killing and the Psychology of Genocide,* and the second, Christopher Browning's *Ordinary Men: Reserve Police Battalion 101 and the Final Solution in Poland.* Lifton, who struggles with the paradox of the physician transformed from a healer to a killer, points out that the German psychiatrists he deals with were usually, as they identified themselves, servants of the state. This made it difficult for them to contemplate defying the state.[21] But they also were affected by the ideal of "scientific" racism and by the desire to remain loyal to the collective will they saw themselves as expressing. The result, in Lifton's term, was that their private consciences were "doubled" by an adaptive, public one:

> The way in which doubling allowed Nazi doctors to avoid guilt was not by the elimination of conscience but what can be called the *transfer of conscience.* The requirements of conscience were transferred to the Auschwitz self, which placed it within its own criteria for good (duty, loyalty to group, "improving" Auschwitz conditions, etc.), thereby freeing the original self from responsibility for actions there . . . The Nazi doctors knew that they selected, but did not interpret selection as murder. One level of disavowal, then, was the Auschwitz self's altering of the meaning of murder; and on another, the repudiation by the original self of *anything* done by the Auschwitz self.[22]

Browning uses the evidence of a battalion of mostly new recruits, middle-aged family men—dock workers, truck drivers, warehouse and construction workers, white-collar workers—men without the experience of battle and without the hatred that moves soldiers whose companions have been killed by the enemy.[23] Three weeks after they arrived in Poland, the battalion's fatherly commander, Major Wilhelm Trapp, assembled his men and, distraught and half crying, told them that they were faced by a frightfully unpleasant task. He did not like the assignment, he said, which was very regrettable, "but the orders came from the highest authorities. If it would make their task any easier, the men should remember that in Germany the bombs were falling on women and children." Besides, the Jews had instigated the American boycott and some of those in the village had relations with the partisans.

The battalion's assignment was to round up Jews in the nearby village, separate out the men of working age, who were to be sent to a work camp, and to shoot all the others. Because this task was difficult, said Trapp, if any older member of the battalion did not feel up to it, he could be excused.[24] A dozen of about the five hundred men stepped out and excused themselves immediately. This act was serious because it "meant leaving one's comrades and admitting that one was 'too weak' or 'cowardly.'"[25] After the actual shooting began, others also excused themselves. But if they wished, even the eighty percent of the men who participated in the killing could have taken advantage of the confusion and avoided shooting anyone.[26] Some of them avoided shooting children; one shot only the children of mothers his neighbor had shot, so as "to release children unable to live without their mothers."[27]

When the men of the battalion returned to their barracks, they were

> depressed, angry, embittered, and shaken. They ate little but drank heavily. Major Trapp made the rounds, trying to console and reassure them, and again placing the responsibility on higher authorities. But neither the drink nor Trapp's consolation could wash away the sense of shame and horror that pervaded the barracks.[28]

By a silent consensus, the massacre was not discussed at all; but some of the men had nightmares. From then on, the battalion was usually relieved of actual killing; but when its men were nevertheless obliged to kill, they proved to be "increasingly efficient and calloused executioners."[29]

Since it had been possible for the men in this battalion to evade killing, the explanation that suggests itself is that these policemen found it too difficult to disobey authority and evade their duty. But many of the policemen who were involved stressed not their obedience to authority but their susceptibility to shame. How would they look in the eyes of their comrades? they asked themselves. When surveillance was lax, many did not comply with their orders. As mature men, they had been trained in pre-Nazi doctrines. Although their Nazi indoctrination as a group was heavy, it is not clear what effect it had. Everything considered, the most likely general explanation is that those who refused to shoot were refusing their share of a difficult collective obligation and risking isolation and ostracism. Those who did not shoot pleaded not morality but weakness and by this excuse allowed the others to feel strong and superior. The conclusion is that

> within virtually every social collective, the peer group exerts tremendous moral pressures on behavior and sets moral norms. If the men of Reserve Police Battalion 101 could become killers under such circumstances, what group of men cannot?[30]

I go on from the pressure the group exerts on its members to the group's response to the hierarchy by it is ruled. As a rule, this hierarchy elicits each individual's tendency to obey the person who stands at its head.[31] Whatever the group's relation to its leader, life within the group makes possible fears and enthusiasms the effect of which is increased by the force of their common acceptance. When the small leader—the leader with small pretensions or authority—is transformed into the great leader and the great leader into the grandiose leader, it becomes increasingly possible for the leader and the led to join in a drama of mutual glorification and euphoric self-worship that more than justify wars of conquest. If the enemy country defends itself strongly or is itself bound on conquest, the reaction is moral outrage. Then the homeland's physical boundaries become moral ones that everyone is obliged to guard, just as the Xinguanos are obliged to guard their land against the savages threatening their moral way of life. Under such circumstances, real or imagined enemies of the parent/leader or the parent/home become personal enemies of each faithful child. The real or imagined enemies are always close by, spies and traitors whose threat is felt to be abetted by the blindness of those who are by nature imperviously kind or unsuspecting. How, then, can one defend oneself except by what looks to an uncomprehending outsider like cunning and brutality?[32]

Should leaders, Machiavellian or not, be expected to sacrifice their welfare for that of the people they lead?

The answer is that leaders say and often believe that they are sacrificing themselves, but that it is so difficult for them to distinguish what gratifies their ego from what is good for others that the line between their egoism and altruism grows thin and can vanish altogether. This is especially true of leaders who pride themselves on their wise cunning and cunning audacity, which are given more than moral force, they believe, by their goal, the good of all those they rule. It is this relation to the more-than-individual whole that makes an act's motive irrelevant to most people. When the selfish act of an artist, scientist, or politician has results that are generally valued, the selfishness is held to be socially good. We accept a kind of *raison d'état* that allows an otherwise immoral act to be praised by the group that benefits from it, the state—Ch'in or Han, Nanda or Maurya, Spartan or Athenian, Pisan or Florentine—that by its supposed intrinsic value ennobles everything that serves its existence.

I have called the act of the artist, scientist, or politician *selfish* because I have assumed that the person who carries it out feels and thinks less of what he can do for his group than of what his group can do to gratify him. But though the selfishness of this person (as I have assumed him) is beyond doubt, it is not clear how, in practice, one distinguishes the desire to do good for others from the desire to win their approval and, with it, the fame, money, power, and self-esteem they can grant. The performer or perpetrator of a useful selfish act probably finds the distinction too difficult to make or irrelevant.

For at least partial enlightenment on this distinction, we can turn to La Rochefoucauld, the connoisseur of egoism. The first three aphorisms of his *Reflections* are as pointed a commentary on the distinction as I know. They leave little room for disinterested goodness because, says the aphorist, of the following reasons:

1. What we take for virtues are often merely a collection of different acts and personal interests pieced together by chance or our own ingenuity and it is not always because of valor or chastity that men are valiant or women chaste.

2. Self-love is the greatest flatterer of all.

3. Whatever discoveries have been made in the land of self-love, many regions still remain unexplored.[33]

Since even the intrepid aphorist qualifies with the word *often*, his first aphorism explains itself and fits experience closely enough to be taken, like the second, with full seriousness. The third aphorism demonstrates something of the explorer's curiosity and hints at future discoveries. Just what La Rochefoucauld thought was still left to be discovered about self-love is not clear from his words. However, I propose that we modify his cynicism by considering that self-love is not understood in and by itself. I mean that it must go beyond the self-loving person and find objects, acts, or persons in relation to which it can express itself. When self-love is creative, it lives by means of the tie with those who love and excuse the creator in the creation's behalf. The expressive nature of self-love makes it as often a mode of attachment and assistance as of exploitation. For this reason, it is often difficult or pointless to distinguish between altruism and egoism or praise modesty at the expense of vanity.

This difficulty becomes relevant to Machiavellism when we try to distinguish between the satisfaction a ruler gets from exercising power and the satisfaction he gets from actually helping those he rules. It is not to be expected that the ruler himself (or the government itself) should take much trouble to analyze the distinction between the exercise in itself of power and the help given to those over whom it is exercised. The distinction is also not very relevant to people whose need to be governed well in the usual sense is weaker than their need to be ruled by a forceful ruler, Machiavelli or not, or their need to venerate the ruler just because he is the ruler. Whatever the reason for the respect granted the ruler, even only fear, his use of deception and force is easy to consider moral, as I have said, in the sense of necessary for the greater good of the state. The people who find it difficult to agree are of several kinds: those who are themselves his victims; those sometimes compulsively kind or honest persons who find it impossible to distinguish between the rules of individual and public morality; those who identify themselves imaginatively, for whatever reason, with the victimized persons or states; and those whose weak identification with their own state or strong identification with some more encompassing human unit—maybe humanity at large—does not allow them to approve.

No conscience can reasonably be thought perfect, but some consciences are too unified and unbending to allow themselves to be divided. As Montaigne saw, a person with an indivisible conscience finds politics more than ordinarily difficult because there are times when either conscience must bend or politics be abjured. A psychologically easy way out of the dilemma is to agree with Robber Chih or Saint Augustine. Their views have been cited, but I add the instance in which Augustine recalls a story (from Cicero) about a pirate chief and Alexander the Great. When Alexander rebukes the pirate chief for terrorism, the answer is: "I am called a terrorist because I infest the sea with my one small ship, while you, who infest it with a whole fleet, are called an emperor."[34]

Buddhists are in partial agreement with Robber Chih and Saint Augustine because they presume that any political ambition is incompatible with full morality or peace of mind. This is the burden of the

Buddhist "birth story" according to which an unfortunate man (in a later life to be Buddha's companion, Ananda) is made co-ruler by the very excellent king named King Udaya (in a later life to be a Buddha of Compassion). The story begins with King Udaya asleep, his head trustingly laid in future-Ananda's lap. Now future-Ananda, unable to control his imagination, imagines that if he does no more than chop off the king's head, he will reign in his place as sole king. Future-Ananda rejects the idea as gross ingratitude but is unable to suppress it and it returns again and again. He awakens the king and confesses his evil thought. What does the superlatively good king do? He offers to rid future-Ananda of the immoral temptation by giving him the whole kingdom immediately. But this is not the Buddhist solution of the problem, so future-Ananda, now awakened to the nature of political ambition, says:

> I have no need of the kingdom, such a desire will cause me to be reborn in evil states: the kingdom is yours, take it: I will become an ascetic: I have seen the root of desire, it grows from a man's wish, from henceforth I will have no such wish.[35]

This moral abstinence is meant not to end but to deepen the Buddhist saint's identification with other Buddhists and, more widely, with all living beings. Is his identification a mere fantasy? Yes, one cannot avoid thinking, in relation to nonhuman creatures, and hardly more in relation to humans. But Buddhist morality apart, is it at all plausible to identify oneself with humanity as a whole, which is so distant from one's own family, so unintelligible in comparison with those who speak one's own, natural language, so uncivilized in avoiding one's own, natural kind of food, and so strange in not living by one's own real, familiar culture? Does identification with all humanity not imply an alienation from the people close at hand and raise the not implausible image of someone who loves all humanity except his own to him hateful family?

I know of no satisfying answer but see no reason why the question must always be put so extremely. The imagination is able to stretch far enough to sympathize with people close by and yet identify itself with large, distant, abstract objects like humanity as a whole. Whether or not a loyalty so large implies a psychological deficit, we know that it is at least possible and by its existence implies that narrower, more immediate loyalties can be overridden. But even if we can feel some closeness with humanity at large, experience teaches us to be cautious in extending our political ideals very far beyond home. To Plato and Aristotle, the ideal state could be only small, smaller than the Athens for whose nurturant sake Socrates was willing to sacrifice his life. The large ideals have had few convincing embodiments—if the ideals are demanding, maybe none at all. Small ideals seem to have had had a larger number of viable examples: New England government by town meeting, early Buddhist monastic rule by discussion, acephalous African tribes and Eskimo villages, and maybe the intensively cooperative *jajami* (caste) system of Indian villages.[36]

The peaceful tribes I described earlier are not easy to generalize from. Each makes the impression of having developed in very particular ways, out of a history that (I venture) took many accidental turns and was changed by persons unforeseeably peaceful, practical, and influential enough to create an ethos of peace strong enough to minimize selfishness and aggression. Each of the peaceful peoples is highly conscious of its peacefulness and of the continuing effort that has to be made to keep peace viable—the peace can continue only if most of the individuals who partake in it go on deciding and acting in a way that supports it.

Another relevant observation is that, in every case, such peace has been bought at a considerable price. The price has included a suppression of anger and other negative emotions, suppression paid for in fear of malevolent powers and witches and in a polarization of the good within the community against the chaos and evil outside it. It may also be considered a price of a sort that, among the Buid and perhaps the Semai, devotion to the community is inversely related to devotion to particular persons.

The crucial question we have raised is the relation of peace and violence to the simplicity or complexity of societies. It is reasonable to speculate that the smaller the society, the more necessary it is for it to preserve good personal relations and the easier it is to remain egalitarian—blunt condemnation and severe, objective punishment are too damaging to the inescapable intimacy of a small society. To illustrate this influence of intimacy, an anthropologist asks, How shall I become reconciled with my brother's hangman?[37] Better, if possible, to treat the offense as a family quarrel, make excuses, redefine the crime, and leave the rest to the informal responses of public opinion.

No one person dominates a small society completely, and the degree to which it exhibits or represses violence, whether internal or external, varies in accord with circumstances that cannot remain the same for long. Hostilities conducted against other groups require aggressiveness and strong leadership and lead to alliances and conquests that create larger social units and more pronounced distinctions between followers and leaders. In turn, these units and distinctions can develop into a clearer, more complicated hierarchy and stimulate greater specialization, especially in the skills needed to make war. The greater the differences in specialization—grossly between what is religious, political, and military—the greater the differences among ordinary people, subordinate officials, higher officials, and leaders, and the greater the differences in the information each individual receives and, all considered, in the individual's interests and power.

It is is true, as we have seen, that small societies can show highly Machiavellian characteristics. However, the larger the society and, correspondingly, the more complex its organization, the more likely it is to produce the forms of industry, technology, art, and science that depend on this complexity, and, along with them, the great bureaucracies and armies that support great political structures—great kingdoms or empires, great, consciously pluralistic democracies, and massively organized tyrannies—and, with them, the enormous wars of which only great states are capable.[38] And the greater and more complex the state, the greater the scope for Machiavellian maneuvers. The individual's impulse remains the same, but it can be expressed and magnified in powerful new ways.

However, even if it is true that there is such a relation between the complexity of a state and the force and deceptiveness it needs and is able to use, this truth is a highly variable one, and the peaceful and other societies we have described show together how permutable— infinitely permutable—human society can be. Thomas Gibson, who describes the Buid along with comparable but more violent societies, concludes that violence is not a necessary part of social life. There are societies, he says, that systematically devalue it, as against other societies or ruling groups within them that regard violence, in the right context and against the right enemies, as the ultimate good.[39]

All this is so important because one's morality, Machiavellian or not, depends on what or whom one joins in imagination. At one extreme, there is the narcissist, who, unable to join anyone else in imagination, identifies with himself everything he has, wants, and values: he is the sole object of his devotion. At the other, at least doctrinal extreme, the Buddhist identifies with and wants the good of all living things, and the Neo-Confucian, of the whole universe. Between these extremes, the personal or impersonal objects of identification can be a family, clan, caste, political party, nation, dialect, language, art, institution, profession, sect, or religion.

One's identification, or, rather, set of identifications, is equivalent to the range of one's loyalties and determines who or what one supports. The support is always at the potential expense of someone or something else. Identification with a small unit such as the family or clan is likely to be especially powerful because it is made up of the people to whom one is most deeply related by biology and intimacy. Because one absorbs loyalties from others, identification with family members or intimate friends leads one to absorb, that is, to inherit, their identifications. There is also a reversal of identification: by some union of identity and rebelliousness, one grows close to someone or something whose opposition to the values of parents bears their face reversed. But however one establishes one's identification, it determines to whom or to what one will be loyal and antagonistic. Maybe, the narrower one's identifications, the more numerous the hostilities into which one can naturally enter. And maybe, conversely, the wider one's identifications, the better the chance that one will regard conflicts as internal and try to solve them in the spirit of self-survival.

The narrowness or breadth of one's identification is selective in a rather particular way. I have contended that there is a genuine equivalence between the isolated narcissist or egoist and the great egoistic leader. The selfishness of their plea that their acts are motivated by necessity, by which they really mean the necessity of their own welfare, is psychologically the same. It is hard to imagine the egoist or the egoistic leader, the Napoleon, sacrificing himself for anyone else, though in psychologically weaker individuals, less insulated from the opinion of others, a public loss of honor may be insufferable. In contrast to the isolated egoist and the egoistic leader, very many individuals and many small groups have willingly sacrificed themselves for the sake of some larger group, such as a nation, or some cause or ideal with which they identify themselves. But it is hard to conceive of a nation sacrificing itself for anything at all. One reason may be that a small group can unite itself around a few individuals whose presence and dramatic resolve are psychologically too difficult to resist. Again, for most of those in the group it is a case of What will the others think? and even What will all the many who are not here think?

A whole nation is not so directly united and contains egoists, dissidents, and subgroups, all of which serve to generate currents of opinion for those who prefer to save themselves. But I think that the members of the large groups—the nations, the speakers of the same language, the adherents of the same religion—are connected with one another in imagination and conscience and therefore constitute what it is easiest to call an organic whole. By this I mean not only that each member feels himself most competent and complete when he or she lives in and with the group, but that the threatened death of the group is felt as the threatened semideath of the member. This need for and loyalty to the large group seems to be the adult's recapitulation of the child's envelopment in the family: the most natural self-sacrifice is for the sake of someone with whom one shares a deep intimacy and, in this sense, a deep union. Remarkably, in self-sacrifice, for example, a bodiless abstraction such as a nation becomes the equivalent of a parent. What this equivalence demonstrates is the great power of emotional identity and the expansiveness of imagination that makes this possible.

Loyalty to the point even of death is significant to our basic theme because the welfare of the large, organically unified group tends to become the value by which all others are measured. To those who resort to it, the plea of necessity for Machiavellian acts derives its plausibility from (and may be proportionate to) the size of the group in whose behalf it is used and the degree of its hold on its members. This relation of the plea to the group's size and degree shows that the favorite excuse for political amorality depends on the ways in which the human imagination works.

The usual political Machiavellism requires that one's primary identification should be with nothing either smaller or greater than the state. Under most circumstances, the Machiavellian insistence that everyone's welfare depends on the ruler's is exaggerated and made for the self-evident purpose of protecting the powers that be from disagreement and replacement. As Machiavelli often says in favor of republics, active disagreement can be constructive and energizing. Philosophy, artisanry, scholarship, and science all give examples of unwarlike, constructive contention. There are stories, especially in Hindu and Buddhist literature, of murderously jealous philosophers and of winners of philosophical or religious disputes who convert, kill, or banish the losers and their adherents. But philosophical battles are only rarely fatal because the combatants share an underlying loyalty to philosophical over military values and victories. Like a philosopher, an ambitious artist is in natural competition with others of his kind, who form competitive groups that have different techniques, values, and forms of imagination; but although denunciation is likely to be part of the tactics of such competing groups, violence—even murder, of which history does show examples—is rare, because artists have an underlying respect for or identification with art and art's nonmilitary means.

Contemporary scholars and especially scientists are likely to find it harder than anyone else to confine their loyalty to a political entity or even culture. Not that they do not often very willingly act for parochial or self-serving ends or bow to the coercive or fatherly power of their state; but, by the nature of their professions, both scholars and scientists develop a loyalty to their rules of analysis and evidence, as well as to the practice of working in cooperation with all the others of their kind. Within the limits of their enterprise, the identification of scholars and scientists is, in effect, with scholar-humanity or science-humanity, and the struggles they wage with antagonistic scholars, scientists, or points of view are always recognized in theory and fairly often in fact as subject to the judgment, demonstrated over a reasonably long time, of their peers everywhere. In spite of local evidence to the contrary, scholarship and science are by inherent tendency both democratic and universal. But who is to say just how powerfully inherent an "inherent" tendency may be, and even if it is inherent, as is believed, how it will work itself out in the unpredictable vagaries of history?

How can we understand the reckless boldness of great Machiavellian leaders?

The answer is that they are adventurers whose most profound satisfaction is to overcome great dangers, make great conquests, and dominate everyone and everything by force of their will. Let me explain my answer step by step. We are bound to one another by the ties of parental and sexual love, friendliness, empathy, sympathy, the need for help, and the tedium and fear of loneliness. However, these mutual ties do not prevent us any more than other, less intelligent primates from frustrating, exploiting, hating, hurting, and killing one another. We are Machiavellian, anti-Machiavellian, and neither, and all of these at once, so that even under the best circumstances, ambivalence is inescapable and creates complicated webs of relationship. We learn soon enough that the love of those who are close to us entails the devaluation and perhaps hatred of those who appear to pose them a threat, sometimes only by being different from them in some sensitive respect. In view of such entangled ambivalences, which, for all their ordinariness, are hard to analyze in clear detail, thinkers who assume either that human beings are fundamentally good or fundamentally bad cast light on their own nature rather than the human nature they presume to describe. But perhaps such extreme views are stated in order to recommend the practices supposed to follow from them rather than to establish the claim that the views are literally true.[40]

Whether human nature is good, bad, or neither, it is a fact that it requires everyone to learn to make and give in to demands, to rule and obey. In a relationship of no more than two people, one of them is likely to be dominant in word or act, or be dominant in relation to certain subjects or kinds of words or acts. In this sense, all human life tends to be hierarchical, first, and most intimately, in the nuclear family and then in the extended family, which in some cultures is the primary context of life. For a time, parents dominate the close family, the father in certain respects, the mother in others; and at first the older children dominate the younger. But coalitions form, of some children against others or against one or both parents; and one or both parents may side with a particular child or particular children, in general or in certain respects. Because of the need of children to remain protected and, all the same, to achieve independence, they cannot merely obey but must also react with anger and concealed or open revolt—the concealed anger in which a person reacts to a parental regime is the anger by which the same person imposes the regime on the next generation.

It is therefore plausible to assume that the desire and ability to obey and to rule are developed first within the nuclear family and then, later, by analogy with familial relationships—this is the very analogy on which Confucianism is based. Typically, the ruler thinks of himself and is thought of by his subjects as a father. In any case, people seem to want either to rule, at least in a small way, or to be ruled; most often, probably, they want both. Circumstances, the force of desire, and the tactics that are used determine the outcome in fact, which is the balance between ruling and subordination in one's life.

Among the tactics used, some are clearly unconscious. One's training, appearance, manner of speech, knowledge, self-assurance, and many other factors play their roles. So does one's ability to gain and hold allies, make attractive promises, and give emotional and physical rewards. Beginning with the nuclear family, therefore, all the tactics we identify as Machiavellian come into play, even though the members of the family know one another so well that some tactics, such as lying or boasting, may be ineffective.

In spite of the differences between societies, from small acephalous tribes to great empires, well-defined hierarchical relations make for the smooth functioning of society and, to that extent, for satisfaction with society. When it is not clear who gives what orders or whether some authority should or should not be obeyed, the result is uncertainty, social friction, wasted effort, and general dissatisfaction (as is true, we know, of the society of chimpanzees). Further confusion may be created by the potential leaders whose hopes are raised by the possibilities they sense in an uncertain situation. Such leaders may prefer a hierarchy unclear enough to allow them to rise by irregular means. This unclarity may also be preferred by someone who likes the feel of impending disorder, the smell of chaos-to-be, or who hopes to gain some advantage with the help of disorder.

For all these reasons, the relation of the leader to the led—even if only as the first among equals—is primal and universal. But how is this related to Machiavellian deception and ruthlessness? The answer is, through ambition: While it is usual for a leader to be conscientious, extreme ambition, especially of a political sort, is unlikely to be compatible with scrupulous truthfulness and the avoidance of even illegal force. The success of great political ambition does not require cruelty and lying in themselves, but, rather, an elastic or selective attitude toward cruelty, kindness, lies, and truth. Such elasticity comes most easily when the ambitious person persuades himself of the truth of two conclusions. The first is that the cause served is so great that cruelty or lying in its service is not a moral fault, any more than a surgeon's operation is cruel or that the surgeon lies when he expresses his own and his patient's hopes. In his essay "Politics as a Vocation," Max Weber comments on this conclusion:

> From no ethics in the world can it be concluded when and to what extent the ethically good purpose "justifies" the ethically dangerous means and ramifications. . . . Whoever wants to engage in politics at all, and especially in politics as a vocation . . . must know that he is responsible for what may become of himself . . . I repeat, he lets himself in for the diabolic forces lurking in all violence.[41]

The second conclusion the ambitious leader needs in order to justify the elasticizing of truth and kindness is that he or she is so vital to the success of the great cause that any act committed to ensure the leader's well-being is justified by the importance of the enterprise as a whole. There is also the auxiliary conviction that anyone else in the leader's position would have no choice but to commit the same acts.

So far, I have not mentioned the ambitious persons whose conscience is either weak to begin with or becomes weakened with experience as they discover how many others fail to regard them with the respect they, the ambitious, accord themselves. But the joining of ambition with consciencelessness or cynicism is rarely enough for success. In politics, great success usually requires the ambition to be linked with an ideal—the motif of the leader's public conscience—that arouses the enthusiasm of leader and followers alike. It is not hard to imagine that a leader may combine belief in such an ideal with a cynical understanding of its usefulness in furthering his own power and with no more than a simulated interest in the welfare of people other than himself. As I will point out, maybe Stalin was of this type.

There is one crucial trait of the Machiavellian leader, suspiciousness, that needs to be mentioned at this point. A certain degree of suspiciousness is no more than a response to one's experience; one learns to anticipate that persons, like events, are not always what they seem. Some persons, as I have mentioned, find it hard to trust others. Their suspiciousness may be the result of the unreliability of their parents, of their life in a hostile human environment, or of their own unreliability projected onto others. But the suspicions of otherwise unsuspicious persons are aroused by their active pursuit of a great ambition or by their possession of great power for which there are dangerous competitors. Because the importance of a failure is proportional to the strength of the ambition it thwarts, it is natural to ascribe the failure not to chance or one's own shortcomings but to the ill will of others. Impelled by this conviction, the greatly ambitious person is driven to use devious methods against competitors; and the more the same methods are ascribed to them, the more readily the ambitious person will resort to them in the future.

The position of the ambitious leader who fears rivals (which one does not?) is the same, and his imagination, like that of Li Ssu or Kautilya, is apt to multiply clever expedients and draw on the vague but powerful fears that inhabit everyone's fantasies. The suspicious leader then builds up a perhaps inherited force of people skilled in spying out and countering hostility; but these people, no less expert in cheating than in detecting cheating in others, must themselves be suspected. The classic means by which the leader guards himself against these guardians is to set them to guarding against one another. This increases the general level of suspiciousness and mutual scrutinizing of the experts in suspicion and leads to the exacerbation of the leaders' own suspicions to a possibly paranoiac extreme. Italo Calvino recreates the extreme when he describes a suspicious king's suspicion-filled palace:

Here the walls have ears. Spies are stationed behind every drapery, curtain, arras. Your spies, the agents of your secret service: their assignment is to draft detailed reports on the palace conspiracies. The court teems with enemies, to such an extent that it is increasingly difficult to tell them from friends; it is known for sure that the conspiracy that will dethrone you will be made up of your ministers and officials. And you know that every secret service has been infiltrated by agents of the opposing secret service. Perhaps all the agents in your pay work also for the conspirators, are

themselves conspirators; and thus you are obliged to continue
paying them, to keep them quiet as long as possible.[42]

Of course, even paranoiac suspicion may fit usefully into the context of plotting, counterplotting, and universal suspiciousness. No
wonder that in such an atmosphere loyalty becomes a precarious and
precious virtue.

Great, unscrupulous ambition destroys, and yet it also has great
constructive power. Perhaps this can be driven home imaginatively by
recalling that the trickster is a culture hero because his/her spontaneous acts of egoism create human culture. The moral applies to morality
itself no less than to material culture. To be renewed, virtue must first
be endangered or destroyed; repentance, which can only follow transgression, is regarded as superior to a merely fixed virtuousness. Just as
the condition of great saintly acts is likely to be the sinfulness, perhaps
of the saint himself, that preceded them, the condition of great political
acts is likely to be a Machiavelli's audacious selfishness. We have seen
this in the creation of the first Chinese empire by Li Ssu and Huang Ti,
in the creation of the Indian empire by Chandragupta and, later, by
Ashoka, whose great desire to be kind emerged out of his great ambition to conquer, and in the creation of the Zulu nation by Shaka. Europeans think first of Alexander the Great and Napoleon. Robespierre,
too, fits the role. So, maybe, does a scholar-politician such as Marx. So
do great explorers. Columbus discovered the New World by luck, skill,
and unrelenting, unscrupulous ambition. Cortés, who destroyed one
civilization and started another, is characterized by his latest historian
as someone worthy of applause by any Machiavelli:

> The word which best expresses Cortés action is "audacity": it con-
> tains a hint of imagination, impertinence, a capacity to perform
> the unexpected which differentiates it from mere valor. Cortés
> was also decisive, flexible, and had few scruples . . . One does not
> have to be a believer in any special theory that great men domi-
> nate history to see at once that Cortés' combination of intelligence
> and prudence, bravery and originality were decisive in the
> extraordinary events in Mexico between 1519 and 1521.[43]

That brings up the issue of conscience and of those who, because
they lack it, are called *psychopaths* or *sociopaths* (in current professional
terminology, those affected by an "antisocial personality disorder").
Experience shows how attractive their freedom from inward moral

restraints can be. When successful, they have a crowd of admirers and, maybe, some friends, even though it must be conceded that they miss satisfactions of which many quite ordinary people are capable: genuinely friendly relations, genuine trust, and the genuine closeness to others that is the best antidote to fear and loneliness. These satisfactions are also likely to be weakened by the at least residual Machiavellism of greatly ambitious persons of any kind. Ironic examples of the danger are such public saints as Tolstoy (the master, in his novels, of empathy) and Gandhi (able to retain sympathy for his enemies), whose sainthood was the obverse of their insensitivity or ruthlessness toward those members of their immediate families who were taught, in act by the saints themselves, to hate them (Gandhi's erring son was much better at angering him than were Gandhi's enemies).

However, since they act in accord with their characters, the practitioners and advocates of Machiavellism cannot be expected to change or, except under unusual circumstances, to want to change. Max Weber says that the leaders he calls charismatic have emerged in all places and epochs "in the two figures of the magician and the prophet on the one hand, and in the elected war leader, the gang leader and *condotierre* on the other."[44] Persons like these may well begin their lives in relative human isolation, for which the dream and reality of success compensates them just as they most want. Take the simple example of such an antisocial Machiavellian as a gang leader. Why does so able a man take so dangerous a path? When a leading member of the Mafia, turned informer for his own selfish reasons, was asked what had been so good about being a mobster, he answered:

> It's the greatest thing that a human could experience. The flavor is so good. The high is so natural. When you sneeze, 15 handkerchiefs come out. I mean, everywhere you go, people just can't do enough for you ... It's unbelievable. In the Mob, you've got friends; you belong to an army, something that is so powerful. You're with the élite. Your word is the law, you're like the judge and jury. Anything you say is final.

Asked what, apart from arrest and the need to disguise his whole life, was the downside, this mobster's answer was the one we have learned to expect:

> The killing. And the treachery. Everybody's jealous of something in "this thing." There's no security, and you're never safe. You learn how to read eyes. You gotta be a good manipulator. You

gotta meet somebody; you don't even know if you're gonna come back.[45]

As for the war leader, he may be such out of necessity rather than desire, but he may be of the type that believes, in the words of Carl von Clausewitz (1780–1831), the author of *On War*, that today (he is speaking of his own time) no other means but war can educate a people in the spirit of boldness.

Nothing else will counteract the softness and the desire for ease which debase the people in times of growing prosperity and increasing trade. A people and nation can hope for a strong position in the world only if national character and familiarity with war fortify each other by continual interaction.[46]

This statement has the ring of the advice given by Shang Yang and other Machiavellians. Friedrich Nietzsche (1844–1900), whose career in the army was not successful by any standard, had fantasies of warlike accomplishment and of the necessity and heroism of actual war. In one passage he speaks of "every great war" with all the enthusiasm at his ably rhetorical command:

For the present we know of no other means by which that rude energy that characterizes the camp, that profound impersonal hatred, that murderous coldbloodedness with a good conscience, that common fire in the destruction of the enemy, that proud indifference to great losses, to one's own existence and that of one's friends, that inarticulate, earthquake-like shuddering of the soul . . . Culture can in no way do without passions, vices and acts of wickedness.[47]

In the same passage, Nietzsche supposes that the attempt to find surrogates for war will perhaps show that the humanity of the European has become so enfeebled that it can be renewed only by "the greatest and most terrible wars." In another, rather later fantasy Nietzsche speaks of the possible day when "a people distinguished by wars and victories" and the highest military discipline and thought will, of its own free will, "demolish its entire military machine." This fantasy is accompanied by the idea that every individual state must and can accept as its supreme maxim that it is "better to perish than to hate and fear."[48]

War or peace, Nietzsche's emphasis is on extreme, fearless adventure. A recent philosopher, J. Glen Gray, who served in various capacities for four years in the American army during World War II, confirms that many men both hate and love combat, and that there is even "a delight in destruction."[49] A contemporary military expert says, discouragingly for most of us, that war is a response to and manifestation of the feeling of power that results from coping with the unknown. War can make sense more than any other activity, he says,

> only to the extent that it is experienced not as a means but as an end. However unpalatable the fact, the real reason why we have wars is that men like fighting, and women like those men who are prepared to fight on their behalf.[50]

These words may be too simple and categorical, but our past history has not shown them to be mistaken. They fit the sense of militant heroism that impels the more audacious Machiavellians, who see life as a great adventure. While all the Machiavellis we have studied advise that boldness should be restrained by intelligent caution, their heroes are not cautious men, and the caution they advise should not be taken as fear of a dangerous goal but as the caution of the mountain climber choosing the rock faces best for climbing and driving his piton into rock as solid as he can find above him. Or if we use the analogy of the criminal—because the Machiavelli's bold ambition is matched by the reticence of his conscience—the caution is like that of the criminal whose response to the greatness or complexity of the crime he proposes is to plan it carefully and keep in mind that the plan will most likely have to be corrected by improvisation on the spot.

It therefore does not impress a great, bold Machiavelli if one points out to him that his audacity may easily lead to failure. The great gamble that fires his imagination is even more important than its success, and while he surely prefers to succeed, failure, too, has its charms: Persons who lead others into spectacular disasters also enter into history, and there, in the serenity of print and the turbulence of imagination, they gain admirers and imitators. It is precisely the appeal of danger and the skill that circumvents it that tempts the heroic Machiavelli. Even if he is somehow religious, the moral cautions of ordinary religion cannot impress him very seriously; ordinary moralizing sets his teeth on edge; and he laughs at the warning that great villainy is very risky. I imagine that in practice the great Machiavellian combines a degree of fatalism—something unavoidable, he knows not what, may thwart or prove fatal to him—with faith in himself and his freely exercised ability to make his own fateful decisions. Much of his success or failure must depend on chance, and something of the success or failure must depend on his insight into people, into how he can use them for his own ends, and sometimes on his ability to exercise an intelligent restraint on his appetites.

I now abandon these generalizations and go on to three twentieth-century examples that are inescapable in any discussion of Machiavellism. These examples show how a great Machiavelli can be the conductor of a whole nation, which performs its public life to the rhythm set by his baton. If a Machiavelli's ability lies in the silent balancing of persons and acts, he is unlikely to be acclaimed as great. But if he dares to do much more, his acts give outward evidence of his genius, to which his rhetoric adds a compelling voice and the ideal he professes a seductive leitmotif. Shaka's Zulu state, too, had a professed ideal—his achievement of intertribal peace at the cost of intratribal terror seems a fair exchange to at least the *post factum* members of the Zulu community. The three great tyrants of the twentieth century, Hitler, Stalin, and Mao exploited ideals they found half-ready for use. Thanks largely to these ideals, each of the three became an omnipotent father whose terror oppressed his children but whose death diminished them.[51]

Mao, to whom I will return only in the following chapter, held the ideal of the Marxist regeneration of China. The ideal of Hitler was the Nazi regeneration of Germany. Persuaded by those who insisted on racial purity, he decided to ensure the "purity" of German blood and do "the Lord's work" by destroying the Jews, who were using their Marxist creed, he was convinced, to defeat all Germans and, possibly, all humanity.[52] For the sake of this ideal, he took on himself to prove the superiority of the German national community *(Volksgemeinschaft)* over Marxism, which set class against class, and to revive the German will to make war and conquer "life-room" for the Germans in the East.[53]

Because of his desire to strengthen his nation by war and because of his brutal use of force, internal spying, and denunciation of citizens by one another, Hitler fits the image of the Legalistic and Kautilyan ruler and Machiavellian prince. Like them, he regarded the force of will as politically decisive. He calculated the effect of his decisions on the public, to which he was well attuned, dramatized himself to great public effect, used bold surprise and subterfuge, and, though personally squeamish, was thoroughly ruthless. His self-dramatization did not prevent him from adopting the Machiavellian's care to keep secrets hidden. "I have an old principle," he confided, "only to say what must be said to him who must know it, and only when he must know it"; and he played off one person against the other, as all the Machiavellians recommend. His tactics were a mixture "of effrontery, terror and reassurance."[54]

Hitler's willingness to work in disregard of law is formally contrary to the principles of the Chinese Legalists, though they would not have denied him the right to pass whatever universally applicable laws seemed necessary to him. Hitler's early paranoid anxieties were over faceless enemies such as the Jews and Marxists, but defeat in Russia turned his suspicions against his officers and intimates.[55] His concern over enemies and his attempts to hunt them down fits the suspiciousness recommended by Han Fei and Kautilya. However, the Holocaust for which he is responsible makes the impression of an act that only a paranoiac fanatic could actually carry out.

Will, which in practice meant his own will, has a paramount role in Hitler's thought. He writes in *Mein Kampf*, "From among the host of millions of men, who as individuals more or less clearly . . . sense these truths . . . *one man* must step forward in order with apodictic force to form granite principles."[56] When this man's will becomes collective, the German community will be "closely bound by sacred oath, ready for every decision, never willing to capitulate" and "master of every affliction."[57] As Martin Heidegger proclaimed in 1933 on his inauguration as Rector of Freiburg University, "The Führer himself, and he alone, is the present and future reality for Germany and its law." By the basic law of 1939, "all public power in the state as in the movement stems from the Führer's power," the Führer himself being conceived as "the executor of the whole people's will."[58]

Historians point out that Nazi Germany was far from internally monolithic; its new agencies competed with one another and with the old ones. But Germany was dominated by Hitler's racial, warlike ideal, and, all things told, he was successful in keeping any law or bureaucratic procedure from limiting his use of power.[59] To a believer, his Machiavellism fits Hegel's declaration, long before, that "world history occupies a higher ground" than morality, because

> moral claims which are irrelevant must not be brought into collision with world-historical needs and their accomplishment. The litany of private virtues—modesty, humility, philanthropy, and fairness—must not be raised against them.[60]

When things were going badly for him toward the end of his life, Hitler spoke of his great nervous suffering but added, "Just the same, I am grateful to Destiny for letting me live, because I believe . . . "[61] This statement is most likely sincere in spite of its self-conscious dramatization. The same historian who says, caustically, that Hitler stands alone because of "the grandiose barbarism of his political vision and the moral emptiness of his character," also tells of his extraordinary political and histrionic talents, which he summarizes in the words:

> As a political animal, he was a nonpareil in his own time. In his person were combined an indomitable will and self-confidence, a superb sense of timing that told him when to wait and when to act, the intuitive ability to sense the anxieties and resentments of the masses and to put them into words that transformed everyone with a grievance into a hero in the struggle to save the national soul, a mastery of the arts of propaganda, great skill in exploiting the weaknesses of rivals and antagonists, and a ruthlessness in the execution of his designs that was stayed neither by scruples of loyalty nor by moral considerations.[62]

Like Hitler, Stalin needed both his own faith and the faith of the public over which he tyrannized.[63] He read Machiavelli with enormous respect, we are told, and he was certainly a Machiavellian genius in the use of force and fraud, which he exercised in the service of Marxist doctrines the exact form of which he himself determined.[64]* The old Bolshevik Fedor Raskolnikov, an ambassador who defected out of fear for his life, described Stalin as a narrow sectarian with a superhuman strength of will. Stalin, he said, tried to force life into a narrow framework, and when it resisted, mangled it to fit. He used passing events to entrench himself and destroy rivals who appeared to be far more intelligent than he was; their superior culture and rhetoric were no match for the Machiavellian skills that Stalin deployed.[65]

Like Hitler, Stalin valued ruthlessness, for which he gave the ideological excuse he at least half-believed that it was all for the sake of a just society. Despising the softer emotions, he did everything to inspire his

---

*Stalin's intimate, Kamenev, wrote the preface for a volume of Machiavelli's writings. "It lauded *The Prince* for offering 'a magnificent picture of the zoological features of the struggle for power in a slave society, in which a rich minority ruled over a toiling majority.' This was quite probably an Aesopian message about the Soviet State. But what satisfaction Kamenev derived from making it must have been eclipsed by that of the Machiavellian from whom— very possibly—there had emanated the suggestion that he dig his own grave deeper by writing that essay on the Florentine. It became evidence against him in the 1936 show trial" (R. C. Tucker, *Stalin in Power*, p. 287).

colleagues' fears. A biographer who consulted a large number of Stalin's personal acquaintances came to the conclusion that his cruelty "was quite simply an inalienable attribute of his being."[66] For a long time, his associates thought that this cruelty was necessary. As Khrushchev later wrote, "We justified what was happening in a lumberjack's terms: when you chop down a forest, the chips fly."[67]

In 1927, a Russian neurologist who visited Stalin at his own invitation (then suddenly died) told his assistant that Stalin was a dangerous paranoiac.[68] But Stalin's paranoia, if it was such in a clinical sense, did not make him the less effective as a political leader; he remained an efficient, which is to say, sane planner and ruler. "His actions were perfectly logical from his point of view and even somewhat in keeping with Leninist policy," and he had the ability "to run the State for decades, unchecked and unopposed."[69]

Stalin had a profound need for enemies, but, as close-mouthed as Han Fei's ideal ruler, he hid his aims, disconcerted people by his questions, confronted them abruptly, and shifted with practiced ease from small but terrifying threats to charming nothings and then back again to threats.[70] He was able to give friendly reassurances to a person on the very day the person was to be arrested as a prelude to his execution. His secret informers, willing and reluctant, proliferated in every byway; and it became a deadly crime to fail to denounce everything in the least suspicious, even (or particularly) in one's own family. As *Pravda* informed its readers, it was "a crime against the party and people for a Communist not to see through the enemy in good time and expose him, if only in some small matter, for a larger hostile action can be concealed behind a smaller one."[71]

Loyalty and trust were not qualities in which Stalin put much stock, any more than gratitude. His suspicion never slept: it was precisely the Bolshevik Old Guard which he distrusted most. Even men who had been closely associated with him in carrying out the Second Revolution as members of the Politburo or the Central Committee were executed, committed suicide or died in the camps.[72]

Hitler trusted his close associates such as Göring, Himmler, and Göbbels, but Stalin, who, in suspiciousness, was a quick student, learned to trust no one. From his standpoint, even his wife betrayed him, by committing suicide. He proved the equal of the most meticulously suspicious Machiavellian when he forbade his closest associates to assemble in groups of any size, whether at home, in their offices, or in their villas, without his express permission.[73]

Stalin has been judged to have been a combination, like Hitler, of profound mediocrity with extraordinary strength of will. His intellectual limitations were more than concealed by the sycophancy of those who had no choice except to glorify his virtues, give his statements scriptural authority, and publish his *Problems of Leninism* in seventeen million copies in fifty-two languages, and his boring *Short Course* in over forty-two million copies in sixty-seven languages.[74] Stalin needed all the evidence he could get (actually, more than he could get) that he was a truly great leader, whose enemies opposed him in order to thwart the expression of his greatness—his version of Marxism was unusual in emphasizing the role of men great enough to alter history. Therefore those whose memories misrepresented the truth as he wanted it had to be silenced along with their lies.[75]

To make his victories complete, Stalin would put real or imagined rivals on show trials, at which, persuaded by deception, threat, or torture, they incriminated themselves in persuasively invented detail. In one case a prisoner was induced to confess by a form of moral torture, which was the murder of persons who were absolute strangers to him.[76] It is not surprising that Stalin's faculty for human relationships was only vestigial.[77] Yet he remained human and social in the sense that he needed to be persuaded not only of his greatness but also of his innocence. An expert actor, he could throw himself into a role with such conviction that he was able in some odd sense to believe in his own deception. For instance, he carefully read and annotated a two-volume dossier of fatal evidence, all, as he knew, fabricated, against a writer he wanted dead.[78] His readiness to sacrifice innocents was meant, it seems, to unmask the guilty among the crowd of those accused, persons whose guilt, as proved by their own words, exonerated him from any blame. He insisted on being informed of what went on in the interrogation of important prisoners, and if any of them refused to sign a confession, he would grow restless and unable to sleep.[79] His victims were often links in a chain in which the accuser or assassin would in turn be accused or assassinated. Stalin's always renewed suspicions were turned into a suspiciousness in which every Russian was ordered to take part. Every enterprise and institution held ritual meetings at which the "enemies of the people" were condemned and their deaths demanded. The announcement of a death sentence would be greeted "with thunderous applause. And since it is not always pleasant to lie, people persuaded each other and themselves that all this was right and good."[80]

Stalin's pattern of action was meant to allow him to rule over not only his own time but over Russian history, with which he was obsessed, and to verify his own image of himself as the great man, the doer of great deeds, in a world full of enemies, who, if not destroyed, would destroy him. So he cut down all possible rivals until he alone remained politically visible. "The Stalin era can be symbolized by this scene, later recounted by Khrushchev, however apocryphal or not: Stalin strolling with maniacal delight among his own statues" (the number of which he could deprecate when he acted the role of the selfless, modest leader).[81]

His inner world, it appears, was one of dramatic fantasies in which he played a heroic part as a fighter for the just revolutionary cause in a protracted struggle culminating in triumph over powerful, scheming, hatefully villainous hostile forces.[82]

Stalin's death left Russians dismayed and disoriented. Andrei Sakharov reports that

people roamed the streets, distraught and confused, with funeral music in the background. I too got carried away . . . It was years before I fully understood the degree to which deceit, exploitation and outright fraud were inherent in the whole Stalinist system. That shows the hypnotic power of mass ideology.[83]

Some of those who mourned Stalin were well aware of his nature and deeds. I have heard two speculative reasons assigned for the mourning. The first is that, terrible as Stalin was, he had succeeded in becoming the mourners' father or, even more, the world in which their lives were enacted. The second, more touching and ironical, is that if they had not mourned, they would be accepting the intolerable conclusion that all the suffering the Russians had undergone under Stalin's regime had not been for the cause he had proclaimed but only for a fraud. Both reasons join in the sense that even a cruel Stalin's will that one cannot escape determines the reality in which one lives. His will is like the will of Heaven, so that when the reality dies, one's world of fears and expectations dies with it.[84]

Was Stalin's satisfaction the pleasure he took in his power as such, in his juggling of good with evil and life with death, or in the black humor the point of which was the exquisite corpse of a friend whose love could no longer appease Stalin's suspicion? Like Mao, Stalin was successful in the elementary sense that he died a natural death, a tribute to the tactics that claimed an enormous number of victims without drawing on him the retribution all the Machiavellian thinkers warned would result from excessive cruelty. Such was the last, we must hope, of the twentieth century's deadly Machiavellis, each one evidence that Machiavellism is most fearful when it abandons the restraints of tradition and common sense, heroizes the leader beyond human measure, and lives by a fantasy of cruel greatness.

∴7∵

Nonutopian Observations

The nonutopian temper, poised between optimism and pessimism, continues to rule in the questions and answers that follow.

Does an established moral tradition make it more difficult for a Machiavelli to succeed?

The answer is, usually yes, because every tradition evolves so as to maintain the social and moral equilibrium. However, in the course of its evolution, it develops ways of justifying the use of deception and force, even when these contradict its old, literal ideals. The most obvious reason is that the leaders of a tradition find it convenient or necessary to enforce it by the aggressive maintenance of the conformism they preach. A Machiavelli can therefore work within a tradition and by means of its institutions.

Let me spell out these statements. Societies of every kind create instruments to protect themselves against social chaos and unbridled, opportunistic Machiavellism. The western democracies defend their democratic character by their (variable) insistence on freedom of expression, freedom of information and choice, judicial protection of citizens' rights, institutional checks and balances, and election of leaders for limited tenures. But political deception and violence have to be curbed not only within democratic but also within traditional nondemocratic societies, those that have in principle accepted the values of a particular tradition and have regarded their rulers as its executants.[1] Since the past cannot be maintained exactly and is taught in an idealiz-

217

ing light, the advocates of tradition may in fact be reformers who, in the name of a past that never existed, urge an end to social ambiguity and the ills that stem from it, they believe. However, here, too, devotion to principles can be hard to distinguish from their use for selfish ends.

Like the exponents of other social attitudes, traditionalists argue their case by giving reasons and by making promises and threats. The reasons are experiential, theological, and philosophical; the promises and threats relate to one's welfare in the present life and, to make things as sure as possible, to one's future life as well. In the West, this extra assurance comes in doctrines of paradise, purgatory, and hell, and in the East, in those of heaven, hell, and karmic reexistence, or—as the highest of rewards—entry into nirvana or transformation into one's true, inexpressibly spiritual being. Where, as in China, intellectual tradition can have naturalistic resonances, the future life is considered to be that, perhaps alone, of one's descendants and one's reputation.

Whatever the beliefs it teaches, tradition *always* objectivizes, that is, makes the claim that what it teaches is the fundamental nature of things. Traditional thought is therefore also cosmological: The universe is such that only action in accord with its nature gains the rewards it offers. This is taken for granted from the beginning of every particular tradition; the religious thought or philosophy that follows works out the details. In this context, openly egoistic Machiavellism—action unconcerned with either the intuitive or the formalized rules of decency—is simply outlawed. It is outlawed because, to the complete Machiavellian, nothing is sacred and the past is useful only for the lessons in expediency that it teaches.

It is necessary to make two qualifications to this judgment. The first is that every tradition has rules for sacrificing what is less important to what it takes to be more important. And so, by transforming certain natural human ends into means, every tradition arrives at a criterion by which desires or principles of one sort are sacrificed for those meant to support another. In Hinduism, social life and even family life are supposed to be sacrificed in the end for the sake of one's higher self (but for most people in India, the qualification *in the end* is enough to reconcile the demands of practical with ideal life). In Buddhism, *everything* is to be ultimately sacrificed for the sake of escape from suffering (but *ultimately* gives time and space enough to pursue an ordinary social life). In Rabbinic Judaism, for which every individual's life is a world with its own quasi-absolute value, life is nevertheless to be sacrificed to prevent the denial of the one true God (but this demand has, in practice, been rare); and in Confucianism it is taught that persons lower in the hierarchy should, if necessary, be sacrificed for the sake of those above—in the family, children should sacrifice themselves for their parents, the wife for her husband, and so on; and much the same is true of Hinduism (but in practice the relations are more complex and in some ways reversed). In Confucian life, too, self-sacrificing officials, among them historians, have demonstrated the priority of truth, in an especially Confucian sense, to life itself (but such sacrifices have been rare acts of heroism). To put it in other words, every tradition has a hierarchy of offices and values that determines its hierarchy of sacrifices. In this sense, every tradition has an equivalent of the Machiavellian *raison d'état* (but like cautious Machiavellianism, tends to subordinate such sacrifices to moderate customary practices).

The second qualification of the anti-Machiavellian temper of tradition is an obvious one: By Machiavellian tactics, tradition is maintained to the advantage of one or another person or group. When such an advantage is given formal sanction, tradition provides the casuistic rationale. Such is the justification given by Buddhists and Jains for traditionally approved killing or war: as the casuist reasons, these are meant to save villains from accumulating still more evil karma and suffering in future lives.

It would extend my argument too far if I tried to apply it with the necessary care to more than one religion. In any case, for such a subject I prefer a religion relatively distant from the probable readers of this book, so I represent all religions by the example of Buddhism. I choose Buddhism not only for its distance but also for its ethics: of the world religions, it is the most insistently and universally kind. The choice of Buddhism is good, furthermore, because it depends in principle on experience and reason, not on divine, often, to humans, inexplicable commands.

Buddhist morality can be summed up in the five abstentions, three holy states, and ten good deeds it teaches. Its abstentions are from killing, stealing, sexual misconduct, lying, and intoxication; its holy states are loving-kindness, compassion, and sympathetic joy; and its ten good deeds, which I will not enumerate, include respect for others and joy in their merit. Such moral recommendations are dwelt on and amplified in Buddhist scriptures. For example, the old, eloquent verses of the *Sutta Nipata* wish all living beings whatever—weak, strong, small, large, far, near, born and unborn—to be happy, safe, and gain inner joy. These verses also claim that a persons's mind should be as all-embracingly friendly to the whole world as a mother is to her only son.[2] The *Dhammapada (Verses on Doctrine)*, a work much beloved by Buddhist laymen of the Theravada countries, tells the Buddhist that hatred is never appeased by hatred but only by love; that victory breeds hatred because the defeated live in pain, so that the truly peaceful give up both victory and defeat; and that one should conquer anger by love, evil by good, the stingy person by giving, and the liar by telling the truth (verses 5, 201, 223).

Buddhist morality does not end at even this humanitarian level. The more expansive tradition of Mahayana Buddhism dwells on "enlightenment beings" or Bodhisattvas, who are superlatively compassionate. In a memorable description of the seventh century A.D., a Bodhisattva resolves not to be affected by the malice, sins, heresies, anxieties, corruption, or quarrels of human beings, but to save them; and because one form of life transmigrates into another, the Bodhisattva's resolve is to save all living creatures, so he takes on himself the burden of all their pain and evil karma. "I have resolved," he says to himself,

> to save them all . . . from the forest of birth, old age, disease, and rebirth, from misfortune and sin, from the round of birth and death, from the toils of heresy . . . I must free them from all misfortune, ferry them over the stream of rebirth. For I have taken upon myself, by my own will, the whole of the pain of all things living . . . I must be their guide to safety . . . And I must not be satisfied with small successes.[3]

To Buddhists, the Buddha himself is the great teacher and the exemplar of all virtues. Early Buddhist literature portrays a Buddha-person who is at least semi-miraculously knowing and inspiring and, in this sense, much more than the almost modest human being he often seems to be.[4] Unlike other founders of religions or sects, the Buddha is represented as intellectually uncoercive. "Think about what I say," he in effect repeats. "Do not take it on trust, and if you have any questions, ask them. And remember the answers are not relevant to the great problem of life, which is suffering and its cure. I am, as I prefer to be, the sure therapist rather than the impossible metaphysician.*

It seems likely enough that the real Buddha, like the mythical one, had great respect for the truth. To drive this home, one of the Jataka tales (tales about the Buddha in his previous existences) says that there

---

*Buddhists are likely to assume that the Buddha knew the answers to the metaphysical questions he dismissed but that he thought them useless to his auditors. In philosophical Buddhism, it is more likely to be assumed that both the questions and any proposed answers are meaningless because language is invariably empty, that is, makes no final sense at all.

are cases in which a Bodhisattva may, for a good enough purpose, commit deeds—theft, adultery, or murder—that in others would be considered crimes, but that he may not tell a lie, for this would violate "the reality of things."[5] Another Jataka tale tells that the evil Devadatta, the archenemy of Buddha in innumerable life cycles, told the very first lie. On hearing of it, the people, who still had no conception of what a lie might be, could only ask, "What kind of thing is a lie? Is it blue, yellow, or some other color?"[6]

It would be easy to continue with Buddhist teachings, but my point is not that Buddhism recommended many humane virtues, but that social reality was able to give Buddhism, the religious epitome of humane behavior, a Machiavellian face. I say this neither as a criticism of Buddhism nor indirectly of any other religion, but only because human social life is such that *any* of its institutions, even a religion like Buddhism, takes on Machiavellian characteristics. To the Buddhists themselves, this was no surprise, and they attributed it conventionally, as I have pointed out, to the cosmic cycle, which by their reckoning had reached a stage of great degeneracy.

Signs of deception and the amoral use of force appear in the traditional accounts of the Buddha's own life. We have already heard the name of their villain, Devadatta, the Buddha's cross-cousin and the first schismatic among Buddhist monks.[7] These accounts tell us that when the Buddha grew old, he often deputed his favorite disciples to speak in his place. This practice aroused Devadatta's hopes and once, when the Buddha was preaching before a large audience including the king, Devadatta said out loud that the Buddha was now too old and should make him, Devadatta, the head of the monks' order. The Buddha refused, and when Devadatta persisted a second and third time, Buddha grew angry and said that he was unwilling to turn the order over to his favorite disciples, so why should he turn it over to him, the despicable Devadatta. The Buddha then had a formal announcement issued that Devadatta was no longer a member of the order.

According to the canonical story, Devadatta suggested to the prince of the country, who favored him, to kill the king, his father, who favored the Buddha.[8] Although the plot was discovered, the king pardoned his son and abdicated in his favor. Having become king, the son imprisoned his father and starved him to death. Devadatta then got the new king to send soldiers to kill the Buddha. The first soldier to encounter the Buddha was afraid, and the devious plot (whose Machiavellian details I omit) failed. So did two further attempts, one, to kill the Buddha by hurling a huge stone down the peak of the mountain in the shade of which he was pacing, and the other, by means of a vicious bull-elephant, a man-slayer, who was so overcome by the loving-kindness radiating from the Buddha that he bowed and became instantaneously tame.

Devadatta then proposed to the Buddha that five of the disciplinary rules for monks be made more strict and compliance with them made compulsory. As the wily Devadatta anticipated, the Buddha refused, and people of little faith thought that Devadatta was conscientious while the Buddha had become fond of a luxurious life. The king, Devadatta's ally, established and supported a monastery for him and his disciples.

We see that according to tradition, Devadatta used both force and guile. Told from his point of view, the story would certainly have been different; but it is significant that the Buddha himself seems to have shown un-Buddhistic anger and made un-Buddhistic insults and threats of punishment. Anyone who has read Buddhist exegesis knows that it will be denied that Buddha was *really* angry or insulting. The exegete is forced to assume that what the Buddha said was not in order to relieve his feelings but for the good of the person at fault. Such, too, is the message of the "Discourse to Prince Abhyaha," where it is suggested that the Buddha be asked about his apparently un-Buddhistic talk. "How is it, revered sir," the suggested question goes, that the Buddha caused Devadatta anger and displeasure by saying "Devadatta is doomed to a sorrowful way after death, Devadatta is doomed to Niraya Hell . . . Devadatta is incurable."[9] When the Buddha is actually approached and asked if it is ever right to utter anything disagreeable to others, his answer is that if what is said is true, relevant to the great goal, and said at the right time, the remark is justified, in the same way as it is justified to pain a baby by pulling a stick or stone out of its throat:

> Whatever speech the Tathagata [the Buddha] knows to be fact, true, connected with the goal, but not liked by others, disagreeable to them, the Tathagata is aware of the right time for explaining that speech . . . The Tathagata has compassion for creatures.[10]

If this were not the omniscient Buddha speaking, he might be suspected of rationalizing an act that is not permitted to less percipient beings. The same would have to be said of Buddha's words to Devadatta when the latter asked him a third time to give up his leadership and was called by Buddha (in the words of an uncompromising translator) "vile one, to be vomited like spittle."[11]

Compassion demonstrated in such ways leads to conclusions that make Buddhism seem paradoxical. The *Mahavamsa*, the old chronicle of

Sinhalese (Sri Lankan) history, tells approvingly how the heroic King Dutugamunu, when told that killing non-Buddhists is not really killing, supports Buddhism by making war against the Tamils.[12] When one day the king recalls his victory, he does so without joy because it caused the deaths of millions of people. But a group of *arahats* ("worthy ones," who have penetrating insight) reads his thoughts from the distance and sends eight representatives who inform him that he really killed only one and a half persons, the rest being only "unbelievers and men of evil" not worthy of more esteem than beasts. A later chronicle says that they told the king that the Tamils he had killed "were not only barbarians and heretics but their deaths were like those of cattle, dogs, and mice."[13]

The psychologically minded anthropologist whose account I am using says that although the king violated the axiomatic basis of Buddhism as a religion of nonviolence, the king's guilt—like that of other Buddhist kings—had the virtue that it drove him to support religion and act for the people's welfare. It should therefore not be surprising "if monks justify all sorts of violent acts such as regicides, mass killings, sexual violation by kings—all except the act of parricide" (which some of those excused committed symbolically).[14]

Out of such justifications of explicitly forbidden acts, Mahayana Buddhism created the doctrine of *skilful means, ingenuity,* or *expediency,* as the term *upaya* may be variously translated. This doctrine, according to which Buddha uses the means most appropriate to teaching or acting, allows his wholly insightful, compassionate aim to take precedence over an act's prohibition to lesser beings. A Bodhisattva (one who has achieved "the wisdom-seed of emptiness, signlessness, nonaction, and nonself") will not fall to "the miserable planes of existence" even though he indulges in what in others would be sinful lust and desire.

To drive the point home, Buddha is represented as telling how in a previous life, out of purity and compassion, not lust, he married and had sexual intercourse with a woman in order to save her from committing suicide for love of him. He also tells how in order to influence others to avoid sinning, he pretended to be punished for sins that, in him, were no sins at all. And he tells how, out of compassion, he speared to death a man who wanted to rob and kill five hundred traders. The Buddha's means were skilful because by this act he not only saved the lives of the five hundred (Bodhisattvas, he says) but also saved them from the sin of hating and killing their would-be murderer if, as otherwise obliged, he would have told them of the threat to their lives. Lastly, by his compassionately economical act of killing he allowed the murderer to be reborn in heaven and not in the hells to which he would otherwise have fallen.[15]

To the above stories and their accompanying doctrine, I should add something about the relation of Buddhism to politics. For practical reasons, I will limit myself to China, Tibet, and Japan. In the case of China, I can make the point briefly by recalling the career of the Empress Wu, who turned to Buddhism because Confucianism made it difficult to legitimize a woman ruler. Toward the end of the 680's A.D., a group of ten Buddhist monks was enabled or ordered to find a scripture, a sutra, in which a female deity and appropriate oracles identified the empress as the Buddha-to-come (Maitreya Buddha) to whom the traditional Mandate of Heaven had now passed. The empress reciprocated the discovery of the document by favoring the Buddhist clergy and sponsoring translations of Buddhist scriptures. She also supported two new Buddhist schools, the antiphilosophical Ch'an (Zen) sect, and the highly philosophical Hua-Yen (Flower Garland). A title she assumed hinted clearly at her likeness to the Buddhist Universal Monarch.[16]

The Tibetan history of the official institution of Buddhism tells of the contest between Indian and Chinese Buddhists in which the Indians succeeded in driving out the Chinese, who were of the Ch'an persuasion. But the Chinese succeeded in murdering the leading Indian master and causing his Tibetan supporter to commit suicide. There followed severe persecutions of Buddhism, which put a temporary end to the community of foreign scholars, Tibetan translators, and monks.[17] In time, however, the power of the Buddhist monasteries of Tibet came to supplement or replace that of the hereditary feudal nobility. These monasteries were not simply religious but also political and economic organizations that cooperated or conflicted with one another as their interests dictated. The Dalai Lama became the theocratic but fairly tolerant ruler.[18]

The doctrine of skillful means is prominent in the Lotus Sutra, a scripture that was the main inspiration of the Japanese Buddhist monk Nichiren (A.D. 1222–1282). Nichiren somehow became convinced that the truth and power of this sutra were concentrated in its title, so that the chanting of "Hail to the Lotus of the Perfect Truth" could ensure salvation. He also convinced himself that he was a prophet, the reincarnation of the Bodhisattva meant to protect Japan and realize the sutra's ideal in a world suffering from many calamities. Nichiren's list of recent Japanese calamities included the unprecedented earthquake of 1257, the great wind of 1258, the great famine of 1259, and the rampant disease that begin in 1259 and continued to rage during 1260, a year in which more than half of the ordinary citizens of Japan died. The prayers ordered by the alarmed rulers of the country proved useless. This was evidence to Nichiren that the age was such that Buddhist truth was no longer effective and the world was now ruled by demons, not by gods. Then, in 1264, on the fifth day of the seventh month, according to Nichiren, all Japan saw the light of a comet, "an evil portent such as has never been seen before since the beginning of history."[19] Such disasters and such an omen, wrote Nichiren, were the result of the prevalence of false forms of Buddhism, which the government was obliged to suppress.

In support of his version of Buddhism, Nichiren levelled an extraordinarily harsh attack on the Buddhist sects that did not teach the priority of the Lotus Sutra, which, he believed, every person was obliged to acknowledge in order to rescue Japan from its difficulties. The ethics preached by Nichiren were this-worldly and populistic and justified violence. Under questioning, he admitted that he had named five temples he wanted burned and two high priests he wanted beheaded. A further problem for the government was that his attack on Zen was an implicit attack on the regent himself. Convicted of treason, Nichiren was arrested in 1271 and condemned, officially to exile but in fact to death. As he describes it, when he was arrested, he was struck with a scroll of the Lotus Sutra, the other scrolls of which were unrolled, trampled on, and strewn about the floor. Nichiren then said loudly, "You gentlemen have just toppled the pillar of Japan!"

Taken to his execution, Nichiren continued his defiance, and (as he tells it) was saved by the miraculous appearance of an orb as bright as the moon that shot across the sky from southeast to northwest. Blinded, the executioner fell on his face and the soldiers panicked. That very evening, a letter of reprieve arrived from the regent. Despite further dramatic signs and portents that Nichiren describes, he was exiled, this (second) time for three years, after which he was pardoned. As he had predicted, the Mongols invaded. Their double defeat, primarily by the elements, was attributed by the Buddhist enemies of Nichiren to the efficacy of their prayers.[20]

Nichiren's denunciation of the other sects of Buddhism shows him to have been almost completely intolerant. He repeats that the Lotus Sutra predicted that in the evil age there would be monks who were perverse, fawning, crooked, and boastful, and there would be, as well, forest-dwelling monks who wore clothing of patched rags but were greedy for power and honor and would spread lies about true Buddhism, which they would call heretical.[21] To justify violence against these sham Buddhists, Nichiren points out that the Nirvana Sutra quotes Buddha as saying, "Men of devout faith, defenders of the True Law need not observe the five precepts or practice the rules of proper behavior. Rather they should carry knives and swords, bows and arrows, prongs and lances."[22] Nichiren continues that the Nirvana Sutra says that one may give alms to an ordinary sinner but never to anyone who has slandered the Law. Whoever kills even an ant will suffer for it, "but he who helps to eradicate slander of the Law will ascend to the state from which there can be no retrogression."[23]

According to Nichiren, the Lotus Sutra can be taught either by gentle arguments or by means of strict (severe) refutation. Japan, he says, requires the strict kind because its sins are not the result of ignorance but of deliberate defiance. The leaders of the perverse sects teach by means of twisted view and private opinions. They enter the service of the ruler and military leaders and preach so as to destroy the Buddhist Law and the country.[24] Zen, in particular, is a false doctrine that appeals to the children abandoned by their parents because they are unfilial, to retainers dismissed for outrageous conduct, to priests too lax to study, and to prostitutes.

> Even though its followers have all embraced the precepts, they are no more than swarming locusts feeding upon the people of the nation. That is why Heaven glares down in anger and the gods of the earth shudder.[25]

In criticism of the Shingon sect, with its sensuous brilliance and esoteric ritual, Nichiren says that although widely respected and patronized by the government, it is delusive and fraudulent, and its prayers and curses proved useless in helping Japan against the Mongols—as long as the shogun and his intimates use the services "of priests who invite grave disaster by ignoring the Lotus Sutra, the nation will in fact face certain destruction."[26]

In the heat of his enthusiasm, Nichiren makes a great vow:

> Though I might be told that my father and mother will have their heads cut off if I do not recite the Nembutsu—whatever obstacles I encounter, as long as men of wisdom do not prove my teachings to be false, I will never yield! All other troubles are no more to me than dust before the wind.
>
> I will be the Pillar of Japan. I will be the Eyes of Japan. I will be the Great Ship of Japan. This is my vow, and I will never forsake it![27]

Nichiren was sincere and, in this sense, Machiavellian only in justifying the use of force to gain his ends. But like the other Buddhist sects
of Japan, Nichiren's underwent a process of institutional development
and division into branches. This process was inevitably accompanied
by Machiavellian tactics. Organizers competed for power within the
sect by trying to become the administrators of temples that had close
connections with Nichiren.[28] "Ordinary adherents had little to say in
the organization's administration. . . . Powerful supporters also began
to place members of their own families in positions of influence as religious leaders and organizers in the temples."[29] The major supporters of
the Nichiren school were mostly samurai, and much of the financing of
Nichiren's movement came, it seems, from local warlords. These warlords established what in effect were clan temples, in which the sons of
the patrons were often the priests.

Nichiren's disciples divided into different schools, sometimes
with all his dogmatism but little of his spiritual forcefulness.[30] Some
Nichiren sects were inclined to peaceful relations with other Buddhist
sects and avoided the severe methods of confrontation sometimes used
to spread the faith (as in the conversion of wives, employees, or retainers).[31] By the sixteenth century, there were twenty-one Nichiren sects in
Kyoto, many of whose temples were armed fortresses with standing
armies that could be used to force the solution of doctrinal debates. For
whatever reasons, a war broke out in 1536 with the Pure Land monks
of Mt. He, whose army attacked Nichiren temples in Kyoto, burned
twenty-one of them, and killed perhaps tens of thousands of Nichirenites; but this defeat affected the Nichirenites only temporarily.[32]

The history of Zen is just as edifying and unedifying. The larger
Zen monasteries, with their thousands of monks and their meditative
practices and artistic interests, were allied with the warrior elite and the
imperial court. Hungry for land and donations, the monasteries were
the sites of competition for high offices, which might be sold to anyone
who could pay the price. Sometimes, too, the monasteries were the sites
of armed conflict among groups of monks. The monks of Soto Zen, who
were often farmers and local warriors, worked their land with conviction, built bridges, dug wells, served the local population, and were
concerned with the interests of ordinary laymen.[33] But as Nichiren's not
very balanced attack leads one to expect, there was much criticism of
Zen, internal and external, much sectarian strife within it, and tales that
showed the Zen monks in a less than favorable light.[34] It is, no doubt, the presence of many warriors among the patrons
and practitioners of Zen that created the relationship, so strange in the

abstract, between Zen Buddhism and the military arts, especially swordsmanship and archery. The relationship was always loose and as much with Confucianism as with Zen. Zen, in particular, was useful to warriors because it taught them to take spontaneous advantage of every opportunity to kill an opponent while themselves losing all consciousness of ego and fear of death. Takuan Soho (1573–1645), the swordsman, argues that the swordfighter does not fight for victory nor defeat, nor to kill his opponent. Conscious striving purpose makes the accomplishment more remote and destroys one's spiritual accomplishment, for which reason he advocates the Zen paradox of the identity of stillness and dynamism, of "original mind," which is "to melt the mind and to let it work, like flowing water, in every part of the body—that is what is meant by "original mind."[35]

I have summarized the complicated facts incompletely but in enough detail to lend substance to my generalization about the religious use of violence and deception. The point having been made, I feel absolved from going into the history of the Hinayana countries and I return to the generalization itself.[36] It is beyond doubt that the religious precepts of even so humanitarian a religion as Buddhism are spelled into human existence in ways that are also inevitably Machiavellian. This Machiavellism begins with the traditional story of the Buddha (as it probably began with the real one), continues with Buddhist rivalries and schisms, and comes to explicit expression in the principle of skilful means. This principle is regarded as essential to preserve the interests of the apparent victim but also assumes the appearance and, I take it, the substance of the Machiavellian *raison d'état*.

Nichiren gives an impressive historic lesson. He is an idealist rather than than a conscious Machiavellian. But to anyone without faith in him, his argument that in this degenerate age every version of Buddhism but his ought to be suppressed by force, must appear to express his struggle for existence against other Buddhist leaders, a struggle maintained in an openly Machiavellian temper by his heritors. Buddhism begins as limitless mercy but transforms itself into a political instrument, learns to justify lying, adultery, coercion, murder, and war, learns to become the official religion of warring bands of monks, and learns to be used as the psychological prelude to the efficient practice of swordsmanship and archery.

Because religions are historical amalgams of everything human, they cannot be summed up in merely moral, rational, dogmatic, or symbolic forms. All a religion's preachings, reasonings, dogmas, ceremonies, and humanitarian ideals cannot prevent its ideals from being adapted to the ambitions of those to whom victory in whatever social sense demands Machiavellian practices. In the final analysis, Machiavellism is not only compatible with religion but indispensable to it, for the single but sufficient reason that no religion can dispense with human beings. Given time, these indispensable persons explore the variations of which their life is capable and learn to regenerate their perception of themselves by means of fantasies that include force, destruction, and re-creation. Given time, therefore, Buddhism, the reasonable, totally compassionate religion, is able to turn into paradoxical variants of itself in tantric (magical-rite) theories that teach the ambiguously symbolic and literal practice (confined to accomplished yogins) of killing, lying, stealing, and adultery, each of which is specifically forbidden in authoritative old texts, but each of which is compatible with the tantric Buddhist's love for the identity of opposites and his ambition to become totally, omnipotently, really (because unreally) real.[37]

Does history teach whether or not Machiavellism has been successful?

The answer is that history teaches no lessons or predictions of interest that are at all certain. Just that, the uncertainty of its lessons, is history's greatest value, because it sensitizes us to the usual within the unpredictable and the unpredictable within the usual. The inexactness of its lessons corresponds to their endless variety and indefinable subtlety. When we are hungry for history as such, it is more often in order to keep our thoughts free, unconfined to a fixed moment, especially our own, than to learn an immediately practical lesson. Yet though the most useful lessons of history are implicit ones, historians can go beyond description and make plausible analyses of fragments of the past. To speak of what is relevant to the question I have asked, such an analysis can show, I believe, that large-scale Machiavellian policies can be relatively successful for a relatively long time.

Not to appear arbitrary, I have to explain in some detail. To begin with, if what I have said about Buddhism is accurate, it teaches an important though general historical probability. Would Guicciardini, who once claimed that history teaches nothing except that one cannot learn from it, deny the possibility of learning a general lesson of the kind we derived from Buddhism? I think he would not. But whatever his answer, in claiming that history teaches nothing he is right in the sense that history teaches nothing that can be applied exactly. The historical situation we face at any given moment is different enough from any preceding one to make even a painstaking forecast hardly better than a guess. Arising and subsiding in unpredictable variations within shifting contexts, the events we isolate out of the historical flux are most sensibly viewed as having not causes but constellations of causes. It is only after the event that we have some chance to learn which, if any, of the component-causes were critical, what shifted, and how and where, to give just these results, which have added up, maybe, to defeat or victory in a war, or, less calculably, the rise of decline of a civilization.

While this is not the place to go into the possible component-causes of history, something of their depth, variety, and interdependence ought always to be kept in view. Most of these causes are referred to sporadically if at all in historical writing—this despite the *Annales* school—except when they intrude on politics in the most direct, extreme way. Thanks to Thucydides (alone), historians of ancient Greece remember the devastating outbreak of the plague in Athens that for a time disoriented the Athenians, helped lead to the downfall of Pericles, and after he was voted back into office, killed him. Historians who describe the conquest of Peru cannot neglect the ravages of the smallpox, caught from the Spanish invaders, that killed the Inca emperor, Wayna Capac, his heir apparent, and many of the governing elite, and led to the revolution that made Pizzaro's success possible. Nor can historians of the fall of the Aztecs forget that Cortes's conquest of Mexico depended on the near immunity of the Spaniards to the smallpox that devastated the Aztecs. Historians of particular nations also recall the storms that influenced the history that concerns them. For instance, Japanese historians cherish the memory of the "divine wind" that saved Japan from the invading Mongols in 1274 and, again, in 1281, just as English historians cherish the memory of the storm that helped defeat the Spanish Armada in 1588.

But these are isolated intrusions of diseases, storms, and the like into the evenly political tenor of most historical writing. And though European historians cannot avoid considering the effects of the Black Death on fourteenth-century Europe, they are rarely interested in following the plague back to the Mongol army from which it spread, and from this army back to its probable origin in China under Mongol, that is, Ming, rule. Mostly, historians have continued to be the chroniclers of the acts, pronouncements, and difficulties of governments—historians prefer anything that rests on an archival source, that can be quoted and dated exactly, that fits an quite limited conception of what constitutes history, and that goes easily into narrative form. But except for sporadic instances of the kind I have recalled, such a narrative review of politics neglects the influences that, hard as they are for the historian to reckon with, are usually far deeper than the political ones considered in bare isolation. The Machiavellians, unafraid to believe in the importance of accident (or "fate"), emphasize the need to react to it quickly and efficiently. Given the human dependence on the forces of nature, it is easy to understand why the earliest, mythical rulers of China were believed to have tamed them as far as possible and to have taught human beings how to remain in harmony with the universe. All religions have attempted to propitiate the forces supposed to cause floods, famines, and diseases. And as we have seen, the Machiavellis, who make use of and compete with religions, have argued that people should be willing to accept a harsh government because its efficiency protects them against social disorganization, such as that which accompanies flood, famine, and disease.

Of the component-causes of the deeper sort I would like to mention, economics is the least neglected. Created as it is by human relationships, it is not usually considered beyond human ability to understand. But even now, when statistics are far more accurate than in the past and when statistical theory is so much further developed, economists, equipped with their models and computers, are not conspicuously successful in forecasting either short-term or long-term economic trends. So-called behavioral finance, which explains economics with the help of psychology, may well make economics more intelligible, because more intelligibly irrational, but not necessarily more predictable.

Since no one disputes the profound importance of economics for history, history must share its obscure nature, which is only somewhat relieved by our ability when looking back to invent doubtful explanations. But economics, whatever the degree of its intelligibility, is itself dependent, like everything in human life, on other, incompletely understood factors. Among these factors, the most obvious are those that affect a population's supply of food and its health—flood, famine, and disease. Without studying the effects of parasites on river dwellers, how deeply can we understand the history of the farmers who worked in the great river valleys, the early sites of civilization? How deeply can we grasp African history. If we remain ignorant of the influence on it of sleeping sickness? And then, apart from the plague of smallpox, already mentioned, there are tuberculosis, typhus, syphilis, cholera, malaria, and the bubonic and pneumonic plagues, with their devastating effects.*

---

*William McNeill ends his book, *Plagues and People*, with the following passage: "In any effort to understand what lies ahead, as much as what lies behind, the role of infectious disease cannot properly be left out of consideration. Ingenuity, knowledge, and organization alter but cannot cancel humanity's vulnerability to invasion by parasitic forms of life. Infectious disease which antedated the emergence of mankind will last as long as humanity itself, and will surely remain, as it has been hitherto, one of the fundamental parameters and deter-

But these—flood, famine, and disease—can in turn be understood only in relation to still other factors. There is the weather, of course, or, rather, the weather in relation to all the ecological factors to which it is relevant. But the weather, too, is not very well understood or, if in a sense, understood, not easily predictable. Even short-term weather predictions are intrinsically fallible because they are so often falsified by the quick amplification of unobservably small changes. And long-term weather prediction is highly uncertain because it depends, among the rest, on the sun's not well understood changes in radiation, the earth's changes in inclination, the relations between the different layers of the atmosphere, the oceans' heat, and the land masses' makeup and topography.

But to know how the weather works is far from enough to enable a historian or anyone to understand the changes in plant and animal growth and in human health. One must also understand genetics as it affects organisms, considered alone and in groups, affects ecology, and affects evolution. It is true that there has been extraordinary progress in understanding genetics, but, as usual, the more we have come to know of it, the better specified our great remaining ignorance has become. The result is that we realize, or should realize more clearly, that history is unpredictable not only because human actions are unpredictable in enough relevant detail, but also because *all* the deep component-causes that converge in historical change are unpredictable, surely to us, here and now. History can therefore be conceived as the temporal succession of humanly interesting changes that result from the interactions, either unpredictable or unpredictable in much detail, of natural forces, non-human biological organisms, and human beings.

I quickly abandon this desperately inclusive conception of history and concentrate on human purposes and actions alone, which are in themselves difficult enough to understand. To illustrate the problems involved in predicting human reactions even when they are isolated from the other components of historical causation, I choose a case as simple as possible to manipulate intellectually, that of two opposed political leaders. I ask: How can the outcome of a clash between the two be predicted when the intelligence that inspires one leader's act is countered by the equal intelligence of the other? Prediction becomes still more guesslike when the leaders' acts are not, as I have assumed, equal

---

minants of human history." Immediately following this passage, there is a long list (pp. 259–69) of epidemics in China from 243 B.C. to A.D. 1911. This list is testimony to Chinese need to record all information that had a possible official use.

in intelligence and opposite in purpose, but incommensurable, that is, not measurable on the same scale of purpose. How, I ask, can the outcome be predicted when an intelligent act is met with one too "irrational"—too far off the scale by which intelligence is being measured—to be predicted by anyone who expects only an intelligent—intelligently self-serving—response? Further, how can it be known in advance that a certain devious act for which a devious response is expected will in fact get an undevious one, or that a violent act will get an unexpected peaceable one? Can a compulsive planner and an impulsive nonplanner understand one another, or a truculent person and a mild one, or a blind one and a deaf one? And how can anything useful be predicted when the situations involved are so complicated or so fluid that, to be clear, an analysis must be greatly oversimplified?

We counter such difficulties by the systematic gathering of information, which we analyze by advanced statistical methods and models as sophisticated as we can construct. But the information itself is often inaccurate and, if much is at stake, may be intentionally misleading. As for statistics, even assuming they are roughly accurate—for politics and history can they ever be more?—they cannot be counted on to yield trustworthy advice on particular acts meant to deal with complicated real issues. This is so if only because statistics smooth out the deviations of which they are composed while some, many, most, or all individual events (depending on their details that are considered relevant) are deviant events, and because even a small deviation can lead to quite different results. Nor is a formalistic, logical procedure, such as game theory, very promising for actual life because, as we discover, the real analogues of theoretical games have critical factors of which the games take no account. The difficulty in prediction is repeated on another level when sophisticated real-life gamesters competing against one another, in the stock market, for instance, or, as may one day happen, in a war, make use of the same theories and compete in the invention of better ones.

When they deal with human relations, formal models such as are translated into computer programs, may be highly suggestive, but they are possible only because they leave out the essentially incalculable complications that occur in fact. On the assumption, clarified by use, that such a computerized program contains no serious bugs, it may be regarded as exact in itself. But it depends on a probably over-simple analysis, is confined to a highly simplified, perhaps misleadingly construed context, and is highly dependent on the correctness of the data it uses—even a slight mistake or a necessary rounding off of numbers can create large errors when multiplied. All these hazards are self-evident to those who develop the programs, but not necessarily to those who use them. Yet the discovery of the importance of what a model or program has left out is itself enlightening: not only are the models improved, but those who use them in full awareness of their nature may improve their very human intuition by grasping how certain flaws make even the best of models imperfect.[38]*

Psychology, though also very uncertain in practice, sometimes offers more retrospective enlightenment than analysis by formal theory. Let me give a modern example. It has been said that Lenin was very mistrustful from childhood on. In later life, his mistrust made it difficult for others to betray him; but, for better and worse, his mistrust was allied with a good deal of pessimism. This pessimism was for the worse (it is claimed) when the failure of the July 1717 Bolshevik uprising in Petrograd sent him into hiding in Finland and weakened his effectiveness until power had already been taken over. But his pessimism proved justified when it led him to suspect the Germans at Brest-Litovsk and to conclude that the Russians would be unable to resist them.

Mistrustful and pessimistic by nature, Lenin was relatively little bound to others by feelings of personal loyalty or the need to cooperate. This personal ability to isolate himself was often politically helpful to him. Trotsky, however, was more optimistic and trusting than Lenin, always surprised by the antagonistic responses of others to himself and unable to see the world in the harsh, decisive manner of Lenin. His vitality and optimism gave him great successes in organizing the Red Army. However, at Brest-Litovsk his optimism led him astray, and his indecision, which qualified his optimism, often made him vulnerable. So did his pride.[39]

---

*The philosopher Robert Nozick emphasizes the extent to which the study of rationality has become technical: "A sleek and powerful theory of rational action—decision theory—was developed in this century by mathematicians, economists, statisticians, and philosophers, and now this theory is applied in a wide variety of theoretical and practical contexts." Unfortunately, "the common culture of intelligent, educated, and serious people has lost its grip on many topics that are central to understanding and thinking about society or people or the universe at large." Nozick predicts that philosophers will lose their old function and be replaced by cognitive and computer scientists, who work by rules whose surface validity is by nature unclear (Nozick, *The Nature of Rationality*, pp. xiii, xvi, 76). However, the technical procedures Nozick mentions must be used and interpreted with the help of ordinary human judgment. Though I guess above that game theory may be used for real wars, I doubt that the persons responsible will be able to abdicate their human judgment to technically ingenious but fallible models.

One moral is sound if also in practice difficult: As Kautilya and Machiavelli say, it is enlightening to grasp the character of enemy leaders on the assumption that they may be different from oneself. Think of the kind of dilemma I have suggested, a dilemma on both sides, when a person sensitive to individuals and their emotions is pitted against a Machiavelli who is sensitive to neither because, like Lenin, he is interested only in practical goals. Hard as it is to fathom the character of opponents quite different from oneself, it is harder still to fathom one's own because this requires getting outside of one's skin and looking at oneself from the outside in. Such looking is foreign to the leader who loves himself too much to be able to see his own weaknesses clearly. How many ambitious leaders are realistic about their abilities, and how can they be realistic about them until they have taken the chances that demonstrate their own limitations? And if, like Napoleon after his first exile, they continue to be ambitious after failure, what leads them to suppose that the one failure will not be succeeded by another? Perhaps the conclusion should be that, when joined, history and psychology can help us to understand better than either alone; but it is unfortunately true that the most convincing analyses of history and character are retrospective. Wisdom is much easier to achieve in relation to the past, when we already know that Napoleon's second try was a failure.

A more convincing conclusion might be that what history shows most clearly is that pretensions to (non-retrospective) political understanding must be exaggerated and that there cannot be a true science of politics. Historical reflection

is not a constant beacon and does not mark a stage on the route taken by humanity. The road twists and turns. The truth does not direct it toward the horizon. Nor are its vagaries molded on the powerful contours of an infrastructure. The road winds haphazardly. Most of the time the travelers do not care. Each one believes that his road is the true one, and the turns that he sees others take scarcely disturb him.[40]

Vividly expressed though it is, this conclusion seems to me too complacent. Guicciardini and Paul Veyne (whom I have just quoted) are right only in a narrow sense. In a wider sense, they are wrong because we in fact think less in terms of exact repetitions than of analogies that experience helps us to adapt as events prove necessary. More or less exact repetitions hold true only of the mechanical activities that demand them. Intelligence (even, often, what is considered animal instinct) gives the ability to make intuitive reassessments of what has already been learned (or, for instinct, apparently fixed). This ability is the equivalent of a conscious re-analysis of our previous experiences into their newly relevant and irrelevant components.

Guicciardini and Veyne are also wrong because history gives us the chance to assimilate experience—thin, yet intellectually helpful experience—we can never otherwise have and, in this way, to be exposed to thousands of eventful years and innumerable kinds of lives. The importance of this exposure is not contradicted by the frequent failures to learn from history: No experience, direct or historical, can open the eyes of a person with too limited an imagination or intelligence. Lack of experience, however, can be fatal even to those with a receptive imagination—they too can be blind to dangers they have never known—and limit the intelligence even of the natively intelligent. Intelligence needs experience to feed on, to quicken it, and to transform it into understanding.

I do not mean that the study of history can guarantee understanding, or understanding, success. However, by supplying many more or less analogous experiences and by encouraging their comparison, analysis, and imaginative reassembly, history teaches us how to examine events closely and how to react to them discerningly. The discerning reaction I mean reinforces personal memories with impersonal, that is, historical ones and strengthens one's intuitive ability to reach judgments the nuances and intelligence of which are based on experiences varied enough to suggest not only what is usual but how and why there are variations from the usual. Discernment is an informed intuitive adaptation by way of analogy—intuition is needed because the number of possibilities is far too great for anyone to take into conscious account.

Let me put this idea in another way: To our most vivid, personal experiences we add those that, in the course of time, we assimilate from history. Together, all these experiences define an area of possibilities in which they are, so to speak, registered and arranged in relation to one another and to the unknown for which they prepare us. The many experiences, each with its implicit record and aura of success or failure, may be visualized as a relatively dense scattering of points all contained within the area of the possibilities to which we may still have to respond. When something occurs that turns out, as often, not to coincide with any of these points, our thought moves, more or less unconsciously, to some new, previously unoccupied point. We move there by a kind of search for the optimal position between the points that represent other, previous experiences; and then, having found the optimal position, we make a new response by means of a subtly adjusted analogy to perhaps many experiential reference points, none of them quite the same as or quite different from the point we have searched for.

All honest, careful history can nourish the ability to discern in this sense. The historians' passion to record accurately and understand deeply, which animates persons as distant from one another as Ssu-ma Ch'ien and Thucydides, is a craving to understand by means of the accumulation of experience. It is the need to increase both the range of experience and the skill to navigate in thought within it. It is also a craving to live again, as a particular form of discernment, in the thought of every person who will one day study the particular historian's works.

The histories of Ssu-ma and his Chinese successors seems to me especially good for lessons in discernment. This is because the records the Chinese kept make it possible to think in coherent detail about the history of large numbers of people over long periods of time. Non-Chinese sources for (written) history apply to smaller territories or briefer stretches of time, or, if not, lack essential detail and credibility. The archives of the old Italian cities, for example, have provided material for interesting historical and socioeconomic analysis; but the history of these individual city-states is not as useful for wide-ranging study as that of a great, long-lived empire like China, which by its size, age, and complexity allows the vagaries of its constituent territories to be be averaged out, if desired, or, if not, retained for themselves; and it gives time, place, and detail enough for the creation and testing of general hypotheses.

I cannot persuade the reader that this is so unless I explain how and why Chinese history was composed. Its relative coherence is mostly the work of the bureaucracy that ruled over China for some two thousand years, kept meticulous records of everything that seemed important to it, and wrote factually (mostly) faithful although heavily stylized accounts of the lives and deaths of the successive dynasties.[41] A learned translator of Ssu-ma Ch'ien, writing in the late nineteenth century, at a time when it was easier to believe in the objectivity of history, compares him, in part very favorably, with the Greek and Roman historians. He says that Ssu-ma and those who imitated his method preserved material invaluable for reconstructions that we may want to undertake:

> We can admire the marvelous historians of Greece and Rome, but they do not satisfy our intellectual exigencies; we try to disengage the material they made use of from the art with which they have dissimulated it. Ssu-ma Ch'ien almost completely frees us from this work because his intervention has not altered the original

texts at all [this is an exaggeration] . . . It is not possible to be enthusiastic about Ssu-ma Ch'ien [another exaggeration, expressing a French scholar's literary sensitivity]: a patient collector of old documents, he astonishes us more by his erudition than he seduces us by his genius; but his work has become great by the greatness of its subject.[42]

The Chinese themselves were sure they could learn from history, though the main lesson they got from it was usually the one they had formulated in advance, so that only the many details of its application remained in question. Out of respect for this preestablished lesson, most of the official Chinese historians gave up the effort to think independently; but they showed their historians' connoisseurship by selecting just those phrases and passages that would most faithfully transmit what appeared essential to them. They saw their function as that of preservation and transmission—in annals, biographies, tables, and monographs—to enable future generations to judge the preceding ones.[43] As defined in A.D. 819 by a historian writing to the emperor to protest against the corruption of historiography,

the duties of the historian are to encourage good and reprove evil, to express opinions in just speech with a straight brush, to record the merit and virtue of our divine dynastic house, to write down the deeds and accomplishments of the loyal and sage [ministers], to make a record of the shameful conduct of evildoers and sycophants, that may be handed down for ever.[44]

Is it possible to become somewhat the wiser about Machiavellism by studying history written by men with such ideals? In answering, we should note that all of civilization seemed to these historians to depend on China's bureaucrats, among whom they too were numbered. In spite of galling favoritism, many of the bureaucrats were chosen not for their social standing or the eminence of their patrons but for their ability. The way in which their ability was tested appears odd to us. It was by the mastery of certain conventional essay forms, which gave them the chance to exhibit their erudition in allusions and prove the depth to which they had assimilated the official culture.

Because the ideological interests of the recording bureaucrats remain fairly transparent, their stereotyped verdicts on history can be neutralized. However, information of a sort they were not interested in recording is difficult or impossible to recover, at least from the official histories, which underwent an elaborate process of editing and condensation. The official account represents China from the standpoint of someone who is either within or reporting to the bureaucratic center, from which China appears far more uniform than from peripheral points of view. These must be reconstructed from local records. The focusing of interest on the center is the price paid for the unity of the bureaucrats' history.[45]

The Chinese belief in history was such that the past and future verdicts of the historians were of surpassing interest to bureaucrats and rulers. A Chinese official who thought he had paid a heavy price (loss of office or punishment) for his loyalty to ideals might justify himself by writing an autobiography. By the fourteenth century, it had become fairly usual among officials to preempt the necrologist's verdict by writing death notices for themselves. To give an eminent example, when the first Ming emperor, Chu Yan-chang (1368–98) saw in a mirror how time had affected him—his face had grown pale and his hair white—he decided to put down the truth about himself as only he knew it. Instead of waiting for "the embellishing literary officials," he wrote, he would take the occasion to narrate his "own hardships and difficulties and clarify the imperial fortunes so that successive generations can see for themselves."[46]

Considering the moral pressure that Confucian tradition exerted on the individual, it is not surprising that during the Ming period (1368–1644) there were many scholar-officials who, like so many Benjamin Franklins, kept diaries in which they did moral bookkeeping, a practice others rejected as too mechanical and utilitarian, or simply recorded their faults ("I frequently lose my temper over small matters . . . In my moral indignation, I ignore consequences") or castigated themselves in a temper that now and then recalls Saint Augustine.[47]

Although such guilt reflects a particularly difficult period for officials, it is also reflects a deepened moral tradition, whose influence on individual officials should keep us from judging their whole group too cynically. The morally serious among them were sincere in judging themselves and their times by the precedent of the ideally familial, ceremonial, hierarchical, responsible, inspiring past that Confucius had found in the Chou dynasty. Ironically, this Confucian ideal of government was supported by political methods inherited from the Ch'in dynasty. Whether this adoption reflected Hsün Tzu's warnings, the ideas of the hated Legalists, practical necessity, or—as is most most plausible—all of these together, the government of China ruled in fact by Legalistic attitudes and expedients. Yet it was impossible for the government to give up the Confucian declaration that human beings are by nature kind and decent. A moral rather than merely utilitarian ideology was essential to keep the sense of fairness alive—the sense that the government was not an opportunistic system designed only to further the interests of the elite. The values taught a Confucian official were better fitted to make him conscientious and lend his work dignity than were rewards and punishments alone. A scholar argues that the Confucians' practical weakness lay not in what they advocated but in their lack of desire or ability to establish their own base of political power.[48] But this explanation may be just another way of saying that the true Confucian could not be a true Machiavellian or the true Machiavellian a genuinely moral Confucian.

As might be expected, there were well-defined limits to the authority of each Chinese official. His work was periodically reported on, he was interviewed by his superiors, he was rewarded for efficiency and punished for failure by fines, transfers, dismissals, and sometimes worse. Such measures enabled the central government to govern by means of its officials and yet guard its power from them by putting them under one another's supervision and so dividing them against themselves. The relations between the emperor, the central bureaucracy, the many local bureaucracies, and the populations they all ruled together became very complex. Each bureaucratic level, kind, and region developed interests of its own and methods of resisting unwelcome commands from above. The resistance was expressed in the ways in which the officials interpreted the commands, transferred them to one another, and reported their results. In other words, the bureaucratic machine that put the emperor's power into effect also limited him. Despite the Legalism in Chinese practice, the control over the apparatus of government exercised by the quasi-divine person at the center, the very emperor, was more than routinely effective only if he were a very forceful person served by an efficient, not too obstructive bureaucracy, one that could identify itself with his aims.

The Chinese experience shows that emperors, although so near to divine, made their lives more difficult by any desire they had to improve society. Theoretically supreme, the emperor was likely to become trapped in a hard-working career made up of ceremonies from which, as the emperors sometimes complained, they could find no rest; and all an emperor's protests and attempts to break out of his ceremonial confines and make effective changes might come to very little. He could too easily be defeated by the passivity, prudence, routine, favoritism, and concealment practiced by the officials he ruled— they also had the choice of making self-interested or truly virtuous appeals to their tradition.[49]

With its many small, persistent Machiavellisms, Chinese tradition made unimpeded tyranny very difficult, as the following recent reaction, written in acid, makes clear:

Nobody mourns the old Chinese bureaucracy. The social harm it did, even by the standards of its day, went well beyond the crushed ankles of helpless vagrants. Yet its nature impeded zealotry of any sort, whether for good or for ill. Without that great sheet-anchor, China yaws wildly in the storm. Without a workable alternative, leaders can manipulate mass fears and turn them with terrible force against the deviants and scapegoats of our own day—anyone vulnerable to labeling, either for his social origins or his exotic beliefs—with none to stand between.[50]

The records kept by the bureaucracy, which culminated in the last two dynasties in enormous collections of statutes and regulations, show a "cumbrous, gigantic machinery of government" with snags and quantities of red tape, that, all the same, functions efficiently.[51] If used critically and compared with other evidence, the records allow empirical tests of Machiavellian (and other) theories on subjects such as the effectiveness of the government's rule and the success of its attempts to maintain social peace.

The example of such testing I especially want to refer to is a research on the rule of the Ming dynasty, whose records provide information on local problems and disturbances of all kinds.[52] As usual with complex historical testimony, the answers arrived at are not always clear-cut. Yet they come as close as such evidence and research methods allow to verifying the Legalistic, Kautilyan, Machiavellian view that the social fabric can be preserved by a government that is intelligently repressive and maintains its army, keeps its taxes tolerable, and relieves famine effectively.

What grounds are there for this conclusion? Autocracy was not rare in China's previous history, but the early Ming dynasty was the most autocratic it had ever known. Quite aware of the temptations of power, this autocracy was careful to spread it so as to prevent any official body, bureaucrat, general, or eunuch or other inhabitant of the palace, from accumulating enough to become a serious challenge to the emperor. This preventive policy begins with the reign, from 1368 to 1398, of the first of the Mings (Chu Yan-chang, officially titled Huang-wu), the emperor whose obituary of himself I mentioned earlier.

The only surviving son of a peasant family of a starving, plague-ridden village, this emperor was proud of his origin and compassionate to ordinary farmers. His compassion led to him to reassure village elders, restrain soldiers from looting, and extend relief to areas ravaged by war. But though he identified himself with the peasants, he was soon persuaded that he needed the help of the literati and of a bureaucracy adapted from that of the preceding dynasty. "Rites and laws *(li fa)"* he said, "are the network sustaining the state. . . . When a state is being newly established they constitute the first order of priority."[53]

Because he hated the abuses of the preceding regime's bureaucrats, the emperor did his cruel best to terrorize his own bureaucrats into compliance and decency. The frankness he solicited from them was rewarded, to speak ironically, by ruthless punishment—the first prominent official to be frank got death, the second, hard labor. Public beatings were prescribed to humiliate erring officials, and harsh regulations were adopted to keep all the officials under surveillance and to overcome their laziness, over-staffing, and corruption. Nepotism was attacked by forbidding officials to appoint their own subordinates and by forbidding relatives to enter government service without imperial permission. An official who took a bribe above a certain sum "was decapitated, his head was spiked on a pole, and his corpse was skinned and stuffed with straw."[54] In keeping with Kautilyan precepts, "investigating guards," who included monks and nuns and Koreans and Muslims, were sent to collect information on officials of all the high ranks. Organized spying

> was carried out by a special secret agency, the Embroidered Guards [accountable to the emperor alone], who were empowered to investigate, arrest, and try special cases of corruption and organized opposition to the throne, especially conspiracy cases among the bureaucracy and rebellious sects. From 1382 to 1393, the Embroidered Guards handled at least three major purges of the bureaucracy, each of which resulted in some 10,000 executions.[55]

For fairness' sake, I should add that the emperor I have been describing would repeat, "If I am too lenient, people say I am muddleheaded, the law ruined and discipline lax; and if I am harsh, people call me a tyrant."[56] But freedom in the sense we are familiar with was not allowed, and it was in vain that a critic called on the emperor to abolish collective responsibility for crimes.[57] The Ming Code did whatever its authors could imagine to ensure order: It prescribed that professions should be hereditary, that commoners who entered or left a village should notify the authorities, and that no one without an official pass could travel a certain distance beyond a registered place of residence. The code regulated the activities of monks and permitted the execution or banishment of the members of sects who, by divination, prophecy, or other means, might cast doubt on the legitimacy of the regime. Merchants needed licenses to pursue their trades and innkeepers had to report monthly on their merchant-guests. In schools and civil service examinations, only the Confucian classics were allowed. Families virtuous by Confucian standards were rewarded and their deeds set down in local gazetteers.[58]

The research I have been summarizing shows that this repressiveness served its purpose well, that is, was successful in controlling the number and danger of armed disturbances and so in keeping the regime stable. The research points out that banditry and rebellion increased under two conditions. One was when times were bad and the government was not helpful enough with food or local construction. The other was when punishment became uncertain because government troops were far away, mutinous, or otherwise ineffective. The statistics show that revolts of tenants or bondservants, revolts that are easy to interpret as class conflict, were relatively infrequent. Just as a Legalist would have predicted, the combination of government aid when really necessary, vigorous social control, and quick, severe punishment made rebellion difficult and infrequent. Control of travellers and the distancing of heterodox sects must also have helped to maintain social stability. The same desire to keep life stable made indoctrination with Confucian precepts important to the government. For the sake of this indoctrination, regular village assemblies were held at which moral lectures were given and imperial decrees read exhorting the people to obey their parents, respect their superiors, live in harmony with their neighbors, educate their sons and brothers, rest content with what they had, and refrain from evil.[59]*

The historical evidence is, then, that the centralized, rigorous, paternalistic Ming autocracy was by and large effective for a long time. It underwent many threats. Under the less vigorous Ming govern-

---

*These findings fit in fairly well with a recent analysis of revolutions in Europe. According to this analysis, revolutions broke out when a state was unable to induce its best organized citizens to fulfil its demands, or when it made insupportable threats to strong collective identities or the rights attached to such identities, or when the ruler's power was visibly diminished by that of competitors. Control over military force was almost invariably essential. "Peasant revolts occurred repeatedly in Europe, but they almost never maintained themselves unless they allied with magnates or municipalities that had their own armed forces" (Tilly, *European Revolutions 1492–1992*, pp. 237, 241 [quoted]).

ments, traditional bureaucratic evils multiplied: Officials took bribes, bribed their superiors to maintain or better their appointments, squeezed the peasants unconscionably, appropriated government relief funds, and sentenced innocent people for the sake of the fines they paid. The army was troubled by absenteeism and desertion or used by its commanders for their private purposes. Army training was often neglected and morale was often low—in 1550, when the Mongols raided the outskirts of Peking (Beijing), the members of the elite Imperial Guards, who had a proud past, are said to have been so frightened that they broke into tears. Military spending on fortifications and mercenaries grew very high. Court extravagance joined with laxness and corruption led to a fiscal crisis, which led to new, more burdensome taxes, tax rebellions, and reduced sums for famine relief.[60]

Of course, no ideology or set of tactics is successful forever. The whole Ming system broke down when, as the Chinese would say, the dynasty lost its virtue. The loss became decisive under the Wan-li Emperor, who reigned from 1573 to 1620. Becoming aware that his Confucian officials preached the virtues more earnestly than they practiced them, he turned cynical. His officials took to criticizing him, and he began to resist them, although uncertainly, and ended by growing quite alienated from them. In the effort to keep his distance from them, he began to conduct most of his business on paper rather than in person and left important posts without incumbents; but though unwilling to cooperate with the bureaucracy, he was unable to reform the system. Nevertheless, he remained the official fount of the moral responsibility that he refused to assume. He still had too many papers to attend to, he complained, famine relief was still handed out, and rebellions were still crushed. But he ignored the day-to-day work of the court functionaries, did not answer memorials submitted to him, and ignored the need to fill vacancies in government posts—with the exception of those needed to replenish his own funds. The civil service lost its sense of direction and became impossible to manage. Individual magistrates, whose integrity could protect the population from being exploited by the local gentry, usually worked alone, and now, to their discouragement, their merit went mostly unrecognized. The imperial administration was demoralized at every level.[61]

The analysis of Ming government I have summarized is undoubtedly subject to correction. But it shows how historical records can be used to understand the Machiavellian practices of government in China and, I assume, elsewhere—with the necessary reasoned and intuitive adjustments. Another, though implicit lesson is the deep influence of history on the Chinese imagination. Even the most radical attempts to transform China have been influenced by the style of its historical record.

Radical attempts? I am referring to later history, in particular to Mao Tse-tung. Mao began as the rebellious son of a farmer and then became a kind of anarchist and student of Mill, Spencer, and Rousseau. Then he changed to the dynamic Marxist revolutionary who, in fact and theory, gave Marxism its Chinese form. During the last stages of his life, he turned into an embattled, finally paranoid sort of emperor. Much of his now malign activity was spent in persecuting intellectuals, whom he was unable not to suspect of treason. Yet this rebel, Marxist, and irregular emperor, turns out to have been a diligent student of Chinese history. Even during his army's Long Retreat, he kept reading, studying, and discussing it. Later he studied the official dynastic histories—printed for him in his last years in large type—especially the parts that deal with the winning and losing of thrones and, most especially, with the change from the native Ming to the alien Ch'ing dynasty.[62] Among emperors, he singled out for praise Shih Huang Ti, founder of the Ch'in dynasty.[63]

During the last year of Mao's life, when secretiveness and growing senility isolated him from direct action as much as Han Fei's ideal emperor, he undertook, by someone's count, his eighteenth reading of a work famous in Chinese historiography—he hardly could have paid equal attention to all its 9,612 pages. This work, the *Comprehensive Mirror for Aid in Government*, was a chronological history from 403 B.C. to A.D. 959. Compiled in the eleventh century by the great historian Ssu-ma Kuang and four assistants, it took in "all that a prince ought to know" by way of good and bad historical examples. Ssu-ma Kuang, whom Mao had also studied during the Great Retreat, explains how dynasties fall because they contravene the timeless principles of order. In practice, this means that rulers must maintain an unambiguous structure of authority that works by means of virtue, which is the ability to see and support the right. But it also means that the structure of authority is supported by appropriate rewards and punishments. Ssu-ma Kuang explains (as Mao must have had the chance to ponder) that because the ruler is responsible for choosing his advisers, it is his fault if their advice leads him to failure.[64] Mao's successor, Teng Hsiao-p'ing (Deng Xiaoping in the now more usual transliteration), is known to have studied Ssu-ma Kuang's book with an interest like Mao's in the shift of power from one to another emperor.[65]

It is not incidental that Mao's most influential adviser in the later, imperial part of his career was the highly Machiavellian Kang Sheng.

Kang Sheng was more successful personally than Li Ssu in that he died a natural death. His interest in traditional Chinese art, including the theater, and his ability as a calligrapher (with either hand) put an aesthetic face on acts that stand comparison for ruthlessness with those of the other great tyrants of our time. It is said that it was he who incited Mao to carry out, that is, to commit, the Cultural Revolution against the elite, the educated, and the other privileged persons. He did all he could to earn his informal title, The king of Hell. The number of actual executions during this revolution has been estimated, by extrapolation from statistics in several Chinese counties, as 2,200,000. The number of deaths that resulted from the revolution must have been much larger.[66]

How adequate is the Machiavellian description of political life?

The answer is that, at critical points, Machiavellian description is often more realistic than any other; but its realism is limited by two faults: its inability to grasp the depth of the human need for trust and intimacy and its tendency to fall into a self-defeating suspiciousness. These faults are faults in political understanding. Therefore, if we think of Machiavellism as a general doctrine of *raison d'état*, it suffers not from being objective but from not being objective enough.

I will be brief in explaining this answer because it has been the burden of so much of this book. Machiavellism penetrates the facade behind which politics is so often concealed; it refuses to engage in the futile scolding with which moralists confront actual politics; and it emphasizes the contingency of human affairs. These are strengths, but it is a weakness of Machiavellism that it relegates all optimism relative to uncoerced humans to an ancient, now impossible past. At its extreme, Machiavellism speaks in the voice of a criminologist who runs an organization with nothing in mind but the potential criminality of its members.

There is no disputing the Machiavellian conclusion that whoever uses deception and force effectively has the political advantage. But the qualifying word *effectively* makes the conclusion circular because it says no more than that whoever succeeds is successful. The conclusion is circular because the use of deception and force often fails, and what may cause them to fail may be the opponent's qualities of truthfulness, faithfulness, resourcefulness, and un-Machiavellian, straightforward intelligence. Therefore, if a Machiavelli is taken to say that deception and force are most successful when used with the fewest scruples, he will often be wrong: scruples, too, can be politically effective. And if the

Machiavelli says that the pursuit of glory—in the sense of political might and territorial conquest—is the only worthwhile political aim, he is revealing no more than a subjective preference; and his belief that a country can flourish only if its people engage in frequent wars is unproved and can have an extraordinarily high human cost.

Let me put my criticism in another way. As we know very well, it is characteristic of Machiavellian thinkers to say that human nature is bad, and of their opponents to say the opposite, that human nature is good; and it is not uncharacteristic of people with a cynical attitude toward politics to say that all politicians (or rulers, or governments) are corrupt. All such statements and counterstatements, we have concluded, are gross oversimplifications that make it harder, not easier, to understand what really goes on. Those who accept the statements do not take into account the attitudes and purposes of those who make them and do not undertake a searching enough examination of the evidence by which the statements are supported. The statements rest on the absurd assumption that our understanding can be furthered by giving a categorical answer to the question, Is human nature good or bad? or by responding with a simple yes or no to the conclusion that human nature is such that it must always be curbed by strict laws and heavy punishments, the stricter and heavier the better. If the Machiavellis, speaking honestly, avoid or qualify some of their characteristic assertions, they are harder to criticize; but the more they qualify, the less Machiavellian they become.

It is, has been, and will be true that—given the more or less instinctive utilitarianism of human beings—the plea of political necessity will continue to excuse any and every political act. This situation is so usual in fact, so resistant to moral responses, and so awkward for moral analysis that we often stop moralizing about it and accept it as necessary. To stop moralizing about it is natural because, to recapitulate, Machiavellian tactics are incorporated into the intrinsic life of every human group, beginning with the family and going on to the nonfamilial assembly of all nations. But though the tactics are the nature and need of the social, human animals we are, they are limited by many factors, including tradition and the habits of decency. We are complex creatures that change in more directions than the Machiavellis allow. They are not right enough to allow us to neglect alternatives to the politics they describe (with the pleasure of disenchantment). Their Machiavellism would be more convincing if it could open itself to the unideal but optimistic possibilities from which it habitually turns away.

Have philosophers raised any decisive arguments against Machiavellism?

The answer is that philosophical arguments cannot in themselves be decisive. If we set aside those based on religious dogma or doubtful metaphysics, the most cogent of the classical ones are those of Kant. It appears to me to serve clarity and brevity best if we refer to the arguments as Kant himself put them rather than to the varied forms they take among the political philosophers now influenced by him. Everyone can adapt him as wished to the present.[67]

As I have noted, Kant has a Machiavellian eye for human nature but argues that a good future is likely to emerge out of the evil present. If this good future comes, he adds, it will be the outcome of human selfishness. Kant's unsentimental judgment of humans combined with his passion for truth and justice make him the most considerable anti-Machiavellian philosopher of whom I know. I represent his thought mainly as it appears in his essay "Perpetual Peace," all of which is directly relevant to our theme.[68]

"Perpetual Peace" suggests a compact between states that rules out all present reasons for future wars and all acquisitions of one independent state by another. A radically anti-Machiavellian provision of the treaty rules out the use in wartime of any means that would make mutual confidence impossible in the peacetime that follows. Such means, Kant specifies, include the use of assassins or poisoners, the breach of agreements, or the instigation of treason within the enemy state. He argues that these means should be outlawed even in wartime because if all trust in the enemy is destroyed during the war, it will be impossible to conclude a peace and the war will turn into one of extermination. Such means as assassination, poisoning, and the encouragement of treason are not only despicable in themselves, Kant says, but, once used in times of war, can no longer be confined to them. A practice such as spying, which exploits others' dishonesty, will survive into peacetime and, in doing so, will nullify its purpose.[69]

"After all," Kant says, "war is only a regrettable expedient for asserting one's rights by force within a state of nature, where no court of justice is available to judge with legal authority." When a judge is lacking, there can be no formally unjust action nor any war of punishment for unjust actions. Lacking the possibility of true legal adjudication or just punishment, wars easily turn into nothing but opportunities to exterminate the enemy. In a war of extermination, the victims are likely to be both of the combatting sides. Along with them, the right itself falls victim. Such simultaneous annihilation "would allow perpetual peace only on the vast graveyard of the human race." Therefore, "a war of this kind and the employment of all means which might bring it about must be absolutely prohibited."[70]

In agreement with Hobbes (whom he ordinarily opposes), Kant declares that a state of nature is a state of war, because even when there are no hostilities, there is the constant threat that they will break out. "Thus the state of peace must be *formally instituted*, for a suspension of hostilities is not itself a guarantee of peace."[71] Kant is convinced that an effective agreement to keep the peace forever requires every state that is party to the agreement to be republican, that is, a state all of whose members are recognized to be genuinely human and therefore free. The legislation in such a state applies to all of them; as citizens, they are all legally equal to one another. The republican constitution, says Kant, is the only one that can be derived from the idea of an original contract. With respect to the right, it is "the original basis of every kind of civil constitution."[72]

In a republic, Kant goes on, the consent of the citizens is required to decide on a declaration of war. Because this commits them to great misery, they give their consent only with great hesitation. In contrast, under a constitution that is not republican, the head of the state, who is the state's owner, finds it very simple to go to war—the decision, says Kant (who cites no historical evidence), will not force the head of state to make the slightest sacrifice.*

Kant is adamant that a republican form of the state is not a democracy, which he understands, in the Greek sense, as a state that allows all its citizens to make decisions concerning the individual without his or her consent. Unlike the so-called republics of antiquity, he declares, the government that accords with the concept of right must be based on the

---

*Perhaps surprisingly, Kant thinks that a rightly fought war is ennobling and a long peace possibly degrading. Some five years before *Perpetual Peace*, he writes: "War itself, provided it is conducted with order and a sacred respect for the right of civilians, has something sublime about it. . . . On the other hand, a prolonged peace favors the predominance of a mere commercial spirit, and with it a debasing self-interest, cowardice, and effeminacy, and tends to degrade the character of the nation" (*Critique of Judgment*, trans. Meredith, pp. 112–13 [para. 28]). Hegel objects to Kant's vision of perpetual peace. He argues that a league of states "must generate opposition and create an enemy. Not only do people emerge from wars with added strength, but nations [*nationemen*] by civil dissension gain internal peace as a result of wars with their external enemies" (Hegel, *Elements of the Philosophy of Right*, trans. Nisbet, p. 362 [para. 324, add. G]. See O'Hagan, "On Hegel's Critique of Kant's Moral and Political Philosophy," pp. 155–59).

representative system. For the sake of its own security, each nation must demand that the others accept a constitution that secures the rights of each. This demand would require the establishment of a federation of equal states, which is essentially different from an international state, in which the superior, who is the legislator, rules over an inferior, the people who obey the laws.[73]

Although he does not mention Machiavelli, Kant spends much of his essay denouncing Machiavellism as it has been described here. Of course, his denunciation does not conceal his opinion that human nature is highly though not totally depraved. Much of the depravity is concealed, he says, by the constraints that rule a society; but the same depravity continues to be displayed in the unrestricted relations between independent nations. In his characteristic way, he explains that every state justifies its military aggressions by appealing to principles that show that the state pays an at least verbal homage to the concept of right. To him, this homage is one of the proofs that man has the (still dormant) moral capacity to overcome the principle of evil within him and to hope that others will do the same. How else could it be explained that even the states that intend to go to war against one another speak in the name of the right?[74]

Kant's view of the relation of human nature to politics is not unlike Machiavelli's and, except for his preference for a republican state, not unlike that of Hsün Tzu. His belief that humans are evil by nature means to him that they are not merely weak, but contain within themselves a deep, radical, inextinguishable principle of evil, the source of which he does not pretend to understand. However, he adds, humans also have a moral instinct that, despite everything, will win by virtue of the principles that universal reason suggests and that the state, armed with severe but reasonable punishments, will apply without partiality.

Kant's world resembles Hsün Tzu's in that it embodies the equivalent of Hsün Tzu's (usually) impartial moral Heaven. That is, Kant believes that nature takes on for us the appearance of a wise higher cause and shows the way to the objective goal of human beings, so that providence, as we name it, fosters the economic and social conditions that in the long run tend to create a perpetual peace.[75] Likewise, as Kant puts it in his essay, linguistic and religious differences separate nations and at times create mutual hatred and give pretexts for war, but as culture develops, human beings are led to greater mutual understanding and peace:

Hard as it may sound, the problem of setting up a state can be solved even by a nation of devils (so long as they possess understanding)... For such a task does not involve the moral improvement of man; it only means finding out how the mechanism of nature can be applied to men in such a manner that the antagonism of their hostile attitudes will compel one another to submit to coercive laws, thereby producing a condition of peace within which the laws can be enforced.[76]

Sooner or later, in Kant's view, the spirit of commerce, which cannot coexist with war, takes hold of people, and states feel compelled, out of quite nonmoral motives, to promote the peace. When this happens,

wherever in the world there is a threat of war breaking out, they will try to prevent it by mediation, just as if they had entered into a permanent league for this purpose ... In this way, nature guarantees perpetual peace by the actual mechanism of human inclinations.[77]

Such a response by the states of the world is by no means certain, says Kant, but its likelihood is enough to make it the duty of human beings to work toward it.[78] He continues to explain this view in an appendix on the "the disagreement between morals and politics in relation to perpetual peace." Experience, he there says, does not show that honesty is the best policy. Nonetheless, "honesty is better than any policy" because honesty "is an indispensable condition of any policy whatsoever." Careless of this truth, "worldly-wise politicians resort to despicable tricks, for they are out only to exploit the people (and if possible the whole world) by influencing the current ruling power in such a way as to ensure their own private advantage." They resemble the lawyers who enter politics and think and act as they do because, they claim, they know men; but "they do not know *man* and his potentialities, for this requires a higher anthropological vantage-point." They and their likes have learned to expropriate for their own benefit the rights of a state over its own or a neighboring people. If, for instance, they commit a crime in leading their people to desperation and rebellion, they deny any guilt and attribute it to others, or they blame the nature of man because this nature leads them to anticipate that if they do not preempt the violence of others by means of their own violence, they will themselves be overpowered by it.[79]

In a subjective sense, Kant continues, that is, in relation to the self-ish disposition of human beings, the conflict between morality and politics "will and ought to remain active, since it serves as a whetstone of virtue." A whetstone because it is our unqualified duty to confront the evil within ourselves and make whatever sacrifices are necessary to overcome its wiles. This remains possible because there is no objective or theoretical conflict

> between morality and politics . . . And although politics in itself is a difficult art, no art is required to combine it with morality. For as soon as the two come into conflict, morality can cut through the knot which politics cannot untie.[80]

Kant combines this argument with another according to which, whatever the reason, it is in the highest degree wrong for people to rebel. They do have inalienable rights against the head of state, as he says elsewhere, contradicting Hobbes. But they do not the right to use force to claim these rights.[81] The reason, stated before, is that the right to rebellion would defeat the very purpose for the state's existence. By the logic of moral relationships, it is impossible for the people to proclaim their rightful authority over the ruler whose authority over them makes the state possible. Yet, by the same logic, if they rebel successfully, the former head of state, now a subject, would have no right to rebel in order to restore his former position.[82]

In the later *Metaphysics of Morals*, Kant puts the emphasis differently: "The head of state has only rights against his subjects and no duties (that he can be coerced to fulfill)." Anyone who rebels and, above all, attacks the person or life of the head of a state, "must be punished by nothing less than death for attempting to *destroy his fatherland (parricida)*." The formal execution of the head of state, such as that of Charles I or Louis XVI, is a formally evil crime inexpiable in both this world and the next.[83]

Despite this argument against the right to rebel and the severity he thought justified against it, in a somewhat later publication, Kant shows himself to be partial to the French Revolution, the revolution, as he calls it, "of a gifted people."* He says that the sympathy the revolu-

---

*Earlier, Kant was ready to argue that the French Revolution was not truly a revolution because the king, Louis XVI, had abdicated his authority to the Estates General. Returned by his abdication to the state of nature, Kant said, the Estates General had the right to legislate in the absence of a sovereign. See Henrich, "On the Meaning of Rational Action in the State," p. 111.

tion aroused in the hearts of its spectators was evidence that its cause could be only "a moral predisposition in the human race."[84] Although in principle unqualifedly opposed to revolution, Kant adopts the unqualified principle that "the rights of man must be held sacred, however great a sacrifice the ruling power may have to make . . . For all politics must bend the knee before right."[85]

What makes Kant's thought most valuable to us at this point is his insistence on the possibility of universalism by means of selfishness guided by reason and inspired, as if from another, nonselfish world, by the inner voice of conscience. To him, there is no escape from the constant struggle for primacy between good and evil, between *ought to*, on the one hand, and *like to* or *take pleasure in*, on the other, which is to say, between universal principle and subjective preference. Since he takes the coordination of these two opposites to be impossible, Kant preaches the supremacy, through struggle, of principle, which by its free decisions is able to overcome contingent and subjective preferences. The autonomy of the human will depends on this inner conflict and its leavening by reasonable hopes. What we discover, says Kant, is the force of the impossible and yet reasonable ideal. For we discover that universal reason and the moral law it teaches always demand more than can either be fulfilled or explained—ordinary human reason is confined by Kant (as it is by Buddhists) to the world of phenomena.

To deal with this limitation of reason to the world of phenomena, Kant argues, three things must be postulated, none of which can be proved. The first is God, by the idea of which the moral person is enabled to judge. The second is immortality, belief in which is necessary for a plausible relation between one's conduct and one's well-being. The third is freedom, the idea of which is the condition by virtue of which we make choices and demonstrate our moral worth. These three postulates are the modes in which reason complements itself and allows itself to have faith in universal reason.[86]

This is not the place to go further into Kant's reasoning or to react seriously to his opinion—to me an almost excruciating combination of faith and doubt—that we are compelled to believe in God, immortality, and freedom even though they are beyond proof. More disturbingly still, we are told by Kant that we must believe in freedom even though it is in direct contradiction to the laws of causality that express the very structure of our thought. How the Machiavellians would answer his political views it is by now unnecessary to repeat. However, I feel compelled to respond in their name to Kant's argument that, even in wartime, the breaking of agreements and the use of spies and assassins makes peace impossible and turns the war into a war of extermination.

He is right in saying that these Machiavellian methods turn war into an arena of cruel deceptions; besides, we now have stronger reasons than Kant's to fear that the peace we finally inherit will be, in his phrase, the peace of the graveyard. Yet almost nothing of what Kant argues about deception is historically plausible.

What can be counted as true in Kant's argument is expressed in the fear of leaders, even in wartime, to encourage the practice of assassination. They obviously prefer the rule of an eye for an eye to that of a leader for a leader. But Kant's fear that the use of spies will be carried over from war to peace ignores the fact that peacetime spying was already widespread in his time. If his statement that such spying will vitiate its purpose means that it rewards lying, teaches error as often as truth, and creates double agents, he is right. Yet to require leaders, especially in wartime, to give up spies is like requiring them to stop lighting their way on dangerously dark nights. Kant is also not convincing when he argues that the destruction of trust will make it impossible to conclude a peace. It is possible to conclude a treaty with leaders other than those who conducted the war. In any case, the character of the persons who sign a treaty is not very important because what guarantees that it will be kept is not their trustworthiness—they may soon be displaced—but the military superiority of the victors and, even more, the situation that makes the keeping of the treaty advantageous to both winner and loser. When the situation no longer remains so, in the absence of a body to enforce it, the treaty's validity in practice comes to an end.

What I should most like to retain of Kant is his preference for republicanism—which we call democracy—and his stress on the endless, inevitable battle within humans of good and evil. The battle is such that the potential for good is never fully realized. But, as he says, persons are free in that they accept or can accept the rules for their own conduct. Inherently autonomous in this sense, they have inherent dignity and deserve to be fully equal before the law. In saying this, Kant seems to be expressing in philosophical terms what everyone feels about fairness and unfairness. Principles like his seem to be the only ones on which human beings everywhere may possibly agree.[87]

As we have seen, Kant's view is that the human need for autonomy is best served in a "republican," that is, democratic state, which best cultivates the freedom that can make people truly responsible to themselves and therefore to one another. Such democratic states coexist best, he says, with others of their kind. Kant may be right. By now, there is empirical evidence that stable democracies, unlike authoritarian states, are reluctant to take up arms against one another—where other democracies are concerned, the Kantian pact, though not formalized, does in fact guard the peace.[88]

As to the battle of good with evil, Kant accepts that political life runs largely as the Machiavellians have described it. He is, on the whole, plausible when he continues that it is selfishness guided by reason that legislates the moral laws that bring subjective desire into a slowly increasing conformity with what he calls the general will. As we can sense from this argument, to Kant the premise and desideratum of morality is the unity that is created by free, if selfish choice, while the lack of unity in the world as a whole is the source of all its evils. The end, the endlessly distant end, is wholly good. And everything that controverts itself—whether dogmatic metaphysics, politics as the history of wars, or faith as a war to exterminate others faiths—is an evil that destroys itself.[89]

Kant's forbidding view of human nature was disputed by contemporary thinkers, among them his admirer Friedrich Schiller. In his "letters" *On the Aesthetic Education of Man* (1794–95)—a discussion of the impulses that make up human nature—Schiller tries to persuade the reader that the aesthetic impulse, the impulse to play, is able to create the human unity that Kant thinks impossible. He agrees with Kant that our nature is dual and that feeling and thinking exclude one another, but he believes that the enjoyment of beauty achieves a momentary union between matter (what the senses show) and form (by which thinking shapes what the senses show). To Schiller, this union proves that our two natures are compatible and that the infinite can be realized in the finite (a conclusion Kant is sometimes obscurely ready to accept). Truth is potentially included in beauty, says Schiller, so that the possibility of passage from the one to the other need not be questioned as Kant questions it. This conclusion allows Schiller to conclude that there can be a higher type of political organization, which he calls *aesthetic*, in which freedom becomes the fundamental law and in which the will of the whole is consummated through the nature of the individual. Only the aesthetic mode of perception, he thinks, can make a whole of man and unite the sensuous and spiritual parts of his being.[90]

I cite Schiller's view because I believe that the imagination displayed in art has a decisive effect on the social life of human beings. This is not because everyone is deeply interested in art, but because art, or, more broadly, the work of imagination, acquaints people with each other's inward perceptions and gives them the ability to share in a common culture. Art tells the truth in the sense that it reveals one persons's feelings and fantasies to another and creates the same intangible foci of experience. Art therefore belongs to that aspect of social life that I earlier called *social attentiveness and reciprocity.* By forming human beings' imaginative relationships with one another, art is essential to the process of identification by which the members of every group see themselves as the same as or different from those of every other—the people who share their imaginative lives share their social and political identities.

I find Kant's reasoning satisfying and yet deeply inadequate—in making it more adequate, Schiller draws its sting, denatures it. Kant is so committed to human intractability that he is ready to say, without qualification, that human selfishness, antagonism, and competitiveness are permanent human characteristics, immune to all attempts to eradicate them. He should be applauded for his courage in saying so, and for his courage in trying to see beyond this ineradicable evil, as he calls it. But his extreme polarization of human impulses into good and bad and his refusal to see the good except as it comes to expression in an absolute, unrealizable, purely formal principle makes his philosophy too remote from the psychodramatic human reality—unless one takes him as bringing to light, without metaphysics, what the human sense of fairness entails.

To Kant, human beings live a diametrical opposition: their inborn, pure selfishness, desire, and feeling opposed to their inborn, pure, objective reason. Schiller unites the opposites, the purely selfish and the purely reasonable, with play that is art. Bound strictly to his logic, Kant, though sometimes tempted by such a union, is in the end too formalistic to allow it (except as an unprovable hope). When the union is accepted, as Schiller wants, the human being no longer appears irredeemably selfish, which is to say, radically evil. By his rigid polarization, Kant abandons the middle area in which human beings in practice mostly live and have their being. For all the extensive knowledge he has of what he calls, in the terminology of his time, anthropology, his dualism makes the therapeutic middle (as I see it) much more difficult to inhabit. But though Kant's meliorism and his absolutism continue to be at odds, as a philosopher he is honorable, by which I mean, too honestly observant and wise to be utopian.

Does the prevalence of Machiavellism rule out the likelihood of a better political future?

The answer is that there can be no answer in the shape of a prediction, but that the fear of disaster is so widespread that, as Kant foresaw, the fear itself makes hope more reasonable. In trying to think realistically without giving in too much to Machiavellism, I would start with the Machiavellis' sensitivity to change. I would agree with them that circumstances and people are variable but add, as they might accept, that people's reactions oscillate around formulable but uncertain states (construable as attractors in the sense of the mathematics of chaos). I would emphasize (is it with Guicciardini?) that people pay only moderate attention to moral rules and political generalizations and react more in keeping with the local situation at a particular time, a situation too composed of nuances to be grasped by the bare abstractions of ordinary intellectual analysis: just as the color of butterflies' wings comes off as plain dust when you touch them, the living color of a local situation comes off as plain words when you analyze it. Therefore people, including politicians and rulers, understand or feel—as theorists may not—that because of the contingency in life, it may be as harmful as it is helpful to guide oneself by strict principles, even those of Machiavellism.

The role that principles play in relation to circumstance, character, and social pressure, is not a usually dominant one. This is so in part because principles clash with one another in ways that cannot often be solved by turning to still another principle. To be effective, principles must in any case be embedded in character; and, as I have repeated, we cannot get much insight into character by assigning it any constant nature. Though pessimistic about human nature, Machiavelli knew that habits of mind and action—the humans' varieties of ethos—are changeable. He finds a stably decent people only in the past, and other Machiavellians concur; but in idealizing the distant or mythological, as they could not the present, the Machiavellians (often) denied that the present "human nature" could change much for the better. But "human nature" remains as changeable as it has always been. Very much depends on habits that are a sometimes prolonged inheritance of families, neighborhoods, or any relatively cohesive, stable group of people. Civic responsibility is less a set of conscious ethical conclusions than of social attitudes that are maintained or destroyed by local approval and disapproval:*

---

*These near-platitudes reflect the variations in the ethos of people who live in different areas or countries. I am told, for example, that in Denmark the outright corruption of officials is hard to conceive, but that free income is almost universally concealed from the income-tax authorities. In defense of what I say in the text above, I cite a study of the regional governments established in Italy in 1970. These governments, which correspond approximately to the historic divisions of Italy, restore a good deal of local control in urban affairs to the citizens. Some of the local governments have proved far more successful than others. The study claims that the differences cannot be accounted for by obvious

Fabrics of trust enable the civic community more easily to sur-
mount what economists call "opportunism," in which shared
interests are unrealized because each individual, acting in wary
isolation, has an incentive to defect from collective action . . . Toc-
queville observed that "feelings and ideas are renewed, the heart
enlarged, and the understanding developed only by the reciprocal
action of men upon one another."[91]

At the opposite pole there are the areas in which participation in
political life is not decided by collective needs but by personal depen-
dency or greed:

Corruption is widely regarded as the norm, even by politicians
themselves, and they are cynical about democratic purposes.
"Compromise" has only negative overtones. Laws (almost everyone agrees) are made to be broken, but fearing others' lawless-
ness, people demand sterner discipline . . . Nearly everyone feels
powerless, exploited, and unhappy.[92]

In the end, chance, social pressure, and character determine the
degree to which each of us uses Machiavellian tactics and the degree to
which amoralism or "amoral familism" proves itself to be a reasonable
strategy for survival. Impossible to avoid in private life, Machiavellian
tactics on a large scale pervade politics, sacred and profane. But speaking in general—not of particular painful situations—none of this ought
to cause the (relative) non-Machiavellian to despair or adopt a merely
cynical attitude toward society. That is, a moderate Machiavellism,
human in scale and sociability, is attractive even to most ambitious persons; and the minimal Machiavellism of most of us—which might as
well be called anti-Machiavellism—is just as compatible with a satisfac-
tory life as its more drastic varieties.

All the possibilities are open: Machiavellis can fail, the extreme
ones as easily as the moderate, and basically non-Machiavellians can

---

socioeconomic reasons but only by the level of a culturally inherited sense of
civic responsiblity. This level determines the willingness to trust others and
work for the communal good. Remarkably, the centers of greater trust and civic
responsibility are such communities as Florence, Bologna, and Milan, all with
an old and (says the research) still deep commitment to civic life, while the for-
merly monarchical South has a fragmented social life and "a culture of distrust" (See Putnam, *Making Democracies Work*, pp. 114, 115). This observed
difference between different areas of Italy appears to be reflected even in the
currently revealed, extraordinarily widespread corruption.

succeed; and Machiavellis, too, remain with unsatisfied ambitions and unassuaged suspicions, so that there is no good reason to envy them very much. Even people with the desire for an equitable life may be lucky or effective enough to witness its partial fulfillment, with the help of persons whose Machiavellism is tempered by a still active conscience. The wicked have as much trouble inheriting the earth as do the rest of us. Whoever does not try to escape the human condition excessively in any particular direction can enjoy it, luck permitting, as well as can reasonably be hoped.

This near-optimism is the more persuasive if one is occupied to one's limit with something greater than oneself, some enterprise, craft, art, or science, to which Machiavellism, in any strong, consistent sense, is likely to be more destructive than helpful. The truth can still attract and help: Truth in its sense of discovery and communication can make the need to lie socially more transparent and innocuous and can expose political lying and ruthlessness for exactly what it is. The fantasy of the discovery of truth, which is the fantasy of fantasies among the really curious, can be directed against the fantasy of political power.

Does religion have a reasonable place in such hopes? The moral standards that religions preach sometimes lead them a way beyond dogmatism. To some religions, ecumenical passions seem more natural than to others. Considered in the abstract—abstracted from history—at least two of the great religions, Buddhism and Neo-Confucianism, are often rather close to a humanitarianism without excessive dogma. Buddhism in some of its forms and Confucianism in perhaps all are so strongly oriented toward a rational ethics that it has been doubted whether they are religions at all; but, in the end, this doubt is a rather idle one of definition that cannot survive a close look at what actual Buddhists and Confucians believe and do.

Of Buddhism I have already spoken. Neo-Confucianism is Confucianism sensitized by Buddhism to become, out of its own resources, more systematic, metaphysical, and carefully humane than before. Both religions can be interpreted as ethical standpoints able to dispense with magical dogmas. In principle, we know, Buddhism requires the utmost kindness to any living being in any condition, and Neo-Confucianism teaches innate sympathy with all human beings, with living beings of any kind, and with everything in nature, of which, it teaches, we are an integral part.

It seems that ethical positions such as these, though affected and sometimes dominated by Machiavellian impulses, are naturally favorable beginnings for identification with humanity at large. I believe this to be so in spite of earlier tragicomic attempts to create a framework common to all forms of Buddhism and in spite of the unique connection between Confucianism and Chinese civilization. A belief in humanity at large is possible, with modification, in other religions. However, the briefly encouraging episodes that history records do not justify any more than modest hope in the ability of religions to go beyond their dogmas, defensiveness, and selfishness—maybe the conditions by which they, like other human institutions, can exist at all.

Seeing beyond one's dogma and one's birthplace are no longer as unnatural as they were. It is no longer difficult to understand and to feel that the world is an interdependent economic unit, that it is a geographical and ethological unit, that it is not far from one in art and literature, or that it is morally and even selfishly united by the demand that those who are better off help the others. Philosophy, which has up to now only pretended to be universally human, can become more nearly so by the mutual awareness of its different traditions. Science, by its very conception, goes beyond all national, religious, and linguistic bounds.

Suppose that, keeping in mind everything that has been said here, we recall all the arguments—of the Legalists and their like, of the Confucians and other traditionalists, of the philosophers, most notably Kant, who believe in an absolute rational ethics, and of the anthropologists, psychologists, and sociologists on whom I have often depended. Should we conclude that, all things considered, what we need in order to minimize our Machiavellian tendencies is a morality that is impartial as the Legalists recommend, is taught by reason, precept, and practice, as the Confucians recommend, and is developed by compromise out of clashing interests as Machiavelli and Kant recommend? Should the constructive selfishness of Kantian universality be instilled into the individual by the psychologists' means and into the prevailing ethos by the means the anthropologists and sociologists know best?

The sad and laughable confusion that would follow any conscious attempt to merge all these tells us how resistant human life is to full analysis or to full theoretical synthesis. Life is simple in the sense that it has such an obvious animal basis. But life is infinitely complicated in the sense that we are intellectually unable to mimic the subtle variability of our natural responses—instinct and intuition are often superior to intellect alone—so our doctrines are too gross to describe what happens and too insensitive to predict will happen if we follow one course rather than another.

We can be sure that, like crime, Machiavellism will never disappear because it exists in the complex entanglements of social life: of the legal with the illegal, the moral with the immoral, the kind with the cruel, and the truthful with the deceptive. But though Machiavellism is immortal, circumstances, which have so often pushed us in its direction, are now also pushing us in the direction of the universalism that Kant foresaw. The plea of necessity will continue to be made to excuse any and every act; but the same plea is now turned against Machivellism's worst excesses. The world is now so interdependent, its tensions so many, and its armaments so effective, that it seems to be heading toward disasters beyond any that human beings have ever caused themselves. It is therefore more reasonable than before to transfer one's deepest loyalty from a nation to humanity, or, in more practical terms, to an effective union of nations or, at the extreme, a world government.

Neither sentiment nor reason can decide how good the prospects are for such a union or government and, if it is created, whether or not it will be of a kind more to be honored or loved than belittled or hated. It is possible to escape an oppressive tribe, village, or state, but there may be nowhere to escape from an oppressive universal government. So while the smaller loyalties no longer answer our interdependence, there is no way of being sure that the larger ones will prove themselves to be more satisfying. Because there is no way to make very plausible guesses about the future, it is everyone's temperament that takes over at this point and gives the answers for which reason is inadequate. The optimist, born or made, will imagine success, while the pessimist, with more visible evidence to command, will be convinced beforehand of failure. As should be apparent, I myself am of the intermediate sort, hopeful but doubtful, deeply convinced of the need, but not of what will actually answer it.

While history does not encourage utopianism, it does not exclude the hope to limit Machiavellian deception and violence. The hope is supported by testimony that there have been societies and times in which Machiavellism has been muted. The ability to identify ourselves with a broader human culture, although still much less natural than cultural nationalism, is already at least feasible. Human beings have proved so fantastically inventive that they may even find ways to invent a humane political future for themselves.

CONCLUSION

To end as pointedly and clearly as I can, I repeat my main thesis and follow it with eleven subtheses, which summarize the answers I have given to the questions on which the two preceding chapters are based. As I have said in somewhat different words, the main thesis is that Machiavellism has been integral to the political life of every civilization and of many or most smaller societies. Whoever ignores the persistence of Machiavellism gives up the chance to understand the morality that in fact governs organized social life.

The subtheses are as follows:

1. Machiavellian behavior is normal, that is, usual and to be expected. Indignant as we may be at its excesses, it is naive to be surprised by them. Machiavellism or, briefly, political amorality, is not a special problem to which a special solution can be given but behavior inseparable from being human.

2. The virtues of truthfulness and fairness contradict Machiavellism, but they are not an adequate defense against it. Truth, as we learn in practice, plays different roles, each subject to its own social imperatives. Because it does social harm to be consistently truthful in everyday life, the measure of the truth and untruth by which we relate to one another is fitted to the mood, the occasion, and the individual. As for fairness, we learn in practice that it is an ambiguous, often impractical ideal. We also learn that conscience is selective and that conspicuous virtuousness attracts resentment and may isolate one socially.

3. The desire to discover and communicate the truth can be very strong and it affects Machiavellis no less than others. A Machiavelli who teaches the truth that the truth has to be sacrificed for the

263

good of the state is quite willing to be caught in an existential dilemma, which is that his explanation of Machiavellism limits the ability to practice it.

4. Most of us need to follow a leader and all of us to belong to a group. The need is so powerful that leaders and groups not only fix what is publicly allowed and forbidden but influence what individuals themselves prefer to do, avoid, and even be. The result is that the impulse to act morally is often much the same as the impulse to conform and be accepted. An individual's willingness to regard Machiavellian tactics as desirable or moral depends on the strength of that individual's identification with the group in whose behalf the tactics are exercised. However, moral scruples are widespread enough to create a constant struggle at each social level between the desire to escape Machiavellian tactics and to profit by them either as a group or an individual.

5. Leaders find it difficult to distinguish their private ambitions from their public goals. This conjunction or confusion of private with public welfare, of egoism with altruism, is characteristic of the leaders of groups of every size and nature. The egoism of an imperviously ambitious leader may increase rather than diminish the devotion of followers—his egoism becomes theirs. Their readiness to accept the Machiavellian plea of necessity is proportionate to their devotion to the leader and to the size and internal unity of the group on whose behalf they accept the plea.

6. We cannot understand the great Machiavellian leaders unless we grasp that they are adventurers of a ruthless sort, who, like all adventurers, are exhilarated by the risks they take. When the risks are in the name of a professed ideal, all those who are drawn either to the leader or to the ideal, share the leader's exhilaration—at least as long as the adventure, having become their own as well, does not cause them more suffering than they want to bear.

7. Moral tradition is constructed over a long period of time with the purpose, among others, of maintaining the social equilibrium. It therefore tends to restrict any leader whose ambitions or acts threaten the equilibrium, which is the social consensus. But moral tradition, as embodied in its institutions and titular leaders, develops the casuistic ability to justify Machiavellian tactics that, on their face, contradict the explicit ideals the tradition professes. Conformism, too, can be devious and violent.

8. History allows no accurate predictions and teaches no lessons that changing circumstances will not sooner or later modify. But history multiplies the reserves of experience on which intelligence can draw. There are stretches of history that were recorded well enough for us to judge, by whatever standard, the success or failure of the political tactics that were used. Chinese history, which is extensively documented, provides an example of the relatively prolonged success of Machiavellian tactics on a large scale.

9. Machiavellis describe much of political life accurately. They go to its heart, or to one of its heart's chambers. They are able to do so because they recognize that humans are not very moral by their own standards, and because they assume that necessity, the *raison d'état*, governs most of politics. Yet the Machiavellis are usually one-sided in their reasoning and have always undervalued the need for trust and intimacy. Not only do they discount trust and intimacy, but they undermine them by their theory and practice. The uncompromising realism with which they try to view social and political reality can easily turn into a caricature. And by using suspicion as an instrument with which to dominate others, they themselves fall repeated victims to its excesses.

10. Philosophical arguments cannot in themselves be decisive. If we rule out such as are based on religious dogmas or doubtful metaphysics, we find that of the great classical philosophers, it is Kant who has provided the most cogent set of arguments. These arguments are his characteristic translation into philosophy of the stubborn human preference for fairness: he sets natural morality to the music of abstraction and adapts disillusionment to hope. In what concerns social progress, his hope is based on the disillusioned idea that it is the innate selfishness of human beings that is in time likely to force all governments to respect human rights and renounce war.

11. It is idle to believe that violence and deception can be eliminated from political life. But as Kant foresaw, humans are now afraid that war will destroy them along with the structures, tangible and intangible, of their civilization. At moments of crisis the fear grows acute, so acute that it may yet drive them to invent effective ways of limiting Machiavellism, at least of the sort that leads to war. The human condition has never been static and is still open to exploration and improvement.

My theses stated, I rest my case.

NOTES

1 The Machiavellis Introduced

1. Ekman, ed. *Emotion in the Human Face*. For a more abstract and complex discussion of the issues involved in the assumption that certain emotions are universal, see Lazarus, *Emotion and Adaptation*, pp. 190–213.

2. I argue this position in detail in Scharfstein, *The Dilemma of Context*. For a variety of responses of British anthropologists, see Holy, ed., *Comparative Anthropology*. Mostly American anthropologists respond to this and related problems in Clifford and Marcus, eds., *Writing Culture*.

3. I know of only a few knowledgeable comparisons, none very extended, and all of Kautilya and Machiavelli. These include Kautilya, *The Kautilya Arthaśastra*, vol. 3, pp. 269–73; Drekmeier, *Kingship and Community in Early India* pp. 158, 205; Ghoshal, *History of Indian Political Ideas*, pp. 153–54; and Sil, *Kautilya's Arthaśastra: A Comparative Study*, pp. 75–108.

4. Kautilya, *The Kautilya Arthaśastra*, trans. Kangle, vol. 3, pp. 279–81. In discussing Kautilya, I have throughout used *The Kautilya Arthaśastra*, trans. Kangle, 3 vols. (henceforth cited simply as *The Kautilya Arthaśastra*). Vol. 1 contains the Sanskrit text, vol. 2 is the annotated English translation, and vol. 3 is a detailed introduction. The 3 vols. have been reprinted by Motilal Banarsidass, Delhi.

5. *Complete Works of Han Fei Tzu*, trans. Liao, trans. Liao, chap. 54, vol. 2, p. 326.

6. Ibid., chap. 14, vol. 1, p. 328.

7. *The Kautilya Arthaśastra*, vol. 2, pp. 10–11 (1.4.11–15).

8. N. Machiavelli, *The Prince*, chap. 17, in *Chief Works and Others*, vol. 1, p. 61.

9. Shang Yang, *Book of Lord Shang*, trans. Duyvendak, chap. 1, par. 4, pp. 200–201.

10. *Complete Works of Han Fei Tzu*, trans. Liao, chap. 14, vol. 1, p. 121.

11. *The Kautilya Arthaśastra*, vol. 2, p. 10 (1.4.7–10).

12. Machiavelli, *The Prince*, chap. 17, in *Complete Works and Others*, vol. 1, p. 62.

13. See Ghoshal, *History of Indian Political Ideas*, pp. 529, 531–32, 548, 562–64.

14. *Complete Works of Han Fei Tzu*, trans. Liao,vol. 1, p. 29.

15. *The Kautilya Arthaśastra*, vol. 2, p. 13 (1.15.17).

16. Machiavelli, *The Prince*, chap. 7, in *Chief Works and Others*, vol. 1, p. 34.

17. *The Kautilya Arthaśastra*, vol. 2, pp. 364–65 (61.3.5).

18. Ibid., p. 368 (6.2.12).

19. Machiavelli, *The Prince*, chap. 14, in *Chief Works and Others*, vol. 1, p. 55.

20. *Complete Works of Han Fei Tzu*, trans. Liao, vol. 1, p. 31.

21. Ibid., pp. 31, 32.

22. Ibid., vol. 2, p. 331.

23. Ibid., vol. 1, p. 32.

24. Ibid., vol. 1, p. 28.

25. *The Kautilya Arthaśastra*, vol. 2, p. 31 (1.9.10), p. 20 (1.13.9).

26. Ibid., p. 342 (5.1.57).

27. Ibid., p. 44 (1.17.1).

28. Machiavelli, *The Prince*, chap. 22, in *Chief Works and Others*, vol. 1, pp. 22, 85.

29. Machiavelli, *The Prince*, chap. 19, in *Chief Works and Others*, vol 1, p. 70.

30. Spinoza, *Ethics*, bk. 5, prop. 34.

31. For Hegel's opinion of Machiavelli, see chap. 4, below.

32. On Aristotle, see Nussbaum, *Fragility of Goodness*, especially chaps. 1, 2, 10, 11.

2 The Machiavllian Legalism of Ancient China

1. Lewis, *Sanctioned Violence in Early China*, p. 36.

2. Ibid., pp. 90–96.

3. Ibid., chap. 3; Knoblock, *Xunzi*, vol. 2, pp. 211–34 ("Debate on the Principles of Warfare"); and Sun Tzu translated by Ames (as *The Art of Warfare*), Griffith, or Sawyer. Sawyer, *Seven Military Classics of Ancient China*, contains additional texts, of which T'ai Kung's has also proved to be early. The figure on the number of combatants is taken from Sawyer, p. 11.

4. Sawyer, *Seven Military Classics of Ancient China*, p. 16.

5. Ibid., p. 56.

6. Sun Tzu, *Art of War*, trans. Ames, pp. 104–5. See the corresponding translation in Sawyer, *Seven Military Classics of Ancient China*, and his introductory comments, pp. 149–55.

7. Sun Tzu, *The Art of War*, trans. Ames, p. 169.

8. Lewis, *Sanctioned Violence in Early China*, p. 65.

9. Based on Bodde, "State and Empire of Ch'in."

10. Eno, *Confucian Creation of Heaven*, pp. 188–89. Eno describes three theories of the origin of T'ien and suggests that it makes no real difference which of these T'ien fits, and that he might have been or become all of the T'iens at once.

11. For Chinese mythology see S. Allan, *Shape of the Turtle*; Bodde, "Mythology of Ancient China"; Birell, *Chinese Mythology* (now probably the best general reference for ancient Chinese mythology); Girardot, *Myth and Meaning in Early Taoism*; and the account by Kaltenmark in Bonnefoy, ed., *Mythologies*, vol. 2, pp. 1007–24. I have also made use of Knoblock, *Xunzi*, vol. 2, chap. 1.

12. From the account quoted in the appendix to Ssu-ma Ch'ien's history, as quoted in Kaltenmark (preceding note), p. 1019. For further details, see Birrell, *Chinese Mythology*, pp. 44–47; and for Shen Nung, pp. 47–50.

13. *Shu ching* (in English known as *The Book of History, The Classic of History*, or *The Book of Documents*), p. 4. For Ssu-ma Ch'ien's version of early history see E. Chavannes, trans., *Mémoires Historiques de Se-ma Ts'ien*, vol. 1. For the mythology bearing on the Yellow Emperor, see Birrell, *Chinese Mythology*, chap. 6.

14. *Shu ching*, pp. 6–7, 12, 14, 17. For mythology bearing on Shun see Birrell, *Chinese Mythology*, pp. 74–77.

15. Knoblock, *Xunzi,* vol. 2, pp. 15–21.

16. Ibid., pp. 9–12.

17. See the *Shu Ching,* pp. 62–63; Birrell, *Chinese Mythology,* pp. 108–10; Kaltenmark, in Y. Bonnefoy, *Mythologies,* vol. 2, pp. 1023–24; and J. Knoblock, *Xunzi,* vol. 2, pp. 17, 21–22. Sawyer, *Seven Military Classics of Ancient China,* p. 5, contains an excerpt from the Shang Annals (as preserved in Ssu-ma Ch'ien's history). Allan, *Shape of the Turtle,* is a new attempt to understand the Shang by correlating the shreds of mythology with recent archeological findings. See especially chapter 4, "From Myth to History."

18. Knoblock, *Xunzi,* vol 2, pp. 7–8, 9–10; *Shu Ching,* p. 41; and, for the Huang-Lao school, Peerenboom, *Law and Morality in Ancient China,* pp. 85–87.

19. Mo Tzu, *Ethical and Political Works of Mo Tzu,* trans. Yi-Pao Mei, pp. 24–25.

20. On him and his political theory see especially Kung-chuan Hsiao, *History of Chinese Political Thought,* vol. 1, chap. 3, which contrasts him systematically with Hsün Tzu. For translations see *The Works of Mencius,* trans. J. Legge; and *Mencius,* trans. D. C. Lau. Appendix 4 of Lau's translation is the essay, well-known to Sinologists, "Ancient History as Understood by Mencius."

21. L. H. Yearly, "Confucian Crisis," p. 315.

22. The translation is from *The Works of Mencius,* trans. Legge, pp. 279–83. The italicized words are those the translator added to make the text clear.

23. *Mencius,* trans. Lau, p. 117.

24. *Chuang-tzu,* trans. Graham, p. 234.

25. *Complete Works of Chuang Tzu,* trans Watson, pp. 327–28.

26. Ibid., pp. 117–18. See pp. 116–18 (for denigration of the Yellow Emperor and intellectual and moral culture), and pp. 119–20 (for praise of the Taoist accomplishments of the Yellow Emperor). See also Girardot, *Myth and Meaning in Early Taoism,* pp. 197–99, which explains the possible historical origin of the opposite assessments of the Yellow Emperor.

27. *Book of the Lord Shang,* Duyvendak, pp. 225–27.

28. Ibid., pp. 284–85.

29. Ibid., pp. 314–15.

30. *Complete Works of Han Fei Tzu,* trans. Liao, vol. 2; also in Watson, trans., *Han Fei Tzu: Basic Writings.*

31. Hsiao, *History of Chinese Political Thought,* vol. 1, p. 418. For the immediately preceding remarks, see Hsiao, pp. 413–18.

32. See, above all, Shang Yang, *Book of Lord Shang*, trans. Duyvendak. See also Hsiao, *History of Chinese Political Thought*, vol. 1; Schwartz, *World of Thought in Ancient China*, pp. 321–38; and Graham, *Disputers of the Tao*, pp. 267–78. A thinker traditionally but, perhaps, too laxly classed with the Legalists is Shen Pu-Hai, an early advocate of bureaucratic administration. On him see *Shen Pu-Hai*, trans. Creel. Two further books of interest are *Kuan-tzu*, trans. Rickett, vol. 1; and Ames, *The Art of Rulership*.

33. Watson, trans., *Ssu-ma Ch'ien*, pp. 44, 46–47 (46 quoted).

34. *Shen Pu-Hai*, trans Creel, pp. 142–44; Ames, *Art of Rulership*, chap. 4; Graham, *Disputers of the Tao*, pp. 273–76.

35. Schwartz, *World of Thought in Ancient China*, pp. 323ff.

36. Hsiao, *A History of Chinese Political Thought*, vol. 1, p. 373.

37. Shang Yang, *Book of the Lord Shang*, trans. Duyvendak, pp. 145–46. There is a more modern translation of lord Shang's biography in the third volume of Watson's translation of Ssu-ma Ch'ien.

38. Shang Yang, *Book of the Lord Shang*, trans. Duyvendak, pp. 8–11.

39. Ibid., pp. 13–14.

40. Ibid., pp. 15–16.

41. Ibid. p. 15.

42. Ibid. pp. 16–17.

43. Ibid., pp. 19–30.

44. Ibid., p. 197.

45. Ibid., p. 201.

46. Ibid., p. 223.

47. Ibid., pp. 229–30.

48. Ibid., p. 331.

49. Knoblock, *Xunzi*, vol. 1, pp. 32–33, which includes the critical references.

50. Hsün Tzu, *Basic Writings*, trans. Watson, p. 158.

51. Ibid., p. 157.

52. Ibid.

53. Ssu-ma Ch'ien, "The Biography of Han Fei Tzu," in *Complete Works of Han Fei Tzu*, trans. Liao, vol. 1, p. xxvii.

54. On Li Ssu's relations with Han Fei, see Bodde, *China's First Unifier*, pp. 62–77.

55. Bodde, *China's First Unifier*, pp. 64–67 and Liao, *Complete Works of Han Fei Tzu*, trans. Lao, vol. 1, pp. 13–16.

56. *Complete Works of Han Fei Tzu*, trans. Liao, vol. 1, p. 17 (with slight changes); see the (more sober) translation in Bodde, *China's First Unifier*, p. 68.

57. *Complete Works of Han Fei Tzu*, trans. Liao, vol. 1, pp. xxviii–xxix (with slight changes); for another translation see Bodde, *China's First Unifier*, pp. 63–64.

58. *Complete Works of Han Fei Tzu*, trans. Liao, p. xxix; Bodde, *China's First Unifier*, p. 64.

59. *Complete Works of Han Fei Tzu*, trans. Liao, vol. 2, pp. 326–27).

60. Ibid., pp. 327–28.

61. Ibid., pp. 26–27.

62. Ibid. vol. 1, pp. 127–28.

63. Ibid., vol. 2, pp. 254–55; vol. 1, p. 121.

64. Ibid., vol. 1, p. 128.

65. Ibid., vol. 2, p.. 311.

66. Ibid., vol. 1, pp. 275–6; vol. 2, p. 200.

67. Ibid., vol. 2, p. 201.

68. Ibid., vol. 2, pp. 204–6 (and see Ames, *Art of Rulership*, pp. 92–94).

69. Ibid., pp. 134–41.

70. Section 15 (chap. 15 in Liao's translation), and *Han Fei Tzu: Basic Writings*, trans. Watson, pp. 84, 85.

71. *Complete Works of Han Fei Tzu*, trans. Liao, vol. 2, p. 331.

72. Ibid., vol. 1, pp. 259–60.

73. Ibid., vol. 1, p. 32.

74. For the principle of nonaction (*wu-wei*) in the political theory of the period, see Ames, *Art of Rulership*, chap. 2, which points out that the principle appears, though far less emphasized, in Confucian literature as well. The combination of doing nothing and seeing nothing is ascribed to an earlier Legalist called "the elder of Cheng." For Ames' exposition of Han Fei's version of *wu-wei*, see pp. 47–53.

75. *Complete Works of Han Fei Tzu*, trans. Liao, vol. 1, p. 33.

76. Ibid., vol. 2, p. 27.

77. Bodde, *China's First Unifier*. Bodde draws from Ssu-ma Ch'ien, in this instance from his biography of Li Ssu. The third volume of Watson's translation of Ssu-ma Ch'ien contains the basic material on the First Emperor and the biography of Li Ssu. In the two earlier, now reprinted volumes and the third, new one, Ssu-ma Ch'ien's name takes the pinyin form Sima Qian, while Li Ssu becomes Li Si.

78. Ibid., p. 13.

79. Ibid., p. 15.

80. Ibid., pp. 15–21.

81. Ibid., pp. 21–22, 77ff.

82. Ibid., p. 79; see also pp. 121–23.

83. Hulsewé, "Ch'in and Han Law"; and Bodde, "The State and Empire of Ch'in," pp. 36–38.

84. Bodde, "The State and Empire of Ch'in," pp. 61–66.

85. Bodde, *China's First Unifier*, pp. 147–61.

86. Ibid., pp. 162–66; and Kramers, "Development of the Confucian Schools," pp. 760–64.

87. Bodde, *China's First Unifier*, pp. 22–23.

88. Ibid. pp. 23–24.

89. Ibid., p. 24.

90. Bodde, "The State and Empire of Ch'in," pp. 95–96.

91. Ibid., p. 29.

92. Ibid., p. 35.

93. Ibid., pp. 40–41.

94. Ibid., pp. 43–44.

95. Ibid. pp. 48–49.

96. Ibid., pp. 50–52.

97. Ibid. p. 52.

98. Ibid., pp. 53–54.

99. Bodde, "The State and Empire of Ch'in," p. 85; from "The Faults of Ch'in," by Chia I (201–169 B.C.).

100. Bodde, "The State and Empire of Ch'in," pp. 85–89 (89 quoted).

101. Ssu-ma Ch'ien, *Records of the Grand Historian of China*, trans. Watson, vol. 2, p. 398.

102. Peerenboom, *Law and Morality in Ancient China*, chap. 7. See also Loewe, "The Religious and Intellectual Background," pp. 693–95.

103. Peerenboom, *Law and Morality in Ancient China*, chaps. 2, 3. Schwartz, *World of Thought in Ancient China*, pp. 237–54. Hsiao, *History of Chinese Political Thought*, chap. 9. On the concept of *wu-wei* in early Chinese thought, see Ames, *Art of Rulership*, chap. 2.

104. An early version may have been presented to the Han court in 140 B.C., during the lifetime of Ssu-ma Ch'ien. See Ames, *Art of Rulership*, p. xiv and note 2. See also Creel, *Shen Pu-hai*.

105. Ibid., pp. 183, 190–91 (quoted).

106. Ibid., pp. 13–20, 206.

107. Ibid., pp. 13–20.

108. Gale, *Discourses on Salt and Iron*, pp. xxv–xxvi.

109. See Gale, *Discourses on Salt and Iron*; and Loewe, "Former Han Dynasty."

110. Gale, *Discourses on Salt and Iron*, pp. 40–41.

111. Ibid., p. 47.

112. Ibid., p. 49.

113. Ch'en, "Confucian, Legalist, and Taoist Thought in Later Han," pp. 783–94. See also Balasz, "Ts'ui Shih, or the Attempt to Revive Legalist Doctrines," in Balasz, *Chinese Civilization and Bureaucracy*; and Chang, "Metamorphosis of Han Fei's Thought in the Han."

114. Ssu-ma Ch'ien, *Records of the Grand Historian of China*, trans. Watson, vol 2, pp. 419, 420.

115. Ibid., pp. 440, 441.

116. Ibid., p. 445.

117. Ibid., pp. 450–51.

118. Ibid., p. 451.

3 The Machiavellian Political Science of Ancient India

1. Philips, ed., *Historians of India, Pakistan and Ceylon*, pp. 20–25.

2. Rhys Davids, *Buddhist India*, p. 269. On Chandragupta, see Rhys Davids, "Early History of the Buddhists," pp. 190–92; and Thomas, "Chandragupta, the Founder of the Maurya Empire." See also Sastri, ed., *Age of the Nandas and Mauryas*, chap. 4.

3. Rhys Davids, *Buddhist India*, p. 270; from Justin 15.4.

4. Bevan, "India in Early Greek and Latin Literature,"pp. 402–11, 419–20. Bevan's chapter contains a full summary of the Greek and Latin evidence on India of the time. See also the full summary in chap. 3 of Sastri, ed., *Age of the Nandas and Mauryas*.

5. Bevan, "India in Early Greek and Latin Literature," pp. 416–18.

6. Ibid., p. 413.

7. Sastri, in Sastri, ed., *Age of the Nandas and Mauryas*, p. 165.

8. Sastri, in Sastri, ed., *Age of the Nandas and Mauryas*, p. 202.

9. Nikam and McKeon, *The Edicts of Aśoka*—the immediately following quotations from the edicts are taken from this source; Thomas, "Aśoka, the Imperial Patron of Buddhism." Van Zeyst, "Aśoka," and Dutt, "Aśoka: A Comparison and Contrast between the Legends and the Edicts"—both in the *Encyclopedia of Buddhism*, vol. 2, fasc. 2, pp. 178–93; Sastri, ed., *Age of the Nandas and Mauryas*, chap. 6; and Strong, *Legend of King Aśoka*.

10. Although some doubt that Ashoka was an actual convert to Buddhism—Buddhist legend naturally stresses his adherence—the evidence seems decisive. See Dutt, "Aśoka: A Comparison and Contrast between the Legends and the Edicts," pp. 190–93.

11. Strong, *Legend of King Aśoka*, p. 39. My summary is from the *Aśokavadana*, as translated in this book. What I refer to as "the legend" takes different forms, discussed in Strong, pp. 18–26, and in Dutt, "Aśoka: A Comparison between the Legends and the Edicts." See also Obeyesekere, *The Work of Culture*, pp. 157–59, who places Ashoka in a line of real or symbolic parricidal Buddhist kings—in Indian tradition, he says, the eldest brother is regarded as a kind of father.

12. Strong, *Legend of King Asoka*, p. 215.

13. Ibid., pp. 220, 232, 285.

14. Ibid., pp. 42–43.

15. Ibid., pp. 50–53, 76–83.

16. Ibid., p. 288.

17. Ibid., pp. 289–92.

18. Scharfe, *State in Indian Tradition*, pp. 234–36, drawing on Eisenstadt, *The Political Systems of Empires* (London, 1963), pp. 10, 132–37; and J. Baechler, *La solution indienne* (Paris, 1988).

19. Strong, *Legend of King Asoka*, pp. 5–15.

20. Thapar, *A History of India*, pp. 86–91. The preceding quotation is from Scharfe, *State in Indian Tradition*, p. 236.

21. Valleé Poussin, "Ages of the World (Buddhist)," in Hastings, ed., *Encyclopaedia of Religion and Ethics*.

22. Davids and Davids, trans., *Dialogues of the Buddha*, vol. 3, p. 82 (*Agganna Suttana, Digha Nikaya* 3.80–98). There is a more modern translation in Embree, *Sources of Indian Tradition*, vol. 1, pp. 129–33. The best translation is now the annotated one of Collins, "Discourse on What Is Primary (Agganna-Sutta)," which I most often follow just below.

23. Davids and Davids, trans., *Dialogues of the Buddha*, vol. 3, p. 88; Collins, "Discourse on What Is Primary (Agganna-Sutta)," p. 345.

24. Davids and Davids, trans., *Dialogues of the Buddha*, vol. 3, pp. 89–93; Collins, "Discourse on What Is Primary (Agganna-Sutta)," pp. 346–48.

25. For an explanation of this Buddhist, anti-Brahmanic myth of social devolution see Reynolds, "Multiple Cosmogonies and Ethics: The Case of Theravada Buddhism," pp. 209–213. On the contrast between the Brahmanical and Buddhist goals see the brief summary in Scharfe, *State in Indian Tradition*, pp.212–20; and see the relevant passages in Ghoshal, *History of Indian Political Ideas*. On the inacceptability to Buddhist kings of the Buddhist idea of an original contract, see Collins, "Discourse on What Is Primary," pp. 387–89.

26. Ghoshal, *History of Indian Political Ideas*, chap. 1.

27. Pollock, trans., *The Ramayana of Valmiki*, vol. 2, pp. 16–29 (22, 29 quoted).

28. Pollock, trans., *The Ramayana of Valmiki*, vol. 3, p. 44, quoting the *Mahabharata* 12.68.37ff.

29. Scharfe, *State in Indian Tradition*, p. 61, citing *Mahabharata* 12.67.2–29. For a summary of the initial development of the state as seen in the Puranas, see Prakash, *Political Ideas in the Puranas*, pp. 30–45. The basic themes appear to be the same as those expounded in the epics and in Manu.

30. . *The Laws of Manu*, trans. Doniger and Smith, pp. 3–9 (*Manu* 1).

31. Ibid., p. 11 (*Manu* 1.68–74). For a description of the Indian cycle see Jacobi, "Ages of the World: Indian" in Hastings, ed., *Encyclopaedia of Religion and Ethics.* For a summary account of the world cycle as it appears in the Puranas, see Rocher, *Puranas*, pp. 124–25.

32. *The Laws of Manu*, trans. Doniger and Smith, p. 13 (*Manu*, 1.92).

33. Ibid. (*Manu* 1.96).

34. Ibid., p. 128 (*Manu*, 7.5–6, 8).

35. Ibid., pp. 229–30 (*Manu* 9.303–11). Fully summarized in Ghoshal, *History of Political Ideas*, pp. 163–64.

36. Ibid., p. 230 (*Manu* 9.313).

37. Ghoshal, *History of Indian Political Ideas*, pp. 194–95.

38. Ibid., pp. 197–98 (from *Mahabharata* 12.68.1–47).

39. van Buitenen, trans., *The Mahabharata*, vol. 2, p. 596 (*Mahabharata* 3 (37) 186).

40. Ibid.

41. Ibid., pp. 587–88.

42. Ghoshal, *History of Indian Political Ideas*, p. 541 (as in the Jain *Nitivakyamritam* and [inconsistently] the Shukranitisara).

43. *The Laws of Manu*, trans. Doniger and Smith, pp. 130–32, 188–89, 230–31 (7.27–29, 7.39, 8.346–48, 9.313–14). On the deposition of the king in theory and in fact, see Scharfe, *State in Indian Tradition*, pp. 66–71.

44. Scharfe, *State in Indian Tradition*, p. 66.

45. Ghoshal, *History of Indian Political Ideas*, pp. 207–9 (from *Mahabharata* 12.79.12–18, 13.61.31–3).

46. Ghoshal, *History of Indian Political Ideas*, p. 203 (from *Mahabharata* 12.66.35, 12.79.26–8, 12.72.28–9).

47. Scharfe, *State in Indian Tradition*, pp. 210–11 (from *Mahabharata* 12. 129–67, 12.34.20, 12.128.15, 12.138.61).

48. van Buitenen, trans., *The Mahabharata*, vol. 1, p. 268 (*Mahabharata* 1.7.122).

49. Scharfe, *State in Indian Tradition*, p. 39 (from *Mahabharata* 12.81.39, 12.86.32, 12.137.69, 12.120.4–6)

50. Ghoshal, *History of Indian Political Ideas*, pp. 42–49; Lingat, *Classical Law of India*, chaps. 1, 2, 4; Scharfe, *State in Indian Tradition*, pp. 220–27.

51. See Kautilya, *The Kautilya Arthaśastra*, trans. Kangle, vol. 2, p. 593 (*Arthaśastra* 15.1.1); and Ghoshal, *History of Indian Political Ideas*, p. 81.

52. Ghoshal, *History of Indian Political Ideas*, pp. 111, 371; Winternitz, *History of Indian Literature*, vol. 3, pp. 634–35.
In discussing Kautilya, I have throughout used *The Kautilya Arthaśastra*, trans. Kangle, 3 vols. (hence forth cited simply as *The Kautilya Arthaśastra*).

53. For the arguments on the author and date of the *Kautilya Arthashastra* see Ghoshal, *History of Indian Political Ideas*, pp. 111–13; *The Kautilya Arthaśastra*, vol. 3, chap. 4; Sastri in Sastri, ed., *Age of the Nandas and Mauryas*, pp. 190–201; Scharfe, *State in Indian Tradition*, p. 21 (esp. notes 93, 94); Sil, *Kautilya's Arthaśastra* (there is a later American edition), pp. 18–20, 24–25 (esp. p. 24, note 68); and Winternitz, *History of Indian Literature*, vol. 3, pp. 626–34, the translator of which has inserted (p. 633) the views of Louis Renou.

54. *The Kautilya Arthaśastra*, vol. 2, pp. 13–14 (*Artha.* 1.6.4–10). See also, Scharfe, *State in Indian Tradition*, pp. 21–22.

55. *The Kautilya Arthaśastra*, vol. 2, p. 15 (1.7.3–7 [6–7 quoted]).

56. Ibid., pp. 51–52 (1.19.1–24).

57. For these last, Machiavellian traits see ibid., sections 1.11, 12.5, 13.2. And see Ghoshal, *History of Indian Political Ideas*, pp. 125–26 (Kautilya's geopolitical ideas) and pp. 149–50 (Kautilya's attitude toward religion and morality).

58. *The Kautilya Arthaśastra*, p. 7 (1.2.10), especially note 10. The texts I am referring to are quoted in *Dialogues of the Buddha*, trans. Rhys Davids, vol. 1 (London: Pali Text Society, 1899), pp. 167–70.

59. *The Kautilya Arthaśastra*, vol. 3, pp. 6–11 (1.2–4, 5–15 [13–14 quoted]); Ghoshal, *History of Indian Political Ideas*, pp. 112–13.

60. *The Kautilya Arthaśastra*, vol. 2, p. 286 (3.18.2,4).

61. For a full classification and enumeration, with some rather casual comparison with other premodern legal systems, see Agrawal, *Kautilya on Crime and Punishment*.

62. *The Kautilya Arthaśastra*, vol. 2, pp. 317–20 (4.8.1–29).

63. Ibid., pp. 319–20 (4.8.22).

64. Ibid., pp. 327–29 (4.8.1–26).

65. Ibid., pp. 20–23 (1.10).

66. Ibid., pp. 23–25 (1.11.1–20). For a clear summary of Kautilya on spies see Scharfe, *State in Indian Tradition*, pp. 159–65.

67. *The Kautilya Arthaśastra*, vol. 2, pp. 23–36 (1.7–1.14).

68. Ibid., pp. 338–42 (5.1).

69. Ibid., pp. 31–33 (1.12).

70. Ibid., pp. 211–12 (2.35.8–15).

71. Ibid., pp. 29–30 (1.12.19–25).

72. Ibid., pp. 31–36 (1.10–11).

73. Ibid., pp. 44–48 (1.17).

74. Ibid., pp. 54–61 (1.20–1.21).

75. Doniger, trans., *The Laws of Manu*, p. 150 (7.216–20); *The Kautilya Arthaśastra*, vol. 2, pp. 58–60 (1.21.4–16).

76. *The Kautilya Arthaśastra*, vol. 2, pp. 368–69 (6.2.13–22). On the circle or mandala of kings, which constitutes a state–system, see Ghoshal, *History of Indian Political Ideas*, pp. 93–99.

77. *The Kautilya Arthaśastra*, vol. 2, pp. 372–76 (7.1).

78. Ibid., p. 379 (7.3.10).

79. Ibid. pp. 378–83 (7.3).

80. Ibid., p. 388 (7.5.16).

81. Ibid., pp. 409, 413, 431 (7.10.12, 7.11.18, 7.16.3–9).

82. Ibid. p. 510 (10.3.43). The whole of the tenth book is on actual war.

83. Ibid., pp. 510–11 (10.3.45, 47).

84. Ibid., pp. 533–49 (12).

85. The two aphorisms are respectively from ibid. pp. 525 and 482 (10.6.51, 9.3.42).

86. Ghoshal, *History of Indian Political Ideas*, is relatively full in his summaries of political ideas as expounded in literature. See chaps. 10–13 for the *Mahabharata*, chap. 15 for the *Ramayana* and the *Panchatantra*, and chap. 20 for the classical Sanskrit literature of the fourth to eighth century A.D.

87. As translated in Smith, *The Oxford History of India*, p. 107.

88. Gupta, *Somadev Suri's Nitivakyamritam* (tenth century Sanskrit treatise on statecraft), p. 44. On Somadeva's thought see also Ghoshal, *History of Indian Political Ideas*, chap. 27.

89. See van Buitenen, trans., *Two Plays of Ancient India*; Dimock, ed., *Literatures of India*, pp. 106–13; and A. K. Warder, *Indian Kavya Literature*, vol. 3, pp. 257–76.

90. Van Buitenen, trans., *Two Plays of Ancient India*, p. 269 (act 7).

91. See Ryder, trans., *Panchatantra*, and Edgerton, trans., *Panchatantra*. See also Ghoshal, *History of Indian Political Ideas*, chap. 15; Keith, *History of Sanskrit Literature*, pp. 243–56; Winternitz, *History of Indian Literature*, vol. 3, pp. 307–46; and Dimock, ed., *The Literatures of India*, pp. 198–200.

92. *Panchatantra* 1.116–77, as told by Ghoshal, *History of Indian Political Ideas*, p. 279. Ghoshal says it is the frame-story of book 1, but in the translations by Ryder (*Panchatantra*, pp. 134–41) and Edgerton (*Panchatantra*, pp. 57–60), it is only one of the many framed stories and, for our purposes, is less interesting. The first, frame-story in Ryder is a somewhat analogous one about a lion, two jackals who act as his advisers, and the lion's faithful friend, the bull he eventually eats. The verse I quote, taken from Ryder's frame-story, is on p. 208.

4 The Machiavellism of Renaissance Italy

1. For Europe in general, see Hale, *Civilization of Europe in the Renaissance*, esp. chaps. 3("Divisions of Europe"), 8 ("Civility in Danger?"), and 9 ("Control of Man"). In conformity with Chinese and Indian attitudes, Hale declares (p. 467) that "to guard the palace was seen as at least as important as to police the realm." For Italy in general, see Bock, Skinner, and Viroli, eds., *Machiavelli and Republicanism*; E. Garin, "Kultur der Renaissance"; F. Gilbert, *Machiavelli and Guicciardini*; and *Cambridge History of Renaissance Philosophy*.

2. Gilbert, *Machiavelli and Guicciardini*, p. 35. For the inheritance of medieval political thought, see Skinner, "Political Philosophy." See also Viroli, *From Politics to Reason of State*, chap. 1. On the "new urban system" of medieval Europe, with its independent centers, each with its own physical configuration, differentiated activity, and civic pride, see Benevolo, *The European City*, chap. 2.

3. Skinner, "Political Philosophy," pp. 408–19.

4. For an assessment of the humanists' social and economic position, see Martines, *Social World of the Florentine Humanists 1300–1460*.

5. Skinner, "Political Philosophy," pp. 416–18, and Holmes, *The Florentine Enlightenment 1400–1500*, chaps. 3, 5.

6. This description of the change in Florentine civic life is based on Martines, *Social World of the Florentine Humanists 1390–1460*. For Aristotelian ethics as taught in the Renaissance, see Kraye, "Moral Philosophy," pp. 328–48 (331 quoted). For "the philosophy of the city and the political man," see Viroli, *From Politics to Reason of State*, chap. 2.

7. Kraye, "Moral Philosophy"; Aristotle, *Nichomachean Ethics*, 4.2.

8. The preceding pages are based on Martines, *Social World of the Florentine Humanists* and on Skinner, "Political Philosophy," pp. 423–30.

9. Rubenstein, "Machiavelli and Florentine Republican Experience," pp. 15–16.

10. De Grazia, *Machiavelli in Hell*, pp. 5–8, 107–8; Skinner, *Machiavelli*, pp. 12–13.

11. Villari, *Life and Times of Niccolò Machiavelli*, vol. 1, pp. 203–14.

12. Gilbert, *Machiavelli and Guicciardini*, pp. 7–20.

13. Ibid., pp. 20–28.

14. Ibid., p. 33.

15. Ibid., p. 41.

16. Ibid., pp. 42–44.

17. Ibid., pp. 112–113, 81 (quoted).

18. Ibid., p. 95 (from *Dialogo e Discorsi del Reggimento di Firenze*).

19. Ibid., p.. 99 (from *Dialogo e Discorsi*).

20. Ibid., p. 120.

21. Ibid., pp. 128–43 (136, 137, 142, 143 quoted).

22. De Grazia, *Machiavelli in Hell*, pp. 5–6; Villari, *Life and Times of Niccolo Machiavelli*, vol. 1, chap. 1. For Machiavelli's studies, see also Black, "Machiavelli, Servant of the Florentine Republic," pp. 73–75.

23. . For Machiavelli himself on the past, see de Grazia, *Machiavelli in Hell*. There is a full enough and yet compact account of early Greek views in Guthrie, *History of Greek Philosophy* vol. 2, pp. 473–76, and vol. 3, chaps. 4 ("The 'Nomos'-'Physis' Antithesis in Politics") and 5 ("The Social Compact"). For Hesiod I have depended on Fränkel, *Early Greek Poetry and Philosophy*, pp. 116–21. Loraux, "Origins of Mankind in Greek Myths," pp. 390–95, is an interesting summary essay in the inventive manner of Vernant and other contemporary French mythologists (*mythologists* somewhat in both senses of the word). A brief review of the Renaissance attitudes can be found in Burke, *Renaissance Sense of the Past*, and Weisinger, "Ideas of History during the Renaissance."

24. Machiavelli, *Chief Works and Others*, vol. 2, p. 735–36 ("Tercets on Ambition," lines 13–63 [58–60 and 63 quoted]).

25. . For the difficulty, see, e.g., the account in Loraux, "Origins of Mankind in Greek Myths."

26. See Fränkel, *Early Greek Philosophy and Poetry*, pp. 116–19. I have used Hesiod, *Theogony and Works and Days*, in trans. West.

27. Fränkel, *Early Greek Poetry and Philosophy*; Hesiod, *Works and Days* 105–201.

28. Guthrie, *History of Greek Philosophy*, vol. 2, pp. 473–76; vol. 3, chaps. 4, 5. See also. Edelstein, *Idea of Progress in Classical Antiquity*; and Dodds, *Ancient Concept of Progress*, chap. 1—the quotation is from p. 4 (Xenophanes, frag. 18).

29, Plato, *Protagoras* 320–23.

30. *Republic* 546a, as translated in Plato, *Republic*, trans. Shorey, vol. 2, p. 245. For the succession of cities and typical individuals see Guthrie, *History of Greek Philosophy*, vol. 4, pp. 444–49, 471–76, 483–86, 527–37.

31. *Metaphysics* 1074, as translated in *Complete Works of Aristotle*, ed. Barnes, vol. 2, p. 1698; and, for cosmology, *On the Heavens* (De caelo), 1.10.

32. Sources are conveniently assembled in Long and Sedley, trans., *The Hellenistic Philosophers*, vol. 1, pp. 274–79, 308–13).

33. Aristocles (second century A.D.), as reported in Eusebius (A.D. 260–340) in ibid., p. 276.

34. See the exposition in ibid., pp. 277–79.

35. Ibid., p. 309; from Nemesius (fl. c. A.D. 400).

36. Ibid., pp. 308–13.

37. This passage and the quotations from Polybius that immediately follow are from Polybius, *Rise of the Roman Republic*, trans. Walbank, pp. 305–10 (*Histories*, bk. 6. 5–9).

38. Machiavelli, *Chief Works and Others*, vol. 1, p. 195.

39. Ibid., pp. 199, 200.

40. Machiavelli, *Chief Works and Others*, vol. 3, p. 1232 (*History of Florence*, 5.1).

41. Polybius, *Rise of the Roman Empire*, trans. Walbank, p. 44 (*Histories*, bk. 1.4).

42. Watts, *Nicolaus Cusanus* (Leiden: Brill, 1982), pp. 191–207.

43. Polybius, *Rise of the Roman Empire*, p. 537 (*Histories*, bk. 36.17).

44. Ibid., pp. 537–39.

45. See Walbank's introduction to Polybius, *Rise of the Roman Empire*, pp. 27–30.

46. On this subject see especially Parel, *The Machiavellian Cosmos*.

47. Machiavelli, *Chief Works and Others*, vol. 1, p. 90 (*The Prince* chap. 25).

48. Ibid., p. 90.

49. Ibid., p. 92. Skinner, *Machiavelli*, p. 37, points out that Seneca had expressed the idea that Fortune should be opposed violently, and Piccolomini had added erotic overtones to this suggestion.

50. Parel, *The Machiavellian Cosmos*, pp. 32.

51. Machiavelli, *Chief Works and Others*, vol. 2, p. 747 ("Tercets on Fortune," 118–20).

52. Parel, *The Machiavellian Cosmos*, p. 33 ("The Golden Ass," 3). For the same passage in Gilbert's translation, see Machiavelli, *Chief Works and Others*, vol. 2, p. 758.

53. . I am following Parel, *The Machiavellian Cosmos*, pp. 105–12, who gives the references to Machiavelli. That from *The Prince* is chap. 9. Gilbert's translation in Machiavelli, *Complete Works and Others*, makes the word *humors (umori)* unrecognizable. In Bull's translation of *The Prince*, chapter 9 has *dispositions* for *humors*.

54. Parel, *The Machiavellian Cosmos*, pp. 107, 109.

55. For "An Exhortation to Penitence," see Machiavelli, *Chief Works and Others*, pp. 171–74. The translator's introduction (pp. 170–71) contains other references to Machiavelli's religiousness. See also de Grazia, *Machiavelli in Hell*, chap. 3. The quotation on fear of God is Machiavelli, *Chief Works and Others*, vol. 2, p. 567 (*The Art of War*, "Preface").

56. De Grazia, *Machiavelli in Hell*, pp. 64–69. The quotation from Machiavelli, which is from the *Discourses* 51.6, in Machiavelli, *Chief Works and Others*, vol. 1, p. 311.

57. Black, "Machiavelli, Servant of the Florentine Republic," pp. 71–72.

58. Mallett, "Theory and Practice of Warfare in Machiavelli's Republic."

59. Angelo, *Machiavelli* (London: Gollancz, 1969), p. 50. From *The Historical, Political, and Diplomatic Writings of Niccol Machiavelli* (Boston, 1882), vol. 4, pp. 419–20.

60. Angelo, *Machiavelli*, p. 47.

61. Angelo, *Machiavelli*, p. 49.

62. Ibid., pp. 51–53; Guarini, "Machiavelli and the Crisis of the Italian Republics, pp. 26–29. See Machiavelli's *Description of the Affairs of Germany; The Prince*, 10, and *Discourses*, 1.55.

63. Angelo, *Machiavelli*, p. 34.

64. Ibid., p. 23.

65. Chabod, *Machiavelli and the Renaissance*, p. 130 (Machiavelli's letter of September 3, 1500).

66. Najemy, "The Controversy Surrounding Machiavelli's Service to the Republic," In Bock, Skinner, and Viroli, p. 107.

67. Ibid., p. 116. The letter, written on November, 29, 1509, is to Luigi Guicciardini.

68. Chabod, *Machiavelli and the Renaissance*, p. 9.

69. Ibid., pp. 116–17 (116 quoted).

70. Machiavelli, *Chief Works and Others*, vol. 3, pp. 1031. See also Bock, "Civil Discord in Machiavelli's *Istorie Fiorentine*," which discusses Machiavelli's possible ambivalence on the positive effects of civic discord.

71. Machiavelli, *Chief Works and Others*, vol. 3, pp. 1140–41 (*History of Florence* 3.1).

72. Ibid., p. 1141.

73. I have adopted the account of the writing of the two books as in Chabod, *Machiavelli and the Renaissance*, pp. 38–41. On the relations between the two books see also "On the Unity of 'The Prince' with the 'Discourses' in Tejera, *City-State Foundations of Western Political Thought*.

74. Machiavelli, *Chief Works and Others*, vol. 1, p. 62. (*The Prince*, chap. 17).

75. Machiavelli, *Chief Works and Others*, vol. 1, pp. 10–11.

76. Villari, *Life and Times of Niccol Machiavelli*, vol. 2, p. 161.

77. Machiavelli, *Chief Works and Others*, vol. 1, pp. 189–90, 191 (*Discourses*, dedication and preface to bk. 1).

78. For these passages from the *Discourses* see Machiavelli, *Chief Works and Others*, vol. 1, pp. 328–33, 202–4, 211.

79. Bock, "Civil Discord in Machiavelli's *Istorie Fiorentine*."

80. See. e.g., Chabod, *Machiavelli and the Renaissance*, pp. 106–8. For Machiavelli's republican ideal, see Viroli, *From Politics to Reason of State*, chap. 3.

801. *Basic Writings of Saint Augustine*, vol. 2, p. 643, *City of God*, bk. 22. For Augustine on Adam's sin see *City of God* 4.4. and Kirwan, *Augustine*, p. 139.

82. Machiavelli, *Chief Works and Others*, vol. 2, pp. 736, 737, 738 ("Tercets on Ambition," lines 55–57, 73–84, 157–59).

83. Machiavelli, *Chief Works and Others*, vol. 2, p. 738, footnote.

84. De Grazia, *Machiavelli in Hell*, pp. 34–38. See Villari, *Life and Times of Niccolò Machiavelli*, vol. 2, pp. 29–37. For a consecutive translation see Machiavelli, *Chief Works and Others*, vol. 2, pp. 1013–13. Villari (p. 37) conjectures that they were "written for amusement, as a capricious, ironical, even cynical outburst" in a moment of ill-humor. Allan Gilbert prefaces his translation (p. 1013) by saying that the sonnets "present the unquenchable humor with which Machiavelli accepted his misfortunes." Villari and Gilbert seem to me to miss the pain and horror that can accompany humor, too. If this is humor, it is of the black kind.

85. Machiavelli, *Chief Works and Others*, vol. 1, p. 62 (*The Prince*, chap. 17).

86. ; Machiavelli, *Chief Works and Others*, vol. 1, p. 201 (*Discourses* 1.3).

87. *Discourses* 1.1, as translated in Skinner, "Political Philosophy," p. 439. Skinner's translation is slightly more emphatic than the Italian, which he gives in a footnote. If the translation in Machiavelli, *Chief Works and Others* is not based on a different text, it appears to obscure or lose some of these words. In any case, the words are an accurate representation of what Machiavelli is saying.

88. Plato, *The Republic*, trans. Shorey, vol. 1, pp. 213–14, 301–2, 461 (389b–d, 414b–415d, 459c–d). On Plato's advocacy of certain forms of lying, see Guthrie, *History of Greek Philosophy*, vol. 4, pp. 457–59, 462–64.

89. Thucydides, *Peloponnesian War*, pp. 400–408 (402, 404–5 quoted) (*Peloponnesian War* 5.89, 105). For the whole debate in Athens at the time, see Guthrie, *History of Greek Philosophy*, vol. 3, chap. 4. On Thucydides in general, see Hornblower, *Thucydides*.

90. My interpretation follows that of de Romilly in *Thucydides and Athenian Imperialism*. See especially pp. 103–4, 306–10, the whole of chap. 3, and pp. 357–69. For a brief attempt to grasp the situation as he himself might have grasped it, see A. Andrewes in *The Cambridge Ancient History*, vol. 5, *The Fifth Century*, pp. 444–46. In the same volume (pp. 1–6, 13–4) D. M. Lewis gives a summary analysis of the method, structure, and reliability of Thucydides' history and praises him for his competence and devotion to truth. A more cynical attitude is, of course, possible. There is a brief but cogent comment on the dialogues' authenticity in Hornblower, *Thucydides*, pp. 52–53. See also his comments on pp. 184–90 on the exact nature of Thucydides' "amorality."

91. See MacKendrick, *Philosophical Books of Cicero* (London: Duckworth, 1989), especially pp. 262–63, on Cicero's influence on Machiavelli. I have also used Cicero, *On Duties (De Officiis)*.

92. Machiavelli, *Chief Works and Others*, pp. 64, 62 (*The Prince*, chaps. 18 and 17).

93. Machiavelli, *Chief Works and Others*, vol. 1, pp. 64–65 (*The Prince*, chap. 18).

94. See Gilbert, *Machiavelli and Guicciardini*, pp. 169–70; and Skinner, *Machiavelli*, pp. 18–20, 25–26.

95. Machiavelli, *Chief Works and Others*, vol. 1, p. 62 (*The Prince*, chap. 17).

96. De Grazia, *Machiavelli in Hell*, pp. 269–70.

97. Machiavelli, *Chief Works and Others*, vol. 1, p. 324 (*Discourses* 2, preface). See Viroli, *From Politics to Reason of State*, pp. 176–77.

98. Gilbert, *Machiavelli and Guicciardini*. Ridolfi, *Life of Franceso Guicciardini*. Viroli, *From Politics to Reason of State*, chap. 4.

99. Gilbert, *Machiavelli and Guicciardini*, pp. 239–41. See also the introduction of Guicciardini, *Selected Writings*, trans. Grayson; and Chabod, *Machiavelli and the Renaissance*, pp. 109–15, a psychological contrast.

100. Ridolfi, *Life of Francesco Guicciardini*, p. 124.

101. Gilbert, *Machiavelli and Guicciardini*, pp. 275–76.

102. See, e.g., Thomas More's description, which I came upon in Hale, *War and Society in Renaissance Europe*, p. 72.

103. Ridolfi, *Life of Francesco Guicciardini*, pp. 210–15.

104. In my account of Guicciardini's career I have, for the most part, followed the introduction to Guicciardini, *Selected Writings*. For the *History of Italy*, see Gilbert, *Machiavelli and Guicciardini*, chap. 7.

105. The first quotation is from Procacci, *History of the Italian People*, p. 139. The second quotation is from Chabod, *Machiavelli and the Renaissance*, p. 110.

106. Gilbert, *Machiavelli and Guicciardini*, pp. 282–85.

107. Ibid., pp. 288–94.

108. Gilbert, *Machiavelli and Guicciardini*, p. 278 (ricordo 66).

109. Ibid., p. 284.

110. Guicciardini, *Selected Writings*, p. 66 (bk. 1, chap. 2).

111. Ibid., pp. 104–5 (bk. 1, chap. 58).

112. Gilbert, *Machiavelli and Guicciardini*, p. 277. On Guicciardini's conception of "the art of the state," see Viroli, *From Politics to Reason of State*, chap. 4.

113. Gilbert, *Machiavelli and Guicciardini*, pp. 278–79 (ricordo 10).

114. Guicciardini, *Selected Writings*, p. 7 (ricordo 6).

115. Gilbert, *Machiavelli and Guicciardini*, p. 279 (ricordo 6, 35, and *Scritti Politici*, pp. 8, 11). On Machiavelli's not always appropriate use of historical examples, see Butterfield, *The Statecraft of Machiavelli*, chap. 2; and on Machiavelli's conception of warfare, Gat, *The Origins of Military Thought*, introduction.

116. My remarks on the Machiavelli's rhetorical and particularistic modes of thought are based on Tejera's "Of the Unity of 'The Prince' with the 'Discourses,'" in his book *The City-State Foundations of Western Political Thought*.

117. Gilbert, *Machiavelli and Guicciardini*, p. 290.

118. Guicciardini, *Selected Writings*, p. 15 (ricordo 37).

119. Ibid., p. 35 (ricordo 133).

120. Ibid., p. 47 (ricordo 186).

121. Ibid., p. 22 (ricordo 73).

122. ibid., p. 17 (ricordo 46).

123. Ibid., p. 35 (ricordo 134).

124. For compressed sketches of the history of Machiavellian thought, see Gilbert, "Machiavellism," pp. 116–26; and K.-H. Gerschmann, "Machiavellismus," pp. 580–83. F. P. S. Donaldson, *Machiavelli and Mystery of State* is a study of a number of sixteenth- and seventeenth-century writers on politics who associated Machiavelli's doctrine with an ancient, secret knowledge of the mystery of kingship or state. Meinecke, *Machiavellism* is a classic study that ranges from Machiavelli himself up to German thinkers of the eighteenth and nineteenth centuries such as Hegel, Fichte, and Ranke.

125. Hill, *Intellectual Origins of the English Revolution*, p. 32; drawing from Raab, *English Face of Machiavelli* (London, 1964), pp. 52–53, 96, 274–75.

126. See Shakespeare, *King Richard III*, ed. A. Hammond (London: Routledge, 1981), pp. 97–119; and Vickers "Shakespeare's Hypocrites," *Returning to Shakespeare*, esp. pp. 97–102.

127. Vickers, "Shakespeare's Hypocrites," p. 117.

128. Donaldson, *Machiavelli and Mystery of State*, chap. 1, esp. pp. 7–9, 30.

129. Ibid., chap. 6.

130. Exod. 2.12.

131. Ibid., pp. 194, 196.

132. Since I have not read Gentillet, I rely almost completely on Meinecke, *Machiavellism*, pp. 51–56.

133. *Essays of Michel de Montaigne* , trans. Screech, p. 744 ("Of Presumption" 2.17).

134. Ibid., p. 737.

135. Ibid., p. 745.

136. Ibid., pp. 776–77 ("On Bad Means to a Good End," 2.24).

137. Ibid., p. 902 ("On the Useful and the Honorable," 3.1).

138. Ibid., p. 902.

139. This is a leading theme of Schaefer's full, carefully reasoned book, *The Political Philosophy of Montaigne*. See especially chap. 12.

140. Montaigne, *Essays of Michél Montaigne*, p. 35 ("On Liars," 1.9), quoted; and pp. 897–98 ("On the Useful and the Honorable," 3.1). For interpretation, see Schaefer, *Political Philosophy of Montaigne*, pp. 19–24, 32–38, 354–56.

141. Montaigne, *Essays of Michél Montaigne*, p. 1124 ("On Vanity," 3.9). For many references and a discussion of their inconsistencies, see Schaefer, *Political Philosophy of Montaigne*, pp. 357–65.

142. Schaefer, *Political Philosophy of Montaigne*, pp. 380–95.

143. Bacon, *De Augmentis Scientiarum*, bk. 7, chap. 2, trans. F. R. Headlam, as quoted in Machiavelli, *The Prince*, trans. Adams. On Bacon's political philosophy in relation to his ambition to reform science, see Martin, *Francis Bacon, the State, and the Reform of Natural Philosophy*. See the quotations from Bacon praising Machiavelli on pp. 144 and 171. See also Raab, *English Face of Machiavelli*; Rossi, *Francis Bacon*; Zeitlin, "Development of Bacon's Essays"; and Luciani, "Bacon and Machiavelli."

144. Bacon is cited from the second book of *The Advancement of Learning*— see *Selected Writings of Francis Bacon*, ed. Dick, pp. 353–54.

145. Bacon, *Essays*, pp. 62, 61.

146. Ibid., p. 78 and, in order of their quotation, pp. 155, 152 ("Of the True Greatness of Kingdoms and Estates"), 116 ("Of Empire").

147. Hobbes, *Leviathan*, reprinted from the edition of 1651, chap. 11, p. 75.

148. Ibid., pp. 96–97 (chap. 13); 128, 132 (chap. 17); 134 (chap. 18). For Hobbes' subsequent Machiavellian reputation in England, see Mintz, *The Hunting of Leviathan*.

149. Spinoza, *Ethics*, bk. 4, def. 8; prop. 22, cor.; appendix, viii (pp. 547, 558, 589). In "Virtue and Sociality in Spinoza," Barbone distinguishes between Machiavelli's and Spinoza's conceptions of virtue as power on the grounds that

Machiavelli "relates his notion of virtue only to the community leaders, while Spinoza insists that virtue . . . extends to the community at large" (p. 383).

150. Ibid., p. 263 (1.4).

151. *The Political Works*, trans. Wernham, p. 312 (*A Treatise on Politics*).

152. Ibid., p. 277 (2.14).

153. Ibid., p. 425 (9.13).

154. Ibid., p. 275 (2.11).

155. Ibid. p. 309 (5.2); for many further likenesses or borrowings see the index of the work cited and see McShea, *Political Philosophy of Spinoza*.

156. Hegel, *Political Writings*, trans. T. M. Knox, pp. 219–20; as cited in S. Avineri, *Hegel's Theory of the Modern State*, pp. 53–54.

157. From G. W. F. Hegel, *Gesammelte Werke*, Rheinish-Westfaelischen Akademie der Wissenschaften, vol. 8, pp. 1–24, 256–60, as paraphrased in Harris, *Hegel's Development*, vol. 2, pp. 503–4.

158. Ibid., p. 504.

159. Kant, "Idea for a Universal History from a Cosmopolitan Point of View," Fourth Thesis, in *Kant: Selections*, ed. Beck, p. 418.

160. Ibid., Sixth Thesis, p. 419 and note.

161. From the memoirs of Kant's disciple J. G. Hasse, in *Lezte* [sic!] *Aeusserungen Kant's* [sic!], pp. 28–29.

162. Kant, *Religion within the Limits of Reason Alone*, trans. Green and Hudson, p. 25.

163. Ibid., pp. 27, 32.

164. Henrich, "On the Meaning of Rational Action in the State," pp. 107–11.

165. Kant, *The Metaphysics of Morals*, pp. 131–32.

5 Machiavellism Everywhere?

1. The literature of ancient Mesopotamia, Egypt, and Israel gives many relevant examples. To compare the status theoretically (or theologically) assigned to rulers, one might begin with Frankfort's *Kingship and the Gods*. Mendel's recent book, *Rise and Fall of Jewish Nationalism*, considers such relevant matters as nationalism in the Hellenistic world, nationalism and the concept of

'history' in the Ancient Near East, the status of Jewish (and adjacent) kings, and the use of native and mercenary troops.

2. Although it cannot easily be dispensed with, the term *tribe* has been the subject of a great deal of controversy among anthropologists. For a brief explanation of part played by administrators and missionaries in the formation of African tribes, see Oliver, *The African Experience*, pp. 148, 185.

3. What I say about the difficult of generalizing has become so common-place in contemporary anthropology that I do not think it necessary to give a bibliography. But just to whet nonanthropologists' skepticism for conventional interpretations of old sources, I can cite the intelligent observations in Obeyes-ekere, *Apotheosis of Captain Cook*.

For my subsequent remarks on aggression and war, I have made much use of two anthropological symposia on war: Friend, Harris, and Murphy, eds., *War*; and—more in tune with current anthropological views—Haas, ed., *The Anthropology of War*. Silberbauer's "Ethics in Small-Scale Societies"is admirably nuanced and sensible.

4. Moseley, *The Incas and Their Ancestors*, pp. 9–16. For details, see Cobo, *History of the Inca Empire*, bk. 2, chaps. 12–15.

5. Ibid., pp. 194–97.

6. For the description of Inca laws, see ibid., pp. 203–207 (207 quoted).

7. Ibid., pp. 238–41. For the state disposition of children, ibid., pp. 235–38. On the prohibition of mourning, see Cobo, *Inca Religion and Customs*, p. 8.

8. Ibid., pp. 239 ff. For the prohibition of sadness see Cobo, *History of the Inca Empire*, pp. 240–43.

9. Ibid., p. 243. For a recent, less emotional view of Inca government see Moseley, *Incas and Their Ancestors*, chap. 3.

10. For the Mayas, see the reading of the evidence of the statuary and monuments in Schele and Miller, *Blood of Kings*; and the reading of the historical evidence (from the monumental records themselves) in Schele and Freidel, *A Forest of Kings*—see pp. 128 and 212 for my quotations. Freidel, Schele, and Parker, *Maya Cosmos* is an attempt to enter into Maya thinking—including their view of war (chap. 7)—from the ancient records and from the contemporary descendants of the Mayas. For the words "war as statecraft," see p. 317.

11. For the Aztecs, I have depended on Anawalt and Berdan, "The Codex Mendoza"; Bierhorst, trans., *Cantares mexicanos*—severely criticized by Leon-Portilla (see below); Brundage, *Fifth Sun*; Clendinnen, *Aztecs*; Davies, *Ancient Kingdoms of Mexico*; Davies, *The Aztec Empire*; Duran, *Book of the Gods and Rites and The Ancient Calendar*; Leon-Portilla, *Fifteen Poets of the Aztec World*; and Townsend, *The Aztecs*. Thomas, *The Conquest of Mexico*, is a new, detailed his-

tory of the interaction between the Aztecs, whom he calls the "Mexica," and the Spaniards.

12. Townsend, *The Aztecs*, p. 66; see also Davies, *Ancient Kingdoms of Mexico*, p. 175.

13. From the *Codice Matritense de la Real Academia* 8, fol. 192 v., as translated in Leon-Portilla, *Pre-Columbian Literatures of Mexico*, p. 119. Translated excerpts from various versions of the Aztec Migration myth can be found in Markman and Markman, *The Flayed God*, pp. 381–409.

14. Townsend, *Aztecs*, pp. 84–85, based on the work of Jerome Offner, *Law and Politics in Aztec Tezcoco* (Cambridge: Cambridge University Press, 1988).

15. I am following mainly Townsend, *The Aztecs*, chap. 4.

16. Davies, *The Aztec Empire*, p. 197.

17. For the suspicion that the numbers are exaggerated, Davies, *The Aztec Empire*, pp. 241–42.

18. Brundage, *Fifth Sun*, p. 196. On the Aztecs' motives for sacrifice, see Davies, *The Aztec Empire*, chaps. 9, 10. For fertility rites and sacrifice, see pp. 222–23.

19. Davies, *The Aztec Empire*, p. 233.

20. Brundage, *Fifth Sun*, pp. 205–8; Davies, *The Aztec Empire*, pp. 223–25 (on sacrifice), 232–36 (on flower war).

21. Brundage, *Fifth Sun*, pp. 203–4; Davies, *The Aztec Empire*, pp. 179–80.

22. Clendinnen, *Aztecs*, p. 92.

23. Davies, *The Aztec Empire*, pp. 284–90.

24. Ibid., p. 133. And see Townsend, *The Aztecs*, p. 188.

25. Clendinnen, *Aztecs*, p. 134; from the *Florentine Codex* 9.5.21.

26. Ibid., pp. 117–18.

27. Brundage, *Fifth Sun*, p. 199; from Bernardino de Sahagun (1499–1590), the Franciscan monk who wrote an indispensable if very Christian description of Aztec culture as it was at the time of the Spanish conquest.

28. Bierhorst, *Cantares Mexicanos*, pp. 151, 357, 365. Leon-Portilla, *Fifteen Poets of the Aztec World*, pp. 128 (rhetorically very different from Bierhorst's equivalent, p. 327).

29. See Oliver, *The African Experience*, chaps. 10, 12.

30. Ibid., pp. 145–46.

31. Mair, *Primitive Government*, p. 205.

32. Ibid., pp. 99, 126–27, 152; and Smith, *Kingdoms of the Yoruba*, chaps. 3, 9, 10. On the Oyo empire and its art, see Drewal, Pemberton, and Abiodan, *Yoruba*, chap. 6.

33. See, for example, Balandier, *Political Anthropology*, pp. 102–3, summarizing the researches of the anthropologist J. H. M. Beattie on the African kingdom of Bunyoro.

34. Bascom, *Yoruba of Southwestern Nigeria*, pp. 9–10, 29–31. For another version of the Yoruba creation story, see Courlander, *Tales of Yoruba Gods and Heroes*, pp. 30–38.

35. Roberts, *The Zulu Kings*, p. 162. For a brief background to the African states of the time see Oliver, *The African Experience*, chap. 12; and also pp. 167–68. For a more formal account, see Omer-Cooper, "The Nguni Outburst"; and Ngcongco, "The Mfecane and the Rise of New African States."

36. On the value of the testimony, see Roberts, *The Zulu Kings*, pp. 156–53.

37. Ngcongco, "Mfecane and the Rise of New African States," pp. 103–4; Walter, *Terror and Resistance*, p. 120.

38. Walter, *Terror and Resistance*, pp. 138–39. For a wider perspective, see Omer-Cooper and, particularly, Ngcongco.

39. Roberts, *The Zulu Kings*, p. 131, quoting J. Y. Gibson, *Story of the Zulus* (London, 1911), p. 37.

40. Walter, *Terror and Resistance*, pp. 134–35 (quoted), 37. "Terrible declination of his head" is from Isaacs, *Travels and Adventures in Eastern Africa*, p. 150.

41. Isaacs, *Travels and Adventures*, pp. 153, 156.

42. Ibid., p. 156.

43. Walter, *Terror and Resistance*, p. 141.

44. Ibid., p. 145.

45. Roberts, *The Zulu Kings*, pp. 120–23; Walter, *Terror and Resistance*, pp. 170–72.

46. Walter, *Terror and Resistance*, p. 161.

47. Ibid., pp. 147–48, 163.

48. Ibid., pp. 165–66.

49. Ibid., p. 168.

50. Ibid., p. 176.

51. Ibid., p. 177.

52. Walter, *Terror and Resistance*, p. 174; Roberts, *The Zulu Kings*, p. 148.

53. Isaacs, *Travels and Adventures*, p. 143.

54. Ibid., pp. 174–75.

55. Ibid., p. 219; Roberts, *The Zulu Kings*, pp. 170–72.

56. Walter, *Terror and Resistance*, pp. 186–209; Roberts, *The Zulu Kings*, pp. 187–89.

57. Walter, *Terror and Resistance*, pp. 178–211.

58. Ibid., p. 218.

59. Carneiro, "Chiefdom-level Warfare as Exemplified in Fiji and the Cauca Valley, in Haas, *The Anthropology of War*, pp. 190–91. The worse-than-average despots are mentioned in Oliver, *Oceania*, vol. 2, p. 1175.

60. On the role played by Europeans in increasing the scope and violence of Native American tribal warfare see Ferguson, "Tribal Warfare." See also Service, "War and Our Contemporary Ancestors."

61. Driver, *Indians of North America*, pp. 320–24. The quotation is from p. 320.

62. See the impressive account in Maybury-Lewis, *Millennium*, pp. 240–45. The remark on obedience in wartime is based on Wallace, "Psychological Preparations for War," pp. 176–77. A general reference, which makes clear the precarious nature of received histories of the Iroquois is Jennings, *The Ambiguous Iroquois Empire*.

63. Maybury-Lewis, *Millennium*, pp. 239–41.

64. Ibid., pp. 251–57.

65. Oliver, *Native Cultures of the Pacific islands*, pp. 101, 114–15, 149. For greater detail, see the same author's *Oceania*, vol. 1, chap. 11.

66. Trompf, *Melanesian Religion*, p. 52; and Oliver, *Oceania*, vol. 1, pp. 427–30.

67. Oliver, *Oceania*, vol. 1, p. 434.

68. Trompf, *Melanesian Religion*, pp. 55–58. Oliver, *Oceania*, vol. 1, pp. 484–500.

69. Oliver, *Native Culture of the Pacific Islands*, pp. 71–74; *Oceania*, vol. 1, pp. 460–63, 467–75.

70. Gregor, "Uneasy Peace," p. 110.

71. Ibid., p. 114.

72. Ibid., p. 117.

73. For generalizations and examples see Roberts, *Order and Dispute: An Introduction to Legal Anthropology*, chaps. 7, 9; Lesser, "War and the State"; McCauley, "Conference Overview."

74. E.g., Lesser, "War and the State," p. 94.

75. Berndt and Berndt, *World of the First Australians*, pp. 356–59.

76. Spencer, *North Alaskan Eskimo*, pp. 71–72. The preceding references to the Eskimos are all from Damas, ed., *Handbook of North American Indians*, vol. 5, *Arctic*, pp. 112, 115, 177. For further references see "warfare" in the index to this volume.

77. Evans-Pritchard, *The Nuer*.

78. Ibid., p. 181.

79. Ibid., esp. pp. 90, 151–55, 169, 162–76.

80. Chagnon, *Yąnomamö: The Fierce People*—unless otherwise noted, quotations are from this first edition, of 1968, which is sometimes more detailed, not from the fourth, 1992 edition, which gives a fuller, more rounded picture, contains answers to the author's sometimes very sharp critics—he has been accused of inventing his data—and is minus the former subtitle; "Yąnomamö Social Organization and Warfare"; and "Reproductive and Somatic Conflicts of Interest in the Genesis of Violence and Warfare among Tribesmen." For a complementary, more intimate, and on the whole gentler impression, see Lizot, *Tales of the Yanomami*. See also the criticism especially of Chagnon, in Ferguson, "Tribal Warfare."

81. Chagnon, "Yąnomamö Social Organization and Warfare," pp. 130–32.

82. These statistics are from the fourth edition of *Yąnomamö* . p. 205.

83. Chagnon, *Yąnomamö* , p. 123.

84. Chagnon, "Effects of War on Social Structure," pp. 138–39. See also Chagnon's *Yąnomamö* , p. 123, with a specific example in the fourth edition, pp. 2–3.

85. Chagnon, "Reproductive and Somatic Conflicts of Interest," p. 95. See also pp. 97–98; and see the fourth edition of *Yąnomamö* , p. 205.

86. Ferguson, "Tribal Warfare," pp. 94–95. Chagnon, *Yąnomamö* , 4th ed., pp. 85–87. On the general problems involved in Chagnon's contentions and the criticisms of his opponents see Symons, "On the Use and Misuse of Darwinism in the Study of Human Behavior."

87. See Gibson, "Raiding, Trading, and Tribal Autonomy in Insular Southeast Asia"; Gregor, "Uneasy Peace: Intertribal Relations in Brazil's Upper Xingu"; and Robarcheck, "Motivations and Material Causes: On the Explanation of Conflict and War." See also McCauley "Conference Overview."

88. Gibson, "Raiding, Trading, and Tribal Autonomy in Insular Southeast Asian Cultures," pp. 132–33.

89. Robarchek, "Motivations and Material Causes," p. 61.

90. Ibid., p. 66.

91. Ibid., p. 68.

92. S. F. Moore, *Law as Process: An Anthropological Approach*, p. 1; as cited in Edgerton, *Rules, Exceptions, and Social Order*, p. 13. On the whole subject, see also Roberts, ("Rules and Power"), chap. 10 in *Order and Dispute*.

93. Roberts, *Order and Dispute*, pp. 180–81, quoting P. H. Gulliver, *Social Control in an African Society* (London, 1963), p. 123.

94. Krige and Krige, "The Lovedu of the Transvaal," p. 78.

95. Edgerton, *Rules, Exceptions, and Social Order*, p. 133, quoting C. Turnbull, *The Forest People* (New York: Simon and Schuster, 1961), p. 125.

96. Edgerton, *Rules, Exceptions, and Social Order*, pp. 133–34, on the basis of Turnbull's reports.

97. Edgerton, *Rules, Exceptions, and Social Order*, pp. 155–56, and 163–72 (a careful and rather puzzled summary of the evidence on the Walbiri). For a general description of law among the Australian aboriginals, see Berndt and Berndt, *World of the First Australians*, chap. 10, together with the additional comments on it. Williams, "Studies in Australian Aboriginal Law 1961–1986," is a discussion of various interpretations of Aboriginal law and the insufficiency of the research in the period she discusses.

98. For a general description of tricksters, see consulted two general reference books: Bonnefoy, ed., *Mythologies*, vol. 2, pp. 1153–56, 1217–20; and Leach, ed., *Funk and Wagnall's Standard Dictionary of Folklore, Mythology and Legend*—the entry "Trickster" and the entries on such different particular tricksters as Anansi (the Spider, of Africa), Coyote (the Native American trickster), Legba (the Dahomeyan trickster), Maui (the Polynesian trickster and culture hero), and Reynard.

For the African trickster, I have read Abrams, *African Folktales*, pt. 3; Haring, "A Characteristic African Folktale Pattern"; Evans-Pritchard, *The Zande Trickster*; and Knappert, *Myths and Legends of the Congo*.

For the Native Americans, see Alexander, *North American Mythology*, pp. 141–45, 158–62; Bierhorst, *The Mythology of North America*, pp. 12–37, 141–49; Bright, *A Coyote Reader* (this contains contemporary poetry and comments; in his own translations and adaptations, Bright tries for esthetic authenticity by means of a measured-verse style); Erdoes and Ortiz, eds., *American Indian Myths and Legends*; Norman, *Northern Tales*, pt. 3; Radin, *The Trickster*; and Thompson, *The Folktale*, pt. 3, chap. 3, and *Tales of the North American Indians*, chap. 3.

Finally, for the Polynesian trickster, see (apart from Bonnefoy) Alpers, *World of the Polynesians*, pp. 92–105.

99. Radin, *The Trickster*, pp. 29–30.

100. Alpers, *World of the Polynesians*, pp. 92–105; and see note pp. 373–74. The atoll of Manihiki is in the northern Cook Islands. For a summary of the varied Maui myths, see Poignant, *Oceanic and Australian Mythology*; and for a critical background to Oceanic mythology, which I ignore here, see Guiart, "Religions and Mythologies of Oceania," in Bonnefoy, ed., *Mythologies*, vol. 2, pp. 1208–24.

101. Knappert, *Myths and Legends of the Congo*, p. 177.

102. Abrams, *African Folktales*, pp. 107–8; W. Bascom, "African Dilemma Tales," in Dorson, *African Folklore*.

103. Abrams, *African Folktales*, pp. 142–43; from H. A. S. Johnston, *A Selection of Hausa Stories* (Oxford University Press, 1966), pp. 48–49.

104. Gbadamosi and Beier, *Not Even God Is Ripe Enough*, p. 13.

105. See, e.g., the report on selfish genes, including one called "Medea," "Mother's Little Favorite," in the *Scientific American*, July 1992, pp. 15–16.

106. In general, see Cronin—who is trained in both biology and philosophy—*The Ant and the Peacock*; Cosmides and Tooby, "Cognitive Adaptations for Social Exchange; Dawkins, *The Selfish Gene*—the edition of 1989 contains interesting answers to his critics, including M. Sahlins, *The Use and Abuse of Biology* (London: Tavistock, 1977); Mayr, "The Origins of Human Ethics," and "Philosophical Aspects of Natural Selection" in Mayr, *Toward a New Philosophy of Biology*; Ruse, *Taking Darwin Seriously*; and Wilson, *Sociobiology*. On parasitism as a form of mutuality, see Rennie, "Living Together."

107. For an introduction to the ugly but intriguing mole-rat, see Braude and Lacey, "The Underground Society"; or Sherman, Jarvis, and Braude, "Naked Mole Rats." For the social insects (as, in other chapters, for biology in general), see the summary in Wilson, *Sociobiology*, chap. 20; and, for ants in particular, Hölldober and Wilson, *The Ants*.

Cosmides and Tooby, "Cognitive Adaptations for Social Exchange," analyzes the empirical evidence for the theory of altruism and for rejecting the view that humans have "a single 'reasoning faculty' that is function-general and content-free" (quotation p. 205).

108. Davies and Brooke, "Coevolution of the Cuckoo and Its Hosts."

109. The literature I have consulted includes Byrne and Whiten, eds., *Machiavellian Intelligence: Social Expertise and the Evolution of Intellect in Monkeys, Apes, and Humans*; Cheyney and Seyfarth, *How Monkeys See the World*; Hamburg and McCown, eds., *The Great Apes*; Heltne and Marquardt, eds., *Understanding Chimpanzees*; Jolly, *Evolution of Primate Behavior*; Goodall, *The Chimpanzees of Gombe* and *Through a Window: 30 Years with the Chimpanzees of Gombe*; Smuts et al., eds., *Primate Societies*; Strum, *Almost Human: A Journey into the World of Baboons*; Symons, "On the Use and Misuse of Darwinism in the Study of Human Behavior"; and de Waal, *Chimpanzee Politics: Love and Sex among Apes* and *Peacemaking among Primates*.

110. Cheyney and Seyfarth, *How Monkeys See the World*, pp. 207, 304–6 (305–6 quoted).

111. Ibid., p. 195, the remark on pretended friendliness on the basis of a personal communication of De Waal, p. 195. The anecdote about the baboons is from R. Byrne and A. Whiten, "The Manipulation of Attention in Primate Tactical Deception," in Byrne and Whiten, *Machiavellian Intelligence*, p. 217.

112. Heltne and Marquardt, *Understanding Chimpanzees*, p. xiv.

113. Goodall, *Through a Window*, chap. 10.

114. De Waal, *Chimpanzee Politics*, p. 207.

115. See Power, *The Egalitarians—Human and Chimpanzee*. Power favors the view that chimpanzees living under undisturbed, favorable conditions live in accord with a "mutual dependence system," in which competition is indirect, leadership charismatic, tolerant, and fluid, individuals act autonomously, and the whole social system is notably egalitarian. Power derives this model from J. Woodburn, "Egalitarian Societies," *Man*, n.s., 17:431–51, who used as examples six small peoples of foragers, that is, hunter-gatherers.

116. Goodall, *The Chimpanzees of Gombe*, pp. 442, 453, 477–87.

117. Goodall, *The Chimpanzees of Gombe*, pp. 410, 424, 426–28.

118. Ibid., pp. 431–35; and Goodall, *Through a Window*, chap. 13.

119. Goodall, *The Chimpanzees of Gombe*, pp. 412–17, 426–28; de Waal, *Chimpanzee Politics*, pp. 141–42, and "Dynamics of Social Relationships," in Smuts et al., *Primate Societies*, p. 422.

120. Heltne and Marquardt, *Understanding Chimpanzees*, pp. 12–13. See also pp. 161–63.

6 Moral Abstractions and Human Realities

1. Fairly comprehensive guidance to relevant contemporary philosophers can be found in two handbooks, Singer, ed., *A Companion to Ethics* and Goodin and Pettit, eds., *A Companion to Contemporary Political Philosophy*. The intellectual level of Goodin and Pettit's book is high, but much of it is distant from political reality—many of its chapters refer little if at all to empirical studies. Because there are separate chapters on history, sociology, economics, political science, and legal studies, it is surprising that there is none on psychology. Even the index, which has a few references to "psychoanalysis and continental philosophy," contains none to psychology. The book was published too late for me to make much use of it.

2. I dismiss the idea of just war here too cavalierly. For India see Dikshitar, *War in Ancient India*; for the West see Walzer, *Just and Unjust Wars*, and, on a rather different subject, Best, *Humanity in Warfare*. For essays on both the Europe and Islam, see Kelsay and Johnson, eds., *Just War and Jihad*. The quotation is from Shakespeare, *Richard III* 5.3.310.

3. See, e.g., Scott, *Domination and the Arts of Resistance*.

4. For a discussion of the possible evolutionary benefit of self-deception, see Nesse and Lloyd, "The Evolution of Psychodynamic Mechanisms." pp. 603ff.

5. Flanagan, *Varieties of Moral Personality*, speaks of the "the principle of minimal psychological realism" (p. 32), by which he means the assumption that an ethical theory should be constructed to fit creatures of the kinds we really are.

6. Among the books for on which I depend for ideas and empirical support in the immediately following pages there are: Christie and Geis, *Studies in Machiavellianism*; Milgram, *Obedience to Authority*; and Peck and Havighurst, *Psychology of Character Development*. I have also used two books of conversations with criminals: Parker and Allerton, *Courage of His Convictions*, and Parker, *Frying Pan*. To these may be added Sutherland, annotator and interpreter of the autobiographical account that dominates *The Professional Thief*.

These are all relatively old books. Some of them may no longer meet strict professional standards, while others (Christie and Geis, and Milgram) can probably no longer be followed up because the deception of experimental subjects is now forbidden by professional standards of ethics. However, I feel towards these books as to old friends and continue to trust them in a general way.

For a philosopher's informed comments on the work of Milgram and other studies of the influence of particular situations on moral behavior, see Flanagan, *Varieties of Moral Personality*, chap. 14.

7. Aristotle, *The Nichomachean Ethics*, trans. Rackham, pp. 267–69 (1131b). Aristotle's proportional theory of justice is carried over into Islamic thought by the moral philosopher Ahmad Muhammad Miskawayah (d. 1030). See Fakhry, *Ethical Theories in Islam*, pp. 113–15.

8. Confucius, *The Analects*, trans Lau, p. 155 (5.24).

9. Urbach, *The Sages*, vol. 1, p. 589.

10. Matt. 7.12 RSV.

11. Christie and Geis, *Studies in Machiavellianism*, pp. 340, 357

12. Parker, *Frying Pan*, pp. 202–3.

13. Parker and Allerton, *Courage of His Convictions*, p. 144.

14. Parker, *Frying Pan*, p. 202.

15. Parker and Allerton, *Courage of His Convictions*, p. 88. On a criminal's sense of professionalism see also Sutherland, *The Professional Thief*, chap. 6.

17. Diderot, "Rameau's Nephew," in Diderot, *Diderot's Selected Writings*, p. 137.

17. Montaigne, *The Complete Essays*, trans. Screech, p. 892 ("On the Useful and the Honorable").

18. Shang Yang, *Book of the Lord Shang*, trans. Duyvendak, p. 25. On the publishing history of the book, see the introduction, chap. 4.

19. For a philosopher's response to "The Machiavellian Challenge," see Coady, "Politics and the Problem of Dirty Hands."

20. For some empirical support for this statement see Christie and Geis, *Studies in Machiavellianism*, chap. 14, "Overview of Experimental Research." Peck and Havighurst's conformists (see their *Psychology of Character Development*, pp. 168–69) whom they picture as more sensitive to what others think of them than of how they act, may well coincide in part with Christie and Geis's category of persons highly susceptible to social influence—to the point of being influenced, for example, to lie, though to lie unreflectively. It would be interesting to disentangle this overlapping of categories.

21. Lifton, *Nazi Doctors*, p. 113. All of Lifton's writings are centered on the theme of human inhumanity to humans. See, e.g., his essays in *The Future of Immortality* and in Lifton and Markusen, *The Genocidal Mentality*.

22. Lifton, *Nazi Doctors*, pp. 421, 422..

23. Browning, *Ordinary Men*, p. 47.

24. Ibid., p. 2

25. Ibid., p. 72.

26. Ibid., p. 65.

27. Ibid., p. 73.

28. Ibid., p. 69.

29. Ibid., pp. 76–77.

30. Ibid., pp. 170–89 (189 quoted).

31. See Milgram, "Why Obedience?" chap. 10 in *Obedience to Authority*.

32. For a psychoanalytic expression of such self-glorification and defense, see the study by the Group for the Advancement of Psychiatry, *Us and Them: The Psychology of Ethnonationalism*, p. 93. See also Anzieu's adventurous ideas in *Group and the Unconscious*. Two relevant collections of articles are LeVine and Campbell, eds., *Ethnocentrism*, which is anthropological and psychoanalytic in emphasis; and Reynolds and Falger, eds., *The Sociobiology of Ethnocentrism*.

33. La Rochefoucauld, *Maxims*, trans. Tancock, p. 35.

34. Kirwan, *Augustine*, p. 219; from Augustine, *City of God*, 4.4; from Cicero, *De republica* 3.

35. Jones, *Tales and Teachings of the Buddha*, pp. 159–60 (Jataka story no. 421).

36. See the brief, fair discussion in Dumont, *Homo Hierarchicus*, pp. 138–50.

37. Silberbauer, "Ethics in Small-Scale Societies," p. 22.

38. See McCauley, "Conference Overview," pp. 10–13; and for a rather different, more detailed anthropological emphasis, Hallpike, *Principles of Social Evolution*, pp. 237–252 (on societal size) and 252–83 (on the emergence of the state and the rationalization of society).

39. Gibson, "Raiding, Trading and Tribal Autonomy in Insular Southeast Asia," p. 144.

40. Such is the position of A. C. Graham in relation to Mencius and Hsün Tzu, whose traditional polar image in Chinese philosophy I have accepted. See Graham's essay "The Background of the Mencian Theory of Human Nature," in *Studies in Chinese Philosophy and Philosophical Literature*.

41. From Max Weber's famous essay, "Politics as a Vocation," pp. 121, 125–26. For contemporary versions of the typically Machiavellian principle of being cruel only to be kind (e.g., *Hamlet* 3.4.178) can be found in Madsen and Shafritz, eds., *Essentials of Government Ethics*. In this anthology, see especially Bok, "Lies for the Public Good"; French, "Dirty Hands"; Walzer, "Political

"Action: The Problem of Dirty Hands"; and Amy, "Why Policy Analysis and Ethics Are Incompatible." Bok explains her views at greater length in *Lying: Moral Choice in Public and Private Life.*

42. Calvino, "A King Listens," in *Under the Jaguar Sun*, pp. 38–39.

43. Thomas, *The Conquest of Mexico*, pp. 601–2.

44. Weber, "Politics as a Vocation," p. 80.

45. From the interview with Nicholas ("The Crow") Caramandi, a Philadelphia Mafioso, in *Time*, June 17, 1991.

46. *On War* 3.6, as quoted in Gat, *The Origins of Military Thought*, pp. 243–44.

47. Nietzsche, *Human, All too Human*, trans. Hollingdale, p. 176 ("Vol. 1," sec. 477).

48. Ibid., pp. 380–81 (vol. 2, sec. 284).

49. Gray, *Warrior: Reflection on Men in Battle*, pp. 28, 51.

50. Creveld, *The Transformation of War*, p. 221.

51. Mitscherlich and Mitscherlich, *The Inability to Mourn*, pp. 23–24, 57, 193.

52. Burleigh and Wipperman, *Racial State*, pp. 39–41 (40 quoted).

53. Bullock, *Hitler and Stalin*, pp. 500–501. This book has been particularly convenient because of the careful parallel it draws and the questions it addresses. On Hitler I have also consulted Craig, *Germany 1866–1945*; Fulbrook, *Fontana History of Germany*; and Stern, *Hitler.*

54. Bullock, *Hitler and Stalin*, pp. 406, 408.

55. Ibid., p. 406.

56. Stern, *Hitler*, p. 49; from *Mein Kampf*, 17th ed. (Munich, 1943), p. 419.

57. Stern, *Hitler*, p. 51; from a speech of September 1939.

58. Craig, *Germany 1866–1945*, p. 590; and see Bullock, *Hitler and Stalin*, pp. 362, 479.

59. Burleigh and Wippermann, *Racial State*, chap. 1, on the "polycratic" or monolithic structure of Nazi Germany, and their concluding comments on pp. 306–7. See also Fulbrook, *Fontana History of Germany*, pp. 73–81.

60. Ibid., p. 387; from G. W. F. Hegel, *Lectures on the Philosophy of History*, trans. J. Sibree (London, 1902), pp. 31–32.

61. Ibid., p. 955.

62. Craig, *Germany 1866–1945*, pp. 543, 545.

63. For Stalin I have used Bullock, *Hitler and Stalin* and Conquest *Stalin: Breaker of Nations*; Sinyavsky, *Soviet Civilization*; Tucker, *Stalin in Power*; and Volkogonov, *Stalin*.

64. Sinyavsky, *Soviet Civilization*, p. 96; Tucker, *Stalin in Power*, p. 282.

65. Conquest, *Stalin*, p. 193. On Raskolnikov see also Tucker, *Stalin in Power*, pp. 505–6.

66. Conquest, *Stalin*, p. 318.

67. Bullock, *Hitler and Stalin*, p. 127.

68. Ibid., p. 401.

69. Sinyavsky, *Soviet Civilization*, p. 85.

70. Bullock, *Stalin and Hitler*, p. 406.

71. Tucker, *Stalin in Power*, p. 453.

72. Bullock, *Hitler and Stalin*, p. 424.

73. Volkogonov, *Stalin*, p. 550.

74. Tucker, *Stalin in Power*, pp. 160–62, 537.

75. Tucker's interpretation, in *Stalin in Power*, pp. 476–78, 538–40. Bukharin says much the same thing—see Bullock, *Hitler and Stalin*, pp. 405–6.

76. Tucker, *Stalin in Power*, pp. 165–71 (p. 170 for the episode involving the murder of strangers).

77. Conquest, *Stalin*, p. 316.

78. Ibid., pp. 317, 323.

79. Tucker, *Stalin in Power*, p. 475.

80. Sinyavsky, *Soviet Civilization*, p. 93.

81. Bullock, *Hitler and Stalin*, p. 514; Sinyavsky, *Soviet Civilization*. p. 94 (quoted).

82. Tucker, *Stalin in Power*, p. 6.

83. Conquest, *Stalin*, p. 314. See also Sinayavsky, *Soviet Civilization*, p. 104.

84. See Mitscherlich and Mitscherlich, *The Inability to Mourn*, p. 57.

7. Nonutopian Observations

1. For an exposition of the favorable, even ideal nature of tradition, especially Jewish tradition, see Goodman, *On Justice*.

2. *Sutta Nipata*, p. 143ff., as quoted in Embree, ed., *Sources of Indian Tradition*, rev. ed., vol. 1, p. 118.

3. Shantideva, *Sikhasamuccaya (Compendium of Doctrine)*, pp. 278–83, as quoted in Embree, *Sources of Indian Tradition* (note 4), pp. 162–63.

4. Masefield, *Divine Revelation in Pali Buddhism*.

5. Jataka Story 431, in Jones, *Tales and Teachings of the Buddha*, p. 138.

6. Jataka Story 432, in Jones, *Tales and Teachings of the Buddha*, pp. 139–40.

7. I follow the accounts in Schumann, *The Historical Buddha*, pp. 232–38. See also Thomas, *The Life of Buddha*, pp. 131–38.

8. *Vinaya Pitaka, Cullavagga* 7.2, 7.3.

9. Horner, trans., *The Middle Length Sayings (Majjhima-Nikaya)*, vol. II, pp. 60–64. The quotation is from pp. 60–61.

10. Ibid., pp. 62–63.

11. Thomas, *The Life of Buddha*, p. 133.

12. Gombrich, *Precept and Practice*, p. 227, and Obeyesekere, *The Work of Culture*, pp. 166–74. Gombrich reports that the monks and others he interviewed in Ceylon of the 1960s mostly justified this holy war.

13. Obeyesekere, *The Work of Culture*, p. 168.

14. Ibid., pp. 185–86.

15. Keown, *Nature of Buddhist Ethics*, chap. 6, esp. pp. 150–54, 157–63; Williams, *Mahayana Buddhism*, pp. 143–45, 161. The sutra *On the Paramita of Ingenuity*, sutra 38 of the *Maharatnakuta Sutra*, is wholly devoted to "skilful means." For a complete translation of this sutra see Chang, ed., *Treasury of Mahayana Sutras*, esp. pp. 430, 433–35, 451–52, 456–57, 458.

16. Weinstein, *Buddhism under the T'ang*, pp. 37–47.

17. Snellgrove, *Indo-Tibetan Buddhism*, vol. 2, pp. 426–526.

18. Tucci, *The Religions of Tibet*, pp. 39–46.

19. Yampolsky, ed., *Selected Writings of Nichiren*, p. 45.

20. Anesaki, *Nichiren the Buddhist Prophet*; A. Matsunaga and D. Matsunaga, *Foundations of Japanese Buddhism*, vol. 2, chap. 3; Osumi Kazuo, "Bud-

dhism in the Kamakura Period," In Yamamura, ed., *The Cambridge History of Japan*, vol. 3, pp. 557–58; Williams, *Mahayana Buddhism*, pp. 141–66; Yampolsky, ed., *Selected Writings of Nichiren*, pp. 323–28—the description of Nichiren's arrest is from his own dramatic account.

21. Yampolsky, ed., *Selected Writings of Nichiren*, pp. 20–21.

22. Ibid., p. 33.

23. Ibid., p. 35.

24. Ibid., pp. 51, 114, 145.

25. Ibid., p. 218.

26. Ibid., p. 233.

27. Ibid., p. 138.

28. Kazuo, "Buddhism in the Kamakura Period," p. 577.

29. Ibid., p. 579.

30. Matsunaga and Matsunaga, *Foundation of Japanese Buddhism*, p. 175.

31. Ibid., pp. 175–76.

32. Ibid., pp. 176–81; Tamura Yoshiro, "The Ideas of the *Lotus Sutra*, pp. 50–51.

33. Collcutt, "Zen and the *Gozan*."

34. See, e.g., Faure, *Rhetoric of Immediacy*, pp. 21–24, 161, 234–37.

35. Dumoulin, *Zen Buddhism: A History*, vol. 2, *Japan*, pp. 274–97 (287 quoted).

36. For the Hinayana countries see, e.g., Yoneo Ishii, *Sangha, State, and Society: Thai Buddhism in History*.

37. Broido, "Killing, Lying, Stealing, and Adultery: A Problem of Interpretation in the Tantras."

38. Poundstone, *Prisoner's Dilemma*, gives a clear, untechnical survey of game theory and its social applications, including the modelling of wars.

39. Wolfenstein, E. V. *Revolutionary Personality: Lenin, Trotsky, Gandhi*.

40. Veyne, *Did the Greeks Believe in Their Myths?* p. 128.

41. For an introduction to Chinese Historiography see Gardner, *Chinese Traditional Historiography*. Further, see Balasz, "History as a Guide to Bureaucratic Practice," in Balasz, *Chinese Civilization and Bureaucracy*; Beasley and Pulleyblank, eds., *Historians of China and Japan*. Leslie, Mackeras, and Wang Gung-

wu, eds., *Essays on the Sources for Chinese History* gives a clear, readable overview of the rich records available (and sometimes lost). Chavanne's introduction to his translation of Ssu-ma Ch'ien, *Les Mémoires Historiques de Se-ma Ts'ien*, criticizes the historian for his rigidity, uniformity, and rationalism, but praises his basic truthfulness (pp. clxxxii–clxxxvii). Twitchett, *Writing of Official History under the T'ang* gives a relatively full, nuanced picture of official historiography from about the seventh to the ninth centuries A.D.

42. Chavannes, *Les Mémoires Historiques de Se-ma Ts'ien*, vol. 1, pp. ccxxiii–ccxxv.

43. Balasz, "History as a Guide to Bureaucratic Practice," in Balasz, *Chinese Civilization and Bureaucracy*, pp. 130–31.

44. Twitchett, *Writing of Official History under the T'ang*, p. 71.

45. On the overwhelming historical emphasis on the central government and on other editorial bias during the T'ang period, see Twitchett, *Writing of Official History under the T'ang*, pp. 199–200

46. Wu, *Confucian's Progress: Autobiographical Writings in Traditional China*, pp. 25–26. For an example of an autobiography of the kind I mention, see pp. 32–34.

47. Ibid., pp. 217–34 (232 quoted).

48. De Bary, *The Trouble with Confucianism*, p. 49—but the thesis runs through the entire bk..

49. There is a brief and clear account of the changing structure of Chinese government in Hucker, *China's Imperial Past*, chaps. 2, 6, and 11. For a detailed, persuasive, and intelligent analysis of the nature and limits of governmental rule, imperial and bureaucratic, in eighteenth century China, see Kuhn, *Soulstealers: The Chinese Sorcery Scare of 1768*, especially the two last, generalizing chapters. The bureaucratic burden of a conscientious Chinese emperor is expressed by Kang Hsi, who reigned from A.D.1661 to 1722. See Spence, *K'ang-hsi, Emperor of China*, p. 146.

50. Spence, *K'ang-hsi, Emperor of China*, p. 232.

51. Balasz, "History as a Guide to Bureaucratic Practice," in Balasz, *Chinese Civilization and Bureaucracy*, p. 149.

52. Tong, *Disorder under Heaven: Collective Violence in the Ming Dynasty*, which is based on the provincial and prefectural gazetteers of eleven of the fifteen provincial units of China.

53. Mote, "The Rise of the Ming Dynasty, 1330–1367," in Mote and Twitchett, eds. *The Ming Dynasty, 1368–1644*, pt. 1. p. 55.

54. Ibid., pp. 100–103 (103 quoted). For an account of the rise and fall of the Ming dynasty, including the career of Chu Yan-chang, whose reign title was Ming Huang-wu, and a description of Ming historical writing, see Mote and Twitchett, eds., *The Ming Dynasty, 1368–1644*, pt. 1.

55. Ibid., p. 103.

56. Langlois, "The Hung-wu Reign, 1368–1398," in Mote and Twitchett, eds., *The Ming Dynasty, 1368–1644*, pt. 1, p. 155.

57. Ibid., p. 157.

58. Tong, *Disorder under Heaven*, pp. 164–65.

59. Ibid., pp. 192–97. The sentences on Confucian indoctrination are based on Hucker, *China's Imperial Past*, pp. 310–11.

60. Tong, *Disorder under Heaven*, pp. 117–29.

61. Ray Huang, "The Lung-Ch'ing and Wan-li Reigns, 1567–1620," in Mote and Twitchett, *The Ming Dynasty, 1368–1644*, pt. 1, p. 556.

62. Salisbury, *New Emperors*, p. 480, note. 17 and pp. 52–53.

63. Ibid., p. 144.

64. Jenner, *The Tyranny of History*, p. 39. On Mao's interest in the histories of Ssu-ma Ch'ien and Ssu-ma Kuang see the entries *Records of the Historian* and *The General Mirror for the Aid of Government* in the index of Salisbury, *New Emperors*. In speaking of Mao, I have also drawn on Fairbank, *Great Chinese Revolution, 1800–1985* and Ladany, *Law and Legality in China*.

For Ssu-ma Kuang as a historian, see Beasley and Pulleyblank, eds., *Historians of China and India*, pp. 151–59. See also Bol, *This Culture of Our*, pp. 237–46.

65. Salisbury, *New Emperors*, pp. 325–26.

66. Byron and Pack, *The Claws of the Dragon*. This book is a conscientious report as carefully documented as could be expected under current circumstances. The estimate of the number of executions during the Cultural Revolution is given in a footnote on p. 321.

67. Beiner and Booth, eds., *Kant and Political Philosophy*, contains a variety of essays on Kant's own views, on the Kantian legacy of political thought, and on present-day views influenced by Kant. The last group of essays, entitled "Contemporary Debates," are by John Rawls, Jürgen Habermas, Charles Taylor, and Hans-Georg Gadamer. All of these are reprinted from elsewhere.

68. See Kant, *Kant's Political Writings*, trans Reiss.

69. Ibid., p. 97. This reasoning is repeated in Kant's *Metaphysics of Morals*, trans. Gregor, p. 154 ("The Right of Nations").

70. This and the preceding two quotations, Kant, "Perpetual Peace," p. 96.

71. Ibid., p. 98.

72. Ibid., pp. 99–100.

73. Ibid., p. 102.

74. Ibid., p. 103.

75. Ibid., p. 108.

76. Ibid., pp. 112, 113.

77. Ibid., p. 114.

78. Ibid.

79. Ibid., pp. 116–20.

80. Ibid., pp. 124, 125.

81. Kant, *Kant's Political Writings*, trans. Reiss, p. 84 ("On the Common Saying: 'This May Be True in Theory, but It Does not Apply in Practice'").

82. "Perpetual Peace," pp. 124–25. This verdict is repeated in the *Metaphysics of Morals*, p. 133, where Kant raises the question, which he leaves to the right of nations, if other powers have the right to band together in the deposed monarch's behalf.

83. Kant, *Metaphysics of Morals*, trans. Gregor, pp. 130, 131–32.

84. Kant, *The Conflict of the Faculties*, trans. Gregor, p. 153 ("The Conflict of the Philosophy Faculty with the Faculty of Law").

85. Kant, "Perpetual Peace," p. 123.

86. I follow the exposition of Kant's views in Saner, *Kant's Political Thought*, pp. 263–269.

87. See, e.g., the introduction to Beiner and Booth, *Kant and Political Philosophy*.

88. Russet, *Grasping the Democratic Peace* and Singer and Wildavsky, *The Real World Order*. I know these books only from reviews.

89. Saner, *Kant's Political Thought*, p. 306, where the references to Kant are given. The critical references are to the Akademie edition of Kant's works. In the order in which I use the references they are vol. 19, pp. 280ff.; vol. 18, p. 213; vol. 19, p. 491; vol. 4, p. 366. Saner gives further references, which I do not repeat, to the volumes with the Kantian fragments.

90. Schiller, *On the Aesthetic Education of Man*, trans. Wilkinson and Willoughby, pp. 189, 215 ("Twenty-Fifth Letter" and "Twenty-Seventh Letter).

91. Putnam, *Making Democracy Work*, pp. 89, 90.

92. Ibid., p. 115.

BIBLIOGRAPHY

Abrams, R. D. *African Folktales*. New York: Pantheon, 1983.

Agrawal, K. M. *Kautilya on Crime and Punishment*. Almora: Shree Almora Book Depot, 1990.

Alexander, H. B. *The Mythology of North America*. London: Marshall Jones, 1916.

Allan, S. *The Shape of the Turtle: Myth, Art, and Cosmos in Early China*. Albany: State University of New York Press, 1991.

Alpers, A. *The World of the Polynesians*. Auckland: Oxford University Press, 1987.

Ames, R. T. *The Art of Rulership: A Study in Ancient Chinese Political Thought*. Honolulu: University of Hawaii Press, 1983.

Anawalt, P. R., and F. F. Berdan. "The Codex Mendoza." *Scientific American* June, 1992.

Anesaki, M. *Nichiren the Buddhist Prophet*. Cambridge: Harvard University Press, 1949.

Angelo, S. *Machiavelli*. London: Gollancz, 1969.

Anzieu, D. *The Group and the Unconscious*. London: Routledge and Kegan Paul, 1984.

Aristotle. *The Complete Works of Aristotle*. Ed. J. Barnes. 2 vols. Princeton: Princeton University Press, 1984.

———. *The Nichomachean Ethics*. Trans. H. Rackham. Cambridge: Harvard University Press, 1926.

Augustine. *Basic Writings of Saint Augustine*. Ed. W. J. Oates. 2 vols. New York: Random House, 1948.

309

Avineri, S. *Hegel's Theory of the Modern State*. Cambridge: Cambridge University Press, 1972.

Bacon, F. *The Essays*. Harmondsworth: Penguin, 1985.

———. *Selected Writings*. Ed. H. G. Dick. New York: Random House, 1955.

Balandier, G. *Political Anthropology*. Harmondsworth: Penguin, 1972.

Balasz, E. *Chinese Civilization and Bureaucracy*. New Haven: Yale University Press, 1964.

Barbone, S. "Virtue and Sociality in Spinoza." *Iyyun, the Jeusalem Philosophical Quarterly* 42 (July 1993).

Barkow, J. H., L. Cosmides, and J. Tooby, eds. *The Adapted Mind: Evolutionary Psychology and the Generation of Culture*. New York: Oxford University Press, 1992.

Bascom, W. *The Yoruba of Southwestern Nigeria*. New York: Holt, Rinehart and Winston, 1969.

Basham, A. L. *The Wonder That Was India*. 3rd ed. London: Sidgwick and Jackson, 1967.

Beasley, W. G., and E. G. Pulleyblank, eds. *Historians of China and Japan*. London: Oxford University Press, 1961.

Bee, R. L. "Quechuan." In Ortiz, ed., *Handbook of the American Indian*, vol. 10.

Beiner, R., and W. J. Booth. *Kant and Political Philosophy*. New Haven: Yale University Press, 1993.

Benevolo, L. *The European City*. Oxford: Blackwell, 1993.

Berndt, R. M., and C. H. Berndt. *The World of the First Australians*. Rev. ed. Canberra: Aboriginal Studies Press, 1988.

Berndt, R. M., and R. Tonkinson, eds. *Social Anthropology and Australian Aboriginal Studies*. Canberra: Australian Institute of Aboriginal Studies, 1988.

Best, G. *Humanity in Warfare*. London: Methuen. 1983.

Bevan, E. R. "India in Early Greek and Latin Literature." In *Cambridge History of India*, vol. 1.

Bierhorst, J. *The Mythology of North America*. New York: Morrow, 1985.

———. trans. *Cantares mexicanos: Songs of the Aztecs*. Stanford: Stanford University Press, 1985.

Birell, A. *Chinese Mythology: An Introduction.* Baltimore: Johns Hopkins University Press, 1993.

Black, R. "Machiavelli, Servant of the Florentine Republic." In Bock, Skinner, and Viroli, eds., *Machiavelli and Republicanism.*

Bock, G. "Civil Discord in Machiavelli's *Istorie Fiorentine.*" In Bock, Skinner, and Viroli, eds., *Machiavelli and Republicanism.*

Bock, G., Q. Skinner, and M. Viroli, eds. *Machiavelli and Republicanism.* Cambridge: Cambridge Unviersity Press, 1990.

Bodde, D. *China's First Unifier: A Study of the Ch'in Dynasty as Seen in the Life of Li Ssu.* Leiden: Brill, 1938.

———. "Mythology of Ancient China." In S. N. Kramer, ed., *Mythologies of the Ancient World.*

———. "The State and Empire of Ch'in." In *The Cambridge History of China,* vol. 1.

Bok., S. *Lying: Moral Choice in Public and Private Life.* New York: Random House, 1989.

Bol, P. K. *This Culture of Ours: Intellectual Transitions in T'ang and Sung China.* Stanford: Stanford University Press, 1992.

Bonnefoy, E., ed. *Mythologies.* 2 vols. Chicago: University of Chicago Press, 1991.

Braude, S., and E. Lacey. "The Underground Society." *The Sciences,* May/June 1992.

Bright, W. *A Coyote Reader.* Berkeley and Los Angeles: University of California Press, 1993.

Broido, M. M. "Killing, Lying, Stealing, and Adultry: A Problem of Interpretation in the Tantras." In Lopez, ed., *Buddhist Hermeneutics.*

Browning, C. R. *Ordinary Men: Reserve Police Battalion 101 and the Final Solution in Poland.* New York: HarperCollins, 1992.

Brundage, B. C. *The Fifth Sun: Aztec Gods, Aztec World.* Austin: University of Texas Press, 1979.

Bullock, A. *Hitler and Stalin.* London: HarperCollins, 1991.

Burchell, G., C. Gordon, and P. Miller, eds. *The Foucault Effect.* London: Harvester Wheatsheaf, 1991.

Burke, P. *The Renaissance Idea of the Past.* London: Edwin Arnold, 1969.

Burleigh, M., and W. Wippermann. *The Racial State: Germany 1933–1945*. Cambridge: Cambridge University Press, 1991.

Butterfield, H. *The Statecraft of Machiavelli*. New York: Collier Books, 1962.

Byrne, R., and A. Whiten, eds. *Machiavellian Intelligence: Social Expertise and the Evolution of Intellect in Monkeys, Apes, and Humans*. Oxford: Oxford University Press, 1988.

Byron, J., and R. Pack: *The Claws of the Dragon: The Evil Genius Behind Mao—and His Legacy of Terror in People's China*. New York: Simon and Schuster, 1992.

Calvino, I. *Under the Jaguar Sun*. London: Cape, 1992.

The Cambridge Ancient History. 2nd ed., Vol. 5. *The Fifth Century B.C.* Edited by D. M. Lewis et al. Cambridge University Press: Cambridge, 1992.

The Cambridge History of China. Vol. 1. Ed. D. Twitchett and M. Loewe. Cambridge: Cambridge University Press, 1986.

The Cambridge History of India. Vol. 1. Ed. E. J. Rapson. Cambridge: Cambridge University Press, 1935.

The Cambridge History of Renaissance Philosophy. Ed. C. Schmitt, Q. Skinner, and E. Kessler. Cambridge: Cambridge University Press, 1988.

Carneiro, R. L. "Chiefdom-level Warfare as Exemplified in Fiji and the Cauca Valley. In Haas, ed., *The Anthropology of War*.

Chabod, F. *Machiavelli and the Renaissance*. New York: Harper and Row, 1965.

Chagnon, N. A. "Reproductive and Somatic Conflicts of Interest in the Genesis of Violence and Warfare among Tribesmen." In Haas, ed., *The Anthropology of War*.

———. *Yąnomamö The Fierce People*. New York: Holt, Rinehart and Winston, 1968. The fourth edition, published in 1992, drops the subtitle.

———. "Yąnomamö Social Organization and Warfare." In Fried, Harris, and Murphy, *War*.

Chang, C. C., ed. *A Treasury of Mahayana Sutras*. Delhi: Banarsidass, 1991.

Chang, K. D. Art, Myth, and Ritual: The Path to Political Authority in *Ancient China*. Cambridge: Harvard University Press, 1983.

Chang, L. S. "The Metamorphosis of Han Fei's Thought in the Han." In Rosemont and Schwartz, ed., *Studies in Classical Chinese Thought*.

Chavennes, E., trans. *Les Mémoires Historiques de Se-ma Ts'ien*. Vol. 1. Reprint. Paris: Adrien-Maissonneuve, 1967.

Ch'en Ch'i-yn. "Confucian, Legalist, and Taoist Thought in Later Han." In *The Cambridge History of China*, vol. 1.

Cheyney, D. L., and R. M. Seyfarth. *How Monkeys See the World*. Chicago: University of Chicago Press, 1990.

Christie, R., and F. L. Geis. *Studies in Machiavellianism*. New York: Acadmic Press, 1970.

Chuang Tzu. *The Complete Works of Chuang Tzu*. Trans. B. Watson. New York: Columbia University Press, 1968.

———. *The Seven Inner Chapters and Other Writings from the Book* Chuang-Tzu. Trans. A. C. Graham. London: Allen and Unwin, 1981.

Cicero. *On Duties*. Trans. E. Atkins. Cambridge: Cambridge University Press, 1991.

Clendinnen, I. *Aztecs: An Intepretation*. Cambridge: Cambridge University Press, 1991.

Clifford, J., and G. E. Marcus, eds. *Writing Culture: The Poetics and Politics of Ethnography*. Berkeley and Los Angeles: University of California Press, 1986.

Coady, C. A. J. "Politics and the Problem of Dirty Hands." In Singer, ed., *A Companion to Ethics*.

Cobo, B. *History of the Inca Empire*. Austin: University of Texas Press, 1979.

———. *Inca Religion and Customs*. Austin: University of Texas Press, 1990.

Colcutt, M. "Zen and the *Gozan*." In Yamamura, ed., *The Cambridge History of Japan*, vol. 3.

Collins, S. "The Discourse on What Is Primary (Agganna Sutta). An Annotated Translation." *Journal of Indian Philosophy*, December 1993.

Confucius, *The Analects*. Trans. D. C. Lau. Hong Kong: Chinese University Press. 1983.

———. Trans. R. Dawson. Oxford: Oxford University Press, 1993.

Conquest, R. *Stalin: Breaker of Nations*. London: Weidenfeld and Nicolson, 1991.

Cosmides, L., and J. Tooby. "Cognitive Adaptations for Social Exchange." In Barkow, Cosmides, and Tooby, eds. *The Adapted Mind*.

Courlander, H. *Tales of Yoruba Gods and Heroes*. Greenwich: Fawcett Publications, 1973.

Cowan, M., trans. *Humanist without Portfolio*. Detroit: Wayne State University Press, 1963.

Craig, G. R. *Germany 1866–1945*. Oxford: Oxford University Press, 1978.

Creel, H. G. *Shen Pu-hai: A Chinese Political Philosopher of the Fourth Century*. Chicago: University of Chicago Press, 1974.

Creveld, M. van. *The Transformation of War*. New York: Free Press, 1991.

Cronin, H. *The Ant and the Peacock*. Cambridge: Cambridge University Press, 1991.

Crump, J. I., trans. *Chan-kuo Ts'e*. London Oxford University Press, 1970.

Damas, D., ed. *Handbook of North American Indians*. Vol. 5, *Arctic*. Washingon: Smithsonian Institution, 1984.

Davids, T. W., and C. A. F. Davids, trans. *Dialogues of the Buddha*. 3 vols. London: Pali Text Society, 1899–1921.

Davies, N. *The Ancient Kingdoms of Mexico*. Harmondsworth: Penguin, 1983.

———. *The Aztec Empire*. Norman: University of Oklahoma Press, 1987.

Davies, N. B., and M. Brooke. "Coevolution of the Cuckoo and Its Hosts." *Scientific American*, January 1991.

Dawkins, R. *The Selfish Gene*. New ed. London: Oxford University Press, 1989.

de Bary, W. T. *The Trouble with Confucianism*. Cambridge: Harvard University Press, 1991.

Diderot, D. *Diderot's Selected Writings*. Trans. D. Coltman. New York: Macmillan, 1966.

Dikshitar, V. R. R. *War in Ancient India*. 2nd ed. Delhi: Banarsidass, 1948.

Dimock, E. C., Jr., ed. *The Literatures of India*. Chicago: University of Chicago Press, 1974.

Dodds, E. R. *The Ancient Concept of Progress*. London: Oxford University Press, 1973.

Donaldson, P. S. *Machiavelli and Mystery of State*. Cambridge: Cambridge Univerity Press, 1988.

Dorson, R. M., ed. *African Folklore*. Garden City: Anchor Books, 1972.

Drekmeier, C. *Kingship and Community in Early India*. Stanford: Stanford University Press, 1962.

Drewal, H. J., J. Pemberton III, and R. Abiodun. *Yoruba: Nine Centureis of African Art and Thought*. New York: The Center for African Art, 1989; in association with Abrams.

Driver, H. E. *Indians of North America*. 2nd ed., Chicago: University of Chicago Press, 1969.

Dumont, L. *Homo Hierarchicus*. London: Paladin, 1972.

Dumoulin, H. *Zen Buddhism: A History*. Vol. 2, *Japan*. New York: Macmillan, 1990.

Duran, D. *Book of the Gods and Rites and the Ancient Calendar*. Norman: University of Oklahoma Press, 1971.

Dutt, S. "Aśoka: A Comparison and Contrast between the Legends and the Edicts." *Encyclopedia of Buddhism*.

Edelstein, L. *The Idea of Progress in Classical Antiquity*. Baltimore: Johns Hopkins Press, 1967.

Edgerton, F., trans. *The Panchatantra*. London: Allen and Unwin, 1965.

Edgerton, R. B. *Rules, Exceptions, and Social Order*. Berkeley and Los Angeles: University of California Press, 1985.

Eisenstadt, S. N., ed. *Axial Age Civilizations*. Albany: State University of New York Press, 1988.

Ekman, P. *Emotion in the Human Face*. 2nd ed. Cambridge: Cambridge University Press, 1982.

Elster, J. *Political Psychology*. Cambridge: Cambridge University Press, 1993.

Elvin, M. "Was There a Transcendental Breakthrough in China?" In Eisenstadt, ed., *Axial Age Civilizations*.

Embree, A. T., ed. *Sources of Indian Tradition*. Rev. ed. Vol. 1. New York: Columbia University Press, 1988.

Encyclopedia of Religion and Ethics. Ed. J. Hastings. New York: Scribner's, 1928.

Eno, R. *The Confucian Creation of Heaven*. Albany: State University of New York Press, 1990.

Erdoes, R., and A. Ortiz, eds. *American Indian Myths and Legends*. New York: Pantheon, 1984.

Eribon, D. *Michel Foucault*. London: Faber & Faber, 1992.

Evans-Pritchard, E. R. *The Nuer*. London: Oxford University Press, 1940.

———. *The Zande Trickster*. London: Oxford University Press, 1967.

Fairbank, J. K. *The Great Chinese Revolution, 1800–1985*. New York: Harper and Row, 1986.

Fakhry, M. *Ethical Theories in Islam*. Leiden: Brill, 1991.

Faure, B. *The Rhetoric of Immediacy: A Cultural Critique of Chan/Zen Buddhism*. Princeton: Princeton University Press, 1991.

Ferguson, B. "Tribal Warfare." *Scientific American*, January, 1992.

Fisher, N. R. E. *Hybris*. Warminster: Aris & Phillips, 1992.

Flanagan, O. *Varieties of Moral Personality*. Cambridge: Harvard University Press, 1991.

Foriers, P., and C. Perelman. "Law: 'Natural Law' and 'Natural Rights.'" In Wiener, ed., *Dictionary of the History of Ideas*.

Forkosch, M. D. "Law: Due Process in Law." In Wiener, ed., *Dictionary of the History of Ideas*.

————. "Law: Equal Protection in Law." In Wiener, ed., *Dictionary of the History of Ideas*.

Foucault, M. *Politics, Philosophy, Culture*. Trans. A. Sheridan et al. London: Routledge, 1988.

Forde, D., ed. *African Worlds*. London: Oxford University Press, 1954.

Fränkel, H. *Early Greek Poetry and Philosophy*. Oxford: Blackwell, 1975.

Frankfort, H. *Kingship and the Gods: A Study of Ancient Near Eastern Religion as the Integration of Society and Nature*. Chicago: University of Chicago Press, 1948.

Freidel, D., L. Schele, and J. Parker. *Maya Cosmos*. New York: Morrow, 1994.

Fried, M., M. Harris, and R. Murphy, eds. *War: The Anthropology of Armed Conflict and Aggression*. Garden City: Natural History Press, 1966.

Fulbrook, M. *The Fontana History of Germany* London: Fontana, 1991.

Gale, E. M. *Discourses on Salt and Iron*. Reprint. Tapei: Ch'en Wen Publishing Co., 1973.

Gardner, C. S. *Chinese Traditional Historiography*. Cambridge: Harvard University Press, 1961.

Garin, E. "Die Kultur der Renaissance." In *Propyläen Welgeschichte*. Vol. 6. Ed. G. Mann and A. Nitschke.

Gat, A. *The Origins of Military Thought*. London: Oxford University Press, 1989.

Gbadamosi, B., and U. Beier. *Not Even God Is Ripe Enough*. London: Heinemann.

Gerschmann, K.-H. "Machiavellismus." In *Historisches Wörterbuch der Philosophie*, vol. 5, ed. J. Ritter and K. Gründer. Basel and Stuttgart: Schwabe, 1980.

Ghoshal, U. N. *A History of Indian Political Ideas*. London: Oxford University Press, 1959.

Gibson, T. "Raiding, Trading, and Tribal Autonomy in Insular Southeast Asia." In Haas, ed., *The Anthropology of War*.

Gilbert, F. *Machiavelli and Guicciardini*. Princeton: Princeton University Press, 1965.

——. "Machiavellism." In the *Dictionary of the History of Ideas*, vol. 3, ed. P. P. Wiener. New York: Scribner's, 1973.

Girardot, N. J. *Myth and Meaning in Early Taoism*. Berkeley and Los Angeles: University of California Press, 1983.

Gombrich, R. H. *Precept and Practice*. London: Oxford University Press, 1971.

Goodall, J. *The Chimpanzees of Gombe*. Cambridge: Harvard University Press, 1986.

——. *Through a Window: 30 Years with the Chimpanzees of Gombe*. London: Weidenfeld and Nicolson, 1990.

Goodman, L. *On Justice*. New Haven: Yale University Press, 1991.

Graham, A. C. " The Background of the Mencian Theory of Human Nature." In *Graham, Studies in Chinese Philosophy*.

——. *Disputers of the Tao*. La Salle: Open Court, 1989.

——. *Studies in Chinese Philosophy and Philosophical Literature*. Albany: State University of New York Press, 1990.

Gray, J. "Against the New Liberalism." *Times Literary Supplemen*, July 3, 1992.

Gray, J. G. *The Warrior: Reflections on Men in Battle*. New York: Harper and Row, 1967.

Grazia, S. de. *Machiavelli in Hell*. Princeton: Princeton Unviersity Press, 1989.

Gregor, T. "Uneasy Peace: Intertribal Relations in Brazil's Upper Xingu." In J. Haas, ed., *The Anthropology of War*.

Group for the Advancement of Psychiatry. *Us and Them: The Psychology of Ethnonationalism*. New York: Brunner/Maazel, 1987.

Guarini, E. F. "Machiavelli and the Crisis of the Italian Republics." In Bock, Skinner, and Viroli, eds., *Machiavelli and Republicanism*.

Guiart, J. "Religions and Mythologies of Oceania." In Bonnefoy, ed., *Mythologies.*

Guicciardini, F. *Selected Writings.* Trans. M. Grayson. London: Oxford University Press, 1965.

Gupta, S. K. *Somadev Suri's Nitivakyamritam.* Jaipur and Calcutta: Prakrita Bharati Academy/ Modi Foundation.

Guthrie, W. K. C. *A History of Greek Philosophy.* Cambridge: Cambridge University Press, 1962–81.

Haas, J., ed. *The Anthropology of War.* Cambridge: Cambridge University Press, 1990.

Habermas, J. *Nachmetaphysiches Denken.* Frankfurt: Suhrkamp, 1988.

————. *The Philosophical Discourse of Modernity.* Cambridge: MIT Press, 1987.

————. *Theory of Communicative Action.* 2 vols. Trans. T. McCarthy. Boston: Beacon Press, vol 1, 1984; vol. 2, 1987.

Hale, J. R. *The Civilization of Europe in the Renaissance.* London: HarperCollins, 1993.

————. *War and Society in Renaissance Europe.* London: Fontana, 1985.

Hallpike, C. R. *Principles of Social Evolution.* Oxford: Oxford University Press, 1988.

Hamburg, D. A., and E. R. McCown, eds. *The Great Apes.* Menlo Park: Benjamin/Cummings, 1979.

Han Fei Tzu. *Basic Writings.* Trans. B. Watson. New York: Columbia University Press, 1964.

————. *The Complete Works of Han Fei Tzu,* trans. W. K. Liao. 2 vols. London: Probsthain, 1939, 1959.

Haring, L. "A Characteristic African Folktale Pattern," In Dorson, ed., *African Folklore.*

Harris, H. S. *Hegel's Development.* Vol. 2. Oxford: Oxford Univerity Press, 1983.

Hasse, J. G. *Lezte [sic!] Aeuserungen Kant's [sic!].* 2nd printing. Königsberg, 1804.

Hegel, G. W. F. *Elements of the Philosophy of Right.* Trans. A. W. Wood. Cambridge: Cambridge University Press, 1991.

Heltne, P. G., and L. A. Marquardt, eds. *Understanding Chimpanzees.* Cambridge: Harvard University Press in cooperation with the Chicago Academy of Sciences, 1989.

Henrich, D. "On the Meaning of Rational Action in the State." In Beiner and Booth, eds., *Kant and Political Philosophy*.

Hesiod. *Theogony and Works and Days*. Trans. M. L. West. Oxford: Oxford University Press, 1988.

Hill, C. *Intellectual Origins of the English Revolution*. London: Oxford University Press, 1965.

Hobbes, T. *The Leviathan*. London: Oxford University Press, 1909.

Hölldober, B., and E. O. Wilson. *The Ants*. Berlin: Springer Verlag, 1990.

Holmes, G. *The Florentine Enlightenment 1400–1500*. London: Weidenfeld and Nicolson, 1969.

Holy, L., ed. *Comparative Anthropology*. Oxfofrd: Blackwell, 1987.

Hornblower, S. *Thucydides*, London: Duckworth, 1987.

Horner, I. B. trans. *The Middle Length Saying (Majjhima-Nikaya)*. Vol. 2. London: Pali Text Society, 1957.

Hsiao, Kung-chuan. *A History of Chinese Political Thought*. Vol. 1. Princeton: Princeton University Press, 1979.

Hsu, Cho-yun. *Ancient China in Transition*. Stanford: Stanford University Press, 1965.

Hsu, Cho-yun, and K. M. Lindoff. *Western Chou Civilization*. New Haven: Yale University Press, 1988.

Hsün Tzu (Xunzi). *Basic Writings*. Trans. B. Watson. New York: Columbia University Press, 1963.

Huang, R. "The Lung-Ch'ing and Wan-li Reigns." In Mote and Twitchett, eds., *The Ming Dynasty*.

Hucker, C. O. *China's Imperial Past*. Stanford: Leland Stanford Junior University, 1975.

Hudson, C. *The Southeastern Indians*. Knoxville: University of Tennessee Press, 1976.

Hulsewé, A. F. P. "Ch'in and Han Law." In the *Cambridge History of China*, vol. 1,

Isaacs, N. *Travels and Adventures in Eastern Africa*. Revised and edited by L. Herman and P. R. Kirby. Cape Town [sic!], 1970

Ishii, Yoneo. *Sangha, State, and Society: Thai Buddhism in History*. Honolulu: University of Hawaii Press, 1986.

Jenner, W. J. F. *The Tyranny of History*. London: Penguin, 1992.

Jennings, F. *The Ambiguous Iroquois Empire*. New York: Norton, 1984.

Johnson, M. *Moral Imagination*. Chicago: University of Chicago Press, 1993.

Jolly, A. *The Evolution of Primate Behavior*. 2nd ed. New York: Macmillan, 1985.

Jones, J. G. *Tales and Teachings of the Buddha*.

Kant, I. *The Conflict of the Faculties*. Trans. M. Gregor. Cambridge: Cambridge University Press, 1979.

———. *The Critique of Judgement*. Trans. J. C. Meredith. London: Oxford University Press, 1928.

———. *Kant: Selections*. Ed. L. W. Beck. New York: Macmillan, 1988.

———. *Kant's Political Writings*. Trans. H. Reiss. Cambridge: Cambridge University Press, 1970.

———. *The Metaphysics of Morals*. Trans. M. Gregor. Cambridge: Cambridge University Press, 1991.

———. "On the Common Saying: "This May Be True in Theory but It Does Not Apply in Practice." In Kant, *Kant's Political Writings*.

———. "Perpetual Peace." In Kant, *Kant's Political Writings*.

———. *Religion within the Limits of Reason Alone*. Trans. T. M. Green and H. H. Hudson. New York: Harper & Brothers, 1934.

Karlgren, B., trans. *The Book of Odes*. Stockholm: Museum of Far Eastern Antiquities, 1974.

Kautilya, *The Kautilya Arthaśatra*. Trans. R. P. Kangle. 3 vols. Bombay: University of Bolmbay, 1963–65.

Kazuo, Osumi, "Buddhism in the Kamakura Period." In Yamamura, ed., *The Cambridge History of Japan*, vol. 3.

Keith, A. B. *A History of Sanskrit Literature*. London: Oxford University Press, 1920.

Kelsay, J., and J. T. Johnson, eds. *Just War and Jihad*. Westport: Greenwood Press, 1991.

Keown, D. *The Nature of Buddhist Ethics*. London: Macmillan, 1992.

Kirwan, C. *Augustine*. London: Routledge, 1989.

Knappert, J. *Myths and Legends of the Congo*. London: Heinemann, 1971.

Knoblock, J. *Xunzi*. 3 vols. Stanford: Stanford University Press, 1990–1994.

Kramer, S. N., ed. *Mythologies of the Ancient World*. Garden City; Anchor Books, 1961.

Kramers, R. P. "The Development of the Confucian Schools." In *The Cambridge History of China*, vol. 1.

Kraye, J. "Moral Philosophy." In *The Cambridge History of Renaissance Philosophy*.

Krige, J. D., and E. J. Krige. "The Lovedu of the Transvaal." In Forde, ed., *African Worlds*.

Kuhn, P. A. *Soulstealers: The Chinese Sorcery Scare of 1768*. Cambridge: Harvard University Press, 1990.

La Rochefoucauld, F. de. *Maxims*. Trans. L. W. Tancock. Harmondsworth: Penguin Books, 1959.

Ladany, L. *Law and Legality in China*. Honolulu: University of Hawaii Press, 1991.

The Laws of Manu. Trans. W. Doniger and B. K. Smith. London: Penguin Books, 1991.

Langlois, "The Hung-wu Reign." In Mote and Twitchett, eds., *The Ming Dynasty*.

Lazarus, R. S. *Emotion and Adaptation*. New York: Oxford University Press, 1991.

Leach, M., ed. *Funk and Wagnalls's Standard Dictonary of Folklore, Mythology and Legend*. New York: Harper and Row, 1984.

Leon-Portilla, M. *Fifteen Poets of the Aztec World*. Norman: University of Oklahoma Press, 1992.

——. *Pre-Columbian Literature of Mexico*. Norman: University of Oklahoma Press, 1969.

Leslie, D. D., C. Mackeras, and Wang Gangwu, eds. *Essays on the Sources for Chinese History*. Canberra: Australian National University Press, 1973.

Lesser, A. "War and the State." In Fried, Harris, and Murphy, eds., *War*.

Levine, R. A., and D. T. Campbell, eds. *Ethnocentrism*. New York: Wiley, 1972.

Lewis, M. E. *Sanctioned Violence in Early China*. Albany: State University of New York Press, 1990.

Lifton, R. J. *The Nazi Doctors*. New York: Basic Books.

——. *The Future of Immortality*. New York: Basic Books, 1987.

Lifton, R. J., and E. Markusen. *The Genocidal Mentality*. New York: Basic Books, 1990.

Lingat, R. *The Classical Law of India*. Berkeley and Los Angeles: University of California Press, 1973.

Liu, J. J. Y. *The Chinese Knight-Errant*. London: Routledge and Kegan Paul, 1967.

Lizot, J. *Tales of the Yanomani: Daily Life in the Venezuelan Forest*. Cambridge: Cambridge University Press; Paris: Editions de la Maison des Sciences de l'Homme, 1985.

Loewe, M. "The Former Han Dynasty." In *The Cambridge History of China*, vol. 1.

———. "The Religious and Intellectual Background." In *The Cambridge History of China*, vol. 1.

Long, A. A., and D. N. Sedley, trans. *The Hellenistic Philosophers*. Vol. 1. Cambridge: Cambridge University Press, 1987.

Lopez, D. D., ed. *Buddhist Hermeneutics*. Honolulu: University of Hawaii Press, 1986.

Loraux, Y. "The Origins of Mankind in Greek Myths: Born to Die." In Bonnefoy, ed., *Mythologies*.

Lovin, R. W., and F. E. Reynolds, eds. *Cosmogony and Ethical Order*. Chicago: University of Chicago Press, 1985.

Luciani, V. "Bacon and Machiavelli." *Italica* 24 (1947).

Machiavelli. *The Chief Works and Others*. Trans. A. Gilbert. 3 vols. Durham: Duke University Press, 1965.

———. *The Prince*. Trans. R. M. Adams. 2nd ed. New York: Norton, 1992. Trans. G. Bull. Harmondsworth: Penguin, 1981.

MacKendrick, P. *The Philosophical Books of Cicero*. London: Duckworth, 1989.

McNeill, W. H. *Plagues and Peoples*. Garden City: Anchor Press/ Doubleday, 1976.

Madsen, A. P., and J. M. Shafritz, eds. *Essentials of Government Ethics*. New York: Meridian (Penguin Books), 1992.

Mair, L. *Primitive Government*. Rev. ed. Harmondsworth: Penguin, 1964.

Mallett, "The Theory and Practice of Warfare in Machiavelli's Republic." In Bock, Skinner, and Viroli, eds., *Machiavelli and Republicanism*.

Markman, R. H., and P. T. Markman. *The Flayed God: The Mythology of Mesoamerica*. San Francisco: HarperSanFrancisco, 1992.

Martin, J. *Francis Bacon, the State, and the Reform of Natural Philosophy*. Cambridge: Cambridge University Press, 1992.

Martines, L. *The Social World of the Florentine Humanists 1390–1460*. London: Routledge and Kegan Paul, 1963.

Masefield, P. *Divine Revelation in Pali Buddhism*. London: Allen and Unwin, 1986.

Matsunage, A., and D. Matsunaga. *Foundations of Japanse Buddhism*. 2 vols. Los Angeles/ Tokyo: Buddhist Books International, 1978.

Maybury-Lewis, D. *Millenium: Tribal Wisdom and the Modern World*. New York: Viking Penguin, 1992.

Mayr, R. *Toward a New Philosophy of Biology*. Cambridge: Harvard University Press, 1988.

McCauley, "Conference Overview." In Haas, ed., *The Anthropology of War*.

McGrew, W. C., and A. T. C. Feistner, "Two Nonhuman Primate Models for the Evolution of Human Food Sharing: Chimpanzees and Callitrichids." In Barkow, Cosmides, and Tooby, *The Adapted Mind*.

McShea, R. J. The Political Philosophy of Spinoza. New York: Columbia Unversity Press, 1968.

Meinecke, F. *Machiavellism: The Doctrine of Raison d'état and Its Place in Modern History*. New Haven: Yale University Press, 1957. Reprint, Praeger, 1965.

Mellor, R. *Tacitus*. London: Routledge, 1993.

Mencius. *Mencius*. Trans. D. C. Lau. Harmondsworth: Penguin, 1970.

———. *The Works of Mencius*, trans. J. Legge. Reprint, New York: Dover, 1970.

Mendel, D. *The Rise and Fall of Jewish Nationalism*. New York: Doubleday, 1992.

Milgram, S. *Obedience to Authority*. New York: Harper and Row, 1974.

Mintz, S. I. *The Hunting of the Leviathan*. Cambridge: Cambridge University Press, 1962.

Mitscherlich, A., and M. Mitscherlich. *The Inability to Mourn*. New York: Grove Press, 1975.

Montaigne, M. de *The Essays of Michel de Montaigne*. Trans M. A. Screech. London: Allen Lane (Penguin), 1991.

Moseley, E. M. *The Incas and Their Ancestors*. London: Thames and Hudson, 1992.

Mote, F. P., and D. Twitchett, eds. *The Ming Dynasty, 1368–1644*. Pt. 1, vol. 7 of *The Cambridge History of China*. Cambridge: Cambridge University Press, 1988.

Mo Tzu. *The Ethical and Political Works of Mo Tzu.* Trans. Yi-Pao Mei. London: Probsthain, 1929.

Najemy, J. M. "The Controversy Surrounding Machiavelli's Service to the Republic." In Bock, Skinner, and Viroli, eds., *Machiavelli and Republicanism.*

Nesse, R. M., and A. T. Lloyd. "The Evolution of Psychodynamic Mechanisms." In Barkow, Cosmides, and Tooby, *The Adapted Mind.*

Ngcongco, L. D. "The Mfecane and the Rise of New African States." In J. F. A. Ajayi, ed. *General History of Africa,* vol. 6. Paris and Oxford: UNESCO/Heinemann.

Nietzsche, F. *Human, All too Human.* Trans. R. J. Hollingdale. Cambridge: Cambridge University Press, 1986.

———. *The Will to Power.* Trans. W. Kaufmann. London: Weidenfeld and Nicolson, 1967.

Nikam, N. A., and McKeon, R. *The Edicts of Aśoka.* Chicago: University of Chicago Press, 1959.

Nozick, R. *The Nature of Rationality.* Princeton: Princeton University Press, 1993.

Norman, H. *Northern Tales.* New York: Pantheon, 1990.

Nussbaum, M. C. *The Fragility of Goodness.* Cambridge: Cambridge University Press, 1986.

Nyberg, D. *The Varnished Truth.* Chicago: University of Chicago Press, 1993.

Nylan, M. *The Shifting Center: The Original "Great Plan and Later Readings."* Sankt Augustin/Nettetal: Institut Monumenta Serica/Steyler Verlag.

Obeyesekere, G. *The Apotheosis of Captain Cook: European Mythmaking in the Pacific.* Princeton: Princeton University Press, 1992.

———. *The Work of Culture.* Chicago: University of Chicago Press, 1990.

Offner, J. *Law and Politics in Aztec Tezcoco.* Cambridge: Cambridge University Press, 1988.

O'Hagan, T. "On Hegel's Critique of Kant's Moral and Political Philosophy." In S. Priest, ed. *Hegel's Critique of Kant.* Oxford: Oxford University Press, 1987.

Oliver, D. L. *Native Cultures of the Pacific Islands.* Honolulu: University of Hawaii Press, 1989.

———. *Oceania: The Native Cultures of Australia and the Pacific Islands.* 2 vols. Honolulu: University of Hawaii Press, 1989.

Oliver, R. *The African Experience*. London: Weidenfeld and Nicolson, 1991.

Omer-Cooper, J. D., "The Nguni Outburst." In J. E. Flint, ed., *The Cambridge History of Africa*, vol. 5. Cambridge: Cambridge University Press, 1976.

O'Neill, O. "Kantian Ethics." In P. Singer, ed., *A Companion to Ethics*.

Ortiz, A., ed. *Handbook of the American Indians*. Vol. 10, *Southwest*. Washington: Smithsonian Institution, 1983.

Pan Ku. *Courtier and Commoner in Ancient China: Selections from the History of the Former Han*. Trans. B. Watson. New York: Columbia University Press, 1974.

Parel, A. J. *The Machiavellian Cosmos*. New Haven: Yale University Press, 1992.

Parker, T. *The Frying Pan: A Prison and its Prisoners*. London: Hutchinson, 1970.

Parker, T., and R. Allerton. *The Courage of His Convictions*. London: Hutchinson, 1962.

Peck, R. F., and R. J. Havighurst. *The Psychology of Character Development*. New York: Wiley, 1960.

Peerenboom, R. P. *Law and Morality in Ancient China*. Albany: State University of New York Press, 1993.

Peterson, D., and J. Goodall. *Visions of Caliban*. New York: Houghton Mifflin, 1993.

Philips, C. H, ed. *Historians of India, Pakistan and Ceylon*. London: Oxford University Press, 1961.

Plato. *The Republic*. Trans. P. Shorey. 2 vols. Rev. ed. Cambridge: Harvard University Press, 1937.

Poignant, R. *Oceanic and Australian Mythology*. Rev. ed. Feltham: Newnes Books, 1985.

Pollock, S. I., trans. *The Ramayana of Valmiki*. Vols. 2, 3. Princeton: Princeton University Press, 1986–1991.

Polybius. *The Rise of the Roman Republic*. Trans. W. W. Walbank. Harmondsworth: Penguin, 1979.

Poundstone, E. *Prisoner's Dilemma*. Oxford: Oxford University Press, 1993.

Power, M. *The Egalitarians—Human and Chimpanzee: An Anthropological View of Social Organization*. Cambridge: Cambridge University Press, 1991.

Prakash, O. *Political Ideas in the Puranas*. Allahabad: Panchanda Publications, 1977.

Procacci, G. *History of the Italian People.* London: Penguin, 1973.

Putnam, R. D. *Making Democracy Work: Civic Traditions in Modern Italy.* Princeton: Princeton University Press, 1993.

Raab, F. *The English Face of Machiavelli.* London, 1965.

Radin, P. *The Trickster.* New York: Bell, 1956.

Raphals, L. *Cunning Words: Wisdom and Cunning in the Classical Traditions of China and Greece.* Ithaca: Cornell University Press, 1992.

Rawls, J. *Political Liberalism.* New York: Columbia University Press, 1971.

———. *A Theory of Justice.* Cambridge: Harvard University Press, 1993.

Remnick, D. *Lenin's Tomb.* New York: Random House, 1993.

Rennie, J. "Living Together." *Scientific American,* January 1992.

Reynolds, F. E. "Multiple Cosmogonies and Ethics: The Case of Theravada Buddhism." In Lovin and Reynolds, eds., *Cosmogony and Ethical order.*

Reynolds, V., and V. S. S. Falger. *The Sociobiology of Ethnocentrism.* London: Croom Helm, 1987.

Rhys Davids, T. W. *Buddhist India.* Reprint, Delhi: Banarsidass, 1971.

———. "The Early History of the Buddhists." In *Cambridge History of India,* vol. 1.

Rickett, A. A., trans. *Kuan-tzu.* Vol. 1. Hong Kong: Hong Kong University Press, 1965.

Ridolfi, R. *The Life of Francesco Guicciardini.* London: Routledge and Kegan Paul, 1967.

Robarcheck, C. "Motivations and Material Causes: On the Explanation of Conflict and War." In Haas, *The Anthropology of War.*

Roberts, B. *The Zulu Kings.* London: Hamilton; New York: Scribner's, 1974.

Roberts, S. *Order and Dispute: An Introduction to Legal Anthropology.* Harmondsworth: Penguin, 1979.

Rocher, L. *The Puranas.* Wiesbaden, Harrassowitz, 1986.

Romilly, J. de. *Thucydides and Athenian Imperialism.* Oxford: Blackwell, 1963.

Rosemont, H., and Schwartz, B. I. *Studies in Classical Chinese Thought. Journal of the American Academy of Religion,* Thematic issue, 47, no. 3 (September 1979).

Rossi, P. *Francis Bacon.* London: Routledge, 1968.

Rubenstein, N. "Machiavelli and Florentine Republican Experience." In Bock, Skinner, and Viroli, eds., *Machiavelli and Republican Experience*.

Ruse, M. *Taking Darwin Seriously*. Oxford: Blackwell, 1986.

Russet, B. *Grasping the Democratic Peace: Principles for a Post–Cold War World*. Princeton: Princeton University Press, 1993.

Ryder, A. W., trans. *The Panchatantra*. Chicago: University of Chicago Press, 1925.

Sahlins, M. *The Use and Abuse of Biology*. London: Tavistock, 1977.

Salisbury, H. E. *The New Emperors: China in the Era of Mao and Deng*. Boston: Little, Brown, 1992.

Saner, H. *Kant's Political Thought*. Chicago: University of Chicago Press, 1973.

Sastri, K. A. N., ed. *Age of the Nandas and Mauryas*. 2nd ed. Delhi: Banarsidass, 1988.

Sawyer, R. D. *The Seven Military Classics of Ancient China*. Boulder: Westview Press, 1993.

Schaefer, D. L. *The Political Philosophy of Montaigne*. Ithaca: Cornell University Press, 1990.

Scharfe, H. *The State in Indian Tradition*. Leiden: Brill, 1989.

Scharfstein, B.-A. *The Dilemma of Context*. New York: New York University Press, 1989.

———. *The Philosophers*. Oxford: Blackwell; New York: Oxford University Press, 1980.

Schele, L., and D. Freidel. *A Forest of Kings: The Untold Story of the Ancient Maya*. New York: Morrow, 1990.

Schele, L., and M. E. Miller. *The Blood of Kings*. New York/ Fort Worth: Braziller/ Kimbell Art Museum, 1986.

Schiller, F. *On the Aesthetic Education of Man*. Trans. E. M. Wilkinson and L. A. Willoughby. Oxford: Oxford University Press, 1967.

Schumann, H. W. *The Historical Buddha*. London: Arkana, 1989.

Schwartz, B. *The World of Thought in Ancient China*. Cambridge: Harvard University Press, 1985.

Scott, J. C. *Domination and the Arts of Resistance*. New Haven: Yale University Press, 1990.

Service, E. R. "War and our Contemporary Ancestors." In Fried, Harris, and Murphy, eds., *War*.

Shang Yang. *The Books of the Lord Shang: A Classic of the Chinese School of Law.* Trans. J. J. L Duyvendak. London: Probsthain, 1928.

Shen Pu-hai. *Shen Pu-hai: A Chinese Political Philosopher of the Fourth Century B.C.* Trans. H. G. Creel. Chicago: University of Chicago Press, 1974.

Sherman, P. W., J. U. M. Jarvis, and S. H. Braude. "Naked Mole Rats." *Scientific American*, August 1992.

Shklar, J. N. *Ordinary Vices.* Cambridge: Harvard University Press, 1984.

Shu ching, Book of History: A Modernized Version of the Translations of James Legge. Modernized by C. Waltham. London: Allen and Unwin, 1972.

Sil, P. *Kautilya's Arthaśastra: A Comparative Study.* London: Sangam Books, 1985.

Silberbauer, G. "Ethics in Small-Scale Societies." In P. Singer, ed., *Companion to Ethics*.

Simmel, G. *The Sociology of Georg Simmel*, ed. and trans. K. H. Wolff. New York: Free Press, 1950.

Singer, M., and A. Wildavsky. *The Real World Order: Zones of Peace/Zones of Turmoil.* Chatham, N.J.: Chatham House, 1993.

Singer, P., ed. *A Companion to Ethics.* Oxford: Blackwell, 1991.

Sinyavsky, A. *Soviet Civilization.* New York: Little, Brown, 1990.

Skinner, Q. *Machiavelli.* Republished in *Great Political Thinkers: Machiavelli, Hobbes, Mill, Marx.* No editor mentioned. London: Oxford University Press, 1992.

———. "Political Philosophy." In *The Cambridge History of Renaissance Philosophy*.

Smith, R. S. *Kingdoms of the Yoruba.* 3rd ed. Madison: University of Wisconsin Press, 1988.

Smuts, B. B., et al., eds. *Primate Societies.* Chicago: University of Chicago Press, 1986.

Snellgrove, D. *Indo-Tibetan Buddhism.* 2 vols. Boston: Shamghala, 1987.

Socarides, C. W., ed. *The World of Emotions: Clinical Studies of Affects and Their Expression.* New York: International Universities Press, 1977.

Smith, V. A., ed. T. G. P. Spear. *The Oxford History of India.* London: Oxford University Press, 1951.

Spence, J. *Kang-hsi, Emperor of China*. New York: Knopf, 1974.

Spencer, R. F. *The North Alaskan Eskimo*. Reprint. New York: Dover, 1976.

Spinoza, B. *Ethics*, in *The Collected Works of Spinoza*, vol. 1, trans. E. Curley. Princeton: Princeton University Press, 1985.

————. *The Political Works*. Trans. A. G. Wernham. London: Oxford University Press, 1958.

Ssu-ma Ch'ien. *Records of the Grand Historian of China*. Trans. B. Watson. 2 vols. New York: Columbia University Press, 1961.

————. *Records of the Grand Historian: Qin Dynasty*. Hong Kong/New York: The Chinese University of Hong Kong/Columbia University Press, 1992. (In 1992, the two translated volumes of the *Records*, dealing with the Han, were republished with Chinese names in Pinyin transliteration—the historian's name becoming Sima Qian—and with addition of this third, new volume containing Ssu'ma's account of the Ch'in.)

Stern, J. P. *Hitler*. Rev. ed. London: Fontana, 1990.

Strong, J. S. *The Legend of King Aśoka*. Princeton: Princeton University Press, 1983.

Strum, S. *Almost Human: A Journey into the World of Baboons*. New York: Random House, 1987.

Sun Tzu, *The Art of War*. Trans. R. Ames (as *The Art of Warfare*; with additional, recently discovered texts). New York: Ballentine Books, 1993. Trans. S. B. Griffeth (as *The Art of War*). Oxford: Oxford University Press, 1963.

Sutherland, E. H. *The Professional Thief*. Chicago: University of Chicago Press, 1956. (The author of the extensive autobiographical is an anonymous professional thief.)

Symons, D. "On the Use and Misuse of Darwinism in the Study of Human Behavior." In Barkow, Cosmides, and Tooby, *The Adapted Mind*.

Tanabe, Jr., G. J., and W. J. Tanabe, eds. *The Lotus Sutra in Japanese Culture*. Honolulu: University of Hawaii Press, 1989.

Tejera, V. *The City-State Foundations of Western Political Thought*. Rev. ed. Lanham: University Press of America, 1993.

Thapar, R. *A History of India*. Vol. 1. Harmondsworth: Penguin, 1966.

Thomas, F. W. "Aśoka, the Imperial Patron of Buddhism." In the *Cambridge History of India*, vol. 1.

———. "Chandragupta, the Founder of the Maurya Empire." In *Cambridge History of India*, vol. 1.

———. *The Life of Buddha*. 2nd ed. London: Legan Paul, Trench, Trubner & Co., 1932.

Thomas, H. *The Conquest of Mexico*. London: Hutchinson, 1993.

Thompson, S. *The Folktale*. Berkeley and Los Angeles: University of California Press, 1977.

———. *Tales of the North American Indian*. Bloomington: Indiana University Press, 1929.

Thucydides. *The Peloponnesian War*. Trans. R. Warner. Rev. ed. Harmondsworth: Penguin, 1972.

Tilly, C. *European Revolutions*. Oxford: Blackwell, 1993.

Tong, J. W. *Disorder under Heaven: Collective Violence in the Ming Dynasty*. Stanford: Stanford University Press, 1991.

Townsend. *The Aztecs*. London: Thames and Hudson, 1992.

Trompf, G. W. *Melanesian Religion*. Cambridge: Cambridge University Press, 1991.

Tucci, G. *The Religions of Tibet*. London: Routledge and Kegan Paul, 1980.

Tucker, R. C. *Stalin in Power*. New York: Norton, 1990.

Twitchett, D. *The Writing of Official History under the T'ang*. Cambridge: Cambridge University Press, 1992.

Urbach, E. E. *The Sages*. 2 vols. Jersualem: Magnes Press, 1975.

Vallé Poussin, L. de la. "Ages of the World (Buddhist)." In *Encyclopaedia of Ethics*, ed. J. Hastings.

Van Buitenen, J. A. B., trans. *The Mahabharata*. Vol. 2. Chicago: University of Chicago Press, 1975.

———. Trans. *Two Plays of Ancient India*. New York: Columbia University Press, 1968.

Veyne, P. *Did the Greeks Believe in Their Myths?* Chicago: University of Chicago Press, 1988.

Vickers, B. *Returning to Shakespeare*. London: Routledge, 1989.

Villari, P. *The Life and Times of Niccolo Machiavelli*. 2 vols. Reprint, New York: Haskell House, 1969.

Viroli, M. *From Politics to Reason of State.* Cambridge: Cambridge University Press. 1992.

Vogel, S., ed. *For Spirits and Kings.* New York: Metropolitan Museum of Art, 1981.

Volkogonov, D. *Stalin.* London: Weidenfeld and Nicolson, 1991.

Waal, F. de *Chimpanzee Politics.* London: Unwin, 1983.

———. *Peacemaking among Primates: Love and Sex among Apes.* Cambridge: Harvard University Press, 1989.

Wallace, F. C. "Psychological Preparations for War." In Fried, Harris, and Murphy, eds., *War.*

Walter, E. V. *Terror and Resistance.* New York: Oxford University Press, 1969.

Walzer, M. *Just and Unjust Wars.* 2nd ed. New York: Basic Books, 1992.

Warder, A. K. *Indian Kavya Literature.* Vol. 3. Delhi: Banarsidass, 1977.

Wardwell, A., ed. *Yoruba: Nine Centuries of African Art and Thought.* New York: Center for African Art, 1989.

Watson, B. *Ssu-ma Ch'ien: Grand Historian of China,* trans. B. Watson. New York: Columbia University Press, 1958.

Weber, M. *From Max Weber.* Trans. H. H. Gerth and C. W. Mills. New York: Oxford University Press, 1946.

———. "Politics as a Vocation." In Weber, *From Max Weber.*

Weinstein, S. *Buddhism under the T'ang.* Cambridge: Cambridge University Press, 1987.

Weisinger, H. "Ideas of History during the Renaissance." In P. O. Kristeller and P. P. Weiner, eds., *Renaissance Essays.* New York: Harper and Row, 1968.

Wiener, P. H., ed. *Dictionary of the History of Ideas.* New York: Scribners, 1973.

Williams, N. N. "Studies in Australian Aboriginal Law 1961–1986." In Berndt and Tonkinson, eds., *Social Anthropology and Australian Aborignal Studies.*

Williams, P. *Mahayana Buddhism.* London: Routledge, 1989.

Wilson, E. O. *Sociobiology.* Cambridge: Harvard University Press, 1975.

Winternitz M. *History of Indian Literature.* Vol. 3. Trans. S. Jha. Reprint, Delhi: Banarsidass, 1985.

Wolfenstein, E. V. *The Revolutionary Personality: Lenin, Trotsky, Gandhi*. Princeton: Princeton University Press, 1967.

Wu Pei-y. *The Confucian's Progress: Autobiographical Writings in Traditional China*. Princeton: Princeton University Press, 1990.

Xunzi (Hsün Tzu). *A Translation and Study of the Complete Works*. Trans. J. Knoblock. 2 vols. (3rd pending). Stanford: Stanford Universtiy Press, 1988–90.

Yamamura, Kozo, ed. *The Cambridge History of Japan*. Vol. 3. Cambridge: Cambridge University Press, 1990.

Yampolsky, P. B., ed. *Selected Writings oif Nichiren*. New York: Columbia University Press, 1990.

Yearly, L. H.. "A Confucian Crisis: Mencius' Two Cosmogonies and Their Ethics." In Lovin and Reynolds, eds., *Cosmogony and Ethical Order*.

Yoshiro, Tamua, "The Ideas of the *Lotus Sutra*." In Tanabe and Tanabe, eds., *The Lotus Sutra in Japanese Culture*.

Zeitlin, J. "The Development of Bacon's Essays." *Journal of English and Germanic Philology* 27 (1928).

Zeyst, H. G. A. van. "Aśoka." *Encyclopedia of Buddhism*. Ed. G. P. Malalasekere. Ceylon: Government of Ceylon, 1961–.

INDEX